Praise for *Twitter API: Up and Running*

"*Twitter API: Up and Running* is a friendly, accessible introduction to the Twitter API. Even beginning web developers can have a working Twitter project before they know it. Sit down with this book for a weekend and you're on your way to Twitter API mastery."

— Alex Payne, Twitter API lead

"This book rocks! I would have loved to have had this kind of support when I initially created TwitDir."

"*Twitter API: Up* ⋯ ⋯ce—any developer will feel the urge ⋯ ⋯ing the book!"

"A truly comprehensive resource for anyone who wants to get started with developing applications around the Twitter platform."

— David Troy, developer of Twittervision

"An exceptionally detailed look at Twitter from the developer's perspective, including useful and functional sample code!"

— Damon Cortesi, creator of TweetStats, TweepSearch, and TweetSum

"This book is more than just a great technical resource for the Twitter API. It also provides a ton of insight into the Twitter culture and the current landscape of apps. It's perfect for anyone looking to start building web applications that integrate with Twitter."

— Matt Gillooly, lead developer of Twalala

"A wonderful account of the rich ecosystem surrounding Twitter's API. This book gives you the insight and techniques needed to craft your own tools for this rapidly expanding social network."

— Craig Hockenberry, developer of Twitterrific

Twitter API: Up and Running

Twitter API: Up and Running

Kevin Makice

Beijing · Cambridge · Farnham · Köln · Sebastopol · Taipei · Tokyo

Twitter API: Up and Running

by Kevin Makice

Published by O'Reilly Media, Inc., 1005 Gravenstein Highway North, Sebastopol, CA 95472.

O'Reilly books may be purchased for educational, business, or sales promotional use. Online editions are also available for most titles (*http://safari.oreilly.com*). For more information, contact our corporate/institutional sales department: 800-998-9938 or *corporate@oreilly.com*.

Editor: Laurel R.T. Ruma		**Indexer:** Fred Brown	
Production Editor: Sarah Schneider		**Cover Designer:** Karen Montgomery	
Copyeditor: Rachel Head		**Interior Designer:** David Futato	
Proofreader: Sarah Schneider		**Illustrator:** Robert Romano	

Printing History:

March 2009:	First Edition.

 This book uses RepKover™, a durable and flexible lay-flat binding.

ISBN: 978-0-596-15461-5

[M]

1236973332

Table of Contents

Preface xiii

1. Hello Twitter 1
   What Are You Doing?   2
      Rules of Engagement   4
      Opportunistic Interruptions   6
      Twitter Is Like a Side-by-Side Conversation   8
   History of Twitter   9
      A Brief History of Microblogging   10
      Believe It or Not: Twitter Was Inspired by Bike Couriers   12
      Millions and Millions Served   14
      The Rise of the Fail Whale   16
      Who Wants to Be a Millionaire? Gauging Twitter's Profitability   20
      Developers Are Users, Too   23
   Creative Uses of Twitter   25
      Twitter Utilitarianism   26
      Twitter for News   27
      Twitter for Science   28
      Twitter for God   29
      Twitter for Emergencies   30
      Twitter for Marketing   31
      Twitter for Social Change   32
      Twitter for Money   34
      Twitter for Games   34
      Twitter for Anthropomorphism   35
      Twitter for Help   36
      Twitter for Creativity   37
      Twitter for Education   38
      Twitter for Entertainment   38
      Twitter for Sports   39
      Twitter for Evil   40
      Twitter As a Shared Event   41

Twitter for Everyone   42
A Changing Culture   43

2. **Twitter Applications** **45**
Twitter's Open API   46
Finding Inspiration   47
Tools for Publishing   48
    Twitterfeed   48
    SnapTweet   49
    SecretTweet   50
Tools for the Information Stream   51
    Twittervision   52
    Twitter Matrix   53
    Twalala   54
Tools of Appropriation   55
    Track This   55
    LiveTwitting   56
    FoodFeed   57
Tools for Search   58
    TwitDir   59
    Green Tweets   60
    TweetBeep   61
    Tweet Scan   62
    Favrd   63
Tools of Aggregation   64
    Twappi   64
    Twitscoop   65
    Twist   66
Tools for Statistics   67
    What's Your Tweet Worth?   67
    TweetStats   68
    Follow Cost   70
    Twitter Grader   71
    Twitterank   72
Tools for the Follow Network   74
    Does Follow   74
    Qwitter   75
    Friend or Follow   76
    Mr. Tweet   77
    Omnee   78
    Twitree   79
And Many More   80

3. Web Programming Basics 83

XHTML   83
   Web Pages   84
   A Nod to Some Other XML Structures   89
CSS   90
   Assigning Styles to Structure   92
   Laying Out Your Web Page Content   93
   Decorating the Web Page Content   94
   Getting the Browser to Recognize Styles   95
PHP   96
   How to Accept Candy from Strangers   97
   Strings, Arrays, and Objects   98
   Manipulating the Data You Collect   100
   Knowing Your Environment   104
   Controlling the Flow of Logic   106
   File Management   109
   Connecting to the Database   111
   Building a Custom Function   113
   SimpleXML   116
   DOM   117
   cURL   118
   Debugging   120
MySQL   122
   Creating a New Table   123
   Retrieving Information from the Database   124
   Changing Information in the Database   125
A Place to Call /home   126
   Selecting a Host Server   126
   Automation   128
Further Reading   130

4. Meet the Twitter API 133

Accessing the API   134
   HTTP Requests   134
   HTTP Status Codes   137
   Format   139
   Authentication   140
   A Peak at OAuth   141
   Parameters   143
   Rate Limiting   147
   Keeping Development Light   148
Play Along at Home   149
The API Methods   150

Publishing   151
The Information Stream   152
The Follow Network   157
Communication   165
Member Account   168
API Administration   174
Search   176
Other Data Options   181
Gone Phishing: A Word About Passwords   182
Is Twishing Worth the Effort?   184
OAuth Can Help   187

5. **Meet the Output** **191**
User Objects   192
User Elements   195
Status Objects   198
Status Elements   200
Message Objects   202
Direct Message Elements   204
Search Objects   205
Feed Elements   206
Entry Elements   207
ID Objects   208
ID Elements   208
Response Objects   209
Response Elements   209
Hash Objects   209
Hash Elements   210
Errors   211

6. **Application Setup** **213**
Establishing Your Twitter Account   214
Registering a New Twitter Member Account   215
Configuring Your New Account   217
Creating Your Database   222
Making Sure There Is a There There   223
Giving the Database Some Structure   223
Included Functions   227
Creating Your Includes Directory   227
Environment Functions   229
API Configuration Functions   230
Database Functions   234
SQL Queries   235

Data Parsing Functions	240
Password Management Functions	246
Data Validation Functions	249
Data Sorting Functions	252
Statistics Functions	253
Log Management Functions	254
Status Messages	255
HTML Template Functions	257
CSS	260

7. Sample Applications **263**
Meet the Sample Apps	263
Why Are You Asking for My Password?	265
Administration Tool	267
Take the App for a Spin	267
Check Under the Hood	268
Shifting Gears	275
Tweet Publisher	277
Take the App for a Spin	277
Check Under the Hood	278
Shifting Gears	282
Auto Tweet	282
Take the App for a Spin	283
Check Under the Hood	284
Shifting Gears	290
Tweet Broadcast	291
Take the App for a Spin	291
Check Under the Hood	293
Shifting Gears	299
Broadcast Feed	300
Take the App for a Spin	300
Check Under the Hood	300
Shifting Gears	304
Tweet Alert	305
Take the App for a Spin	305
Check Under the Hood	307
Shifting Gears	312
Network Viewer	313
Take the App for a Spin	313
Check Under the Hood	315
Shifting Gears	323
Best of Twitter API	324
Take the App for a Spin	325

Check Under the Hood 326

Shifting Gears 329

8. **Automated Tasks** **331**

RSS to Tweet 332

Check Under the Hood 333

Aggregate Broadcast 338

Check Under the Hood 339

Scan Tweets 342

Check Under the Hood 343

Queue Users 349

Check Under the Hood 350

Collect Favorites 352

Check Under the Hood 353

Appendix: Twitter API Reference **361**

Index **377**

Preface

One reason Twitter resonates with me is its simplicity. I've blogged in some form or another since 2000, when my first son was born. It takes a lot of time and thought to compose even a few paragraphs of meaningful text for a blog. You can add pictures and video, fiddle with the formatting, and reference many other sites with hyperlinks. It is an incredibly useful practice, but rarely does blogging fit into one of those natural moments between tasks. Twitter, on the other hand, won't let you contribute more than a few thoughts or a link or two with each post, and only then if it fits into the 140-character limit. There is no formatting or multimedia embedding; it is just a simple act of thinking, sharing, responding, or emoting.

Since Twitter's award-winning appearance at the South By Southwest (SXSW) conference in 2007, many have called for it to improve on the simple things it does. Why aren't there groups? Can we make our posts longer? Will pictures show up in the timeline? How can I manage my private messages to other users? Although Twitter has on occasion responded to collective behavior or demand by implementing a new wrinkle (as with *@username* replies), the service has largely remained as it began: simple.

It is a credit to Twitter that it has resisted such changes. Making the service less simple would also make it less versatile. The void of unanswered user requests for functionality is filled by an ecosystem of third-party developers. The incentive for the innovation and resources these developers bring to the Twitter community would be critically lowered if the main service tried to do too much. A simple Twitter is better not only for the users trying to post their status updates, but also for the third-party applications trying to find their niches.

The purpose of *Twitter API: Up and Running* is to provide an introduction to using the Twitter API—the means to get at the rich Twitter data—to build web applications. This book has three main parts: an overview of the Twitter ecosystem and culture; background information on the languages and environment you need to create your applications; and working code for a suite of sample applications meant to get you started on your programming adventure. Novice readers should be able to gather working knowledge from the PHP scripts used to create the sample applications and see how the syntax works in context. Experienced readers will likely benefit from the references for the API methods as well as discussions about the context into which your applications will be placed.

As Twitter lowers barriers to publication through its simplicity, so this book will provide easy access to the skills and resources you'll need to build web applications for its API.

Who This Book Is For

The cultivation of open API development represents another level of evolution in Internet participation. We aren't just reading and writing content; we're also cocreating the interactions surrounding that content. Twitter, in particular, has a low barrier for both. The most important property of the Twitter API is not found in the nuances of its syntax, but rather in the imaginative and prolific cocreation it inspires.

This groundbreaking book is for Twitter fans who want to do more than just answer the question, "What are you doing?" In this first book about working with the Twitter API, new and casual programmers are provided with explanations of how each part of the API functions and examples of how those parts can be assembled into web applications. We'll also look closely at the culture of Twitter and how it has inspired programmers to build their own tools and games.

A prerequisite for this book is a basic understanding of how applications are built and hosted on the Web. However, you don't need to be a professional coder to launch a Twitter web application successfully. The XHTML, CSS, PHP, and MySQL code necessary to the construction of the example applications will be provided and explained, as will some suggested criteria for securing a website. You should be able to pick up this book, follow the sample code, and have at your disposal a working application to use and modify.

 The sample code can be downloaded from this book's website (*http://www.oreilly.com/catalog/9780596154615/*). It is open and available for anyone to use.

Among the wide range of readers of this book will be IT professionals in small organizations and Twitter members looking for a programming project. In the former scenario, an IT professional may be looking at Twitter as a potential platform to integrate existing services or products provided by his employer. He can use this book to survey some web tools that might serve as a foundation for a larger web application. In this context, it becomes a project companion with additional long-term value as a reference and directory of sample applications.

In the latter scenario, an active member of the Twitter community may have grown tired of waiting for someone else to provide missing functionality and be thinking about adding it herself. She might read this book first to see what is out there, in case someone has already built the desired tool, and then try to code the web application herself. She may not consider herself a programmer, but she can build off of the sample code and learn details by referencing the chapters on PHP and MySQL functions, selecting the sample application closest to what she has in mind and then making changes to add the desired behavior.

Twitter is a hot topic, but not much has been written about it yet. Therefore, the information this book contains on the history of the Twitter culture will also make it attractive to nonprogrammers who want to understand the phenomenon, such as decision makers for company development teams or active Internet users new to Twitter.

How This Book Is Organized

This book introduces the Twitter API in the context of a greater community culture, offering a suite of sample applications to help illustrate some key programming concepts. Here's a synopsis of what you'll find:

Chapter 1, *Hello Twitter*
> Gives you a comprehensive overview of the Twitter culture, including the history of microblogging, the Fail Whale, the company business model, the API developer community, and creative uses of Twitter.

Chapter 2, *Twitter Applications*
> Reviews more than two dozen existing third-party Twitter web applications you can use as inspiration for your own creations. The applications are grouped into seven tools categories—Publishing, Information Stream, Appropriation, Search, Aggregation, Statistics, and Follow Network tools—and each app is profiled with a screenshot and a description of what it does.

Chapter 3, *Web Programming Basics*
> Provides a comprehensive starter kit for XHTML, CSS, PHP, and MySQL. This chapter is meant to be a primer for new programmers and a convenient reference for more experienced programmers. It also offers some advice on what to look for when searching for a web host to care for your new application.

Chapter 4, *Meet the Twitter API*
> Gives the details on how to make requests of the Twitter API. Included in the general explanation are format differences, HTTP methods and error codes, authentication, and rate limits. This chapter contains a directory of all of the parameters used by the API and a description of each of the 40 methods, grouped into seven categories: Publishing, Information Stream, Follow Network, Communication, Member Account, API Administration, and Search. It also includes a discussion about security issues involving Basic Auth and a brief description of how to use cURL to test the API.

Chapter 5, *Meet the Output*
> Takes a look at what comes out of the API as a response from Twitter. The various types of XML objects you will encounter—user, status, message, search, ID,

response, and hash—are detailed with example output, explanations of the included XML elements, and a list of methods that return that object.

Chapter 6, *Application Setup*

Discusses the things you need to do to get your web environment ready, including creating a master Twitter account, making your MySQL database tables, creating your stylesheet, and uploading custom functions to a directory outside the web path. Each of the custom functions used in the sample applications is discussed in detail, with a description of what it does and PHP code provided as examples.

Chapter 7, *Sample Applications*

Describes the web interfaces from the suite of sample applications. For each of the seven applications, I'll run you through how to use it and what it does, and then we'll look closely at the code. Included are suggestions for how to make this starter code better.

Chapter 8, *Automated Tasks*

Describes the code for the programs from the suite of sample applications that run in the background. It includes a brief explanation of what each of the five scripts does and how the PHP code works.

Appendix

Provides a bare-bones look at the Twitter API, listing the method path, whether it requires authentication, if it is charged against your rate limit, the HTTP method type, and any required and optional parameters.

Conventions Used in This Book

The following typographical conventions are used in this book:

Italic

Used for emphasis, technical terms where they are defined, URLs, email addresses, filenames, file extensions, and pathnames.

`Constant width`

Used for code samples, SQL statements, HTML and XML elements, methods, functions, variables and attributes and their values, objects, and class names.

`Constant width italic`

Used for user-replaceable items in code.

`Constant width bold`

Used for emphasis in code samples.

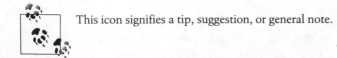 This icon signifies a tip, suggestion, or general note.

This icon indicates a warning or caution.

Using Code Examples

You may use the code in this book in your programs and documentation. You do not need to contact us for permission unless you're reproducing a significant portion of the code. For example, writing a program that uses several chunks of code from this book does not require permission. Selling or distributing a CD-ROM of examples from this book *does* require permission. Answering a question by citing this book and quoting example code does not require permission. Incorporating a significant amount of example code from this book into your product's documentation *does* require permission.

We appreciate, but do not require, attribution. An attribution usually includes the title, author, publisher, and ISBN. For example: "*Twitter API: Up and Running*, by Kevin Makice. Copyright 2009 Kevin Makice, 978-0-596-15461-5."

If you feel your use of code examples falls outside fair use or the permission given above, feel free to contact us at *permissions@oreilly.com*.

Safari® Books Online

When you see a Safari® Books Online icon on the cover of your favorite technology book, that means the book is available online through the O'Reilly Network Safari Bookshelf.

Safari offers a solution that's better than e-books. It's a virtual library that lets you easily search thousands of top tech books, cut and paste code samples, download chapters, and find quick answers when you need the most accurate, current information. Try it for free at *http://my.safaribooksonline.com/*.

We'd Like to Hear from You

Please address comments and questions concerning this book to the publisher:

O'Reilly Media, Inc.
1005 Gravenstein Highway North
Sebastopol, CA 95472
800-998-9938 (in the United States or Canada)
707-829-0515 (international or local)
707-829-0104 (fax)

We have a web page for this book, where we list errata, examples, and any additional information. You can access this page at:

http://www.oreilly.com/catalog/9780596154615/

To comment or ask technical questions about this book, send email to:

bookquestions@oreilly.com

For more information about our books, conferences, Resource Centers, and the O'Reilly Network, see our website at:

http://www.oreilly.com

Acknowledgments

It has always been a dream to write a book. While for a long time I thought it would be about time travel or dragons, I'm delighted that my dream was fulfilled under the banner of O'Reilly Media. For that, I have a number of people to thank.

This book is dedicated to my family—Amy (*@amakice*), Carter (*@cmakice*), Archie, and the TBD baby we were creating during the nine months it took to write this tome— who went out of their way to give me time and space to type, type, type. By now, with me five years into an older-student Ph.D., they are used to helping me get my 3–5 hours of sleep each night, while keeping me fed and entertained. However, writing a book on top of graduate school is like adding a couple more dissertations to the workload. It takes a village to write a tech book. As they supported me, my family received support from Amy's and my parents—Susan Clendening (*@twobigdogs*); Roger (*@rjisb*) and Jean Isbister; Gary and Carol Clendening; Joy and Pete Kottra—and our friends. I am particularly grateful for the supplemental financial support from that group and from my long-time friend, Tim Roessler, who can now take this dedication as a direct request to sign up for Twitter.

From the O'Reilly camp, Laurel Ruma (*@laurelatoreilly*) ran point on this project. Despite my being intimidated by both the brand and the endeavor, she held my virtual hand throughout the process and gently kept me on task. That this book arrived on bookshelves near you is a credit to her stewardship that made this project such a wonderful experience for me. I wouldn't have met her at all if it weren't for Jeffrey Bardzell (*@jeffreybardzell*), my professor and friend, who referred me to his agent Carole Jelen McClendon at Waterside Productions. Carole, now my agent, helped me pitch an idea for a Twitter book to John Osborn (*@johnatlarge*) and Laurel. Nine months later I was holding my first published book. From top to bottom, the O'Reilly Media organization was amazing. Rachel Head, Sarah Schneider, Marlowe Shaeffer, and Rachel Monaghan were also key to completing this project, and I thank them all for their professionalism and patience.

I'd also like to thank the great early tech reviewers that O'Reilly assembled to help improve the content in the book: Alex Payne (*@al3x*), Ed Finkler (*@funkatron*), Eric Stern (*@Firehed*), Cameron Kaiser (*@doctorlinguist*), Bill Ryan (*@wgryan*), Lisa Hoover (*@lisah*), Abraham Williams (*@poseurtech*), Dave Troy (*@davetroy*), Jeff Clark (*@jeffclark*), Matt Gillooly (*@mattgillooly*), Damon Cortesi (*@dacort*), and the Lollicode team. Ed was particularly helpful in answering follow-up questions after his initial review, improving security in the sample code, and taking a second peek at additional sections written into later drafts. I am also appreciative of the fact that Alex was willing to spend so much time looking at my words when he was writing his own O'Reilly book on Scala. This book is all the better for their participation.

My local Twitter community deserves props as well. I am in awe that a small university city could muster over 650 early adopters of the service, many of whom were among my peers at the Indiana University School of Informatics. Their use of Twitter is what makes my timeline so valuable. In the process of testing the code for this book, I had to rely on a number of people in my follow net to make sure I wasn't inadvertently blowing up oil rigs in the Gulf. Thanks to my early reality checkers: Michelle (*@MzHartz*), Allison (*@allisoncooke*), Joel (*@rhythmofself*), Jonathan (*@Jonathan-Branam*), Noah (*@noahwesley*), Steve (*@SoundSystemSDC*), Daniel (*@b00ger*), Chintan (*@tankchintan*), Mike (*@dmikeallen*), Jenny (*@jbhertel*), and several others.

The Twitter version of this would be: "@everyone thanks!"

CHAPTER 1

Hello Twitter

 kmakice For a thing to have meaning, it must have context.

I can remember what life was like without Twitter. The many interesting thoughts popping out of my brain throughout the day had to fight for supremacy. Like an intellectual Thunderdome, only one thought could emerge to become a blog. No one knew when I was sleeping and when I was watching *Battlestar Galactica* on my TiVo. I had no way of being alerted when someone local was heading to Chicago so that I could express to that person my love of Edwardo's stuffed pizzas as a passive hint to deliver.

Before Twitter, my connection with the other people in my academic program was constrained by time and space. I could only inquire about their work or ask what they were eating if we were in the same room with overlapping moments of free time. My news about hurricanes and earthquakes was limited to what I could glean from CNN.com and Weather Underground. There were no personal accounts of mass evacuations, nothing to tell me instantly where someone was when the ground started shaking.

Mercifully, a solution emerged. Twitter—a channel for sharing individual status updates with the world—has brought value to the mundane. We have evolved out of that bygone era and into a world measured 140 characters at a time.

Kelly Abbott (@*KellyAbbott*) of Dandelife introduced me to Twitter through a little Flash widget featured in the sidebar of his blog. It displayed a running list of short journal entries about his life. I clicked and registered my own Twitter account (see Figure 1-1) about a week before the service exploded onto the scene with an award-winning presence at the South by Southwest (SXSW) conference[*] in March 2007.

---

[*] South By Southwest is an annual conference held in Austin, Texas to showcase the latest in music, film, and interactive media. It started in 1987 as a small music festival, and now draws over 11,000 people each year.

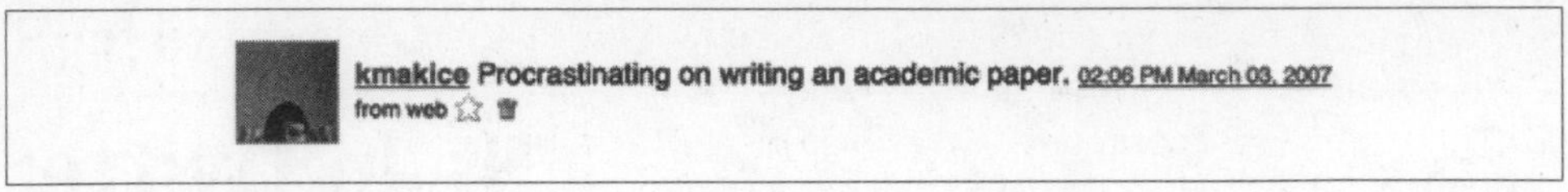

kmakice Procrastinating on writing an academic paper. 02:06 PM March 03, 2007
from web ☆ 🗑

Figure 1-1. My first tweet

The estimated number of Twitter accounts surpassed 3 million during the summer of 2008, according to third-party tools. (Twitter does not provide official statistics on membership.[†]) Compete reported an 812% increase in unique monthly visitors to the Twitter website in 2008, jumping to almost 6 million in January 2009.[‡] Interest in the channel comes not just from the producers and consumers of content, but also from developers of desktop applications, information visualization systems, Internet mash-ups, and completely new services not possible before Twitter existed. *Tweets*—the name given to the brief status updates—are used for many purposes, from alerting local communities about emergency situations to playing games. They can even facilitate the sale of beer. Although Twitter is not without critics, it seems clear that microblogging is here to stay.

You undoubtedly bought or borrowed this book because you are interested in programming some system or widget using the Twitter application programming interface (API). Doing that effectively requires more than just knowing what to code; it is also important to know how your new amazing "thing" is going to fit into the culture Twitter and its users have created. *Don't underestimate the importance of culture*. For a thing to be meaningful, it has to have context. In this chapter, we'll look at the world into which your application will be hatched.

What Are You Doing?

Ian Curry of Frog Design once likened twittering to bumping into someone in a hallway and casually asking, "What's up?" In a 2007 blog post, Curry noted:

> It's not so important what gets said as that it's nice to stay in contact with people. These light exchanges typify the kind of communication that arises among people who are saturated with other forms of communication.[§]

[†] TwitDir (*http://www.twitdir.com*) launched a member directory in the first half of 2007. Among other things, this website tracked the number of unique member accounts encountered while monitoring the public timeline.

[‡] Compete's SiteAnalytics reported 5,979,052 unique visitors to *http://twitter.com* in January 2009, up from 655,067 in January 2008 (*http://siteanalytics.compete.com/twitter.com/?metric=uv*).

[§] From the February 26, 2007 blog article, "Twitter: The missing messenger," by Ian Curry of Frog Design (*http://designmind.frogdesign.com/blog/twitter-the-missing-messenger.html*).

Leisa Reichelt of *disambiguity* called it "ambient intimacy," the ability to keep in touch with people in a way that time and space normally make impossible.‖ For *Wired* magazine writer Clive Thompson (*@pomeranian99*), it's a "sixth sense,"# incredibly useful in understanding when to interact with coworkers. Twitter has also been described as a low-expectation IRC. Brett Weaver considers each tweet the atomic level of social networking.* It is a phatic function of communication, keeping the lines of communication between you and someone else open and ready and letting you know when that channel has closed. All of these terms suggest what experience has already taught millions of people: there is great value in small talk.

The main prompt for all this contact on Twitter is a simple question: "What are you doing?" In practice, that question is usually interpreted as, "What interesting thought do you want to share at this moment?" The variety of potential responses is what makes Twitter such a valuable and versatile channel.

The throwaway answers include messages of context, invitation, social statements, inquiries and answers, massively shared experiences, device state updates, news broadcasts, and announcements. Twitter is used for many purposes, including:

- Sharing interesting web links
- Reporting local news you have witnessed
- Rebroadcasting fresh information you have received
- Philosophizing
- Making brief, directed commentaries to another person
- Emoting and venting
- Recording behavior, such as a change in location or eating habits
- Posing a question
- Rickrolling (*http://en.wikipedia.org/wiki/Rickrolling*)
- Crowdsourcing
- Organizing flash mobs and tweetups (in-person meetups with Twitter friends)

Small comments return big value when shared with the world. Not everyone will read what you post, of course, but those who do get to sample a small bit of your life in a way previously available only to those who happened to bump into you in a hallway or on the street. In this sense, the primary value of Twitter can be found in the small, informal contact it enables between its users.

‖ From the March 1, 2007 blog article, "Ambient intimacy," by Leisa Reichelt of *disambiguity* (*http://www.disambiguity.com/ambient-intimacy*).

Clive Thompson, "How Twitter Creates a Social Sixth Sense," *Wired* 15:7 (June 26, 2007) (*http://www.wired.com/techbiz/media/magazine/15-07/st_thompson*).

* From the January 28, 2009 blog article, "4 Must have tools to automate Twitter," by Brett Weaver, published on Active Rain (*http://activerain.com/blogsview/904695/4-Must-have-tools-to-automate-Twitter*).

Twitter is also about emergence. Individual members each compose their own information streams by posting original content and also by reading the updates of other selected members, so the many uses for Twitter can lead to an infinite number of experiences. Each user can tailor her experience to her own wants and needs. However, the sum of all of those unique parts creates new knowledge and inspires useful tools.

Twitterspeak

The Twitter culture has created its own lexicon, filled with new words you should know. Here are a few of the basics:

Tweet
> The preferred name for a status update

Retweet
> The reposting of an interesting tweet from another twitterer

Detweet
> Craig Danuloff suggests there should be a way to refute someone's post by passing along a tweet with "a degree of disapproval"

Tweeple/tweeps
> Twitter people, Twitter members, Twitter users, twitterers

Twoosh
> A tweet that is a perfect 140 characters long

Tweetup
> When tweeple meet in person

For a more complete list of Twitter words, try Twittonary (*http://www.twittonary .com*), the Twictionary wiki (*http://twictionary.pbwiki.com*), or the Twitter Fan Wiki's Twitter Glossary (*http://twitter.pbwiki.com/Twitter+Glossary*).

Rules of Engagement

While Twitter itself deals with a daily crush of a million or more status updates,[†] the blogosphere is occupying bandwidth talking about Twitter. There are at least 1,500 articles referencing the microblogging channel each day, according to Technorati (see *http://technorati.com/chart/Twitter*), including 50–350 daily references among the blogs with the highest authority. Many of those posts give advice on how best to use Twitter.

One of the strengths of Twitter is its flexibility. Every information stream is unique and can be customized in the way that best fits the individual at that moment. Are you

---

[†] Twitter does not provide or confirm these statistics, but some third-party applications do offer estimates. TweetRush (*http://tweetrush.com*), an analytics engine that looks beyond page views and clicks for evidence of activity elsewhere in the application logic, estimated peaks of about 1.9 million tweets and 380,000 unique users each day in January 2009.

getting too much information? Unfollow some people. Do you not have time to tweet? Don't. Want to chat with your two best buds for an hour and chase away all your other followers? Feel free. Because of this versatility, there are no universal rules for how to behave on Twitter; each user can control his own experience.

Here is a sampling of some of the tips and guidelines that have shown up in blogs over the past two years:

- Watch your Twitter ratios.
- Never follow more than 300 people.
- Follow 1 person for every 10 who follow you.
- Don't follow people you've never met.
- Be active.
- Don't go all mental and tweet four or five times in a row.
- Never tweet more than five times a day.
- Migrate your real-world conversation to Twitter.
- Don't overdo the @ tweets. It's a stage whisper.
- Pre-write some of your material.
- Be original and useful.
- Don't try to share your political, religious, or business views in 140 characters.
- Don't post thoughts across multiple tweets.
- Don't put things into Twitter that aren't designed for Twitter, like photos, audio, etc.
- Don't start posts with "I am."
- Don't gunk up your stream with machine-readable crapola like "#" or "L:".
- Use contractions whenever possible.
- Use numerals, not words, for all numbers.
- Provide links and context whenever possible.
- Don't assume other people are having the same experience you are.
- Remember that the Twitter question is, "What are you doing?"

Each one of these gems may be considered good advice by some people and horrible advice by others. I have my own set of ever-evolving rules—my *twethics*—but although you will see some suggestions scattered throughout this book, I won't lay them all out here, since they apply only to me. You must find your own way, Grasshopper.

 Any firm advice on how to use Twitter might undercut one of the dynamics that makes Twitter work: *authenticity*. It is easy to detect when you treat your relationships with other twitterers as commodities.

Unlike with other channels, each of us has near-complete control over what we see on Twitter. Spammers can only gain a foothold in our tweet streams if we allow their messages in by following them, and we can stop unwanted messages at any point simply by unfollowing the offending users. There are a few basic tells that can help identify a spammer—most notably an insanely unbalanced following-to-follower ratio—but an often-overlooked sign is whether the posts seem authentic. Do the tweets reek of self-promotion? Do they amount to nothing more than an RSS feed? Do you want that?

Everyone has a different experience with Twitter (Figure 1-2‡). We craft our own experiences when we decide who to follow, what we post, and how we choose to see the results. Ultimately, the burden is on the follower, not the followed, to either communicate dissatisfaction or adjust her stream.

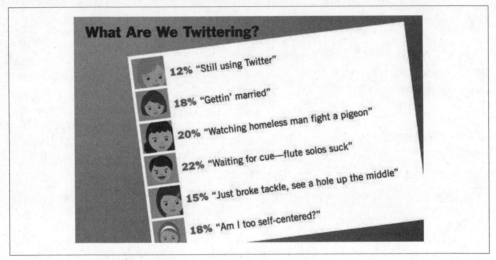

What Are We Twittering?

- 12% "Still using Twitter"
- 18% "Gettin' married"
- 20% "Watching homeless man fight a pigeon"
- 22% "Waiting for cue—flute solos suck"
- 15% "Just broke tackle, see a hole up the middle"
- 18% "Am I too self-centered?"

Figure 1-2. A sarcastic look at twittering content by The Onion

Opportunistic Interruptions

My family used our first tweets to keep in touch with each other over spring break. My wife, Amy, was experiencing Florida with my sons while I was catching up on academic course work and projects. We quickly noticed how much more connected we felt just by reading about little moments that would otherwise have been lost. There are many channels for sharing the bigger things, such as "We're having another baby" or "I just landed a job writing my first book." Blogs, letters, phone conversations, family vacations to Grammy's house—these are all opportunities to share news, but rarely are they used to communicate the smaller experiences that comprise most of our living. Twitter is built for that purpose.

‡ This graphic is reprinted with permission from *The Onion* (copyright ©2008 by Onion, Inc., *http://www .theonion.com*). By the way, *The Onion* is also on Twitter (*@theonion*).

Amy (*@amakice*) lacked Internet access during that first Twitter vacation, so she posted updates exclusively from her cell phone. This allowed her to share good (and bad) moments on the beach or in the car as they happened. I, on the other hand, was attached to an Internet connection for that first week of Twitter. I started out using the website but quickly realized one of the big limitations—a barrier to use—was that I had to go to Twitter to get my fix. It was somewhat disappointing when I loaded up my profile page and didn't see a ping from my family.

My appreciation of Twitter changed when I discovered Twitterrific, a third-party desktop client. Twitterrific runs in the background, starting up automatically when I boot up my computer and requiring no action after the initial configuration. It brings my content to me, adding an ambient quality to Twitter. The notifications can be set to appear for short periods of time before going away on their own, which gives me awareness of activity while minimizing the intrusion.

This approach works because most of us only like to be interrupted in a way that is convenient to us. At about the same time Amy was tweeting about building sand castles, University of Illinois researcher Brian Bailey was making the trip to Indiana to talk to our human-computer interaction group about his work. Bailey and others were painstakingly exploring the nature of interruptions by trying to identify the best times to draw attention away from a current task and alert users to new information. This work turned out to be very influential in the way I think about the design of IT, and it is what comes to mind whenever Twitterrific shows me a new tweet from my personal information stream. Installing Twitterrific on my MacBook greatly increased my consumption and enjoyment of Twitter.

 Twitterrific got a lot of positive buzz when its manufacturer, Iconfactory (*http://iconfactory.com*), released its iPhone application. For Macintosh desktops, there is a free version and a premium version, where you pay to eliminate the advertising. For other platforms, try Twhirl or Digsby. Another popular desktop application is TweetDeck (*http://www.tweetdeck.com*), which is built on the Adobe AIR platform and adds a way to group the tweets from the people you follow. Tools like these are highly recommended to improve your experience reading tweets.

Twitter works in large part because it fits into one's own routine. Although many people publish status updates through the main website, the majority of twitterers use third-party publication tools.§ It is also possible to tweet from a cell phone or via IM. The company maintains a simple API that has spawned hundreds of Twitter applications,

---

§ As of September 2008, 45% of tweets were published through the website, according to "Twitter and the Micro-Messaging Revolution: Communication, Connections, and Immediacy—140 Characters at a Time," an O'Reilly Radar Report published in November 2008 by Sarah Milstein, with Abdur Chowdhury, Gregor Hochmuth, Ben Lorica, and Roger Magoulas. Ed Finkler (*@funkatron*) has recorded similar stats at *http://funkatron.com/twitter-source-stats*.

giving members even more ways to tell the world what they are doing. Desktop and iPhone clients like Twitterrific and Twhirl enhance the way Twitter works, both as a publisher and as an information conduit.

 Twitter disabled its instant message support during the summer of 2008, when the company experienced technical problems trying to handle traffic on its servers. By the fall, Twitter had downgraded the restoration of IM integration to wishful thinking. Third-party developers such as excla.im (*http://excla.im*) are trying to pick up the resulting slack to let members once again tweet via IM.

Twitter Is Like a Side-by-Side Conversation

Although the core concept revolves around individual status updates, there is a communal chat-like quality to Twitter. Sometimes it's used for explicit conversations. Tweets can be directed at specific users with the convention *@username*, which Twitter interprets as a threaded post. About two in every five tweets references someone in this fashion, either as a formal reply—where the *@username* begins the tweet—or elsewhere in the content of the tweet. There is a separate channel just for replies, giving each user the option to include replies from members not in their usual information stream.

The big problem with this kind of directed conversation is the absence of shared context. When I post "@amakice A frog in a blender" to Twitter, it probably won't make much sense to anyone who wasn't following my wife when she tweeted, "What's green and red?" Since everyone's information stream is unique, the odds are good that any reply you post is going to be a response to something some of your followers didn't see. If you aren't providing enough context to make your tweets accessible to everyone, you are losing people in your audience who realize you aren't speaking to them.

The perception of personal connection, in spite of the general broadcast of each tweet, led marketer Ed Dale (*@Ed_Dale*) to dub twittering "side-by-side communication."‖ A traditional marketing perspective is face-to-face. This suggests combat, as if the business and consumer are assuming martial arts poses. Defenses are raised, and to be received, the message must clear several barriers. Dale's observation was that Twitter contact is more personal, like two people walking side by side in the same general direction. There is an embedded nonchalance in the way information is exchanged, lowering the barriers to entry on both ends.

That sacred trust can be fleeting. We all have our own thresholds for how much noise or content we can tolerate before taking action in response. That action can materialize as unfollowing the offending person or, more severely, abandoning Twitter altogether.

‖ From the September 20, 2007 blog article, "The Tao of Twitter," by Ed Dale (*http://mythirtydaychallenge3rdyear.com/date/2007/09/*).

Every tweet, therefore, is as much of a test of your value to others as it is an expression of an idea or desire.

Initially, I vowed to keep my information stream small. I mostly followed people I already knew and avoided anyone using Twitter like a chat client (as in, "@soandso LOL!"). Early in my twittering, my network consisted of four groups of authors: family, colleagues, new acquaintances, and famous people. I thought 50 would be my limit. Two years and several hundred tweeps later, I still feel somewhat conservative in my network management, even if the bars have moved. (You have to follow at least 1,800 others to crack the top 1,000 users, according to third-party Twitter directory TwitDir.)

In 1992, a primate researcher named Robin Dunbar suggested that there is a physical limit, determined by the volume of the neocortex region in the brain, to the number of members in a social group that one person can manage. The Dunbar Number is often reported as 150 people. Some Twitter members follow significantly many more people than that, but the long tail is primarily composed of small balanced networks.[#]

One reason the Dunbar Number likely doesn't apply to Twitter (or many other social networks) has to do with the same cognitive behavior that allows us to recognize information from a prompt more easily than we can recall it on our own. We rely on external resources, like shopping lists and computer searches, to help us remember things our brains would otherwise forget. Likewise, we can use Twitter to maintain relationships that might otherwise wither, giving us a better chance of renewing them.

Our information streams can grow to include hundreds or thousands of other people because not all of them will be communicating at once. The tweeple we follow will presumably have passed some kind of litmus test to prompt us to follow them in the first place, so the relationships tend to persist.

History of Twitter

One of the best descriptions of Twitter came from Australian web developer Ben Buchanan (*@200ok*) a few months before the first explosion of new registrations:

> It's faster than email; slower than IRC (in a good way); doesn't demand immediate attention like IM and has a social/group aspect that SMS alone can't touch. It is quite odd, but I can't help thinking this is a sign of things to come. Communications channels that are flexible and quick, personal and tribal...it's approaching what I imagined when cyberpunk authors talked about personal comm units.[*]

[#] In my own research and that of others, two things are clear. First, people are capable of managing very large and active streams. Second, most people have very small networks that are smaller than the vague Dunbar Number. From a sampling of 64,968 people tweeting about the candidates on Election Day 2008 between poll closing and Barack Obama's acceptance speech, only 7,117 of the 847,007 members in their extended networks were following more than 150 people. That is less than 1% of all members.

[*] From the January 14, 2007 blog article, "Two Weeks on Twitter," by Ben Buchanan, published on the web200ok blog (*http://weblog.200ok.com.au/2007/01/two-weeks-on-twitter.html*).

Ben also disclosed his initial reaction to Twitter: "The first time I heard about Twitter I thought it was a stupid idea." That is an all-too-common refrain from those who haven't tried the service, or worse, tried Twitter under less than optimal conditions (following too few, tweeting too seldom, relying only on the web interface). Almost as common as that initial "stupid idea" critique is the subsequent change in attitude after giving Twitter a fair shake.

Microblogging, a term for the publication of short messages reporting on the details of one's life, made the big time in March 2007 when Twitter became the hit of the SXSW conference in Austin. The company set up large screens to display tweets submitted by conference attendees, who signed up for the service in droves. Twitter creator Jack Dorsey (*@jack*) and early funder Evan Williams (*@ev*) didn't invent communication through text, but their company did construct the scaffolding that gave new power to short messages.

 In August 1935, *Modern Mechanix* magazine published an article describing a robot messenger that displayed person-to-person notes. Dubbed "the notificator," this London-based contraption was like a vending machine for messages. Customers deposited coins to allow their handwritten notes to remain visible in the machine for a few hours. For more information on the notificator, read Dan Hollings's (*@dhollings*) 2008 blog post, "Twitter Invented in 1935? Who Would Have Thunk!" (*http://danhollings.posterous.com/twitter-invented-in -1935-who-w*).

A Brief History of Microblogging

Twitter would not have had the opportunity to befuddle, annoy, and ultimately sway people into daily use without certain technological precursors. Microblogging has its roots in three main technological developments: Instant Relay Chat (IRC), IM chat status messages, and mobile phones.

After a couple decades of computer scientists toying with the idea of distributed chat (see Figure 1-3†), IRC came into existence in 1988. Invented by Jarkko Oikarinen, it was the forerunner to instant messaging tools such as Yahoo! Messenger and Google Talk. The IRC community developed a rich language of protocols using special characters to provide instructions from writers to readers.

Two examples of such protocols are the namespace channel (*#namespace*) and the directed message (*@username*). Both conventions have propagated into current microblogging norms and are sometimes even hardcoded into the services. Twitter is mulling over the possibility of officially recognizing the *retweet*, which is when a twitterer

---

† This image is reprinted with permission from the artist, cartoonist Robert Crumb, who first published this illustration in an issue of *Zap Comix*. A copy of this image can be found on the Web at *http://herot.typepad .com/cherot/2007/10/in-the-60s-r-cr.html* (source: Christopher Herot).

reposts a status update first written by someone else. Members establish new standards by doing things that other people do.

The child of IRC, instant messaging, taught a generation of young Internet users how to chat online with friends in real time. Its popularity grew as it evolved from mere in-the-moment communication into a subculture of creativity expressed via "away" status messages.

Figure 1-3. Cartoonist Robert Crumb predicted Twitter in the 1960s

In most IM clients, a user can select a custom away message to be displayed when the connection idles or when the user explicitly selects a dormant state. Over time, these messages became more and more creative, moving from a standard "Not at my desk" to more specific explanations of absence, such as "Weeping softly in stairwell A. Back in 10." This form of cultural communication also crept into social networking sites, most notably Facebook. It became accepted behavior to express oneself in this manner, as did keeping informed about one's friends by reading their status messages.

The final piece of the puzzle was the mobile phone revolution. This was far more pronounced outside of the U.S., due to late adoption of the technology and a less developed reliance on landline phones. *Texting*—i.e., sending text messages via the Short Message Service (SMS)—got its start in 1992, when Sema Group's Neil Papworth sent the first message, from his PC to a friend's handset: "MERRY CHRISTMAS." It was 1999, however, before SMS was able to allow communication between providers, which sparked its widespread use. Texting became a legitimate use for a mobile phone and soon became as popular a means of communication as simply talking into the mouthpiece. The maximum length of an 8-bit data message is a familiar 140 characters, which gave rise to the signature constraint of Twitter.

Twitter's launch showed strong evidence of all three of these cultures—IRC, IM, and SMS—converging at an opportune moment. By that point, people had gotten used to composing short messages on demand. They sought out such messages to understand how the people they cared about were doing. Mobility meant that our spontaneous urges to communicate could be satisfied, and texting allowed us to do so whether or not everyone in our circle had a computer. That was the world into which Jack Dorsey hatched his idea.

---

140 Characters or Less

The limit of 140 characters is the lowest common denominator for SMS text messages. The Twitter API accepts longer strings of text, but those messages are truncated. Direct messages—a way of communicating with another member outside of the Twitter time-line—can accept up to 255 characters.

In reality, the limit is 140 bytes, not characters. Since Twitter is UTF-8 compatible, special Unicode characters that are part of an operating system are fair game for tweets. However, these characters have a bigger byte size (up to 4 bytes) and therefore shorten the maximum allowed length of a tweet. You can have up to 140 ASCII characters. If you want to use Unicode characters, try TwitterKeys (*http://tinyurl.com/twitterkeys*), a browser bookmark that lets you easily copy and paste these symbols into your tweets.

One of Twitter's original developers, Dom Sagolla (*@dom*), revealed the real motivation for the 140-character limit: the cost of SMS messages. Before the limit was imposed, the company and users took a huge hit to texting bills. 140 characters left room in the message for a username.[‡]

Believe It or Not: Twitter Was Inspired by Bike Couriers

"Like most people, it all started with my mother."

That was how then-CEO Jack Dorsey described the origins of Twitter in a talk he gave in spring 2008.[§] The path he took from that statement to explaining the development of his brainchild was a circuitous one. Try to follow along.

It seems Dorsey's mom liked to shop for bags, a minor obsession that she passed down to her son. Armed with the knowledge of all things bag, Dorsey's ideal model was that of the bike courier: a somewhat magical pouch that carries documents, garments, and other packages all over the city. He became fascinated with the flow of physical information that the courier bag facilitates, and he began to think about the digital information used to coordinate all of those activities—coordination known as dispatch. He

---

[‡] From the January 30, 2009 blog article, "How Twitter Was Born," by Dom Sagolla, published on 140 Characters (*http://www.140characters.com/2009/01/30/how-twitter-was-born/*).

[§] Biz Stone, cofounder of Twitter, posted a video of this talk on May 30, 2008 (*http://vimeo.com/1094070*).

devoted the early part of his career to programming software in Manhattan at the largest dispatch firm in the world.

Through this job, he noticed patterns emerging. Couriers, taxi drivers, and emergency responders all made status and position reports throughout the day via CB radio. Their messages—such as, "Courier 9 / Empty bag at 5th and 57th," "Taxi 054 / Passenger dropped off at LGA," and "Ambulance 12 / Patient having seizure. Going to Bellvue."—offered brief, specific information about particular individuals. Collectively, though, these messages painted a picture of what was going on in the city at any moment.

Dorsey eventually saw parallels between dispatch messages and IM status messages, except that in the latter case, all the action was tied to the desktop: the status messages reflected work and play taking place at the computer. He also noted that the mobile phone had become one of the things we commonly take with us when we leave the computer. By the time he got to Odeo, a podcasting company then owned by Evan Williams and Biz Stone's Obvious group, Dorsey was thinking about ways to merge IM status reports and the cell phone's mobility with dispatch dynamics.

Twitter was built with Ruby on Rails as an internal R&D project, intended to be the thread between devices and social interaction. It was so well received by Odeo employees that Williams decided to release the system—then called twttr—into the wild in July 2006. Robert Scoble (@scobleizer) and other A-list bloggers had already joined by the fall of that year, when it was officially launched, but it wasn't until Twitter bought a few vowels and won an award at SXSW the following March that the general public started to take notice. Dorsey's acceptance speech was appropriate to the new medium: "We'd like to thank you in 140 characters or less. And we just did!"

One of the things that made Twitter the darling of the ball was a giant display showing the tweets of those at the conference (Figure 1-4||). With this visual ROI for participating, hundreds of new users registered for the service and started texting updates in real time. When the conference attendees left Austin for home and work, they were rabid about sharing their excitement, and the Twitter population exploded.

Twitter dealt with its first known security issue about a month after SXSW: in early April 2007, it was reported that if you knew a Twitter user's cell phone number, you could spoof that user and access his Twitter timeline.# An authentication scheme was quickly added to allow for an optional PIN number to further verify that the SMS originator was the account holder. That same April, Williams spun Twitter off into its own company, naming Dorsey as the CEO, a position he held until Williams assumed the role in October 2008.

|| Photo reprinted with permission by Tom Lee (@sbma44), *http://www.manifestdensity.net*. The photo, "twitter's plasma screen," was posted on March 14, 2007 and can be found at: *http://www.flickr.com/photos/sbma44/421143852/*.

From the April 6, 2007 blog article, "Twitter and Jott Vulnerable to SMS and Caller ID Spoofing" by Nitesh Dhanjani, published on O'Reilly's OnLAMP.com, detailing how to post to someone else's timeline (*http://www.oreillynet.com/onlamp/blog/2007/04/twitter_and_jott_vulnerable_to.html*).

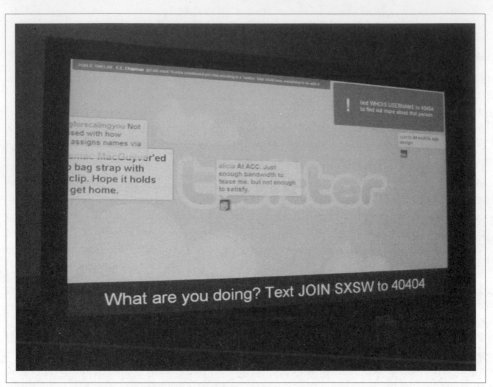

Figure 1-4. Twitter's display at South by Southwest 2007

Millions and Millions Served

According to TwitDir, a third-party search tool that keeps track of the big nodes in the network, a year after its official launch Twitter boasted about 600,000 public accounts, with over 1,000 new members joining daily. By March 2008—one year after the SXSW award—the number of Twitter accounts had passed the 1 million mark, and two years after its launch there were over 3.5 million registered accounts.[*]

The exact number of Twitter accounts is a closely guarded secret. Bruno Peeters (@BVLG), author of the stats blog Twitter Facts (*http://twitterfacts.blogspot.com/search/label/TwitDir*), has paid close attention to the unofficial count provided by TwitDir since April 2007 (Figure 1-5[†]). Aside from a glitch that artificially stalled the count at below 1 million for a couple of months, TwitDir has provided a good estimate of actual Twitter membership figures. TwitDir only accounts for public accounts, however, so the actual figure could be about 10–15% higher when factoring in the private accounts.[‡]

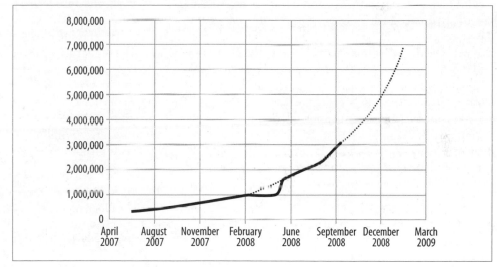

Figure 1-5. Twitter Facts tracks member growth in Twitter

Activity on Twitter is exponentially higher than membership. Before most people knew what microblogging was, Twitter recorded its millionth tweet. In September 2008, Nathan Reed's GigaTweet clock started counting down to the billionth tweet, which

---

[*] TwitDir (*http://twitdir.com*) was launched on March 24, 2007 as a directory of members. It kept a running tally of the number of unique Twitter accounts it had encountered, quickly becoming the best estimate of community growth. Although Twitter has yet to release official membership statistics, these figures are understood to be "in the ballpark."

[†] This graph is inspired by the work of Bruno Peeters, who reported that Twitter passed 3 million members with a blog post on September 21, 2008 (*http://twitterfacts.blogspot.com/2008/09/3-million-twitter-users.html*).

[‡] My own research suggests the number of protected accounts is even lower. Of the 847,007 members in my Election Day sample, 69,722 (8.2%) had protected accounts. Another, smaller data set generated from about 500 local users showed that only 957 of 28,610 members (3.3%) were protected.

arrived in early November 2008.§ After the milestone was reached, Reed (*@reednj*) added a few graphs tracking the number of tweets per day.‖ Another monitor is Twee-tRush (*http://tweetrush.com*), which uses a form of comprehensive use analytics called Rush Hour to look beyond page views and clicks to measure actions and events. According to TweetRush, Twitter gained an additional 150,000 active members and about 1 million tweets each day between November 2008 and January 2009.

Peeters has also spent the past two years tracking the growth of Twitter use by country, everywhere from India to Vatican City. Although the North American market clearly dominates Twitter usage, this may not be the case for long.

Early in 2008, Dorsey and his Twitter pals noticed that 30% of their traffic originated in Japan. Further investigation showed one of the reasons: virtual pets. People had begun giving tamagotchi—digital pets that prompt interaction when they are hungry or lonely or need care—their own Twitter pages through *http://neco.tter.jp* (*neco* is Japanese for cat). Whenever a member registered to adopt a new cat, the site created a corresponding Twitter account to facilitate the interaction. The signature =^..^=, indicating the presence of such an account, began appearing everywhere. This was one of the things that prompted Twitter to launch a Japanese version of its service in April 2008. Japanese quickly became the second most used language on Twitter. The Japanese version is advertising supported, marking the first monetization of the service. As of January 2009, unique visitors to the Twitter website jumped to almost 6 million. A Pew Internet study released at that time found that 11% of online Americans have used a microblogging or status update service like Twitter.#

 The Twitter API is inspiring a wide range of creativity among programmers. Although there is overlap in many of the tools, some developers are creating brand new uses of Twitter beyond simple posting, reading, and following.

The Rise of the Fail Whale

The most recognizable icon for Twitter probably isn't the bluebird used in its branding. Thanks to numerous server failures at a height of growth in the first half of 2008, the Fail Whale claims that honor. This is the story of the bittersweet success of Twitter's most notorious cultural footprint.

§ You can read more about this estimate at *http://www.blogschmog.net/2008/11/11/a-billion-served/*.

‖ Popacular's GigaTweet (*http://popacular.com/gigatweet/analytics.php*) showed that Twitter had reached 2.5 million daily updates by mid-January 2009.

From "Reports: Online Activities & Pursuits" on Twitter and status updating, a memo by Amanda Lenhart and Susannah Fox, published on February 12, 2009 (*http://www.pewinternet.org/PPF/r/276/report_display .asp*).

Because Twitter was initially developed for use by a single, small company, its rapid growth couldn't be anticipated. Somewhere around the half-million-member mark, it became clear that a threshold of use was near. Big conferences and international events, such as Macworld and the Super Bowl, sparked surges of activity that brought Twitter's servers to their electronic knees. Initially, members visiting the website were greeted by an image from lolcats (*http://icanhascheezburger.com*) of a kitten appearing to work on a computer (Figure 1-6). Eventually, that was replaced with a stock image of a whale being lifted out of the sea by a flock of birds (Figure 1-7). That image became beloved as much as despised, which came in handy late in spring 2008.

Figure 1-6. In the early days of Twitter, lolcats warned members of network problems

By the time Twitter celebrated its millionth member, it was clear that the server architecture had to be improved. A return to SXSW in March was a success, but the added interest increased the burden on the servers. In April 2008, vice president Lee Mighdoll (*@mighdoll*) and chief architect Blaine Cook (*@blaine*) left Twitter following another surge in registrations and a period plagued by server downtime and account spamming. This marked the height of a stressful period for the engineers and members of the community alike, as sightings of the Whale were so frequent that the beast became a cultural icon of failure.

Twitter asked users for patience and took measures to stabilize the service. The API rate limit, first invoked six months earlier to battle rogue third-party applications and give the servers some relief, was dropped to a mere 30 requests per hour. Some third-party projects suffered, as they were now unable to ping Twitter for data frequently enough to be effective. The company also disabled some popular features, such as IM support and keyword tracking, to chase away some members. Demand for Twitter was increasing, but experiences were often subpar, with several power users calling for boycotts and migrating to a perceived rival, FriendFeed. Other competitors, such as Plurk and Identi.ca, were able to gain some traction while Twitter struggled. Many compared Twitter to Friendster, which had been a pioneer of online social networking but was long since surpassed by more successful latecomers.

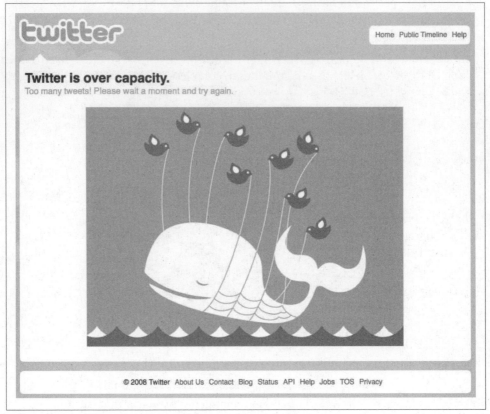

Figure 1-7. Yiying Lu's stock graphic became a celebrated icon

By May, Twitter had started blacklisting spammers, who created accounts and followed members in bulk. The company also emphasized transparency. Engineer Alex Payne (*@al3x*) began using Google Code's issue tracker to keep a running tab on issues with the API and the company's progress in fixing them. Twitter embraced Get Satisfaction, a community source help desk where questions and complaints are addressed in an open forum. It also released a status blog, not served on company machines, to give members information when problems surfaced or solutions were found. The team also added more help, including skilled system administrators Rudy Winnacker (*@ronpepsi*) and John Adams (*@netik*), to work on overhauling the old architecture, which was not meant for millions of users and a daily barrage of a million messages.

These proactive efforts started paying off by midsummer. The first major test was the Steve Jobs keynote address at Macworld announcing the iPhone 3G and a suite of applications, as it was sure to generate high traffic on Twitter. The servers survived. Although downtime continued to be problematic throughout June, by the end of July the Fail Whale sightings were no longer a common topic mentioned in tweets.

According to Pingdom (*http://www.pingdom.com*), Twitter servers were down the equivalent of almost a full day in May and about half a day in June and July. The site was down for about three days combined in all of 2008. The last major incident came in late July. Since then, however, downtime has been measured in minutes instead of hours, with many days passing without any problems. Even a scheduled maintenance job on October 7 took less than 30 minutes to complete. While serving approximately 3 million more users, Twitter managed to double its response time. By the summer's end, the company had raised the API rate limit to 100 hits per hour.

 Alex Payne isn't alone in providing support for developers using the API. The team includes Matt Sanford (*@mzsanford*), who came to Twitter from Summize and is largely responsible for Search API issues, and Doug Williams (*@dougw*), who was hired in March 2009 to outreach to developers through the *@twitterapi* account. Doug is also responsible for whitelisting, source requests, and maintaining the API wiki (*http://api wiki.twitter.com*).

Sarah Perez (*@sarahintampa*) of Read/Write/Web credits Nick Quarantino with giving the signature image the name "Fail Whale,"[*] but blogger Benedikt Koehler tracked down the digital footprint[†] to a video interview Robert Scoble did with Evan Williams at Twitter headquarters, who revealed the name that employees had given the image at just past 24 minutes into the interview.

The designer of that famous image, Chinese artist Yiying Lu (*@yiyinglu*) of Australia, became known only after a Fail Whale fan tracked her down for permission to make T-shirts. Tom Limongello, whose homemade Fail Whale shirt was a hit at a tech party, approached Yiying and urged her to sell her work online through Zazzle, an on-demand retail shopping website. Sean O'Steen started the Fail Whale Fan Club (*http://failwhale .com*) and maintains the Twitter profile for the cetacean. As a show of support, the group of raised almost $400 to buy shirts for the beleaguered Twitter employees, which they sent in late June at the height of the server issues. That gesture prompted Evan Williams to tweet a response of "Mixed feelings," along with a link to the web store.

The Fail Whale Fan Club (FWFC) is the most visible representation of the mixed feelings many Twitter members feel when seeing the beast. On the one hand, it is a sign that tweets aren't flying through cyberspace the way they usually do. On the other

---

[*] From the July 17, 2008 blog article, "The Story of the Fail Whale" by Sarah Perez, published on Read/Write/ Web (*http://www.readwriteweb.com/archives/the_story_of_the_fail_whale.php*).

[†] See the FriendFeed discussion from July 31, 2008 at *http://friendfeed.com/e/af931ac5-d1f1-45a9-82a6 -463c56321644/Who-coined-the-term-fail-whale-Dave-Winer-and/*.

hand, the Fail Whale seems to engender more of a sense of shared community experience than the lolcats did. The Fan Club emphasizes this point on its website:

> This site is here to poke fun at the people who seem to take online social network downtime a little too seriously. Failwhale.com is not affiliated with Twitter. Rather, it's a love letter to the hard working folks at all of our favorite online social networking sites who lose sleep over the concept of scalability.

With whale sightings growing less frequent in 2008, the FWFC directed its energies to other endeavors, such as sponsoring parties and promoting a Fail Whale Pale Ale label design contest.

Use of the icon has extended beyond Twitter to other systems. Mashable held a contest in July 2008 challenging readers to come up with a suitable Fail Whale version for Facebook downtime.[‡] Responses included an image of birds carrying Facebook creator Mark Zuckerberg, a Fail Snail, and the comment, "A picture of me actually working." The "failPhone" image surfaced with a 3G in place of the beluga following Apple's activation nightmare, which bricked many phones. There are even reports of Fail Whale tattoos.[§] Yiyung Lu has kept the spirit of the Fail Whale alive with active use of her own Twitter account and by making appearances at Fail Whale events. She won a Shorty Award for Design, an awards ceremony held on February 11, 2009 in New York City featuring active celebrity twitterers such as Rick Sanchez (*@ricksanchezcnn*), Shaquille O'Neal (*@THE_REAL_SHAQ*), and MC Hammer (*@MCHammer*).[∥]

On October 7, 2008, during a scheduled maintenance break, Twitter members saw a completely new image featuring a caterpillar and an ice cream cone. It was the signature of scheduled downtime, not the unintended variety. Twitter has since survived the election of Barack Obama (*@BarackObama*), New Year's Eve, a major plane crash, and several technology conferences, all while experiencing record growth and traffic. In an ideal world for Twitter engineers, the Fail Whale will never be seen again.

Who Wants to Be a Millionaire? Gauging Twitter's Profitability

Fred Wilson (*@fredwilson*), a venture capitalist and the principal of Union Square Ventures, who invested in Twitter in 2007, has watched the speculation among members of the community and tech business experts about how Twitter is going to make money. In a January 2008 blog response to the ongoing conversation, Fred observed:

[‡] From the July 22, 2008 blog article, "Introducing the Unofficial Facebook Fail Whale" by Adam Ostrow, published on Mashable (*http://mashable.com/2008/07/22/unofficial-facebook-fail-whale/*).

[§] From the February 26, 2009 blog article, "Twitter Fail Whale Tattoo is Awesome, Kinda," by Stan Schroeder, published on Mashable (*http://mashable.com/2009/02/26/twitter-fail-whale-tattoo/*).

[∥] The Shorty Awards recognized the best producers of short-form content in 2008, as determined by Twitter members tweeting votes of nomination and support. Design was one of over 1,500 user-generated categories (*http://shortyawards.com/category/design*).

Every ounce of time, energy, money, and brainpower you spend on thinking about how to monetize will take you away from the goal of getting to scale. Because if you don't get to scale, you don't have a business anyway.#

Twitter's time of reckoning is expected to arrive in 2009, as the company shifts its focus from server stability to accounting stability. It recently cut SMS service in some countries (not the U.S.) after negotiations with local providers stalled. Although some commentators overreacted to the impact this would have on use of the service, the perception was that the move was a sign that the microblogging giant had begun counting pennies. Naturally, the focus of criticism once again turned to whether and how Twitter could make money to keep afloat.

 In a March 1, 2009 article on Read/Write/Web, Todd Dagres of Spark Capital—one of the biggest shareholders on Twitter—claimed that Twitter has known its business model for a long time: "All of a sudden there will be some changes that won't undermine the experience or vitality—but it will be pretty obvious how we're going to monetize it."*

In an article for *Business Week*, writer Ben Kunz calculated the worth of each Twitter user at $12.26† (the math assumed only traditional forms of Internet advertising, such as banner ads and subscription services). For Twitter or any open service to become profitable, he argued, it needs a balance between opportunities to charge and respect for the dynamics that created the community in the first place. Successful monetization may require some nontraditional thinking that enables the service to remain free to most and allows API development to continue.

Charging for service

During the ongoing conversation about Twitter's possible monetization strategy, Internet marketer Samir Balwani noted problems with one common suggestion: the "freemium" option.‡ This approach would constrain use of the service by capping the size of the follower network and the number of tweets a user could send over a specified time period. It might also inject advertisements into the information stream until users paid to get rid of them. The primary trouble with this option, according to Balwani, is that it would penalize the most popular and active users, the core members who drive

---

From the January 2, 2008 blog article, "Twitter's Business Model" by Fred Wilson, published on A VC (*http://www.avc.com/a_vc/2008/01/twitters-busine.html*).

* From the March 1, 2009 blog article, "Twitter VC Laughs at the Idea that Twitter Has No Business Model," by Lidija Davis, published on Read/Write/Web (*http://www.readwriteweb .com/archives/twitter_vc_laughs_at_the_idea.php*).

† Ben Kunz, "The Trouble with Twitter," *Business Week*, August 18, 2008 (*http://www.businessweek.com/ technology/content/aug2008/tc20080815_597307.htm*).

‡ From the July 8, 2008 blog article, "Micro-Blogging Monetization Possibilities," by Samir Balwani, published on Left The Box (*http://leftthebox.com/archive/micro-blogging-monetization-possibilities/*).

the community; alienating them could kill Twitter. Forcing members to pay could also cause them to migrate to Plurk, Identi.ca, or any other free service.

Balwani also noted that the existence of the API could pose problems for monetization plans. Since most users don't go to the Twitter website to use the service, it could be difficult to rely on selling ads there. On the other hand, the API would be a boon if Twitter looks to request-rate surcharges as a source of income. The API could be free for projects with a low request rate—continuing to make it possible for developers to create new visualizations and tools—whereas projects that require a higher request rate or need deeper results returned could be forced to pay.

Self-selecting advertisers

Another money-making possibility that would fit the Twitter culture is opt-in advertising. The company could create fee-paying corporate accounts, and then require that all users select at least three of those to follow. Member accounts not actively subscribed to three or more corporate user accounts could be disabled. Perhaps, as with Twitterrific, Twitter could create a second profit point by offering paid memberships that reduce or eliminate the number of corporate accounts a user needs to follow in order to keep his Twitter account active.

This opt-in strategy might prove effective for two reasons. First, if enough advertisers across enough verticals (technology, politics, family, entertainment, religion, etc.) got on board, a real choice would be available to each member. Don't want to be subjected to Microsoft tweets? Follow Apple. No to Coke? Follow Pepsi. Because the requirement would be modest, a large number of options would make it more likely that the corporate messages would be well received. Second, because the ads would appear in the form of tweets, the advertisers would themselves be members, so the usual follower dynamics would apply to them. Companies that spam or post irrelevant content would be unfollowed and replaced with different advertisers. The beauty of the Twitter channel is that everyone has her own way of using the service and her own tolerance for certain kinds of behavior. This is Ed Dale's idea of side-by-side marketing at work.

Twitter's Biz Stone created a minor stir in early 2009 with some comments that suggested the company planned to charge for corporate accounts.[§] The comments were taken by many to mean that Twitter had found its business model, a rumor Twitter had to dispel a few days later.

Implementing an open source service model

Brad Wheeler, chief information officer at Indiana University, evangelizes that companies can make their open source products profitable by focusing monetization on

---

[§] From the February 10, 2009 article, "Twitter to charge companies for using service," by Claudine Beaumont, published in *The Telegraph* (*http://www.telegraph.co.uk/scienceandtechnology/technology/twitter/4579555/ Twitter-to-charge-companies-for-using-service.html*).

support services. Perhaps the solution for Twitter is not to worry about advertising or membership costs at all, but instead to look at ways of helping individuals trick out and manage their accounts, or to provide development services to companies wishing to leverage the API. The more tweets that pass through the public stream, the easier it is to find people who need help.

Many expected Google to challenge Twitter in 2009 when its 2007 purchase of rival microblogging service Jaiku finally bore fruit, as other such purchases in the past have taken about 18 months to become fully integrated with the search giant. That won't happen, though. In January 2009, Google announced it was releasing Jaiku to open source and discontinuing Dodgeball, a location-based mobile social networking service. Other threats to Twitter's microblogging space may come from FriendFeed, Plurk, or Identi.ca, which received some funding in early 2009. However, Twitter is currently a whole power ahead of them in terms of traffic and membership. In 2008 Twitter was valued at about $80 million, having raised $15 million during the summer of that year and an unsolicited $35 million more in February 2009.‖

Developers Are Users, Too

Alexa.com rankings are only as good as the websites they track. Twitter's API—released in early 2006 with four simple functions—is responsible for a large percentage of server traffic. The community of developers for Twitter has been busy.

Two key design strategies were instrumental to Twitter's success. The first was its simplicity. Unlike some of its microblogging rivals, Twitter doesn't try to be more than it is. Members compose short messages, and Twitter makes sure they are distributed in a self-organizing network. Requests for longer posts, file sharing, threaded commentary, group management, and metadata would make Twitter more complicated than it is now, raising the bar for current and prospective users. Exceptions can be made, however. For example, so many twitterers were using the IRC convention for individual replies that the service added support for the @ command, attaching those tweets to specific user content. With the increased use of microblogging for monitoring the stock market, the $company convention is joining @username, #hashtag, and RT (retweet) as part of the operating language of Twitter.

The second key strategy was an enterprise decision: making access to the membership and content mechanisms available to developers. It is getting more and more common for new systems to provide API methods to allow third-party applications to exchange information. Development from the API not only extends the functionality of Twitter, but also creates a personal investment for the programmers in making Twitter successful. Each new application gathers its own following, expanding the use of the service to a wider audience. Most of the cool Twitter innovations—such as that popular

---

‖ From the February 13, 2009 blog article, "Twitter Raises $35 Million," by Dan Frommer, published on The Business Insider (*http://www.businessinsider.com/twitter-raises-35-million-2009-2*).

Macintosh desktop client, Twitterrific—have not been applications built by the company. There is no need for Twitter to focus on building new tools and features when so many members are sufficiently enamored with the service to want to make it better themselves.

Developers often answer calls for added features by accessing the API in interesting ways. Jaiku, for example, supports channels—a way of defining content around topics rather than individuals—whereas Twitter does not. Nonetheless, developers using Twitter's API have come to the rescue by leveraging traditional IRC conventions in their projects. Hashtags, created by prefixing a keyword with a hash symbol (*#hashtag*), provide a means for topic tracking and are used often enough that Twitter's own search tool (*http://search.twitter.com*) supports them. A number of third-party clients implement similar functionality, either by leveraging Twitter's search API or by following a Twitter account (such as *@hashtags*) that monitors the tweets of its following to form its own database of topical content.

In spring 2008, a third-party company named Summize started tracking the public timeline of Twitter, gathering content to make the tweet corpus searchable. It was widely successful, often up and useful even when Twitter was down. Summize also offered its own API, which spawned a few interesting applications that focused on the content of what was being said rather than on how the networks or streams were constructed. The Twitter team was impressed; it worked with Summize to cover the iPhone application announcements in June and moved to acquire the company in mid-July. The *http://search.twitter.com* subdomain was created to incorporate Summize technology, and most Summize employees went to work for Twitter.

With the integration of Summize, Twitter now allows content to be searched by specific hashtags.

One of the bigger projects for Twitter engineers in 2008 was to fully integrate the Summize API with Twitter's own, as each system used slightly different parameter names and approaches. By mid-2009, the API is expected to be one big happy family.

Since Twitter's splash at SXSW in 2007, other microblogging services have tried to catch that same lightning in a bottle. During the summer of 2007, Jaiku and Pownce—the latter of which closed up shop in December 2008—were Twitter's biggest rivals, leading a host of similar systems such as MySay, Hictu, MoodMill, Frazr, IRateMyDay, Emotionr, Wamadu, Zannel, Soup, and PlaceShout. A year later, it was FriendFeed, BrightKite, Identi.ca, Plurk, and Yammer stealing some of the thunder. Yammer took the top prize at the TechCrunch50 conference in September 2008[#] as a business version of Twitter (ironically, a concept similar to Jack Dorsey's original project). Whenever a

---

[#] From the September 21, 2008 blog article, "Yammer Takes Top Prize at TechCrunch50," by Erick Schonfeld, on TechCrunch (*http://www.techcrunch.com/2008/09/10/yammer-takes-techcrunch50s-top-prize/*).

new startup company involves an information stream, however, the reviews inevitably compare it to Twitter. What separates Twitter from the crowd is its combination of timing, transparency, and simplicity. Whether or not Twitter manages to survive the test of time, microblogging as a communication channel is here to stay.

 The Twitter developer community is filled with generous collaborators willing to share code and feedback. On March 24, 2009, the Twitter Developer Nest (*@devnest*) gathered 90 coders at a Sun Microsystems facility in London to work on applications together. For more information, visit *http://twitterdevelopernest.com/*.

Creative Uses of Twitter

The Academy Awards are great. Each year, about 600 movies are made and about 40 awards are given out (if you count the technical categories). That means there's a 1 in 15 chance that if you make a movie, you'll get an Oscar. Those are great odds compared to the pool available for the Twitties, the annual awards for the best tweets in Twitter.

The first annual Twitties (*http://twitties.com*), held in 2008, accepted nominations in 14 categories, including Best, Funniest, Smartest, Dopiest, and Snarkiest Tweet (Figure 1-8). If the IDs for Twitter status messages are to be believed, the leading microblogging service generated a nomination pool of almost 870 million tweets in two years. By the time the second annual Twitties rolls around in 2009, there will be over a billion new candidates for the handful of awards.

Collectively, tweets can paint a picture of what a community is thinking and doing. Individually, some status updates stand out. A few of my favorites include:

- *@hodgman* flatbush ave=yet another bklyn street named by random compound word generator.
- *@brooksguthrie* "cakey: Can you build websites with firefox? imarock: can you build cars with roads?"
- *@noahwesley* Our government only breaks international law to take lives, but never to save them.
- *@katrina_* Sometimes, twitter is that friend you turn to in class when everyone's being a moron, just to say, "really? Really?!"
- *@ankitkhare* What do you mean, my birth certificate expired?
- *@jennepenne* i think that from now on, when i get cold calls from random marketing people, i will just act like i am drunk.
- *@fluctifragus* The word "webinar" can never be scrubbed from my brain.

People aren't always this witty, but out of the mass of posts some cleverness arises. The same is true of development projects: not every API application is a winner, but Twitter does inspire some neat tools and toys.

Figure 1-8. The 2008 Twitties recognized the best tweets of the year

Twitter Utilitarianism

November 2008 marked the second anniversary of Robert Scoble's first tweet in 2006. At a clip of about 17 tweets a day, this A-list blogger has spent the past two years using Twitter to promote his site and share his life with a mass of readers. Amazingly, Scoble manages to converse with many of his 37,000 followers (most of whom began following him in the past six months). In fact, most of his posts are now directed replies to other users.

Scoble is one extreme on the user spectrum, but he isn't the leader in any category. According to TwitDir, as of November 2008 the Twitter account for Station Portal (*@InternetRadio*) held the record as the biggest producer of content, with over 550,000 tweets and counting. Station Portal monitors about 20,000 Internet radio stations, tracking the number of times each song is played. That account is in the top 1,000 with 1,700 followers, but many Twitter accounts that update über-frequently attract very few followers. In the summer of 2008, the twitterer who attracted the most followers was Barack Obama, whose throng of 107,000 followers outnumbered those of Digg's cocreator Kevin Rose by 40,000—the equivalent of one Scoble. Obama posted about once every three days throughout the campaign.

Most people have balanced networks, which means they follow roughly as many people as they have followers. Imbalances occur mostly with news providers, like @*cnn*, or with spammers, who follow many people who do not reciprocate.

A University of Maryland study published in 2007[*] captured 1,348,543 tweets from 76,177 members over a two-month period between April and May. The researchers analyzed both the content and the network structure of their sample. One of the outcomes was a graph showing the relationship of tweets to followers, which led them to identify three kinds of Twitter members. Members with high numbers of posts and few followers are considered *spammers*, and those with many followers and few posts are *information sources* (e.g., @*BarackObama*). The *authorities*—sources such as @*Scobleizer* and @*InternetRadio*—have high numbers in both areas.

The same study also concluded that there are four common user intentions for Twitter members:

Daily chatter
Talk about daily routines and activities

Conversations
Use of the @ to specifically reference another member

Sharing information
Inclusion of a pointer referenced in the tweet

Reporting news
Manual and automated reporting of new information, typically through mashups with RSS feeds

This first attempt to officially categorize twitterers through academic analysis offers a good road map for understanding how people make use of their 140 characters to contribute to the information stream. Still, much has changed since the study was done in 2007. The ways people use Twitter today are wide-ranging.

Twitter for News

When Washington state Republican Representative Jennifer Dunn died in September 2007, people read about it on Twitter before the news hit traditional media sources or even Wikipedia. On January 15, 2009, Janis Krums was on a ferry crossing the Hudson River when he snapped a photo of a downed plane and posted it to Twitter with a short message. The photo was picked up by news services. It is easier to compose a sentence or two and share immediately with others than it is to prepare an in-depth report. For bloggers and journalists alike, the tweet stream can be a great source of story ideas.

[*] Akshay Java, Xiaodan Song, Tim Finin, and Belle Tseng, "Why We Twitter: Understanding Microblogging Usage and Communities," in *Proc. of the Joint 9th WEBKDD and 1st SNA-KDD Workshop 2007* (2007).

CNN's Rick Sanchez, a Hispanic-American news anchor best known for immersive stunts, solicits tweets for his weekly afternoon news show and features them on the air. ReportTwitters, an effort to strengthen the community of professional and amateur reporters, encouraged its members to tweet about the process of getting and filing a story, offering tips and a transparent look behind the bylines.

The pipeline flows the other way, too. News outlets of all sizes, from the BBC and CNN down to local papers and radio stations, make use of Twitter to share breaking news and provide links to their published articles. Bloggers Blog posted information about the 2007–2008 writers' strike on Twitter, adding to the solidarity base by highlighting the widespread support for the picket line.

 The flip side to news is rumor. As much as we in the Twitosphere like to make a big deal of how quickly we can find out about earthquakes and plane crashes, the desire to keep the information flowing can lead to mistakes. As with any information you find communicated by media, double-check your sources.

Twitter for Science

On May 25, 2008, my wife and I let our two boys stay up late to watch the Phoenix probe land on Mars (televised live on the Science Channel). I remember watching the Space Shuttle Columbia land in the early 1980s—I even took a Polaroid photo of the image on our black-and-white television as it came back to earth, to capture the moment—and I hoped that my sons would remember this in the same way. It probably didn't take, but NASA gave the mission a permanent record of the approach using a Twitter account written in the "voice" of the probe.

The Phoenix tweeted in the first person throughout the event, including an exciting flurry of posts as the probe approached the designated landing site ("parachute must open next. my signal still getting to Earth which is AWESOME!"). It gave the project personality and attracted over 36,000 followers. NASA used Twitter to break the news that ice had been discovered on Mars, earning one of three Twittie awards for its contribution to the public stream.

Mars Phoenix ended its mission in late 2008, but mission support continues to use the @MarsPhoenix account and leverage the community that formed around the probe. Other NASA Twitter accounts include those for the Mars Rovers, International Space Station, and some shuttle missions.

In February 2009, CNN reported about a Detroit doctor who used Twitter during an operation. Dr. Craig Rogers, the lead surgeon at Henry Ford Hospital, wanted people to know that a tumor can be removed from an organ while leaving the organ intact. As Rogers operated, chief resident Dr. Raj Laungani manned the Twitter timeline. This was the second such in-surgery coverage; Robert Hendrick of *https://www.change healthcare.com* had tweeted his own surgery four months earlier while under local anesthesia.[†]

Twitter for God

Westwinds, a church in Michigan, uses multiple Twitter accounts to augment the weekend experience and keep the conversation going throughout the week between services. The integration with offline gatherings began in June 2008 and has attracted 120 followers on Twitter. The tech-savvy church leaders encourage the use of laptops and cell phones to share the religious experience with those not on-site, aggregating a number of accounts into an information stream. They display the feed live on screens during the Sunday services, inviting participants to ask questions or express themselves as the Spirit moves them (Figure 1-9).

Figure 1-9. Tweets from "Twitter Sunday" at Westwinds Church

[†] From a February 17, 2009 article, "Surgeons send 'tweets' from operating room," by Elizabeth Cohen, published by CNN (*http://www.cnn.com/2009/TECH/02/17/twitter.surgery/index.html*).

Organizer John Voelz (*@shameonyoko*) is a bit of a technophile who has spent most of the past two decades bringing religious practice into the Age of the Internet. He noted that Westwinds (*@westwinds*) was reaching thousands more people through its website than the numbers who sat in attendance on any given weekend. He and others added podcasts and streaming video to the toolbox. Twitter was a natural fit for the early adopters in the congregation, as he noted in his blog, Vertizontal:

> In my church, I have seen life-altering small groups formed and forged through Twitter. I have seen teams of people mobilized to do volunteer service like nothing else in the past through Twitter. I have seen needs met financially through Twitter. I have made friends through Twitter. I have witnessed theological discussions, seen prayer answered, seen surprise rendezvous', connected with leaders better, I've seen friends come to the aid of others health....‡

The first Sunday the stream went live, the church buzzed with iPhones, laptops, and 70 people following *@westwindsseries* on Twitter. A big screen displayed the stream as people entered and continued throughout the service. Many of the posts were light, but some reflected on the service with opinions and affirmations of or struggles with faith ("I have a hard time recognizing God in the middle of everything"). The response was predictable, with some loving the experience and others finding it distracting, but Voelz was buoyed by testimony that Twitter helped people feel part of what was happening and connected to others.

Similarly, the microblogging service Gospelr (*http://gospelr.com*) was created specifically for the Christian community. The purpose of Gospelr, which is integrated with Twitter to keep members from duplicating posts, is to provide a channel for sharing thoughts, prayers, and devotionals.

Twitter for Emergencies

The low barrier to reporting makes Twitter an ideal channel for alerting a community to danger. Rampaging fires in San Diego and earthquakes in California and China were well covered through tweets, providing important information about where the dangers were and what damage had been done, and posting links to deeper resources. The emergency channel extends outside the affected area, giving remote friends and family the opportunity to reach out with thoughts of support and to get confirmation that everything is all right with their loved ones.

Even in my town, when we had our own brush with danger, Twitter beat email and blogs to the punch as a means of alerting the community. Greeting me one morning in October 2007 was the tweet, "A possible sniper on 2nd street? Anybody have details?" This came before an email from our university's IT director and another from the dean

---

‡ From the June 3, 2008 blog article, "Twitter Church," by John Voelz, published on Vertizontal (*http://johnvoelzblog.blogspot.com/2008/06/twitter-church.html*).

of our school. A full hour after the tweet was sent, our local emergency information system blog posted an entry.

When Hurricane Katrina hit the Gulf Coast, most of the information flowing from the region came not from FEMA or network news, but from the IRC community, who monitored radio communications and transcribed them to a wiki. The Science News Blog (*http://www.sciencenewsblog.com*) sent hurricane information as tweets, and individuals in affected regions—such as children's storyteller Dianne de Las Casas of Louisiana—tweeted about their evacuation from the area. Reading about strangers' experiences in such circumstances gives others a way to empathize, a precursor to more active engagement.

Since the Virginia Tech shootings in April 2007, universities have been ramping up their own emergency networks to include multimodal communication, such as text messages and automated phone calls. An article in *New Scientist* magazine[§] claimed that researchers at the University of Colorado had found that Twitter and other Web 2.0 media channels did a better job of disseminating information than the traditional channels. According to a study conducted by University of Colorado professor Leysia Palen, instead of rumors and gossip, these channels generate "socially produced accuracy." While traditional media scramble to bring resources to remote locations, social networks benefit from members already situated on-site and preconditioned to share these moments with the world.

At the time of our own "sniper" incident— which turned out to be a frustrated law student using his books for early morning target practice— the number of local twitterers hadn't achieved a critical mass. Two years later, we have hundreds of people around town ready to tweet.

Twitter for Marketing

From the start, the 140 characters allotted by Twitter have been used effectively to sell books, promote concerts, and interact with fans of television shows. Many blog posts about Twitter seem to be related to leveraging Twitter for marketing. There are many different takes on how this is best done, but most agree that the personal nature of tweet-to-tweet contact makes it a good way to reach consumers and potential business partners without raising their defenses. A recent survey of more than 200 social media leaders revealed that 40% picked Twitter as the top social media service, ahead of LinkedIn and YouTube.[||]

[§] The May 2, 2008 article, "Emergency 2.0 is coming to a website near you," by Jason Palmer, published in *New Scientist*, issue 2654, pp. 24–25 (*http://www.newscientist.com/article/mg19826545.900*).

[||] Abrams Research (*http://www.abramsresearch.com*) released results of a social media survey in February 2009 that polled more than 200 social media leaders in the U.S. and Canada during Social Media Week 2009. The survey found that 40% of respondents picked Twitter as the number-one social media service for businesses, followed by LinkedIn (21.3%), YouTube (18.8%), and Facebook (15.3%). When asked what service they would pay for first, however, Facebook won with 32.2%. Twitter was third at 21.8%.

Using Twitter, businesses can announce sales, solicit feedback, and understand customers in a way not really possible through other channels. Because the marketing content is voluntarily included in a personal information stream, it can be highly relevant and tends to be instilled with greater value. Spam is unlikely to become a problem for most users, as the reader must choose to follow the account to get a message. The author must contribute in a way that does not inspire the reader to remove that author's future content from his stream.

Spam definitely exists on Twitter, but it is largely confined to account spam, or *twam*. That is, marketers who never intended to use Twitter to connect with others will sometimes create accounts and follow everyone they can from the public timeline. Since notifications of new followers are usually sent by email, this action can bring a lot of eyeballs to a profile link or a simple first tweet.

Twitter took action in the summer of 2008 to improve spam detection and prevention, even hiring a full-time employee to stand watch.

Businesses use Twitter for everything from customer service to creating positive buzz. Greg Yaitanes (@*GregYaitanes*), director of the new FOX drama *Drive*, tweeted during the premier party in 2007, providing insights about the people at the party and a behind-the-scenes commentary. (It didn't help the show, though; FOX canceled *Drive* not long after the party ended.) Comcast got points for being proactive in responding to complaints posted on Twitter about its cable television and Internet service; Frank Eliason of Philadelphia manages the @*Comcastcares* account, responding to individuals with troubleshooting suggestions and support information. Many other businesses, from Southwest Airlines (@*SouthwestAir*) to Whole Foods (@*WholeFoods*) to Bank of America (@*BofA_help*), have a Twitter presence to interact with customers and inform them about new products and deals.

Twitter for Social Change

Tweeting isn't just an opportunity to share experiences and advertise products and services; it is also a means to express political opinions and persuade others to adopt causes. Among the early adopters of Twitter were several politicians, most notably Barack Obama and John Edwards.

In two presidential bids, Edwards proved to be a leader in Web 2.0 politicking. His staff arguably made the best use of Twitter on the campaign trail, with regular updates about his whistle stops and speeches. Although Obama was more successful both online and offline, Edwards created his account four months earlier, posting 87 times and picking up almost 9,000 followers before his concession and the subsequent scandal dropped his count to 6,000. At the time of his election, Obama was managing a mutual network of over 120,000 followers, the largest following in Twitter.

At the start of the election season in 2008, 7 sitting U.S. senators and 32 congressional representatives had active Twitter accounts.# By the time President Barack Obama addressed the joint Congress for the first time in February 2009, members of Congress were tweeting during his speech. The presidential debates sparked a lot of involvement by Twitter members as the Twitter website added a special Election stream, filtered to include tweets mentioning the candidates, the campaign, or debates. Current.TV included some of those tweets as part of its live video feed, and Twitter Vote Report (*http://blog.twittervotereport.com/*) used SMS and Twitter to keep track of voter experiences on Election Day. Government participation isn't limited to the U.S., either: the British Prime Minister and several Canadian politicians also make use of this medium to communicate with constituents.

 In mid-2007, Twitter cracked down on "identity squatting" on the names of famous people—especially presidential candidates. As a result, politicians such as Dennis Kucinich had accounts that weren't in use. This changed once President Obama took office and elected officials started tweeting regularly.

There are other examples of social activism. Live Earth, a 24-hour, 7-continent concert in 2007 to benefit the SOS environmental project, used Twitter to promote its music event across several sites. Each venue showcased the latest energy efficiency practices and was designed to minimize the environmental impact of the concert. The Sunlight Foundation, whose goal is to create a more transparent Congress, organized a Twitter petition to oppose restrictions preventing elected officials from tweeting in session. They now have their own suite of APIs (*http://sunlightlabs.com/appsforamerica/*) and are encouraging developers to help make government more transparent.

In February 2009, *Guardian* writer Paul Smith (*@twitchhiker*) announced that he planned to "travel by Twitter" in a stunt intending to raise money for charity: water (*http://www.charitywater.org*), a project to improve worldwide access to safe, clean drinking water. (This charity was also a main beneficiary of Twestival [*http://twestival.com*], a global tweetup on February 12, 2009 when twitterers from 202 cities met to raise money—more than $250,000—and awareness for the cause.) Smith's plan was to start in his hometown of Newcastle upon Tyne in the U.K. and attempt to travel halfway around the world in one month, to an island off the coast of New Zealand. His self-imposed rules included relying only on people who followed his *@twitchhiker* account and offered travel and lodging through public replies. Smith documented the experience on his blog (*http://twitchhiker.wordpress.com*) as well as through Twitter.

Sometimes Twitter activism can be reactionary. Parents on Twitter responded strongly to a new ad campaign for the over-the-counter pain-relief drug Motrin®. The

---

Two great sources for finding politicians on Twitter are Tweet Congress (*http://tweetcongress.org/officials/tweeting*) for the U.S. Congress and Tweetminster (*http://tweetminster.co.uk*) for the U.K.

slick-looking ad was very well produced, bringing to mind the great short film *Le Grand Content*.[*] However, the content was, at best, out of touch with the consumer group its producers meant to persuade. With many retweets and a simple hashtag, word spread quickly, and other media (blogs and video channels) were leveraged to organize opinion against Motrin. By Monday morning, the company had announced it was pulling the ad campaign. Although this incident clearly demonstrates the effectiveness of Twitter as a conduit for activism, some people question whether the response was disproportionate.[†]

Twitter for Money

One forward-thinking early adopter decided to use Twitter to sell books. TwitterLit (*http://www.twitterlit.com*)—and the children's book version, KidderLit (*http://www .kidderlit.com*)—provides a daily link to purchase a book online through an Amazon affiliate account. To prompt followers to click, Debra Hamel (*@Debra_Hamel*) posts the first line of a book as a tweet. No author or title is included, which turns the post into a daily guessing game.

Some of the first lines are more recognizable than others:

> "Call me Ishmael."
> "In a hole in the ground, there lived a hobbit."
> "As Gregor Samsa awoke one morning from uneasy dreams, he found himself transformed into a giant insect."
> "It was a dark and stormy night."
> "Dorothy lived in the midst of the great Kansas prairies, with Uncle Henry, who was a farmer, and Aunt Em, who was the farmer's wife."
> "I am an invisible man."

Financial success is difficult to achieve. Other attempts at affiliate linking might be perceived as spam, but Hamel's sites have managed to accumulate about 5,000 followers, and she has faithfully posted some 1,400 first-line links. This is a clever and effective use of Twitter for business.

Twitter for Games

Inspired by the 1924 Richard Connell short story "The Most Dangerous Game," Minnesota resident Aric McKeown (*@aric*) created a community game of hide-and-seek for the Minneapolis-St. Paul area using a Twitter account. Twice a month, Aric spent a Saturday afternoon in a local coffee shop or business tweeting clues about his location for followers to use to find him and earn a little sponsored prize. Unlike Connell's story,

---

[*] *Le Grand Content* is a short animated film from 2007 by Clemens Kogler, Karo Szmit, and Andre Tschinder (*http://www.youtube.com/watch?v=lWWKBY7gx_0*).

[†] Decide for yourself: the ad is on YouTube (*http://www.youtube.com/watch?v=BmykFKjNpdY*).

set on a remote island, Aric's version of the sport of human hunting was nonlethal—he called it the Least Dangerous Game (*http://www.leastdangerousgame.com*). Correctly guessing his location wasn't the goal; rather, the LDG was a multimodal activity where Twitter facilitated a face-to-face meeting. The first follower to find him won a prize and some bandwidth on a weekly podcast.

Following SXSW in 2008, humorist Ze Frank (*@zefrank*) organized a Twitter Color War. Members were asked to choose a team color and had to work to get the most followers. Icons were changed to flaunt color affiliations, and a leaderboard was set up until the war ended two months later. The idea was based on a game played at summer camps, where campers split up into color teams and compete in events like tug-of-war and egg tossing. Frank adapted the concept for Twitter, urging players to form teams and compete for medals in various contests. The activities included:

- Reverse caption, where contestants provide a picture to illustrate a caption
- Mixing a nerd rap with the word "bacon" in the lyrics, to be judged
- Creating a merit badge with Photoshop
- Battle of roshambo (rock-paper-scissors) throw-down photos
- A bingo game, with numbers called through tweets
- The Broom Game, where contestants spin in circles while holding a broom above their heads
- "Young me, Now me," i.e., recreating childhood pictures
- A scavenger hunt using Google Street View to find 31 things

Fifty-four teams earned medals or badges during the color war, which was eventually won by *@teampuce*.

 Twitter games can be a double-edged sword. For all of the community goodwill they generate, they can also create a lot of noise for followers. In effect, each participant becomes two identities: the one you want to follow, and the one playing the game.

Twitter for Anthropomorphism

We have recently entered a new age of Twitter utility. From simple bedroom lights to houseplants to historic bridges, the inanimate world is coming alive in the form of tweets, which both alert and respond to user interactions.

In the U.K., the London Bridge (*@towerbridge*) alerts its 700 followers when the bridge is going up and down. A schedule is available online, but it isn't always at the top of a Brit's mind to check the website. Tom Armitage engineered a way for the bridge to automatically tweet five minutes before it lifts, and again when it closes. The bridge is "friends" with several large telescopes, which similarly tweet whenever they move to observe a different part of the sky.

I'm not clear about the practical applications of being able to use Twitter to turn on and off your lights—beyond being a burglar deterrent or conveniently illuminating the front room as you pull into the driveway—but someone recently figured out how to do it. 2008 was also the year of the twittering plant. Botanicalls.com published a blow-by-blow instruction page explaining how to rig up a houseplant to tweet when it is thirsty (*http://www.botanicalls.com/kits/*). When a plant on the network needs water, it can call users to ask for a drink and then give thanks when it is shown some love. Five different status updates are available: low moisture, critically low moisture, not enough watering, over watering, and thirst quenched. Perhaps most impressively, at least for home movie buffs, is the RoBe:Do robot that responds to Twitter requests to make and deliver popcorn.‡

These feats of simple engineering are likely paving the way for more complicated and useful integrations of Twitter in the future.

Twitter for Help

Members have been relying on tweets to answer their simple questions since the inception of the service. It is not uncommon to solicit opinions about restaurants, websites, or movies by posting an inquiry on Twitter. Sometimes the answers can have life-changing implications.

In April 2008, University of California, Berkeley graduate student James Buck (*@jamesbuck*) and his translator were arrested in Egypt for photographing a protest. Before authorities processed him, Buck used his mobile phone to send a simple status update—"Arrested"—to Twitter. Some of his few dozen followers contacted Berkeley, the press, and the U.S. Embassy in Cairo to get him some help. The detainee continued to update his social circle about his plight until he was released the next day, thanks to the efforts of legal counsel hired by his university. Mohammed Maree, the translator, wasn't as lucky; he was detained in the Mahalla jail until July 6.

For more basic help, the human-guided search engine ChaCha (*http://chacha.com*) offers a Twitter-related option. Users can send questions to ChaCha as text messages or over the phone, and a human will do the work and provide answers. ChaCha also established a Twitter account to post short questions and answers to, but the tweets stopped when Twitter dropped IM support.

The best way to find answers on Twitter is simply to ask your social circle. If your friends don't know, they may retweet the question and find answers from a wider audience. Another option is LazyTweet (*http://www.lazytweet.com*), a community built around answering questions. By including the *#lazytweet* hashtag with your question,

---

‡ From the March 9, 2009 blog article, "Netbook-based robot takes popcorn orders via-Twitter," by Joseph L. Flatley, published on Engadget (*http://www.engadget.com/2009/03/09/netbook-based-robot-takes-popcorn -orders-via-twitter/*).

you automatically post it to a discussion forum, where others outside of your follow network can attempt to answer it for you.

Twitter for Creativity

From Twitter's start, the 140-character constraint has proved both an incentive and an inspiration for people to compose short, efficient messages. Inspired by Ernest Hemingway's famous six-word story—"For Sale: Baby shoes, never used."—one user once offered prizes for the best six-word tweet. More recently, Brian Clark of Copyblogger (*http://www.copyblogger.com*) issued a challenge to write a story in exactly 140 characters (Figure 1-10). If only doctoral dissertations worked that way!

Figure 1-10. "The Hollow Moment"

Clark (*@copyblogger*), whose blog is about effective writing, arranged several sponsorships and drew 331 submissions for his version of the challenge. A panel of five experts gave the first-place booty to Ron Gould (*@rgouldtx*), whose entry was:

> "Time travel works!" the note read. "However you can only travel to the past and one-way." I recognized my own handwriting and felt a chill.[§]

This isn't the only time Twitter and creative writers have come together. Maureen Evans (*@Maureen*) has published her every tweet since September 2006 as a Twitter haiku, or *twaiku*. In December 2007, some writers organized a collaborative story project, Twittories. One hundred and forty Twitter authors signed up on a wiki to compose one line of the work-in-progress, then passing it along to the next person. The effort was never completed, with only 86 authors contributing, but a record of the work ("The Darkness Inside") remains online. Plans for a second project died the following month when just 110 people signed up for the *twequel*.

Intrigued by these writing projects, English teacher George Mayo encouraged his eighth-grade class in Maryland, along with students around the world, to collaboratively write a story using a shared Twitter account (*@manyvoices*). The story took six

§ *http://twitter.com/rgouldtx/statuses/818253230*

weeks for 140 student authors and a dozen teachers to draft, with six different countries represented. The content was then moved to a wiki for revision before being published as a book on Lulu (*http://www.lulu.com*).

Twitter for Education

Educators are making use of the studio qualities of content creation on Twitter. At the University of Texas, assistant professor David Parry (*@academicdave*) created a homework assignment for his "Storytelling for New Media" class that required at least 10 tweets to be posted over the course of a weekend. Parry also required the students to follow at least 10 other classmates, to get the effect that shared status updates bring to the experience.

As a result of the exercise, Parry noticed an increase in student conversation, both in and out of class. The students developed an identity as a class, and Twitter became another channel to give feedback, express frustrations, or ask questions about the course.

At Indiana University, graduate student Jamie McAtee (*@jmcatee*) used her human-computer interaction capstone project to help international students find a voice. One of the problems she observed in mixed classrooms in the U.S. was that language and cultural barriers often prevented international students—those from Asia in particular—from participating in class discussions. Her solution was to create an in-class channel where such students could ask the professor questions via direct messaging, using either their own accounts or a shared anonymous one. One version of the implementation also had a visible display, to encourage all students to comment on the content of the lecture.

The Centre for Learning & Performance Technologies maintains an online directory of learning professionals on Twitter, from both educational and corporate domains. As of fall 2008, almost 500 names were listed. As with Yammer and Present.ly in the business world, Twitter has domain competition from Edmodo (*http://www.edmodo.com*), a private microblogging service for schools with added features for security.

Twitter for Entertainment

A few comedians, including Stephen Colbert and Jim Gaffigan, adopted Twitter early but stopped using the channel fairly quickly. Colbert has 20,000 followers but hasn't posted since May 2007, prompting speculation that the account is a dormant fake. Stolen identities are not uncommon in the online world, and Twitter has worked with celebrities to protect their images if the fake versions are too misleading. In many cases, such as *@FakeSarahPalin* or *@DarthVader*, the phonies are more entertaining than the originals.

If there were ever a comedian made to use this tool, it is that king of dry one-liners, Steven Wright. An account with his name appeared in May 2007 that regularly posted material from his '80s and '90s standup routines. One month later, the real Steven Wright showed up on Twitter, forcing the original account to become *@NotStevenWright*. Neither has been very active since.

One comedian clearly speaking for himself is John Hodgman (*@hodgman*). Known best as the PC in the Apple commercials with Justin Long, Hodgman is a semi-regular on Jon Stewart's *The Daily Show* and a self-proclaimed expert on everything. Hodgman once tweeted his own personal conference—HodgeCon 2008—to poke fun at the real conferences dominating Twitter conversation at the time. He ends most tweets with a signature, "That is all."

History, family pets, and television shows are other sources of entertainment on Twitter. A user posting as 19th century U.S. President Benjamin Harrison tweets as if still in the 1800s using content from Wikipedia and historic events as inspiration. Similarly, Laura Ingalls Wilder is publishing 1867 wisdom in 2008 ("Today I learned not to poke a live badger with a stick."). Numerous cats and dogs tweet regularly, complaining about living conditions with their owners. The most famous of these nonhumans may be Sockington (*@sockington*), a cat belonging to Jason Scott. Sockington's following grew from 13,000 to over 150,000 in the first quarter of 2009.

Television often inspires group efforts. The reimagined science fiction show *Battlestar Galactica* has a fervent following, and more than a dozen cast members have Twitter accounts. In addition to commenting on their respective lives in the show mythology, they reply to each other through Twitter. Not everyone sees the value of free advertising, however, as AMC demonstrated to similarly fervent fans of *Mad Men* by pressuring Twitter to remove those accounts.

Twitter for Sports

In anticipation of their number-one pick in the 2007 NBA draft, the Portland Trailblazers used a Twitter account to engage fans in the debate over whether to select Greg Oden or Kevin Durant. Oden was the man, but he got injured in preseason action, effectively killing the initial Twitter campaign. The Trailblazers brought the account back to life with updates during the season and the 2008 draft. Portland is one of the few major professional sports teams to embrace the medium.

The Boston Red Sox may be another. Their failed effort to win the 2008 American League pennant engendered a following of over 1,300 fans over the course of some 4,000 updates, many of which were essentially play-by-play accounts of big games. Such accounts seem like a natural way to leverage microblogging, but professional league rules and older leadership often get in the way of such innovations, leaving it to dedicated fans and media to fill the void.

Slate Magazine (*http://www.slate.com*), for example, tweeted the 2008 Olympics in China, providing snarky commentary about outcomes, athletes, and the world's hosts. Twootball is a project created by David DiCillo to filter public tweets for references to specific NFL football games, much in the same way Twitter created its 2008 Election site. Similarly, a Clemson University graduate created SportyTweets to follow news on the Tigers college football team. A Twitter account (*@ClemsonTigers*) was created and fed with RSS feeds of helpful websites. This idea was expanded to include all NFL, NBA, MLB, and major NCAA sports teams.

One of the most famous recent adopters of the Twitter service is future Hall of Fame basketball star Shaquille O'Neal (*@THE_REAL_SHAQ*) of the Phoenix Suns. He was prompted to join the service in November 2008 when he found out that an imposter was posting on his behalf, a common problem for corporations and celebrities. Rather than simply demand that Twitter stop the account, Shaq dove in head first. Twitter confirmed he was the real Shaq, and by the NBA All-Star game that year, he had 140,000 followers. Most impressively, he is using the service as a way to break down barriers to his many fans. This was most famously documented by Phoenix resident Jesse Bearden, who responded to a tweet by O'Neal indicating he was at a local diner. Bearden and a friend went to the restaurant, found Shaq, and—after some prompting from the Suns center via tweets—eventually got autographs, a photo, and a story for a lifetime.‖

Twitter for Evil

U.S. military analysts have long feared that the openness of computer and social networks could facilitate terrorist strikes against American targets. According to *Wired* magazine, the Army's 304th Military Intelligence Battalion presented three scenarios in which user-driven applications and mobile technology—including Twitter—could be used as weapons for attacks:#

- Operatives tweet reconnaissance information about the location and strength of troops or other authorities, including cell phone photos, in preparation for an ambush.

- Suicide bombers work with a spotter holding the detonator and viewing on-the-scene images of the location, to help maximize the impact of the explosion.

- Cyberterrorism is conducted against U.S. soldiers by following their Twitter accounts to glean information about an individual's identity, account access, or physical position. The terrorist might even engage in direct communication with the soldiers through replies and direct messages.

‖ Shaq's foray into Twitter is documented in "The Real O'Neal Puts His Cyber Foot Down," by Howard Beck (*New York Times*, November 19, 2008), "His Tweets Are Shaqalicious," by Biz Stone (Twitter Blog, November 20, 2008), and "Finally, A Use for Twitter," by Jesse Bearden (A foot and a half, February 19, 2009). Way to go, Big Daddy.

From the October 24, 2008 blog article, "Spy Fears: Twitter Terrorists, Cell Phone Jihadists," by Noah Shachtman, published in *Wired* (*http://blog.wired.com/defense/2008/10/terrorist-cell.html*).

One of the inspirations for the first scenario was the use of Twitter to monitor Democratic activists at the Republican National Convention. Although officials have monitored some political chatter related to Hezbollah, none of these scenarios has yet come to fruition. Still, it is probably wise to understand the potential dark side of a transparent culture.

Bringing this speculative report a little closer to home was the real-world problem of members of Congress starting to tweet. On February 6, 2009, Rep. Pete Hockstra (R-Michigan) posted an update that he "Just landed in Baghdad." Rather innocuous and seemingly a great example of the new era of government transparency, it also ruffled some feathers in security corners. With the tweet, Hoekstra, a member of the House Intelligence Committee, apparently broke an embargo.* With 69 U.S. representatives and senators known to use Twitter, the sanctioned use or misuse of social media is likely to evolve with some growing pains.†

Twitter As a Shared Event

Once upon a time, watching television was a social event. Neighbors gathered in the homes of the one or two families with a T.V. set to be entertained by the new technology. Even as late as the 1970s, in the pre-cable, pre-VCR days for most households, television shows were events around which entire family schedules were adjusted. More recently, digital video recorders and online media options have taken much of the event out of television programming.

If anything, Twitter is enhancing the sociability of television, turning it back into a shared community event. People commune over cult shows such as *Fringe*, *Lost*, *Heroes*, and major sporting events, tweeting reactions as they watch.

This phenomenon surfaced in fall 2008, when Twitter became a back channel for the U.S. presidential debates. Some 27,000 updates by over 12,000 authors—all commenting in some way on the event—were detected during the fourth and final debate while the candidates' exchange was being broadcast live. Contrary to the traditional view of couch potatoes passively watching moving pictures on the tube, people were spurred, through Twitter, to action. In fact, there was no better way to understand the real-time effect the debates were having on Twitter than to watch the tweets flow over video on Current.TV (*http://current.com*), the text cloud change sizes on Twitscoop (*http://twitscoop.com*), or observations be made by your own social circle on Twitter. This was an active and interactive use of the channel, with some very heady insights mixed with the techno shorthand.

---

* Robert X. Cringely published a nice summary of the issue on February 9, 2009 in the blog article, "Did a US congressman leak classified intel on Twitter?" published on InfoWorld (*http://weblog.infoworld.com/robertxcringely/archives/2009/02/did_a_us_congre.html*).

† According to OpenCongress, there are 19 sitting senators and 50 representatives with active Twitter accounts. Despite Barack Obama being a Democrat, only 24 twitterers are from the party in power (*http://www.opencongress.org/wiki/Members_of_Congress_who_Twitter*).

What critics often overlook when discussing Twitter is that its primary value is not found in a single tweet, in its sentence structure, or in its content. Rather, it is in the casual contact its members make with each other frequently throughout each day. A tweet becomes an act of reconnection. In discussions about social networks, most of the attention is given to how many connections you have to other people (degree) and whether the connection is returned (reciprocity). However, in the real world the most important property of a network may be the ability of one node to engage another. Twitter facilitates this potential to connect very well.

The Internet made three big promises to humanity when it went mainstream more than a decade ago. Most people focus on two of these: universal access to information, and a global economic revolution. For me, the Internet was always about the third promise: personal connection. This is the thing we humans are hardwired to do.

Twitter for Everyone

Among the more interesting Twitter applications to arrive on the scene in 2009 was Twitalyzer (*http://www.twitalyzer.com/twitalyzer*), the latest iteration of metric analysis of a member's use of the service. Twitalyzer examines a user's recent history and converts that statistical footprint into five key measures of use: Influence, Signal-to-Noise Ratio, Generosity, Velocity, and Clout. Although the presentation and explanation of these metrics are well done, each term comes loaded with the implication that there is a preferred way to use Twitter.

Generosity, for example, is Twitalyzer's interpretation of retweeting, or passing along another person's tweet with attribution. It is a particularly loaded term that assumes that retweeting is both universally accepted and must be done using the current version of an evolving convention (RT *@username*: what she tweeted). Some consider retweeting to be noise, particularly when it is done repeatedly within a well-connected group. The same is true for other accepted signs of Twitter success, such as the number of followers one has or how many updates have been posted. One person's treasure is another's junk.

There are many factors contributing to Twitter's success, and among them is its versatility. This is a world in which marketers, conversationalists, family members, conferences, churches, politicians, reporters, investors, fictional characters, artists, sports nuts, and professors can coexist. There is no wrong way to use Twitter; there are only consequences of use. If the individual finds value in doing so, there is no difference between the über-marketer following everyone with a dozen retweets each day and the spouse trying to keep tabs on a small inner circle of family and friends. Twitter is for everyone.

A Changing Culture

Mark Pesce (*@mpesce*), creator of the Virtual Reality Modeling Language (VRML) and author of *The Human Network: Sharing, Knowledge and Power in the 21st Century* (to be published in mid-2009), built his current work on an insight that children learn by imitating their peers. Now, the combination of new mobile technology and our social nature gives us 3.5 billion peers. Because everyone has the potential to see what everyone else is doing, innovative notions spread quickly and spark action within the masses. The days of trying to control such a world are gone. Our interaction is our evolution.

Today, we write about everything. We capture our lives in photos and on video, and we share the links with online acquaintances known only by their login handles. It is undeniable that we live in a transparent age.

The impact of transparency is exhibited in Homeless Man Speaks (*http://homelessman speaks.wordpress.com*), a blog about a man called Tony experiencing homelessness in Toronto, as transcribed by a neighbor. One entry describes a collision between Tony's bike and a car.‡ The driver, a large brute, storms out of the car, ready to confront. He looks at Tony and stops. "I know you. You're homelessmanspeaks.com." Such exchanges are not possible without the decision to share a part of one's life with the world.

As Werner Heisenberg pointed out through his physics experiments, interaction inherently changes the system. By answering Twitter's simple question, "What are you doing?", we are announcing to our corner of the world that we are ready to engage. At the same time, we should also try to answer the question, "What is changing as we do things?"

Jack Dorsey (naturally) is credited with the first tweet, posted on March 21, 2006. Twitter's popularity swelled in the year that followed, and by the end of February 2007, 1 million tweets had been sent. In November 2008, that number reached 1 billion.

Announcing one's presence so frequently and transparently creates issues. Since Twitter is not the only microblogging service, message splintering is occurring as communities form around Jaiku, Yammer, Tumblr, and others. A common solution developers offer is the mass-production of messages to many services. HelloTxt (*http://hellotxt .com*) provides a single web form for message publishing to centralize the process. However, creating redundant messages in all systems can annoy followers who are subjected to duplicate content.

Some people think text is too constraining. Seesmic (*http://www.seesmic.com*) facilitates microblogging with video by inviting members not only to announce what they are doing, but to say it in front of a camera. Although video offers more communication

---

‡ From the November 12, 2007 blog article, "My friends all drive Porsches, I must make amends," published on Homeless Man Speaks (*http://homelessmanspeaks.wordpress.com/2007/11/13/my-friends-all-drive -porsches-i-must-make-amends/*).

cues and context, it is also harder to search and skim, features that Twitter's brevity facilitates.

All of that detail is not universally welcome, either. Time will tell if Twitter's growing popularity (see Figure 1-11§) will elevate it to the level of Facebook, banned by productivity czars in workplaces around the nation. There are cultural differences in the response to transparency as well. The United Arab Emirates has already banned Twitter, stating that its content is "inconsistent with the religious, cultural, political and moral values" of the nation.‖

Figure 1-11. Twitter, Twitter, Twitter (The Gaping Void, by Hugh MacLeod, April 17, 2007)

You are about to create something new for the Twitter community. Fueled by the right idea, that something can change the way people create, view, or find value in their tweets. Keep this in mind as we look more closely at the Twitter API and ways to make it work for you.

---

§ From a comic illustration, "Twitter, Twitter, Twitter," by Hugh MacLeod, which first appeared online on Gaping Void in 2007 (*http://www.gapingvoid.com/history76156.jpg*). Hugh is found on Twitter at *@gapingvoid*.

‖ From the December 6, 2007 blog article, "Success 2.0: Twitter Banned In UAE," by Jason Lee Miller, published on WebProNews (*http://www.webpronews.com/topnews/2007/12/06/success-2-0-twitter-banned -in-uae*).

CHAPTER 2

Twitter Applications

 kmakice What is past is prologue. Draw some inspiration from the Twitter developers who came before you.

Good design is not about originality. It is about improving upon an existing idea and meeting the needs not already being met. For your own new application, your success will likely be tied to understanding the culture of tweeting *and* of developing. You can learn a lot by examining what has already been done.

Twitter developers make up a large and thriving community. Lists of popular and useful tools abound. Brian Solis (*@briansolis*), a PR guru at FutureWorks and cofounder of the Social Media Club, recently created a list of 60 of his favorite Twitter applications.[*] The Twitter Fan Wiki (*http://twitter.pbwiki.com*) has tracked over 300 applications, about half of which are web-based projects. The totals are almost double those from the previous year.

These numbers, however, are only a drop in the applications bucket. Ed Finkler (*@funkatron*) has identified almost 1,000 unique applications in his Twitter Source Tracker (*http://funkatron.com/twitter-source-stats/*), and as of November 2008 Twitter had manually registered over 1,900 applications. By the time you read this, I'm positive that those numbers will have gone up significantly.

The goal of this chapter is not to present you with a directory of the world's best Twitter applications, nor should the inclusion of any given tool be considered an endorsement. The purpose of this list is to show you some of the things that can be done with a web application using the Twitter API. These applications may provide some inspiration for your own projects.

---

[*] From the October 17, 2008 blog article "Twitter Tools for Community and Communications Professionals," by Brian Solis, published on PR 2.0 (*http://www.briansolis.com/2008/10/twitter-tools-for-community-and .html*).

Twitter's Open API

The Twitter team's decision to open up the service to third-party development was brilliant. Some argue it was the key to the company's early success. Access to its simple and well-conceived API led to the formation of a community of communities, with every new application adding its own group of devotees to the Twitter member base. In addition to gaining free development by these programming stakeholders—each with a specific vision of what would make the user experience better—the company also gained an army of evangelists motivating new people to start tweeting.

It was that community—not Twitter itself—that created the desktop applications that uncoupled tweeting from the web browser. Using the Iconfactory's Twitterrific (*http://iconfactory.com/software/twitterrific*) instantly changed my perception of Twitter from "that's interesting" to "that's vital." When Twitterrific enabled tweets to start coming to me and fading away on their own, Twitter stopped interfering with my day and instead fit into what I was already doing. The Iconfactory has since iterated the application several times to incorporate replies and direct messages into its functionality, adding to its appeal. When Apple opened the iPhone App Store in July 2008, Twitterrific quickly became the early mobile application of choice for Twitter users.

At the time of this writing, although the Twitter web interface still accounts for about 44% of all daily traffic, 6% of all tweets are published through Twitterrific.[†] Almost as many are accountable to Twhirl (*http://www.twhirl.org*), an Adobe AIR application with a similarly strong following, and TweetDeck (*http://www.tweetdeck.com*), which eclipsed Twitterrific as the leading desktop application in late 2008. Odds are good that many users of these third-party applications would be less inclined to tweet without their preferred tools.

Encouraging API development is also marketing gold for Twitter. The release of new applications inevitably promotes discussion, typically in the form of blog posts, wiki updates, and inclusion in semi-comprehensive lists like the one that comprises this chapter. The exposure lives on beyond the initial release of the third-party software and expands the Twitter network to reach even more potential members. Similarly, each development cycle brings new iterations and upgrades to generate recurring waves of reaction, inviting both critique and competition. More applications means a larger reach.

None of this, of course, happens without a well-designed, well-supported API.

[†] Ed Finkler's Twitter Source Tracker (*http://funkatron.com/twitter-source-stats/*) keeps tabs on how people are publishing their status updates by looking at the source data returned by the Twitter API. As of January 18, 2009, the top five sources overall were: the Web (44.1%), Twitterfeed (9.9%), Twitterrific (5.5%), Twhirl (4.9%), and Twitterfox (4.3%). However, the monthly stats by spring 2009 showed TweetDeck as the leading third-party application, responsible for just under 9% of all tweets. Twitterfox, Twhirl, and Twitterrific have each fallen to under 4%.

Finding Inspiration

Tracking new applications for Twitter became much easier with the launch of The Birdhouse (*http://birdhouse.tweetcrunch.com*), a Ning group for users and developers of Twitter. Shortly after something is posted to The Birdhouse, it finds its way to Tweetcrunch (*http://tweetcrunch.com*), a multiauthored blog about microblogging. The rate of development and the depth of the tools are increasing, probably buoyed by Twitter's improved uptime and ever-expanding membership.

There are many ways to use the data in the Twitter API. You can create desktop applications or tools for the mobile Web. You can create widgets to add to a blog, or you can build an entire website. In selecting which couple of dozen tools to feature in this book, I filtered out hundreds of options using the following criteria:

- The application must be web-based.
- It should not *require* JavaScript or another API to provide core functionality.
- It should serve some user need.
- It should have the potential to shape Twitter behaviors and culture.
- It must be working at the time of publication.

If you scan through this chapter, you'll notice that not every featured application meets all of these criteria. In some cases—such as Twittervision and TwitDir—the historical significance and longevity of the application merited bending my own rules. The selected websites are included to give you inspiration for what you might build as a useful Twitter web application.

 I am *not* arguing that mashups, JavaScript, or desktop applications are somehow inferior to the tools included in this chapter. Although this book does not cover programming for Adobe AIR or JSON, for example, I do encourage you to explore alternate ways to deliver your cool content without relying on the Web. The best place to start looking for information is the Twitter Development Talk group on Google (*http://groups .google.com/group/twitter-development-talk*).

I review each of the selected applications here with a screenshot of the tool in action and a brief discussion of its relevance to the Twitter community and how it works. I profile a few examples of web applications in each of seven categories of tools: Publishing, Information Stream, Appropriation, Search, Aggregation, Statistics, and Managing Your Follow Network.

Tools for Publishing

Any time I see a new web tool for posting tweets, my first question is, "Isn't there already a web tool for posting tweets?" Though the answer is always "Yes," that shouldn't and doesn't stop programmers from trying to do it better. Not all publishing tools are merely about free-form typing and clicking a button. Many add a new bit of integration or innovation that makes the tool useful.

Twitterfeed

Figure 2-1. Twitterfeed: automatically tweet a link from an RSS feed

People check their Twitter feeds for two basic reasons: to connect with people, and to exchange information. The immediacy of news flow on Twitter, facilitated by the short messages and varied means of access, makes it a great source of information for many members. Connecting other content to these channels, therefore, has value.

One of the simplest and most useful third-party applications is Twitterfeed (*http://twitterfeed.com*). This RSS parser will accept feeds from any XML source—such as Facebook comments, blogs, or other information streams—and automatically convert the newest information into a tweet (see Figure 2-1). Created by Mario Menti (*@mario*), a solutions architect at Global Market Insite, Inc., this web tool allows some customization in terms of how the tweet is constructed, such as how frequently it should check for new content and what text to prefix to every link. Twitterfeed is the most popular third-party publication tool, accounting for about 10% of all tweets in the public stream and sending 80,000 feeds to Twitter.

SnapTweet

Figure 2-2. SnapTweet: publish a link to Flickr photos

One of the important constraints that makes Twitter attractive is also a limitation. Unlike some other microblogging services, such as the now-defunct Pownce, Twitter cannot be used for sharing media files. Digital photography, though, is something many Twitter members do: they take pictures of important events in their lives or interesting things they encounter, and often upload them to photo-sharing communities such as Flickr (*http://www.flickr.com*). SnapTweet (*http://snaptweet.com*), created by Damon Clinkscales (*@damon*) of Austin, Texas, attempts to bridge the gap to Twitter (see Figure 2-2).

SnapTweet lets you automatically or manually post your latest Flickr photos as tweets. After signing up for a SnapTweet account, you can send a direct message to *@snaptweet* specifying the text you want to include with the link to your most recent

Flickr upload. You need to provide your Twitter username and password and a link to your Flickr photostream. SnapTweet will use this information to publish a tweet with a URL to the new photo. You can also configure SnapTweet to scan your photos every 20 minutes and look for the presence of a special tag. Every photo it finds with that tag will automatically be posted to your Twitter stream, with the title and a link directly to the photo.

SecretTweet

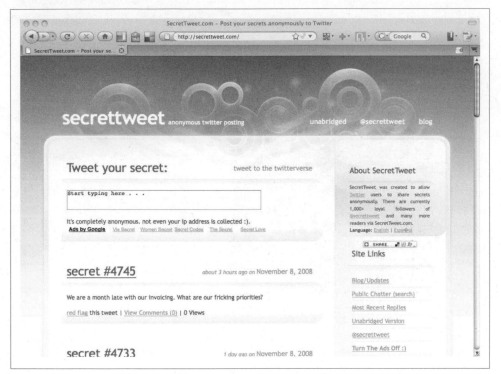

Figure 2-3. SecretTweet: tweet anonymously in a shared account

Twitter is a transparent medium. Not everyone likes sharing personal moments and various minutiae with the world, and there are those who won't tweet simply because other people will know who wrote the messages. One of the benefits of the Internet, however, is the ability to be anonymous when desired.

Inspired by a friend, student graphic designer Kevin Smith (*@mozunk*) of Marshall University created SecretTweet (*http://secrettweet.com*), a communal Twitter account fed from a web interface that allows people to share secrets anonymously (see Figure 2-3). The site already had 750 posts at the height of the Fail Whale period in mid-2008, and another 4,000 were added over the next six months. The following has grown to 1,200 members, and SecretTweet is broadcast in multiple languages. Smith also created Voolia (*http://voolia.com*), a tool to collect multiple URLs into one tweet-able link.

SecretTweet is not entirely automated, as Smith discovered the need for content moderation early on. When a person submits a secret using the SecretTweet web form, an email is sent to Smith with the text and a link to approve the tweet. Clicking on the link triggers a method request to the Twitter API to post the status update. All secrets are saved, stored in a database that feeds the "unabridged" version of the published information stream. Smith censors submissions that contain links to questionable material, racist language, or content not in the spirit of the channel. He also relies on community vetting and feedback, providing a means for commenting on and red-flagging submissions posted to the website.

Tools for the Information Stream

A "stream" is used as a metaphor for the flow of information coming through our computers. In microblogging, Twitter in this case, there are three basic types of streams: individual, public, and personal. Each can be described in terms of *relevance* and *information diversity*.

Content in an individual stream comprises nothing more than a longitudinal diary. The author already knows everything before it is posted; there is no new information to be gained. We might therefore say that the relevance is high, but the diversity is low.

By comparison, the public stream—which contains all tweets from members with public accounts and custom profile pictures—is noisy and lacks context. Since almost every tweet contains new information, the diversity is high. However, relevance for a given member tends to be low.

The sweet spot between the individual and public streams is the personal information stream. A personal information stream is built by its owner, who chooses to follow other twitterers and thus self-selects which content to include. Particularly when the numbers of followers and followed are balanced, the tweets in a personal information stream tend to both be highly relevant and contain a sufficient diversity of information (a feature that grows with the size of the follow network). In other words, any investment in time to acknowledge new information could be seen as worthwhile.

Not so long ago, Digg (*http://digg.com*)—the popular social news and content filter—challenged its community to make use of its API to feed creative and dynamic Flash visualizations. Although Twitter has yet to issue a similar challenge, some developers are using the company's open API to examine the information stream in new ways.

Twittervision

Figure 2-4. Twittervision: tracking tweets around the globe

Among the earliest efforts to view the public timeline was Twittervision (*http://twitter vision.com*), created by Dave Troy (*@davetroy*). This visualization merges the location information in the authors' Twitter profiles with a world map from the Google Maps API to display tweets based on the authors' geography (see Figure 2-4). To be seen on Twittervision, you must have a public account with a custom profile picture and location text that can be parsed. Up to 100 of the most recent public updates during the last half-day are displayed.

With early API developers concentrating on the most easily accessible data, a number of projects similar to Twittervision cropped up in 2007. TwitterFaces, Twitter Planet, and Twitter Earth all did the same thing, albeit with different map platforms. This kind of visualization is interesting because it leverages an available but hidden bit of information—author location—and presents it in an engaging way. However, a lot of filtering is required to find relevant content when reading individual tweets from the public timeline. The real-time map visualization also requires constant attention in order to be of benefit to the user; there is no aggregation of data or any way to replay past tweets. What you see is what you get.

Twitter Matrix

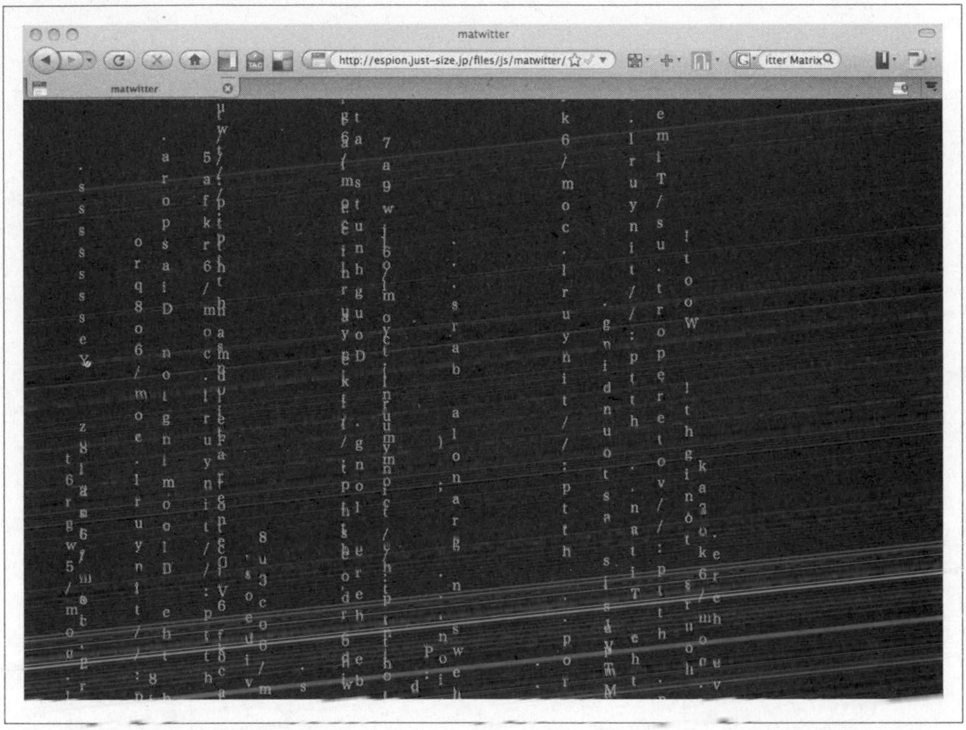

Figure 2-5. Twitter Matrix: tweets flow vertically, green text on black

In June 2007, Biz Stone (*@biz*) used the weekly Twitter newsletter to highlight a unique delivery of the Twitter stream, inspired by the movie *The Matrix* (*http://espion.just-size .jp/files/js/matwitter/matwitter.html*). Initially the treatment was only for the author's own stream (in Japanese), but it now allows members to interact with the Twitter API directly and turn their own tweets into green text flowing vertically on a black screen (see Figure 2-5).

The Twitter Matrix application, created by Kyosuke Takayama (*@takayama*), has no practical value; text rendered in this way isn't readable, nor does it provide any new insights about how you tweet or patterns in your content. Still, it's wicked cool to look at for a while, and it is clearly a unique way to visualize the data flow.

Twalala

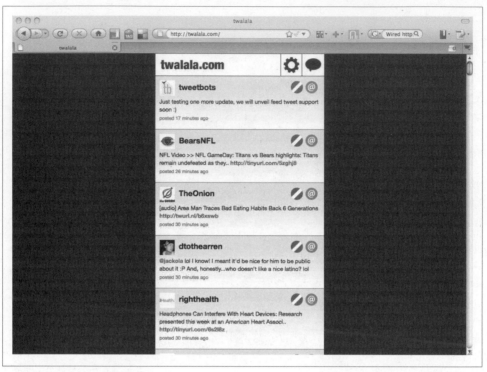

Figure 2-6. Twalala: filter out tweets based on topic or author

Simplicity is an attraction when it comes to posting content, but not so much when it comes to managing a growing number of followers and followed authors. All it takes is one chatty friend attending an all-day conference to realize that your options for getting rid of the noise are limited. Unfollowing that person for a while might be the answer, but she'll find out that you did so when you start following her again. Awkwardness can ensue, which is why a less formal way to filter other people's tweets is a welcome feature of Twalala (*http://twalala.com*).

On the surface, Alex Taylor's (*@goldenmeanie*) web interface is just another way to view your personal timeline (see Figure 2-6). Click on the settings link, though, and you'll realize what Twalala contributes to the Twitter culture. You can filter tweets from your stream by designating keywords, phrases, or specific individuals to block at the presentation level, rather than dealing with a noise problem through Twitter's servers. You can also create a whitelist (*http://twitter.com/help/request_whitelisting*) of designated people or words that you want to exclude from filtering.

This could become a must-have feature for more established tools, like Twitterrific, as business and marketing folk start to push advertising through the Twitter streams: the same hashtag technique used to extract and group status updates by topic can be used against advertisers to effectively remove their content from Twitter. This means businesses such as the new Magpie network (*http://be-a-magpie.com*), which pays individuals for the right to occasionally post in their tweet streams, could find their ads hidden from the eyes they want to reach.

Tools of Appropriation

One of the laws of design is that people will use your products in unanticipated ways. Jack Dorsey didn't build Twitter to be a tool for conversation, but a quarter of a billion *@username* replies later, that's what's happening. Likewise, direct messaging capabilities may have been added for 1:1 human communication, but there are now several applications leveraging that back channel to send commands and statistics and create new functionality. These tools don't use Twitter in the way it was intended, but they get great value out of the available methods.

Track This

Figure 2-7. Track This: track packages over Twitter

For active Twitter members—over 200,000 different people are tweeting on any given day—communicating through status updates and direct messages is often more convenient than sending an email or loading up a website. Most of what we do on the computer involves tasks and information retrieval where connection with others is not the obvious goal; however, it makes sense that the Twitter channel might become useful for these activities, too.

One innovative example is Track This (*http://trackthis.pb30.com*), a tool by Fragmented Tech (*@pb30*) that lets you tweet to get updates about where your packages are as they travel around the world (see Figure 2-7). After following the *@trackthis* account, you can send direct messages with a tracking number and a label that makes sense to you (as in, "d trackthis 123456789123 New Macbook"). Any time your package changes location along the route to its destination, a message will be sent to you with text describing its updated status.

In the first two months after its beta release in April 2008, Track This sent out over 10,000 updates for about 1,500 packages. Major delivery services such as FedEx, UPS, the USPS, and DHL are integrated with the service. In addition to Twitter, the tool accepts tracking numbers through the Web, email, IM, or SMS.

LiveTwitting

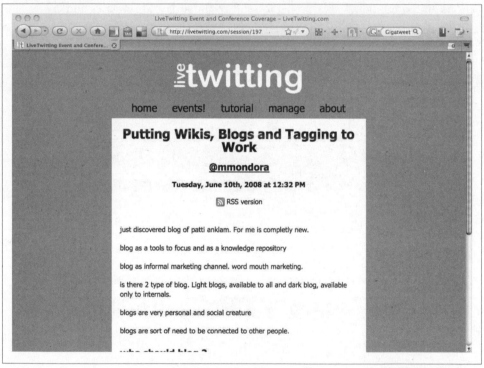

Figure 2-8. LiveTwitting: collect notes from a conference session

There was once a time when conference attendees used pen and paper to take notes on what a speaker said. Then came live blogging, which enabled a person with a laptop to not only capture those notes for posterity but also to share them with others not in attendance. Some people also use Twitter for this purpose, posting short comments throughout long talks. The problem with this is that it can become quite noisy for followers who love you for your occasional tweets about cute kittens and baking bread, not for a stream of snippets about the latest advances in your profession.

Michael Jensen (*@mdjensen*) and Danny Sullivan (*@dannysullivan*) developed Live-Twitting (*http://livetwitting.com*) with this in mind (see Figure 2-8). All of the commands to tell the system what to do with your notes are sent through the direct message back channel—no more flooding your followers with tweets while you enjoy the conference. There is an added benefit of organizing all the tweets into a somewhat coherent document of notes from the live session: you wind up with the same kind of output as you would live blogging, without having to keep a laptop open.

The commands allow you to annotate your messages to *@livetwitting*, not just saving your text but also essentially meta-tagging your content. You can name your session, flag a new topic, identify the speaker, and mark when the question-and-answer segment starts. There are also pause and resume features to allow you to use direct messaging for other purposes before the session has ended. The aggregation of all of the content and formatting can be viewed in the Events section of the LiveTwitting website.

 LiveTwitting went offline at the end of 2008. Such is life in the Twitter ecosystem. I included it in this chapter because the idea behind it is a good one, even if the implementation turned out to be short lived.

FoodFeed

Figure 2-9. FoodFeed: share and track your eating habits

The American people are overweight (well, many of us), and good nutrition is a global issue. Although we techies may eat a lot of unhealthy stuff (mmm, Pop-Tarts) and lead sedentary lives, at least we have some self-awareness about the whole thing, and we occasionally try to get back in shape. For every fast food burger sold, it seems there is a matching tip on how to live a more healthy life. Some of the more successful strategies involve sharing your battle of the bulge with a community.

Vitor Lourenco—a young interaction designer from Brazil who did some coding for Twitter in 2008—built FoodFeed (*http://foodfeed.us*) to encourage people to share details of their eating habits with their followers (see Figure 2-9). Vitor (*@vlourenco*) was responsible for the well-received Twitter website redesign in 2008 and was on the team that created the successful Election feed for the 2008 presidential campaigns. There are a few similar health services out there, but I chose to include FoodFeed here for a few key reasons.

First, it has a great username for the Twitter account that accepts the posts— *@having*—allowing you to both tweet in a more readable way and to answer Twitter's prompt question (as in, "@having scrambled eggs"). The second great decision its developer made was to give users the option of posting what they're eating as replies or as direct messages. This has implications for use, because you don't have to worry about bothering your followers with a lot of food-related data, and also because the private communication option encourages people to feed FoodFeed with more and better data without fearing what others might think.

One thing FoodFeed doesn't do is keep stats. In the site's own words, it doesn't actually do anything: "It's not really useful. It's just fun." If you want to keep track of details such as your calorie intake, try Tweet What You Eat (*http://tweetwhatyoueat.com*).

Tools for Search

Twitter users generate a lot of content. Three and a half million accounts spawn over a million tweets daily from all over the world. That's a lot of stuff flowing through the pipes that needs to be sorted. Summize, the most successful third-party Twitter application (discussed in Chapter 1), brought its tweet search expertise to the mother ship when Twitter acquired it in the summer of 2008. Still, that doesn't eliminate the need for new, better, and more specific kinds of search tools.

TwitDir

Figure 2-10. TwitDir: a directory of public members of Twitter

A year before Summize started searching tweets, a French marketing account manager began creating a directory of all Twitter members. Laurent Pantanacce (*@loran*) launched TwitDir (*http://twitdir.com*) as a way for users to search member profiles that match a given keyword (see Figure 2-10). The site can narrow the search to just parts of the profile, such as the name, username, location, or description. Initially, this was the only way to find other Twitter members in a certain geographic location.

More importantly, TwitDir became a de facto authority for Twitter statistics. By monitoring the public timeline, the site could identify new members posting to the stream and thus keep a running count of memberships. It wasn't precise—private, dormant, and some early adopters' accounts are not visible in the public stream—but it was accurate enough to suggest the arc of Twitter's growth curve. Bruno Peeters, author of the Twitter Facts blog (*http://twitterfacts.blogspot.com*), has tracked the numbers Twit-Dir has published since its launch, using that obscure little number on the main search page to project milestones as Twitter grew.

TwitDir also keeps tabs on the leading users in the four main profile statistics: followed, updaters, favorites, and followers. For the first several months, the Top 10 and Top

100 lists had some meaning. Today, however, even the top 1,000 users lists represent only about .03% of the total membership.

 TwitDir may have disappeared permanently. In late November 2008, the main web page was replaced with a message indicating that the site was down for maintenance and for the LeWeb conference in Paris that December. At the time of this writing, TwitDir is still MIA. It will be sad if it stays that way, but similar functionality is being provided by other Twitter member directories, such as Twellow (*http://twellow.com*).

Green Tweets

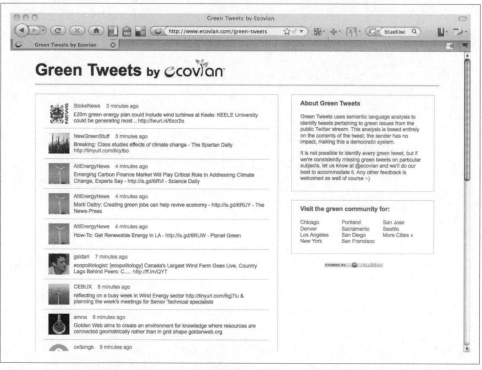

Figure 2-11. Green Tweets: streams tweets about environmental issues

In one sense, Twitter is like a multiverse. There are so many different uses and overlapping interests in what flows through its streams that Twitter has the potential to be all things to all people...but not at the same time. The things I find interesting (Chicago Bears victories, Web 2.0 startups, Joss Whedon) may not be the same subset of things that interest you. We are all using the same channel, but we each find ways to extract the bits that are most relevant to us. One way we do this is by assembling our follow networks, selecting other members whose tweets we want to read. But it is more difficult to filter based solely on content.

Green Tweets (*http://www.ecovian.com/green-tweets*) is one example of a topic filter: it tries to connect what all Twitter members are saying about the environment (see Figure 2-11). The custom information stream applies semantic language analytics to display tweets that mention "green" issues, from global warming to sustainability. The green stream was built by developers at Ecovian (*@ecovian*), a collection of city guides created by local communities of people who are passionate about sustainable lifestyle. Each guide contains user-generated reviews and resources to support local green living. Green Tweets is a great example of how Twitter can be used to help identify a community for another social networking platform, built around a domain topic.

TweetBeep

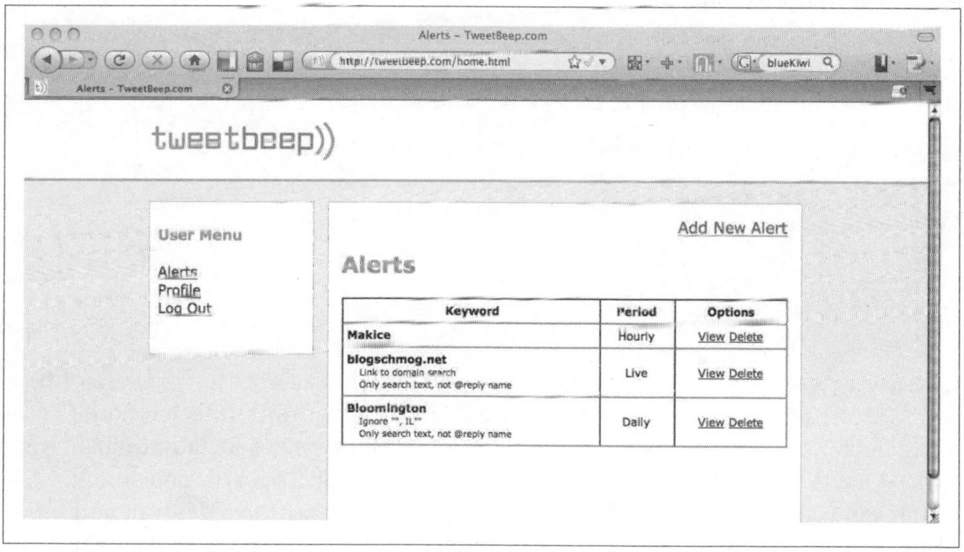

Figure 2-12. TweetBeep: sends emails about keywords found in tweets

Two early features of Twitter that are missed by many were IM integration with Jabber and the ability to track tweets by keyword. Once upon a time, an IM window would pop up with a chat message from Twitter any time someone mentioned a term you had chosen to track, such as "informatics" or "Bloomington." There are other ways to track this information now, but few of them come to me.

TweetBeep (*http://tweetbeep.com*) is billed as "Google Alerts for Twitter" (see Figure 2-12). It is more robust than Twitter's tracker was, with controls for how frequently you are notified, what terms to exclude, and whether you want alerts constrained to a particular location. After you create a new alert, TweetBeep will email you a list of all of the tweets that should be on your radar. Separate domain alerts are available for mentions of your blog or other relevant URLs. Site creator Michael Jensen (*@mdjensen*) is also responsible for LiveTwitting (see "Tools of Appropriation" on page 55) and TweetAnswers, a community sourcing of questions and answers.

Tweet Scan

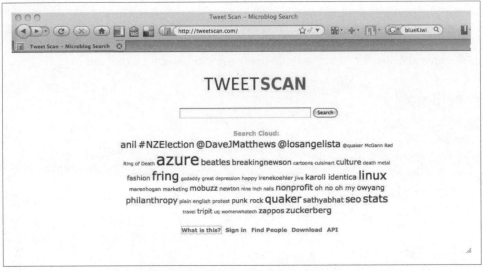

Figure 2-13. Tweet Scan: search public tweets and member profiles

Like TweetBeep, Tweet Scan (*http://tweetscan.com*) offers a way to track use of keywords in the public timeline (see Figure 2-13). Enter a keyword to search both tweets and member profiles; the results are available in several formats, including email, RSS, and JSON. Tweet Scan allows you to track up to five phrases at a time and get the results delivered daily or weekly. The site has added support for Identi.ca and other Laconica-based microblogging channels, which gives the scan a reach that goes beyond Twitter. Tweet Scan maintains its own content database.

Tweet Scan has some other utilities as well. Although the user search hasn't worked well for me, it does offer a tool that lets you download your historical archive of tweets, dating back to December 2007. Creator David Sterry (*@weex*) has also made it possible to include Tweet Scan as a list in your browser's search box, letting you quickly search for terms without loading up the website first.

I have been using Tweet Scan since February 2008 to find local Twitter users. Even when Twitter's own user search is working, it is only as good as the whimsy and diligence of each member choosing to set their location fields. Ironically, iPhone and BrightKite integration wreaked havoc on the trustworthiness of the member location by making the field more accurate. Now that location can change automatically as people travel, tracking who is tweeting as a resident in a college town means many false hits whenever the university hosts a conference or a sporting event. Tweet Scan's daily emails allow me to look at what people say, pointing me to anyone who mentions my hometown so that I can examine the context of their timeline.

Favrd

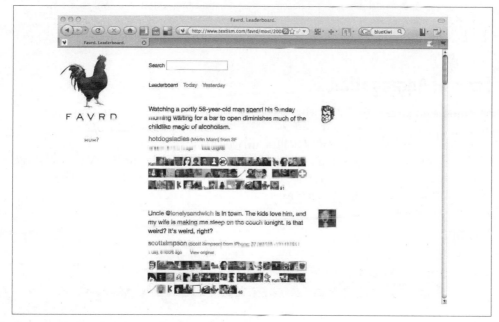

Figure 2-14. Favrd: daily lists of most favorite tweets

A lot of attention has been paid to three key stats that every member compiles: follower count, following count, and total number of updates. These numbers have been prominently displayed on every Twitter member profile page from the start and, as a result, are the most commonly utilized bit of information mined from the API. The black sheep of the profile stats is the favorites count. This is partly due to only a small percentage of people making use of Twitter's bookmarking function, but it is also true that people don't use it because comparatively fewer programmers develop for it.

Dean Allen (*@textism*), a 42-year-old Canadian living in the South of France, developed a website to start mining this underutilized Twitter feature. Favrd (*http://www.textism .com/favrd*) aggregates the favoriting activity of Twitter's members and pulls up the most memorable tweets of the day (see Figure 2-14). Allen tips the hat to Ono Matope's website, Favotter (*http://favotter.matope.com/en/*), which has cataloged almost 900,000 favorited tweets by concentrating on the 950 users that use that feature the most.

Favrd screens out the flotsam and jetsam that distract from the intended use of Twitter: real people commenting on life in their own voices. In addition to automatically crawling to find users who make use of the favorite button, the site also invites any users to add themselves to the voting list by verifying their Twitter credentials once. The site keeps track of the most favorited tweets from that community each day, letting you know who else has favorited the tweets you liked.

 Later in this book, I'll describe code for building a new API tool that keeps track of favorites in the community (see "Best of Twitter API" on page 324).

Tools of Aggregation

Meaning isn't always found in what one person says. Sometimes it can only be found in what many people say. James Surowiecki's 2004 book *The Wisdom of Crowds* (Random House) gave many examples of how smart a group of folks can get when they are following their own localized rules or preserving their own self-interest. With over three million accounts and at least 200,000 active members on any given day, much wisdom can be extracted from the Twitter crowd.

Twappi

Figure 2-15. Twappi: estimates emotion of Twitter users

Twappi (*http://twappi.com*), launched in spring 2008, is a simple tool that scans daily posts from the public timeline and makes a summative assessment of the mood of Twitter's public users (see Figure 2-15). Twitter's advanced search tools allow for search by emoticon, so the "happy" percentage is calculated as a ratio of the use of :) characters out of the tweets that include emoticons.

Twappi isn't just a reporting tool, though. Jacob Friis Saxberg (*@webjay*) of Denmark designed the site to include a single post by a Twitter member who is not in that happy percentage. The text of that user's downer status update is followed by a link—with the text "cheer up"—that invites the viewer to take action. Clicking on the link brings up your Twitter home page, already pre-addressed as a reply to the unhappy tweeter. This is what makes this application so appealing, despite the relatively little it offers in terms of functionality.

Twitscoop

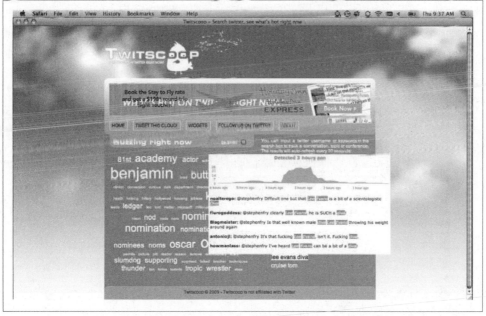

Figure 2-16. Twitscoop: current buzz as a dynamic tag cloud

In 2007 and again in 2008, Twitter got some press for how quickly its members were able to report on and disseminate information about earthquakes and fires, well before the more traditional media could turn the events into stories. The attraction of writing a short tweet as opposed to a longer blog post or newspaper article gives microblogging channels an edge in the speed of information flow. Third-party application developers are trying to leverage the API to allow users to taste some of that breaking news goodness.

Lollicode's Twitscoop (*http://www.twitscoop.com*) is arguably the best at doing this. Inspired by the mathematics of financial markets, the Twitscoop algorithm crawls hundreds of tweets every minute, filtering out the common words and extracting the most often mentioned terms (see Figure 2-16). The results are displayed in a dynamic tag cloud and in a list of top phrases, giving viewers an idea of what people are talking about. One of the better features is the mouseover action on the phrase lists, which reveals some examples of specific tweets and a chart of references in the last 24 hours. Whereas Tweet Scan (see "Tools for Search" on page 58) is most useful for collecting references to specific keywords, Twitscoop is the most advanced tool for understanding what is happening in real time.

What makes Twitscoop so influential and useful, however, is not simply the fancy web work and computation. Twitscoop has its own Twitter account, which it uses to broadcast the more interesting changes in public chatter as they are detected. I've found that I am much more likely to go and explore the site when I'm first prompted that something interesting is going on there. Now, whenever I want to check whether some repetition in my personal information stream has become widespread, I visit Twitscoop to look for the terms in its cloud.

Twist

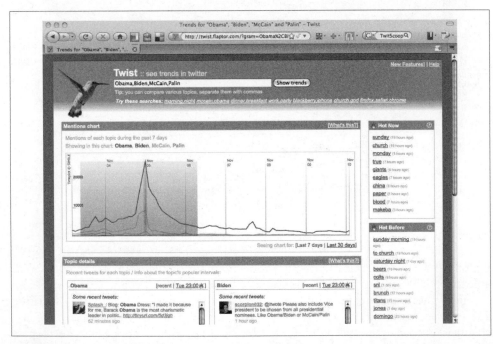

Figure 2-17. Twist: compare graphs of keyword references

Some of the early attempts at trend mining were fixated on basic counts of the number of times a specific word found its way into a tweet. The first tool to do this was Tweet Volume, which compared the total number of references to a few terms with a bar graph. The problem with this approach is that it loses meaning over time. Counting references to Barack Obama isn't meaningful if he is mentioned constantly; the raw numbers of mentions will just continue to go up. The element of time is therefore an important dimension to consider when evaluating a trend.

Flaptor released a similar version of the keyword search that incorporates time into the equation. Twist (*http://twist.flaptor.com*) lets you enter multiple terms and graph the number of daily references in tweets (see Figure 2-17). This allows you not only to see how use of each term has ebbed and flowed over the last week or month, but also to see how that activity compares with that of other terms. Twist highlights the most popular period (sometimes several days long) with a clickable box that reveals more detail. The graph automatically scales to fit the most popular term.

Tools for Statistics

Twitter itself provided the earliest mechanisms for measuring Twitter use, in the form of member profile statistics. The running totals of friends, followers, and total contributions to the tweet corpus were all that early adopters and application developers focused on. Consequently, when the next wave of new users climbed on the Twitter train, they were clearly at a disadvantage: the available stats favored older accounts.

Throughout 2008, the sophistication of the metrics used to describe individual users evolved. Developers moved beyond using the information posted in profiles, and began taking into account the size and composition of a user's follow network as well as the rate and types of posts. The third-party applications discussed in this section offer a few ways to look at the stats that Twitter users can generate.

What's Your Tweet Worth?

The big question during the early life of the company was, "How is Twitter going to make money?" That question is still open, although an answer is expected in 2009. Inevitably, some members have followed it with a second question: "What's in it for me?"

Advertising on Twitter appears to be an emerging industry. Businesses have formed around selling advertising space on Twitter members' profile pages (Twittad), sponsorship of moments during live-tweeted events (such as Glam Media's Academy Awards coverage[‡]), and even selling individual tweets (Magpie). To bring those dollars

---

[‡] From the February 22, 2009 blog article, "Glam edits Oscars Twitter feed and makes money," by Matt Marshall, published on VentureBeat (*http://venturebeat.com/2009/02/22/glam-edits-oscars-twitter-feed-and -makes-money/*).

from advertisers to users, however, investors need some means of evaluating which members will provide the best return on investment.

Figure 2-18. What's Your Tweet Worth?: calculate your value

Lava Row, an emergent social media consultancy firm in Iowa, built a tool specifically for this purpose. What's Your Tweet Worth? (*http://www.whatsyourtweetworth.com*) calculates how valuable you are to the Twitter community and spits out a price tag that you can put on your profile background for Twittad (*@Twittad*) (see Figure 2-18). Although the formula is hidden, the site returns the basic profile statistics, presumably as an indication that they are important in determining worth. If true, this application's contribution is to turn multiple metrics into a single, easy-to-digest dollar figure.

TweetStats

At the close of 2007, Damon Cortesi (*@dacort*) became curious about his own Twitter use and built a little Perl script that would scrape and digest the tweet footprint for a given account. About a month after he released it, he used that script as the base code for a project to teach himself Ruby on Rails, and that in turn became TweetStats (*http://tweetstats.com*).

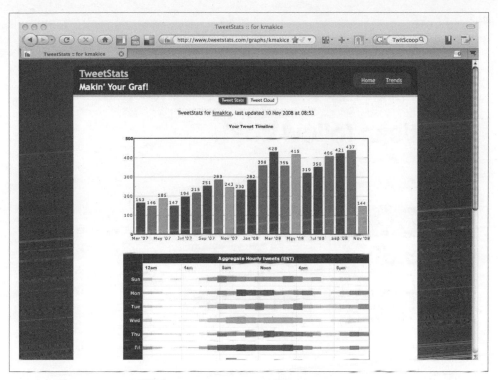

Figure 2-19. TweetStats: graph your tweet history and posting patterns

This web tool examines archival data for a given user and aggregates information about when that user tweets into graphs for different dimensions (see Figure 2-19). TweetStats also shows the people to whom you reply the most and the various ways you publish your status updates. TweetStats graphs are a nice way to understand one's longitudinal usage of Twitter. Cortesi has also added a trends tracker, which tracks the top 10 keywords returned by Twitter's trends API over time. The site includes a historic look at what has been important to twitterers via a tag cloud that includes such terms as iPhone, Obama, and Christmas.

Examining your Twitter history with TweetStats can provide some interesting insights into your daily routine. For example, for the six hours between midnight and dawn, my wife has almost no Twitter activity. Any time she spends conscious during that period is reserved for mild insomnia and needy kids. On the other hand, I have a spike in activity just as my wife is winding down for the night, followed by a low but steady murmur throughout the night. This reflects not only my general lack of sleep but also my irregular sleeping patterns (sometimes I stay up late, sometimes I get up early). It makes me wonder whether TweetStats could be used to reveal patterns in couples' use of Internet technologies.

Follow Cost

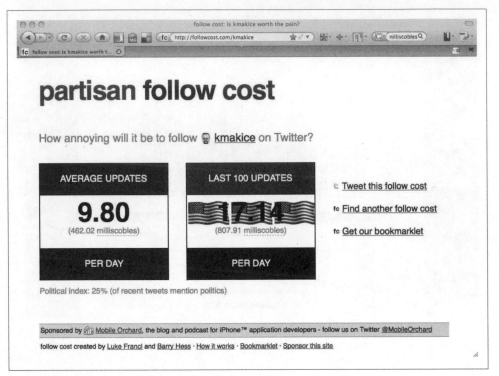

Figure 2-20. Follow Cost: how annoying is it to follow someone?

Whenever I am notified by email that I have a new follower, I do the same few things. First, I pull up the user's profile page and look for a real name and bio information. The more complete and human the profile looks, the more likely I am to keep looking at the rest of the page. I then glance at the statistics for signs of a spammer: high following counts coupled with low follower counts are a red flag. Finally, I start looking at the quality of the member's tweets, shying away from people who only post replies or automated tweets. Not everyone values the same things, but most people have some kind of system they use to determine whether or not to reciprocate.

Follow Cost (*http://followcost.com*) facilitates this process: it attempts to assign an aggregated metric to your Twitter use to give other people another way of evaluating your value. This site only measures tweeting activity. The unit of measurement, however, is defined in a creative way: using über-user Robert Scoble (*@scobleizer*) as the baseline. According to creators Luke Francl (*@lof*) and Barry Hess (*@bjhess*), as of late September 2008 Scoble had tweeted 14,319 times in 675 days, for an average of 21.21 tweets per day. One *milliscoble*—their chosen unit of measure—is defined as 1/1,000th of the average daily Twitter status updates by Robert Scoble, or .02121 tweets per day.

The evaluation tool also has some hidden features. For instance, Figure 2-20 shows my rating shortly after the 2008 U.S. elections, when I spent most of the day and night tracking the Electoral College updates on Twitter. It was a personal record for number of tweets in a day, almost all of which were about voting and the election. Follow Cost picked up on that surge, raising my longer-range stats by 3–4 daily tweets and flagging me as a political junkie. It makes me wonder if I would get a background of footballs instead of flags if I spent a Sunday afternoon tweeting play-by-play for the Chicago Bears.

Follow Cost has at least one more surprise. When I checked, the follow cost for Robert Scoble showed a high level of activity for his last 100 tweets, with a rating of 76.46 posts per day, or over 3,600 milliscobles. The background for that stat was a mushroom cloud, and the title changed to "*nuclear* follow cost."

Twitter Grader

Figure 2-21. Twitter Grader: turn your activity into a 100-point grade

One of the more popular statistical tools to pop up recently is Twitter Grader (*http://twitter.grader.com*), an evaluation site that accumulates several stats and turns them into a single grade on a 100-point scale (see Figure 2-21). Built by the founders of HubSpot, which offers similar graders for websites and press releases, Twitter Grader collects data and adjusts your standing based on your data set. After about a month of service, it had already collected 300,000 profiles.

The grade it gives is the sum of several factors, including the number of followers you have, the power of those followers in the network, how often you update, and how thoroughly you filled out your profile. The single-figure statistic is nice because it is easy to wrap your head around. The metaphor of a test grade, though, unfortunately implies that any number lower than 60 is a failure. Twitter Grader, Twinfluence (*http://twinfluence.com*), and a few other member-ratings tools have drawn criticism for assigning values that some believe are best defined by individual users rather than algorithms.

It isn't the grade that makes this site so interesting, though—HubSpot added a few other features to go with the rating and profile stats. The tag cloud isn't that useful, probably because it doesn't go deep enough into your tweet history to find much useful information to summarize in that way. The list of suggested people to follow, on the other hand, has had an impact on Twitter users. Before Twitter Grader, the people choosing to follow me were largely confined to three groups: people I knew, people from my home state, and spammers. After this app hit the scene, a fourth group became prominent: active users with moderately sized follow networks and some relevant tweet content. I suspect this spike in random follows is in fact not so random, but rather is attributable to people using Twitter Grader to find new members to follow.

Twitterank

Figure 2-22. Twitterank: using PageRank to calculate importance

Sometimes the best inspiration comes from an example of what not to do. One day in early November 2008, the Twitter community took a new third-party application to task, shortly after openly embracing it. At first Twitter was ablaze with signs of interest in the form of self-promoting tweets about a new user-ranking site, but only a few hours later came the backlash, as many speculated about whether the simple application was really a phishing scam. Panic ensued, especially after ZDNet's Oliver Marks posted an article about user gullibility.[§] Passwords were changed. Twitterank's programmer responded. A parody was created.[‖] Twitter spent the latter part of the day responding to user complaints about something it wasn't responsible for, and the Internet had a nice little meme about trust and authentication.

Twitterank (*http://twitterank.com*) was billed as a "PageRank for Twitter users," claiming to ignore follower counts and instead use other indicators to gauge importance in the network. The initial page looked hastily assembled and was littered with a lot of tech slang; it warned users to take caution when giving away their Twitter passwords—and then asked them to enter their passwords. The ROI for granting your trust to this site was a page with a cryptic number and nothing more (see Figure 2-22).

To his credit, the creator of Twitterank—Ryo Chijiiwa (*@ryochiji*), a programmer at Google who made this tool as a side project—responded to the criticism and histrionics about his site being a phishing attack with some fast changes. Not the least of these were adding a method for calculating rank without requiring a password, albeit less accurately; adding context (he included a percentile to let you know where your number fit into the known Twitterverse); and a link to his identity. Those are the types of clues people look for when determining whether to trust a site.

 The Twitterank incident came two months before a real phishing attack on the Twitter community that used direct messages from known friends. For more on phishing, security, and how it affects you as a Twitter API developer, see "Gone Phishing: A Word About Passwords" on page 182.

The Twitterank of yesterday certainly won't be the Twitterank of tomorrow. It is unknown whether Chijiiwa's project will evolve into something useful or permanent, but it is clear that the debut could have gone better. The beleaguered developer tweeted at the end of his long day: "I have a new-found appreciation for people who do PR."[#]

[§] From the November 12, 2008 blog article "Gullible Twitter users hand over their usernames and passwords - did you get your Twitterank yet?!", by Oliver Marks, published on ZDNet (*http://blogs.zdnet.com/collaboration/?p=163*).

[‖] Twitter AWESOMENESS!!! (*http://twitterawesomeness.com*) duplicates the tone and design of the initial Twitterank web page. In the source code was a comment: "<!-- And if you're reading this, then congrats — you're more savvy than the average twitter-bear! -->".

[#] Ryo Chijiiwa's status update can be found at *http://twitter.com/ryochiji/statuses/1003226654*.

Tools for the Follow Network

It's not what you know, it's who you know. People tend to concentrate on the content that flows through Twitter at a clip of about two million tweets a day, but what gives those short status updates value is having other people read them.

Besides statistics, the other big focus of the developer community in 2008 was discovery. People were becoming more and more interested in how to get followers and how to find interesting people to follow. The manual method was to browse through the following lists of people you knew, treating these as tacit endorsements of other members. Over time, however, that strategy can become both redundant and tedious. The applications highlighted in this section help people manage and improve their own follow networks.

Does Follow

Figure 2-23. Does Follow: confirms whether one user follows another

A web application doesn't have to be complex to be useful. A bit of a coding meme started when Twitter API guru Alex Payne (*@al3x*) launched a tool that lets visitors type in an inaccessible web address and confirm whether or not the problem is on that site's server (*http://downforeveryoneorjustme.com*). During Twitter's darker tech days in the first half of 2008, Payne was frequently asked that question about his own company's site. He built Down For Everyone for a friend, after realizing how widespread that line of simple questioning was.

Damon Clinkscales (@*damon*)—the same developer who brought us SnapTweet (see "Tools for Publishing" on page 48)—created a similarly simple web tool, Does Follow (*http://doesfollow.com*), to check whether one Twitter member is following another. It accepts two usernames and then calls the Confirm a Follow API method (see "Confirm a Follow" on page 163) to check with Twitter. The response page returns either a green "yup" or a red "nope." There is also a button to easily switch the order of the names, to check for mutuality.

There's nothing much to Does Follow, but it's useful enough to be bookmarked as a resource (see Figure 2-23). Sometimes simple is good.

Qwitter

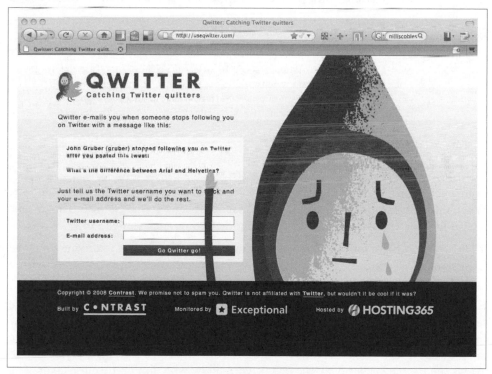

Figure 2-24. Qwitter: monitor who stops following you on Twitter

Managing your follow network is not an easy task on Twitter proper. Sure, you can add someone's content to your personal information stream, and you can unfollow those folks who in the end don't float your boat. When those things happen to you, however, you will only be notified of the follow, not the unfollow. Psychologically, it's probably a good thing not to know when someone loses interest in your Twitter stream or what pushed them over the edge. Sometimes, though, you just need to know.

Enter Qwitter (*http://useqwitter.com*), created by Contrast. Signing up for Qwitter just requires you to enter your Twitter username and your email address (the destination for any future unhappy news when you lose someone from your follower flock; see Figure 2-24). The service monitors your follower list, checking routinely to see if anyone is missing and adding anyone new who might go missing in the future. If Qwitter detects that another user has rejected you, you get an email with a message like:

> John McCain (JohnMcCain) stopped following you on Twitter after you posted this tweet:

> I just voted for Obama in #TwitVote — *http://twitvote.twitmarks.com/*

This tool fills a real gap in the features already offered by Twitter and the extended developer community. Be warned, though: the warm fuzzy feelings you get when someone follows you are twice as intense in the opposite direction when someone unfollows you!

 Sadly, the last Qwitter notifications came at the end of November 2008, with a brief revival in January 2009. I suspect it became too costly to track the size of everyone's network. Whether or not Qwitter is permanently offline, it is a great example of a third-party application filling a need. Another tool you can use to analyze your lost followers is TweetEffect (*http://www.tweeteffect.com*).

Friend or Follow

Your Twitter profile page used to show you up to 100 avatars of the people you follow. When the site was redesigned in mid-2008, that number was reduced to 36. That means that in most cases, many of your flock are hidden from quick view.

If you want to figure out quickly who among that full list is also following you, the fastest way on Twitter is to page through your tweeps 20 at a time and look for the "Direct message" link, evidence that a user is following you back. It's very tedious.

Happily, Dusty Reagan (*@DustyReagan*) has devised an easier way for you to make sense of your contact list. The Texas developer is responsible for Friend Or Follow (*http://friendorfollow.com*), a tool that organizes a follow network of any size into three tabbed pages, separating everyone in your network into three categories. The first tab shows the profile images of all the people you follow who don't return the favor. The second tab shows the people who crave your tweets despite you not liking theirs. The third tab shows the mutuals: those people with whom you freely exchange your little 140-character missives (see Figure 2-25). Members of this last group are the only people with whom you can have a two-way conversation through direct messaging.

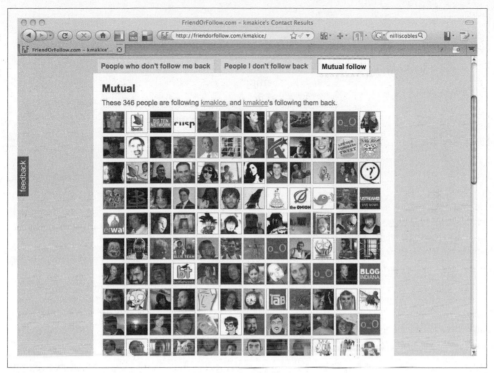

Figure 2-25. Friend or Follow: a pictorial map of your follow network

Mr. Tweet

One of the more personable and effective discovery tools for Twitter was launched in late 2008: Mr. Tweet (*http://mrtweet.com*). Developers Yu-Shan Fung (*@ambivalence*) and Ming Yeow Ng (*@mingyeow*) made an impact in this new development space through a quality product as well as a proactive, open relationship with people using the site (see Figure 2-26). Mr. Tweet quickly jumped onto the crowdsourced customer service site Get Satisfaction, and its developers have been very receptive to making changes to rapidly improve the young application.

Mr. Tweet requires only that you follow *@MrTweet* to join. This allows notifications to be sent via direct messages. Server limitations created an initial backlog of registration requests, but as of January 2009 the site sends out notices of updates to network analyses every two weeks. Mr. Tweet highlights changes in your follow network and gives you details about each Twitter member that follows you to help you make an informed decision about whether or not to follow them.

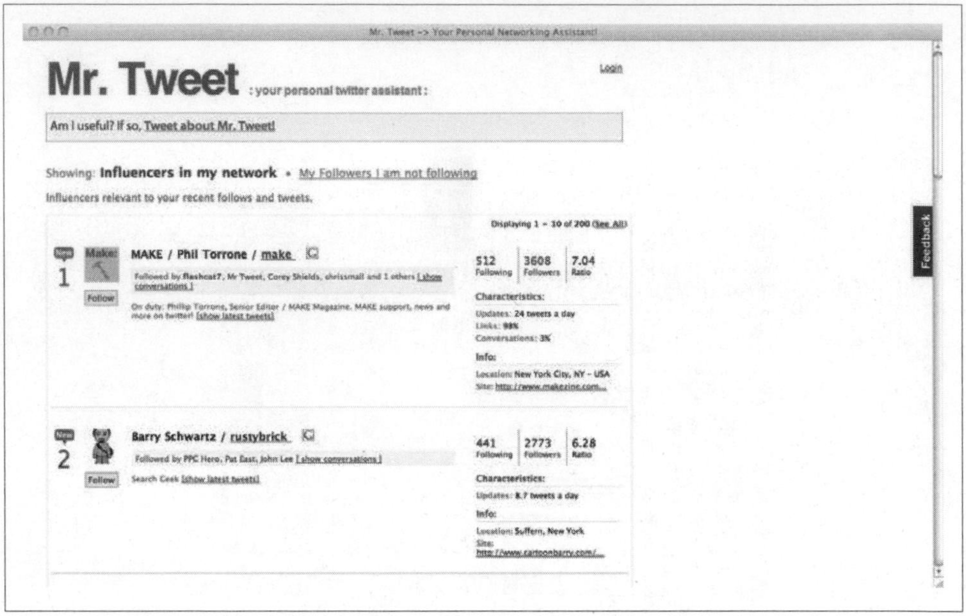

Figure 2-26. Mr. Tweet: gives you info to decide about following

Initially, the site provides three distinct views of your data. Mr. Tweet shows you a list of people that it recommends you follow, but the site also gives you a ranked ordering of people who are following you who might be worth of reciprocation. Finally, it provides a view to show you how others will see you in their lists. The value of these recommendations has improved dramatically since the initial launch, when the same crowd of über-users was always listed first. The algorithm has become quite a bit more nuanced. It is a very stylish site with a respectful appreciation of the Twitter community.

Omnee

The idea for Omnee (*http://omnee.thebubblejungle.com*) came to creator Mark Hawker (*@markhawker*) after he'd compiled a list of top people in health care worth following on Twitter. He quickly realized that maintaining such lists would prove an intractable problem for one person, so he turned to the wisdom of the crowds for help. The tag-based director attracted 100 users on the first day, and its use has grown steadily every since (see Figure 2-27).

The genius behind Omnee is the simple method of self-reported descriptions that each contributing member can add to the site. Rather than completing lengthy web forms or having a central authority assign statuses and classifications, Omnee asks everyone who wants to participate to send a direct message to *@omnee* (or a tweet with the *#omnee* hashtag), using a plus sign (+) before each new descriptive tag. Each submission through Twitter can contain as many keywords or phrases as Twitter length constraints allow. You can use the minus sign (–) to remove existing tags. An automated task runs every five minutes to process new information.

Figure 2-27. Omnee: an organic tag directory of twitterers

Hawker remained busy iterating the site after its launch. Most remarkably, he sought out the second-generation Twitter APIs containing data from other third-party tools to augment his site and give Omnee even more value. These data sources included TwitterCounter (*http://twittercounter.com*), Twitter Grader (*http://twitter.grader.com*), Twinfluence (*http://www.twinfluence.com*), and Monitter (*http://monitter.com*).

Twitree

From the island of Mauritius off the eastern coast of Africa, developer Asvin Baloo (*@asvinb*) released a tool for Twitter that makes the old manual way of searching for new people to follow a lot more efficient. Twitree (*http://twitree.com*) starts with the 100 most recent additions to your friends timeline and lets you browse their own following lists for new names. There is nothing new there. However, because Twitree treats each individual as a directory in a recursive tree structure, you can dive down into the pathways one branch at a time (see Figure 2-28). I navigated through two dozen branches in the tree fairly quickly before the browser response slowed and took another minute to fill the horizontal screen with two dozen more.

Figure 2-28. Twitree: explore your part of the Twitter network

Twitree also adds some other functionality. You can update your Twitter status from its web form, and you can access a suite of actions—follow a twitterer, get profile information, send a direct message, reply, or retweet someone's most recent message—by right-clicking on any of the user icons. Since Twitree knows who you are from the Twitter username you gave it initially, Twitree will also underline in green any Twitter members you encounter whom you are already following.

Much of this interaction only requires you to enter a Twitter username to get started. Authentication is needed so you can do things like post a message, but otherwise Twitree appears to be a well-conceived network exploration tool that takes advantage of what the Twitter API provides and accesses that information in a very efficient manner.

And Many More

The number of Twitter applications created by third-party developers has grown into the thousands. No longer can a single blog post attempt to capture the whole corpus of links and descriptions of every known application. Consequently, a number of collaborative efforts have sprung up to keep track of everything.

Here are a few places you can visit on the Internet to look at the full range of tools and services spawned by the Twitter API:

- Twitter Applications (*http://twitter.com/downloads*)
- The Twitter Fan Wiki (*http://twitter.pbwiki.com/Apps*)
- Twitdom (*http://twitdom.com*), a Twitter applications database
- Twapps (*http://www.twapps.com*), an archive for the best Twitter applications
- Twittown (*http://www.twittown.com*), a blog about widgets and apps
- The Birdhouse (*http://birdhouse.tweetcrunch.com*), a Ning community
- Mark Evans's Twitterati blog (*http://www.twitterrati.com*)
- Programmable Web (*http://www.programmableweb.com/api/twitter*)

Soon, you'll be able to add your own cool new application to these lists.

CHAPTER 3

Web Programming Basics

 kmakice Feeling a little shaky about the whole coding thing? Take a crash course in the languages you will use to build your Twitter app.

As demonstrated in the first two chapters, Twitter is a rich playground for both members and developers. Before we get into specifics on how you can join in the fun, we should spend some time reviewing the mechanics of working with the languages you will be asked to use to build your new Twitter web application.

This chapter provides an overview of the basic knowledge and tools needed to create the applications described later in the book. Although the API can be used to create desktop and mobile applications as well, this book focuses on the web platform built with PHP and MySQL. Even for experienced programmers, it won't hurt to skim this chapter so you understand the scope of what is to come. However, if you are confident in your skills with XML, CSS, PHP, and MySQL, you can skip to Chapter 4 and jump right into the methods available in the Twitter API.

 This chapter reflects what is needed to build and install the suite of sample applications to get you started using the Twitter API. It is not meant to be a replacement for resources dedicated to improving individual skill sets for XHTML, CSS, PHP, MySQL, or server management. Suggested reading on those topics can be found at the end of this chapter.

XHTML

The extra "X" may look intimidating, but Extensible Hypertext Markup Language (XHTML) isn't much different from regular HTML. The main purpose of the revision is to help make web pages better supported by paying more attention to the structure of the data. Whereas HTML did not seek to separate data from presentation, XHTML puts the burden of presentation on the stylesheets.

HTML is not XML. Compliance with XML means that the tags need to be "well-formed," or follow the conventions required by documents of that type. These conventions include use of lowercase in tag names (XML is case-sensitive) and the insistence that all tags are closed, either explicitly with a second tag (`<p></p>`) or implicitly as part of a singleton tag (`<br />`). Attribute values also have to be enclosed in quotes, either single or double. In HTML, you can omit the quotes around integer and Boolean values and the browser will still understand them.

The advantage of XHTML crystallizes when using XML tools. For example, XSLT is used for transforming documents, and XForms lets you edit XML documents in simple ways. Integration with other tools, such as MathML, SMIL, and SVG, is not possible with regular HTML. Of the three versions of XHTML—Strict, Transitional, and Frameset—Strict is the one to use. A lot of problematic tags are deprecated, so using Strict makes your code better prepared for future standards. It also makes it easier for many different devices to properly interpret the page content, since there are fewer unexpected tags and attributes to encounter.

 The easiest way to ensure strict compliance is to use the World Wide Web Consortium's (W3C) validator, at *http://validator.w3.org*. Many text editors also have validation and formatting tools built in.

The rest of the material in this section is pretty straightforward. I include it only to make sure we are all on the same (web) page when it comes to the markup.

Web Pages

Open up any XHTML-friendly text editor (such as TextMate), and you are likely to find a template for a web page that resembles Example 3-1. As soon as it is created, you can forget about these tags; they aren't useful outside of the page definition.

Example 3-1. Sample XHTML for a web page

```
<!DOCTYPE html PUBLIC "-//W3C//DTD XHTML 1.0 Strict//EN"
    "http://www.w3.org/TR/xhtml1/DTD/xhtml1-strict.dtd">
<html xmlns="http://www.w3.org/1999/xhtml" xml:lang="en" lang="en">
<head>
    <meta http-equiv="Content-Type" content="text/html; charset=utf-8" />
    <style type="text/css" media="all">@import url(my_styles.css);</style>
    <title>The Basic Web Page</title>
</head>
<body>
This is the stuff you can see.
</body>
</html>
```

The stuff that is meant to be visible to the person visiting your website is located between the `<body></body>` tags. After changing details such as the name and location of your external CSS file and the title of the page, the tags to focus on are the ones that will describe the content you want to display. Here is some information about the types of tags used in the sample applications for this book:

Block tags

These elements have the inherent property of creating a new line of content when displayed, forming discrete blocks of content when rendered by the browser. The most general block element is the `<div>` tag, which is primarily used to identify each section using the unique `id` attribute. The stuff contained within a given division is isolated from the rest of the page and styled according to the attributes of the enclosing `<div>` tag.

More familiar forms of block elements include the heading tags (`<h1>`, `<h2>`, etc.) and `<p>`. Each has specific properties, such as text size and weight (boldness), for which you can specify values other than the defaults. The break tag, `<br />`, is sometimes considered a block element too, because it forces a new line to be rendered in the page display.

Example: `<div id="me"><p class="others"><br /></p></div>`

Inline tags

For the content contained within block elements, different words may require different presentation. XHTML allows for some special inline elements to handle this without explicitly defining a style. The two most commonly used elements are `<strong>` and `<em>`. By default, the former makes text boldface, and the latter displays text in italics.

Example: This is `<strong>boldface</strong>`.

List tags

List tags are a special category of XHTML element, sort of a cross between block and inline elements. Wrapping content in list tags will force a line break (as with a block element), but these tags are also used to indent or mark specific lines of text. There are tags for three kinds of lists: unordered lists (`<ul>`), ordered lists (`<ol>`), and definition lists (`<dl>`). Which tags you use dictates how the list items are presented.

List tags are nested. Each item in an ordered or unordered list must be wrapped in `<li></li>` tags, and the collection of all the list items must be wrapped in `<ul></ul>` or `<ol></ol>` tags. (Definition lists are a special case that we won't go into here, as the sample applications in this book don't use definition tags.) Unordered lists place bullet characters before each item. Ordered lists use a sequence of numbers, letters, or Roman numerals.

Example: `<ul><li>tom</li><li>jerry</li></ul>`

Hyperlink tags

Arguably the most important tag in the bag of XHTML tricks is the hyperlink tag. Without it, web pages would have to be bookmarked and loaded separately. Linking is what makes Google searches work.

You can make any text, image, or object an active hyperlink by wrapping it in anchor tags (`<a></a>`). Anchors can be used to point to somewhere new, using the `href` attribute and a referenced web document, and to name a particular bit of content. Naming comes in handy to connect XHTML to JavaScript or links from other pages.

Another attribute, `title`, further empowers links. The `title` attribute can store useful descriptive or instructive information that becomes visible in many browsers when you move your mouse over the hyperlink.

Example: `<a href="#" title="hi">click<a>`

Image tags

Adding images to your web page may slow down the page loading a bit, but it also makes the experience more enjoyable for visually perceptive visitors. The bandwidth and access limitations of a decade ago, which discouraged the use of images on web pages, are disappearing, as most U.S. homes now have broadband access.* Graphics—whether they're big pictures dominating the page or a few custom icons used for bullet points in a list—enhance communication and enjoyment.

 Even with faster connections becoming the norm, it is still good practice to be aware of what images and other media do to bandwidth. Optimize your images for delivery on the Web by using PNG or GIF screenshots, or by compressing JPEG photos.

The `<img />` tag—a singleton that does not have a matching closing tag—has an attribute, `src`, that points to a file accessible via the Web. The file can be in any one of a number of formats, but for graphics the most acceptable formats are *.gif*, *.jpeg*, and *.png*.

Although most browsers don't require it, image tags also need an `alt` attribute to be compliant with W3C standards. Alternative text has two important purposes. First, before the browser successfully downloads the image, it uses the text in the `alt` attribute as a placeholder in the page display. More importantly, alternative text is used by web browsers for visually impaired people to describe the images those visitors cannot see. Alt text can be blank for images meant for decoration only, but otherwise, the value should be a short and meaningful description of the image.

The other attributes that are helpful to include are `width` and `height`. These default to the actual pixel size of the image file if not included, but specifying them in the code allows the browser to carve out the appropriate bit of screen real estate while the image loads. The rest of the page is then unaffected by when the graphic decides

---

* According to a Pew Internet & American Life Project report called "Home Broadband Adoption 2008," 55% of American adults now have broadband Internet at home (*http://www.pewinternet.org/pdfs/PIP_Broadband_2008.pdf*).

to show up. These attributes also allow for resizing a graphic on the fly, as their values will override the dimensions of the image for purposes of rendering the web page.

Example: `<img src="hi.jpg" alt="Hi" width="8" height="8" />`

Using the `width` and `height` attributes of the image tag will only resize the display, not the file size. That 10-megapixel shot from your new digital camera will still slowly load into the browser as a giant 4-megabyte file!

Form tags

There is an important group of tags that deserves greater mention. Without them, a web page would not be able to gather information from visitors and respond in a relevant manner. Pointing and clicking on links is fine, but forms are what put the interaction in the Web.

Forms allow people to enter data into a web page and send that data back to the host server. Every blog or wiki uses a form to let people publish information. Every online purchase relies on a web form to manage the transaction. Even a simple Google search consists of an input element and a submit button. Here's a list of the form tags used in the sample applications:

`<form>`

To let the browser know that the aforementioned kind of interaction is permissible, you need to define an area of the web page as a web form. This is done by wrapping content in `<form></form>` tags and specifying a couple of key attributes.

The `action` attribute points to the destination server and file that are expecting the form data. This can be an email or FTP address, but usually it's another web page that will be able to parse the data and formulate some response to the submission.

The `method` attribute lets the browser know how to encapsulate the data as it is sent to the server. GET methods turn the data into a visible query string, whereas POST data is sent with the URL request separately for processing on the server end. Posted data is the most common.

Example: `<form action="process.php" method="post"></form>`

`<input />`

The `<input />` tag is one way to collect information from the person submitting the form. The nature of the input field is dictated by its `type` attribute, which can be filled with values like `button`, `checkbox`, `file`, `hidden`, `image`, `radio`, and `reset`. For the purposes of this book, we are interested in three specific types: `text`, `password`, and `submit`.

Each `text` input is displayed as a one-line box into which text can be typed. You can set the `value` attribute of this kind of field to pre-populate the form field with some text (such as the previously saved value). There is also a `size` attribute that gives you some control over how long the box should be.

Example: `<input type="text" name="user" value="visible" />`

The `password` input is nearly identical to the `text` input. The big difference is that the text being entered is masked with bullets or asterisks. That offers the person doing the typing protection from onlookers. However, the text is still plainly visible in the source and is not inherently secure upon form submission. If possible, use secure protocols and avoid returning the password back to the form.

Example: `<input type="password" name="pw" value="hidden" />`

Text fields are open data entry. That means if it can be typed on the keyboard, it can be sent to the server. This puts some burden on the developer to filter malicious or error-producing content from being fully processed.

This kind of validation can also be done on the client side with JavaScript, but on the server side it must be done with a scripting language such as PHP. Without server-side validation, malicious users (or those that keep scripts disabled for their own browsing safety) can very easily bypass your filters.

The other type of interest is `submit`. This turns the input into a button that can be pressed to send the data to the server. In this case, the `value` attribute becomes the label of the button. By default, the browser will use "Send" as the button text.

Example: `<input type="submit" name="send" value="Go!" />`

Each input tag must also have a `name` attribute. This is what differentiates this particular blob of data from all the rest of the data you may ask for in your web form. If two elements have the same name, the data will look like a list on the server side and may not be interpreted correctly. As with other tags, the name also serves as a hook for JavaScript and other dynamic languages.

`<textarea>`

Sometimes one line of text isn't enough. Imagine trying to blog (or even microblog) with only space for one short line at a time. The brains behind XHTML thought of this when they developed the `<textarea>` tag. This element *does* require a closing tag. Any text between the two tags appears in a big box in the web form.

If you use styles to change the font family, style, or other formatting, the dimensions will change as the size of the characters changes: 3 rows by 70 columns will look smaller with 9pt type than it will with 12pt. It is more effective to use CSS (discussed in the next section) to determine the size of form objects:

```
Textarea {width:400px; height:80px;}
```

Example: `<textarea rows="3" cols="70">My novel</textarea>`

`<fieldset>`

An XHTML element that can be useful for making sense of web forms is the `<fieldset>` tag. The `<fieldset></fieldset>` pair creates a visual grouping of any form elements contained within to make it clear to the visitor that they are meant to be together. You can then add a special nested tag—`<legend>`—that will wrap around the text you want to use for the title of this section. Fieldsets are useful with CSS styles to create tabs, hiding all but the group of form elements that is currently in use.

Example: `<fieldset><legend>Login:</legend><fieldset>`

Forms are used in the sample applications to authenticate Twitter accounts and store some basic configuration information. Example 3-2 shows all the form parts put together.

Example 3-2. XHTML for a simple web form

```
<form action="" method="post">
    <fieldset>
        <legend>
            Authenticate:
        </legend>
        <div id="username">
            Username:<br />
            <input type="text" name="twitter_username" size="25"
                value="you can see this" />
        </div>
        <div id="password">
            Password:<br />
            <input type="password" name="twitter_password" size="25"
                value="you can't see this" />
        </div>
    </fieldset>
    <input type="submit" name="submit_button" value=" Go! " />
</form>
```

A Nod to Some Other XML Structures

Web pages and XHTML are just one form of strict XML structures. The blogs you read typically have RSS feeds, which are formatted using structured tags. The content you will receive from the Twitter API can also be XML.

In this book, we will both read and create new RSS and XML structures. Example 3-3 shows the initial shell for an RSS feed, waiting for dynamic content to be added.

Example 3-3. General RSS structure

```
<?xml version="1.0" encoding="UTF-8"?>
<rss version="2.0">
    <channel>
```

```
        <title>Sample RSS Feed</title>
        <link>http://www.blogschmog.net/feed/</link>
        <description>This is my blog.</description>
        <language>en</language>
        <pubDate>Wed, 10 Dec 2008 13:18:56 +0000</pubDate>
    </channel>
</rss>
```

CSS

If markup languages are all about structure, stylesheet languages are all about presentation. Cascading Style Sheets (CSS) are used most commonly for web page design, but CSS also applies to other XML structures, such as Scalable Vector Graphics (SVG). Once upon a time, rendering instructions were intermixed with the data structure, causing lots of problems with making things look the same when viewed through different system platforms or on different hardware. With separate stylesheets, however, the same structure can be presented in a way that best fits the context of use.

CSS is used to change the appearance and layout of the structured data, spanning everything from colors to fonts to arrangement of content. It can even hide or reveal content, making the web page interactive when associated with event handlers. This is particularly powerful when teamed with a dynamic scripting language like PHP, as you can create a web page that detects a person's browser signature or IP address and then select a stylesheet on the fly that is optimized for display in that context.

Stylesheets are built from three basic parts. The *selector* references the tag element by name, ID, or class. The *property* is the part that indicates what is to be changed, and the *value* indicates how it should be presented:

```
selector { property:value; }
```

 Some related properties and values can be combined to reduce the number of lines of definition the stylesheet requires to display content in the way you want. For instance, borders—the lines surrounding a particular element—have three properties that can be set either separately (`border-width:1px; border-style:solid; border-color:black;`) or as one combination property (`img { border: 1px solid black;`).

The browser will prioritize the style changes and render the display. Sometimes, this may produce unanticipated results—for instance, text in a paragraph that you want to appear in red may show up as blue, forcing you to investigate what is causing (or sometimes preventing) the change. Referencing a selector with a different property value later in the rendering process, or simply not knowing which properties are inherited for which embedded tags, can lead to a lot of hand-wringing.

In Example 3-4, the first line of visible text ("body") is rendered in blue while the next line ("This text is black.") is black.

Example 3-4. Inline style tag

```
<!DOCTYPE html PUBLIC "-//W3C//DTD XHTML 1.0 Strict//EN"
    "http://www.w3.org/TR/xhtml1/DTD/xhtml1-strict.dtd">
<html xmlns="http://www.w3.org/1999/xhtml" xml:lang="en" lang="en">
<head>
    <meta http-equiv="Content-Type" content="text/html; charset=utf-8"/>
    <title>Test of CSS inheritance</title>

<style type="text/css">
*{color:black;}
body {color:blue;}
.my_class {color:gray;}
#my_div {color:red;}
#my_div a {color:green;}
#my_div h4, #my_div p {color:purple;}
</style>

</head>
<body>body
<p>This text is black.</p>
<div id="my_div">
    <p>This text is purple.</p>
    <h4>header 4</h4>
    my_div
    <a href="#">link</a>
</div>
<p class="my_class">This text is gray.</p>
</body>
</html>
```

Be careful when using the * CSS selector—it's easy to accidentally override another style without realizing it. Using a "reset" stylesheet typically addresses this nicely by setting a baseline style for the document body and then telling all child elements to inherit the styles that you don't explicitly specify for them.

The browser's prioritization is based on a weighting formula that calculates how important a particular rule is: more specific style definitions are given a greater weight. A selector of #my_div .my_class p, for instance, would be deemed more important than simply p or .my_class, regardless of the order in which the browser encounters those selectors.

The World Wide Web Consortium officially recognizes CSS1 as the recommended standard. However, there are two newer versions—CSS2 (currently in candidate status) and CSS3 (now in development)—that may one supersede it. These later iterations add support for fine control of positioning, media types, and effects such as shadowing.

I promise that the CSS for the sample applications in this book won't get too fancy.

Assigning Styles to Structure

Example 3-4 shows several ways in which selectors can be constructed to refer to HTML elements and to dictate how the browser displays content. The syntax relies on a handful of characters:

Hash (#)

The hash references a specific ID attribute associated with a tag element in the XHTML structure. Each ID selector can be used only once per page.

Example: `#whoopi { color:purple; }`

Full stop (.)

The full stop, or period, references a specific class attribute associated with one or more tag elements in the XHTML structure. Classes can be used as many times as you want and are great for formatting repeating content, such as dynamic lists.

Example: `.kermit { color:green; }`

They can also be used in conjunction with a specific kind of tag to set a style for that combination of element and class. Because this is more specific, it will take precedence over the class alone.

Example: `h4.kermit { color:black; }`

Asterisk (*)

The asterisk is a wildcard character that can be used to set the default style for any unassigned tag elements in the page. This is often used as the first style declaration, to set the font size and family for the entire page.

Example: `* { font-family: sans-serif; font-size: .9em; }`

You can also use the wildcard to apply styles to everything contained in a specified selector. However, this can lead to frustration if you accidentally overwrite a specific style declared elsewhere in the sheet.

Example: `#sidebar * { color: blue; }`

Space ( )

Spaces are used to build a complex string of selectors into a nested style. A nested style is inherently weighted with greater priority than a single-element selector because it is more specific. You can, for example, define all anchor tags to be underlined (that's the default interpretation by the browser, actually) but turn off the underlining for links in a specific division.

Example: `#subtle a { text-decoration:none; }`

Comma (,)

Commas are used to group several selectors together and assign them the same style properties at once. This is useful when a number of selectors share the same subset of styles. Any differences can be declared separately for each selector.

Example: `#one, #two, #three { color:red; }`

Nested styles are both a blessing and a curse. Such fine control is great, but the more complicated the CSS becomes, the more hair you'll pull from your scalp trying to figure out why a link buried deep in the web page won't turn blue. Maintaining good stylesheets for a large website is an art. Reuse and revise your stylesheets as you build your applications to limit conflicts.

Laying Out Your Web Page Content

In the early days of web design, the people designing web pages often had experience building printed pages, where the position of each bit of text or picture can be finely controlled. The Web, however, is a flexible medium. The same page can be displayed on big monitors and small, with a Mac or a PC, using Internet Explorer or Netscape Navigator. Flexibility and precision didn't always jive.

Although later versions of CSS promise that fine control, even CSS1 provides several properties that let you dictate where chunks of content are presented on the page. The following are the properties used in the sample applications described in this book:

padding and margin
> The "box model" best describes margins, padding, and borders. If you picture the content of an element as the innermost box and the element border as the outermost box, the padding is the space between the content and the inside edge of the border. The margin is the space between the border and the nearest other elements on the page. This extra space is like a force field that protects other content from crowding the parts of the element.
>
> Values for the padding and margin properties can take many forms, including percentages and specific lengths. Lengths are typically measured in terms of pixels (px), which are absolute, or em-length (em), which is a relative measure based on the width of the letter "m" in the chosen font. Margins can also have a special value, auto, which will attempt to balance the spacing between elements. This is often used to center a block of content on a web page.
>
> Example: #content { margin:20px; padding: 1.5em; }

float
> Floating an element moves it to the right or the left of the other elements within the parent element, as content flows around it. Floats are used to create sidebars or to describe the relationship between an image and its surrounding text.
>
> Example: #sidebar { float:right; }

width
> This property sets the horizontal dimension of an element. The width is measured without consideration of the margin, border, or padding values (or as if all three values were set to zero). Remember that there is both a left and a right side to any element, so a division with a width of 100, padding of 10, border of 1, and margin

of 20 would take up 162 pixels across the page (100 + 10 + 10 + 1 + 1 + 20 + 20 = 162).

Example: #column { width:350px; }

text-align

This property sets the alignment of text within a block element. The usual suspects are possible values (left, right, center, justify). text-align cannot be used to affect the placement of a division; instead, use the float property to move divisions to one side of the page or the other.

Example: h2 { text-align:center; }

display

We sometimes take for granted, based on experience, that certain tags will be rendered in specific ways. Header tags result in larger, boldfaced text, with some vertical spacing above and below. List items are indented and have space between each new item. All of that presentation, though, is part of an accepted interpretation of style properties that the browser adds to the page upon seeing those tags.

With the display property, you can assign some of those properties to any tag element. Division tags can become inline objects and anchor tags can become block elements. Either can be displayed as list items. This kind of reappropriation of inherent properties is not frequently done, but display does have one very useful value: none. This effectively hides the element and all of its contents from display. With the incorporation of JavaScript, this value can be changed on the fly, making pop-up content and contextual menus possible.

display differs from another property, visibility, in that with display the hidden elements are not factored into the positioning of the visible elements on the page.

Example: #help { display:none; }

Decorating the Web Page Content

The other big use of CSS is to make the page look pretty. Most presentational control of this fashion revolves around fonts and colors. The sample applications in this book use some of these basic controls to make the web pages look clean:

font-family

In word processors, changing the shape of the letters to match a typographical set of characters is as easy as selecting from a menu. Your computer scans your operating system for the presence of fonts and lists all the ones it finds as options. A web browser has access to this same list of fonts, but the basic list differs from one computer platform to the next and can be expanded by installing extra fonts. To make a web browser try to use a specific font, the CSS must be coded to pass that request on to the client.

The font-family property allows the web developer to send a comma-separated list of font names to the browser, which will use the first one that it recognizes as available in its system. For this reason, any exotic fonts should be either avoided or listed with other, more common fonts that are likely to be available. The list of values should end with a general family type—such as `serif`, `sans-serif`, `script`, or `monospace`—to direct the browser, as a last resort, to pick the system- or user-defined preferred font for that general category.

Example: `* { font-family:Helvetica,Arial,sans-serif; }`

`font-size`

The size of the text is dictated by the `font-size` property, which can accept values that range from percentages to length units to keywords (`smaller`, `larger`, `xx-large`, etc.) that are interpreted by the browser. The values are most commonly expressed in terms of `px` (pixels), `pt` (points, the default), or `em`. Em-length is often preferred, since it is calculated from the current size of the text. A `font-size` value of `.9em` would cause the text to be rendered at 90% of the size it would be without the new style definition, and `2em` would cause the text to be rendered twice as large.

Example: `p { font-size:.9em; }`

`color, background-color`

Colors can be assigned to any object to describe both its text (or border) and the background fill upon which that text rests. There are a number of predefined color names: `aqua`, `black`, `blue`, `fuchsia`, `gray`, `green`, `lime`, `maroon`, `navy`, `olive`, `orange`, `purple`, `red`, `silver`, `teal`, `white`, and `yellow`. The color can also be expressed as a hexadecimal value (`#00ffcc`) or its decimal equivalent (`0,255,204`) to indicate how much red, green, and blue to mix to form the desired color.

The `background-color` property also accepts a value of `transparent`, which means whatever colors, images, or text are underneath the layered object will be visible. This is the default, which is why setting the background color of the body will result in all elements having a background of that color.

Example: `#sidebar { color:green; background-color:black; }`

`text-decoration`

This property deals with some of the less common style changes for text, such as strikethroughs, overlines, and underlines. It's useful if you want to remove an underline, such as the one added to a hyperlink by default. `text-decoration` can also cause things to blink, which is probably a sign that we aren't learning from past mistakes.

Example: `a { text-decoration:none; }`

Getting the Browser to Recognize Styles

Once you've defined your styles, you have to get the browser to locate your styling genius and use it to render your web pages. CSS can be used inline as part of the XHTML or referenced as a separate file outside of the web page.

For inline references, the `style` attribute can be added to any tag and filled with style properties and values, as in:

```
<div style="font-size:36pt;"></div>
```

Whatever styles are defined in this attribute will apply to the content of the tag itself. Since embedded objects can inherit some or all of these properties, the style may cascade down to structures contained within the styled element. Changing the font size of the body, for instance, will also change the size of the text in all of its `<div>` and `<block>` tags, unless that setting is overruled by another style.

Another way to bring styles into a web page is to define a whole block of properties at once using the `<style>` tag. This tag is typically used between the `<head>` tags that are used to define the page. By placing several properties between the style tags, you can define the look of an entire page in one easy-to-edit location in the code.

A third way to assign styles to the elements of a web page is to bring in the defined properties as an external file. There are several advantages to doing so, not the least of which is that it makes the amount of code in your web page much smaller. External files can also be shared across all of your sites, giving you one place to edit a style whose properties you want to affect your entire site.

External files can be brought to the browser in one of two ways. The first is the `<link>` tag, which is placed between the `<head>` tags of the HTML. The browser will look for the file referenced in the `href` attribute, as in:

```
<link rel="stylesheet" type="text/css" href="my_styles.css">
```

The second method is to leverage a CSS convention, `@import`, between `<style>` tags:

```
<style type="text/css" media="all">@import url(my_styles.css);</style>
```

The big advantage of this method is that older browsers can't and won't attempt to interpret this code; they will simply render the page based on the HTML they can see. This increases the chances of compatibility with older systems.

When the browser looks for the specified file, it will start in the directory containing the page it is trying to render. You can use relative paths (*../css/my_styles.css*) that climb up and down the directory structure, server paths (*/css/my_styles.css*) that start at the domain root, or full URLs to point to the file.

PHP

I can remember the early days of web design, when sites consisted of static content, hardcoded into a certain state by the developer/designer/editor/marketer. Small sites with three to five pages were tough enough to maintain. Once a website grew beyond about two dozen pages, time spent making frequent changes could eat up a hefty percentage of the workday.

Dynamic web pages used to be created on the fly using runtime programming languages such as Perl, primarily. There are more options today, including proprietary platforms such as ASP and ColdFusion. PHP—which stood for "Personal Home Page" when it was first released in 1995—is a widely used free server option that powers over 20 million websites, including popular tools such as Wikipedia, WordPress, and even Facebook.

PHP bears a lot of resemblance to Perl, largely because that was what PHP's creator, Rasmus Lerdorf, meant it to replace. It has had five major revisions; the most recent (PHP 5) is now a half-decade old. Although PHP was intended for web page generation, it can also be used from the command line, making it amenable to automation with *crontab*s.

The language is much richer than what you will encounter in this book. My intention here is to explain only the part of PHP that will be used in the sample applications, which are intended to be bare-bones examples of some of the things you can do with the Twitter API.

How to Accept Candy from Strangers

Here you are, ready to set the world on fire with your creativity and build a useful tool for the Twitter community. Your application will require not only data from an API over which you have no control, but also user input typed into web forms and content feeds originating from remote sources. Before accepting such input, you should know about some of the risks in doing so.

SQL injection attacks

Database servers are separate beasts from the rest of the web application. They have their own security and usually reside on a completely different machine. The data they currently contain and are willing to store is of little use if they can't communicate with the web pages that are being rendered, but the necessary connection between the web application and the SQL database creates an opportunity for malicious users.

A SQL injection attack can happen if the data you pass to SQL statements has not been properly filtered to remove escape characters. If these special characters get passed to the database, they could be interpreted as a query. The injected code may be a hexadecimal string that looks like gibberish to you, but the SQL server may still be able to decode and interpret those characters. This kind of attack isn't specific to PHP or MySQL; it can occur whenever one scripting language is embedded within another.

CRLF injection attacks

CRLF refers to the carriage return and line feed combination of ASCII characters often used in Windows applications to indicate a new line (for Unix-based systems, the end of line is denoted with a line feed only). The attack is characterized by a hacker injecting

CRLF commands into the system. Since these characters are often used to parse data, extra end of lines can allow one entry to become several.

Cross-site request forgery (CSRF) attacks

This kind of attack is also known as a "one-click" attack. It is made possible by exploiting ill-conceived browser cookie strategies to send commands to another site that relies only on the cookie for authentication. What makes CSRF so scary is that the links that send the commands can be included as the source of an image file. The act of loading a web page in a browser or viewing an email message in an HTML-enabled email client can be enough to kick-start the attack.

There are a few prerequisites for CSRF to work. First, the attacker has to target a site that is known not to check the `Referer` header. Second, that site must contain a web form that does something useful for the hacker (like transferring funds). The attacker must then simulate that form perfectly, with all the required form names and value constraints, and get the target to load up the malicious web page where the attack is embedded while that person is still logged into the remote site.

 The best way to prevent all these kinds of attacks is to treat all remote data (whether it comes from web form submissions, RSS feeds, or even the Twitter API) as hostile. Escape any variables you don't *know* are filled with good data.

Strings, Arrays, and Objects

The most important concept to grasp is the cornerstone of programming, the variable. This is the entity into which you store data so you can manipulate it and create things such as search engines and blogs showing dogs sleeping upside down. All of this important stuff is dependent on our ability to name and retrieve information as part of the programming logic.

In PHP, strings, arrays, and objects are all referenced in the same way: with a $ and the name of the variable. PHP keeps track of what kind of variable it is based on the context of what you are trying to do with it. A string contains a discrete value, which could be an integer or a bunch of text. An array is a list of strings, referenced with a key that can either be an integer or text. You will use objects whenever you deal with files, databases, or XML structures.

When setting a string, the content is encapsulated in quotes. Single quotes (') cause the content to be taken literally, without interpretation. This means if you include another variable, the value of that variable is not substituted. Double quotes (") cause PHP to attempt to interpret any variables contained in the string and resolve them to the values they represent. Because of this disparity, single-quoted strings will run faster.

If you wish to include a quotation mark of the same type that is encapsulating the string, you have to escape it by adding a backslash (\) before it. This tells PHP to ignore it:

```
$truth = "<div id=\"sarcasm\">The Packers play 'football'</div>";
```

Sometimes short lines of text are not enough. You may want to store a lot of text all at once and not have to deal with all the concatenation and character escaping. Enter the *heredoc*. With this string-creation tool, you signify the start and the end of the text you want to save and just type away between those points. The start point is in the form *<<<EOS*, where *EOS* refers to the sigil text PHP should look for as a signal to stop storing content in the variable. That end text cannot be indented. For example:

```
$truthier = <<<GO_BEARS
<div id="fan">
    <div id="diehard">
        <h4>Chicago Bears</h4>
        <p>$this_person is a diehard fan of #{$player['jersey']}.</p>
    </div>
</div>
GO_BEARS;
```

With a heredoc, you can freely insert quotes and variables without the need to escape them. The only special thing you have to consider is when referencing arrays: array values must be wrapped in curly braces ({}) to let PHP know to evaluate them and use their stored values instead.

Arrays are only a little more complicated. You let PHP know that a variable is meant to be an array by using the array() function. If you do not include data in the parentheses, the variable will simply be set or reset as an empty array. Associative arrays can be created using the convention of *key => value* pairs listed with commas as delimiters:

```
$cURL_options = array(
    CURLOPT_USERAGENT    => 'Twitter Up and Running - '.$app_title,
    CURLOPT_USERPWD      => "$twitter_username:$twitter_password",
    CURLOPT_RETURNTRANSFER => 1
    );
```

Each value is then referenced as *$array[$index]*, where *$index* can be an integer key or, for associative arrays, a string, as in:

```
$UserAgent = $cURL_options['CURLOPT_USERAGENT'];
```

You can add a new indexed value to an array by leaving the index blank. This technique is used within loops as an easy way to build the array iteratively:

```
foreach ($cURL_options as $key => $value) {
    $option_keys[] = $key;
    $option_values[] = $value;
}
```

Arrays can be nested. In this case, instead of storing a string for a given key, an entire array is stored. If $twitter_data were an array that contained the individual arrays containing each Twitter member's most recent status update, a single tweet could be extracted as:

```
$my_tweet = $twitter_data[0]['tweet'];
```

PHP objects will come into play whenever you parse data from the Twitter API. The XML files that are returned are turned into objects that can be manipulated by referencing shared methods within them, as in:

```
$feed_title = $doc->getElementsByTagName('title')->item(0)->nodeValue;
```

In this case, the value being returned is whatever text was wrapped within `<title></title>` tags in the XML structure. The text is extracted from the object and placed into the string `$feed_title` for later use.

Manipulating the Data You Collect

Once you've captured some information in one of the variable forms, you may need to do something to it to make it useful. Like any good programming language, PHP has a number of functions that perform commonly required manipulations:[†]

array_search(*array_to_search,array_of_search_terms*)
> Rather than building a loop to check every value in your array, you can use the array_search( ) function to look for matches with a search string or multiple values stored in an array. The function returns the key for the first match it finds.

base64_encode(*string_to_encode*), base64_decode(*string_to_decode*)
> This function encodes data as base64, returning a new string that is a bit (33%) larger than the original. It is used to make data safe for transfer to destinations where some of the characters may cause problems. The base64_decode( ) function will convert text that has previously been encoded with base64_encode( ) back into its original string.

basename(*path_to_file*)
> This function takes a string containing the path to a file and returns the base name of the file. For instance, if the path is */path/to/file.php*, basename( ) will return *file.php*.

bin2hex(*ascii_text*)
> This function takes an ASCII string and returns the hexadecimal equivalent.

ceil(*value_to_round_up*)
> The math function ceil( ) turns a value into the next highest integer, or the ceiling for the number.

[†] I have boiled down the full list of available PHP functions to just the ones used in the sample applications. For the full list, or for more details about any of the functions listed in this section, check out the official PHP documentation available online at *http://www.php.net/docs.php*.

date(*format_template,timestamp_to_format*)

>The date( ) function turns a numeric version of the time into a formatted string. The template for that resulting string is dictated by the letter codes used as place-holders for the various parts of the date and time. For example, "l, F jS, Y G:i:s a" would produce something like, "Thursday, December 25th, 2008 6:21:34 am."

dechex(*hexadecimal_value*)

>The dechex( ) function converts a hexadecimal string into a number. The input value can be no more than eight characters long. This is the opposite of hexdec( ), which performs the conversion the other way.

explode(*delimiter,string_to_break_into_na_array*)

>The explode( ) function converts a long delimited string into an array of strings. You specify the character(s) to use as a delimiter, and it splits the provided string into parts at every instance of that delimiter. The parts then become separate in-dexed values of a new array. The companion to this function is implode( ).

gmdate(*format_template,timestamp_to_format*)

>This function works in the same way as date( ), turning a numeric timestamp into a formatted string to represent the date and time. The difference is that the time is expressed in Greenwich Mean Time (GMT) rather than in the local server time zone.

hash(*method_of_encryption,string_to_encrypt*)

>Hashing involves use of a specific algorithm, such as sha256, to encrypt a string. This is a one-way process used to store sensitive information, such as passwords, for comparison with user-entered information as a way of verifying access. There is no mathematical way to reverse-engineer this, although lookup lists can be gen-erated to re-map back to the original string. It isn't easy, especially if you salt the password by adding a random string to the password being stored.

>Example: $secured = $salt.hash('sha256',$salt.$password);

htmlentities(*string_to_encode*)

>This function recognizes that some characters—namely, the ampersand (&), double quote ("), single quote ('), less-than symbol (<), and greater-than symbol (>)—have special meaning in HTML and may cause text containing them to be rendered inappropriately. The htmlentities( ) function is often used to prevent text submitted by the user from rendering as HTML by substituting translations for these characters. It is similar to htmlspecialchars( ) but substitutes more comprehensively.

>You can reverse the translation by using html_entity_decode( ).

implode(*delimiter,array_to_make_a_string*)

>This is an important function that bridges the gap between strings and arrays. You can use implode( ) to turn an array into a single string by specifying a delimiter character(s) that will connect each value in the array. This is the reverse of the process performed by the explode( ) function.

in_array(*term_to_find,array_in_which_to_search*)

Like the array_search( ) function, this function is a way to search through the values stored in an array for keyword matches. The in_array( ) function simply confirms with a Boolean whether or not a match is found.

is_int(*value_to_test*)

This function tests to see whether a given variable value is an integer, returning a Boolean as a result.

mt_rand( )

The mt_rand( ) function is one of many random number generators that aren't truly random, but that generate pseudorandom values that work well enough to make programs seem unpredictable. This one is a bit faster than the rand( ) function, which is why it is preferred.

number_format(*number_to_format,decimal_places*)

This versatile function accepts up to four parameters to return a string that adds formatting to a numeric value.

pack(*format_template,arguments_to_convert ...*)

The pack( ) function uses formatting codes inherited from Perl to turn a list of arguments into a binary string. The binary string can be turned back into an array of arguments with unpack( ).

preg_replace(*pattern_to_find,replacement_value,string_to_search*)

This is a search-and-replace function that uses pattern matching to locate the places to insert replacement text into a string.

Example: $x = preg_replace('/&(?!\w+;)/', '&', $x);

reset(*array*)

When arrays are navigated, the internal pointer is incremented to reference items with higher and higher indices. The reset( ) function returns that pointer to the first element in the array.

sizeof(*array*)

This function counts the number of items in an array. count( ) is an alias for sizeof( ).

stripslashes(*quoted_string*)

For most PHP configurations, quotation marks within the user-submitted text are automatically escaped to allow for operations such as saving to a database, where they could mess things up. There are times, though, when that is overkill. The stripslashes( ) function will remove those escaped characters.

str_pad(*string_to_pad,minimum_length,pad_text,instructions*)

Back in the day when all formatting was done with monospaced characters, lining up numbers and text in columns required some padding spaces or other characters. The str_pad( ) function makes that easy by asking for a minimum length for the resulting string and the text you want to use to make a shorter string that target size. By default, the padded characters will be added to the right of the initial string, but you can specify instructions to pad to the left side (for numbers, typically) or on both sides (to center the string).

The sample applications make use of str_pad( ) in password encryption to make sure that the salt strings are all the same size.

str_replace(*text_to_find,replacement_value,string_to_search*)
This function works like preg_replace( ) except it is more straightforward, ditching regular expression matching with a simple string to match. It returns an array with all of the occurrences where the value was replaced.

str_rot13(*string_to_shift*)
This encoding function simply shifts every letter it finds in a string by 13 places in the alphabet. Any numbers or other nonalphabetic characters are ignored. Decoding is accomplished simply by running the result back through the same str_rot13( ) function.

strlen(*string*)
Just as sizeof( ) returns the number of items in an array, strlen( ) returns the number of characters in a string.

strnatcmp(*first_string,second_string*)
Whereas strcmp( ) treats numbers as text, the strnatcmp( ) function is able to order strings based on "natural ordering," or the way a human would read and interpret a string. That is, instead of ordering a list "1,10,2,20...", this function would correctly interpret the order as "1,2,10,20...". It returns an integer value between –1 and 1 to indicate whether or not the first string should be ordered before the second. It is more often used with usort( ) to help order entire arrays of data.

strpos(*string_to_search,text_to_find*)
Like array_search( ) does for arrays, the strpos( ) function returns the position of the first match of the given text found within the specified string. Since it returns the Boolean false if the text is not found in the string, this function is also useful as a conditional to confirm whether a match exists.

strrev(*string_to_reverse*)
This function simply reverses the character order of a given string. The result can be decoded by running it through the same strrev( ) function again.

strtolower(*string_to_convert*)
When case is not important (as is typical of usernames), it is good practice to turn strings into lowercase for storage and comparison. The strtolower( ) function changes any capital letters into lowercase.

strtotime(*datetime_as_text*)
There are many different ways of conveying a date and time. Many of these are variations of the numbers and text we commonly use to report time in a readable format, such as "January 30 2000 11:13:00 GMT." For PHP to be able to do any calculation on that moment in history, the text has to be converted to its numeric

counterpart. This is performed with the function strtotime( ). If no string is provided, the current Unix timestamp will be returned.

substr(*string_to_shorten,starting_position,length_of_substring*)
To extract a part of a larger string, use the substr( ) function to specify the starting point within that string and optionally the length of the new string. If the starting position is negative, the extraction will be done from the end of the original string, rather than the beginning.

trim(*string_to_trim*)
Sometimes data is entered or recalled with leading or trailing whitespace. This can include ordinary spaces as well as tabs, returns, and newlines. The trim( ) function will examine both ends of a string and clip off any whitespace it finds there.

urlencode(*string_to_pass_as_URL*), **urldecode**(*string_passed_in_URL*)
The urlencode( ) function adjusts a string of text to turn any special characters to a URL (such as an ampersand) into characters safe for transfer in a URL query string. Some are converted to a different character (for example, a space is converted to a plus sign, +), whereas most become hexadecimal codes tagged with a % symbol, as in %7E.

This adjustment should be made before any text is passed to a form as a URL query string. The urldecode( ) function will return a string that restores all %## translations back to their original characters.

usort(*array_to_sort,name_of_sorting_function*)
Arrays can be sorted in very complex ways. The usort( ) function allows you to reference another function for comparing two values and use it to order the contents of a given array. The function is typically one of custom design and must provide the same kind of response as an existing comparison function, such as strnatcmp( ). That is, the comparison between two values should return an integer between –1 and 1 to indicate which of the two values should precede the other.

utf8_encode(*string_to_encode*)
The utf8_encode( ) function encodes a string to UTF-8, a Unicode standard that deals with wide character values.

This is not a complete list of all that PHP can do, of course, but it does represent all you need to know to follow along with the programming done in this book.

 For very thorough documentation on PHP's hundreds of functions, visit *http://www.php.net*.

Knowing Your Environment

There are other ways for users to communicate with your PHP program besides explicitly filling out a web form. Every time a visitor clicks on a link on your website, she makes a formal request to the server for content. That action automatically creates a slew of special predefined variables that are available to scripts to let them know something about the context of the request.

One of the more useful of these variables is `$_SERVER`, an associative array that contains a variety of information about the paths and script locations. The `$_SERVER` values are filled in by the web server, so if the script is not requested over the Web, this array will be empty (as is the case with automated tasks configured as *cron* jobs).

 The server does fill in these values, but many of them are based on user input (the HTTP request). As such, even some environmental variables can be used for an attack if not properly sanitized.

Even if the script is requested over the Web, not every variable will be filled with information. For example, `HTTP_REFERER` is supposed to contain the address of the page that the user was on when he clicked a link to your web page. However, if that person loaded your web page from a bookmark, or if the ISP host through which he accesses the Internet doesn't provide that address information, then the value for `$_SERVER['HTTP_REFERER']` will be empty.

Although more information about the server request is made available by PHP, these are the variables that are used in the sample applications for this book:

`__FILE__`
Whereas a `$_SERVER` variable will reflect the file that was requested via the Web, `__FILE__` always refers to the full path and filename of the script in which it is invoked. That means an included file will have a different `__FILE__` value than the main script that called it.

 `__FILE__` is referenced using *two* underscore characters on each side of "FILE."

`$_SERVER['DOCUMENT_ROOT']`
The document root is the directory path on the server from the top of the configured file structure to the directory root under which the current script is running.

`$_SERVER['HTTP_HOST']`
The host usually contains the domain information part of the URI request. `SERVER_NAME` likely holds the same value.

`$_SERVER['QUERY_STRING']`
If there is a query string—the part of a URI that comes after the filename, following a question mark (?)—that entire part of the request string will be stored in this

variable. This information is likely also pre-parsed into name and value pairs in the $_GET associative array.

$_SERVER['REQUEST_METHOD']

Several kinds of HTTP request methods are possible, but most web pages deal with just two: GET and POST. This server variable stores the name of the method used to access the script and can be useful in determining where to find any user-provided input parameters.

$_SERVER['REQUEST_URI']

This variable contains the URI that was used to trigger the web page script, once the request arrived on the server. This does not include the protocol and domain, only the server path after the web root (as in /index.php). The REQUEST_URI will also include the query string, if one exists.

$_SERVER['SCRIPT_NAME']

The SCRIPT_NAME is the current script's path. This is often the same value contained in REQUEST_URI, but without a query string, if one exists. Unlike __FILE__, this variable will reflect the path to the requested file, not the one invoking the variable.

Web forms and links are usually submitted to the server using either the GET or POST HTTP method. These methods encapsulate the data in different ways, and PHP then parses it to fill special associative arrays, $_GET and $_POST. When processing a web form or accepting query string parameters as part of a request, your program can reference these arrays to check for the presence of user input.

 If you accept the same form variables using either method, you will have to determine which method takes precedence. For instance, if posted data is preferred, that means your program only has to check $_GET['*variable_name*'] if $_POST['*variable_name*'] is missing.

Controlling the Flow of Logic

Programming is about more than storage and calculation. It is also about the flow of logic. PHP offers the usual assortment of flow controllers to help your application make decisions about what to do.

if...elseif...else

The if statement acts like a decision tree, checking to see whether a given expression is true before executing a particular part of the program. The expression can be very complicated or involve multiple comparisons, but in the end it is either a true statement or a false one. If the expression is false, the statements between the curly braces are ignored.

The if statement can be extended using elseif and else. The former performs another check on a different expression, proceeding with that section of code if the expression is true and moving on without processing if it's false. Multiple `elseif` statements can be strung together in sequence, but each will be evaluated only if all of the expressions that preceded it proved false. An `else` statement is the last one in the flow structure and serves as a catchall. It does not evaluate an expression; if all of the previous expressions fail, the statements within the `else` brackets are executed by default.

```
if ($a == 4) { $x = 1; }
elseif ($b == 0) { $x = 2; }
elseif ($c == $b) { $x = 3; }
else { $x = 0; }
```

while

A `while` loop will continue indefinitely, for as long as the expression is true. The moment its state becomes false, the `while` block will end and execution will continue with the next line of code. The expression is reexamined with each iteration.

```
while ($row = mysql_fetch_assoc($sql_result)) {
    $rss_feed_stored =  $row['rss_url'];
}
```

 Be careful about the expressions you use in a `while` loop. If you evaluate a condition that never changes, the loop will never exit.

for

A `for` loop will execute the statements in its block repeatedly until the result of its expression reaches a maximum value. The initial state, the expression, and the increment for each iteration are all defined in the initial loop.

The first part of the `for` expression is evaluated once, at the very beginning of the first loop, to set the initial conditions. The second and third parts of the expression are then evaluated at the start and end of each iteration, until the second expression proves false. The three parts are separated by semicolons (;).

```
for ($i=1; $i <= $max_value; $i += 1) {
    echo $i . ' of ' . $max_value;
}
```

foreach

The `foreach` loop is an easy way to iterate over the contents of an array (or, as of PHP 5, objects). At the start of each iteration, the next value in the array is assigned to a variable that can then be referenced in the statements contained in the `foreach` block. For associative arrays, a special form allows the key and value pair to be assigned as separate variables, so both are readily available during execution.

```
    foreach ($array_of_arrays as $this_array) {
        foreach ($this_array as $key => $value) {
            echo $key . ' is filled with ' . $value;
        }
    }
```

switch...case...break

Because some variables may have many different values that trigger distinct responses—this is true for codes for status messages returned to the user as a response to
submitting a form—the `if...elseif` construct can grow unwieldy. The `switch` statement simplifies the code needed in that situation by allowing you to use one variable
expression with many possible values. Each value, or `case`, contains its own set of
statements to process. There is also a `default` that is executed if the variable value does
not find a match.

Unlike in other loops, the `switch` block executes each case line by line, regardless of the
value; it does not stop and ignore all remaining cases automatically when it finds a value
match. After a false value comparison, it simply skips to the next case, ignoring the
statement in between. When it finds a match, PHP starts executing the next line of
code. This will continue until the end of the `switch` block unless PHP encounters a
`break` statement to tell it to stop. If you forget to include a `break` at the end of the
statements for a given case, everything in the entire `switch` block will get evaluated,
including the `default`.

```
    switch ($root) {
        case 'user';
            $thisFeed = $xml->id;
            break;
        case 'status';
            $thisFeed = $xml->user->id;
            break;
        default;
            break;
    }
```

> A `break` can be used elsewhere in your code to stop the execution of a
> loop. It allows PHP to escape the current `for`, `foreach`, and `while` struc-
> tures, too. If they are nested, it will escape only the current block.

try...catch

PHP 5 introduced exception handlers that "catch" errors that the server "throws" when
it tries to run the part of the code contained in the `try` block. Every `try` must have at
least one `catch` block; it can also have more than one to handle each exception differently. If no error is detected, or if there is no `catch` block configured to catch the error,
the rest of the code is executed as normal.

If an exception is caught, any statements in the `catch` block will be executed. This code may or may not be programmed to terminate the program. The purpose of exception handling is to either exit gracefully or allow the program to continue despite the error.

```
try {
    # some statements that cause PHP to choke
} catch (Exception $e) { $form_error = 15; }
```

die( ) or exit( )

There are some cases where errors encountered by PHP should simply stop execution of the script. Both `die( )` and `exit( )` act in the same capacity, killing the running script where it stands and outputting the error message provided as a parameter:

```
$filehandle = fopen($file,$type) or die("can't open file $file");
```

The `exit( )` function can also be useful when debugging, allowing you to temporarily insert the statement before some problem code can be executed to allow you to check the state of the program at that moment.

 It is better to avoid using either `die( )` or `exit( )` in your final scripts. Instead, implement more user-friendly error handling.

File Management

Files that store and later retrieve data are staples of web applications. They are easier to use than databases, since they don't require authentication (although they may require file permissions to be granted to the directory in which they reside). Files can also be used to create static versions of a website through automated tasks to cut down on overhead when databases are required.

In our sample applications, file management functions are used to create log files that report on activity by automated tasks. Here are the methods you'll use:

fopen(*file_name,mode_for_opening*)
> To read from or write to a file, PHP must be able to reference it in some way in the code. The `fopen( )` function creates a file handle that binds to a stream connecting PHP to the contents of the specified file. For this to be successful, PHP must have access to that file, meaning that it not only must be reachable but also must be configured with the appropriate permissions.

 Windows servers reference the path to the file differently than Linux servers do: any backslashes (\) must be escaped, as in *c:\\my_documents\\my_file.txt*. Alternatively, you can use forward slashes and avoid the problem.

There are a few different ways PHP can open the file. fopen( ) asks you to declare the mode (a code that dictates whether you can read from and/or write to the file), where the pointer should be located when it opens the file, and what to do if the file already exists. For logging—where you only need to add a line of text to whatever is already in the file, and worry about reading the contents at a later time—the mode "a", for append, is sufficient.

fwrite(*file_handle,text_to_write*)

Once a file is open in a mode that permits writing, the fwrite( ) function can be used to enter a string of text into that file. The file is referenced through a file handle, not by the path and name of the file itself. Prior use of fopen( ) is required to create that association.

Be aware that different operating systems have different conventions to determine line endings. Unless you are OK with your text running together in one long, wrapped line, using the correct convention is important. For Linux, the newline (\n) is sufficient. Macintosh looks for a carriage return (\r), and Windows machines require both (\r\n).

fclose(*file_handle*)

Assuming the file handle pointing to an existing file is valid, fclose( ) terminates the association between PHP and the file stream.

unlink(*file_name*)

This function deletes the file specified in the parameter, provided it exists and permissions on the server allow it.

file_get_contents(*uri_to_retrieve*)

If you want to create a virtual browser and retrieve content available on the Web, the file_get_contents( ) function can help. Enter an encoded URI, and a string will be returned containing the contents of that file, as rendered by the web server. If the retrieval fails, the function will return a Boolean false.

This function can also point to a local file, acting as three functions in one by opening, reading, and closing the file connection. file_get_contents( ) is used in the sample applications in this book to create a TinyURL that can be included in a direct message to a Twitter member.

file_get_contents( ) won't work if the configuration setting allow_url_fopen is disabled.

Connecting to the Database

Teaming the dynamic programming of PHP with the power of SQL query statements can make for some potent applications. To make this hookup, however, you need to make use of a special group of functions to access and interact with a MySQL database.

With PHP 5, an improved version of this group of old MySQL functions was added. The mysqli extension (the "i" is for "improved") has a procedural interface and an object-oriented interface. Using this extension has several speed and security benefits, and it is recommended that you upgrade your code to take advantage of it.

For more information on converting from mysql to mysqli, see *http:// forge.mysql.com/wiki/Converting_to_MySQLi*, as well as the main documentation at *http://us3.php.net/mysqli*. There are some configuration changes that may be needed for PHP to be able to use the new functions.

mysql_connect(*database_host,username,password*)

This function initiates the connection between PHP and the MySQL database server by specifying the server location with access information. The function mysql_connect( ) returns a link to the database upon success.

mysql_select_db(*database_name*)

A database server can host multiple databases. For your queries to retrieve the data you want, you have to specify one of the available databases on the server. The database name passed to this function will become the current active database associated with the open database link. All communication will be with that database.

The link to the database connection can be specified, but if it isn't, this function will use the link last opened by mysql_connect( ). If no connection has been made previously, it will try to make a new connection without any parameters.

mysql_query(*sql_query_statement*)

The mysql_query( ) function passes a single SQL statement to the current active database through a valid link to the database server. For queries that are meant to fetch data, the function returns a result set. For other queries that are intended to perform some action (like an INSERT or DELETE statement), a Boolean is returned to indicate success or failure.

When you are using the command line or files to run SQL statements, a semicolon is required to let MySQL know when to stop reading the query. This function deals with that internally, and therefore SQL statements passed as parameters should not include semicolons.

`mysql_affected_rows( )`

> For queries where no records are expected, such as `DELETE` statements, this function returns the number of rows that were affected. If the query fails, a negative value is returned.

`mysql_num_rows( )`

> For queries where records are expected, this function returns the number of records in the result set.

`mysql_fetch_array(sql_result_set)`

> Generally, you'll connect to a database to get data from it. The result set stored in the numerical array returned by `mysql_query( )` can be parsed using `mysql_fetch_array( )`, looping each row of data in a `foreach` block. This function automatically moves the array pointer to the next index when called, returning a Boolean false when there is no more data.

`mysql_real_escape_string(string_to_escape)`

> As with URIs, there are characters that have special meaning for MySQL and thus should not be included in the queries you submit. Failing to screen for these characters may lead to trouble, ranging from merely causing the query to return an error all the way to allowing malicious activities with the database. The `mysql_real_escape_string( )` function examines MySQL's own library of special characters and replaces them with safer versions. Because of the potential for disaster and the ease of its use, there is no reason not to escape all text strings before sending them to the database.

`mysql_free_result(result_from_last_query)`

> This function clears the results of the last query, which has two advantages. First, it lets the server know that the memory used to store the previous data is now available for other things. Second, it eliminates the chance that you may accidentally reuse the same result set.

> Technically, the `mysql_free_result( )` function only needs to be called when memory consumption is an issue, typically for very large result sets. For smaller data, using this function can result in higher memory use than not. However, the by-product of its use is a clean break from data that is no longer needed to complete the script.

`mysql_close(database_connection_handle)`

> Assuming the handle representing the database link is valid, this function disconnects PHP from the database server. The link to the database will automatically end when the script finishes running, but it is good practice to close it explicitly.

Building a Custom Function

In any given program, you may decide to write to files or interact with a database. You may do a particular kind of sort on an array, for example. If you only have one program, where you put the code to do these things won't make that much difference. However, if you have several pages that all do the same kinds of things, being able to reuse your code becomes exponentially more important.

Imagine writing a program to build a simple web page with a fancy header menu. Your strategy is to build the page, then duplicate the code for 11 other similar pages, making minor adjustments to the visible content. That may be the quickest and most efficient way to build the pages, but what happens when you want to make changes to the fancy header menu? Instead of updating it in one place, you need to make the changes 12 different times!

Making use of includes and custom functions is one way to make your code easier to maintain and simultaneously cut down on the number of lines of code on any given application page. The sample applications in this book use included files with custom functions to do just that.

Including more code in your application

Bringing additional code into the scope of your PHP script is easy with the `include( )` statement. This function looks in the specified path for the desired file and evaluates its content as if it had been typed into the original script:

```
include $root_path 'environment.php';
```

 The period (.) between the $root_path variable and the rest of the text is a concatenation operator. It connects two or more strings together to form one long string.

Debugging with includes used to be a bit problematic, since problems parsing the included code didn't stop the calling script from running. Now, though, PHP makes sure all of the code it sees is syntactically correct before executing anything.

To do its thing, the `include( )` statement either needs to know the exact path where the file is located or needs to be able to find the file among the locations added to the `include_path` list. If it can't find it, the script will issue a warning but will continue to run until the absence of that code proves fatal. If you don't want that behavior, there is another command—`require( )`—that works just like `include( )` but kills the application the moment it can't find an included file.

Included files don't have to live in the web path, which is another reason to use them. If you have access to your server account's document root, you can move all of your included files into a path that other people can't see from the Web. This eliminates the chance that someone will call that script by accident or intentionally try to make use of it. It also allows you to store hardcoded access information—such as the username and password you are going to use to get into your database—without exposing that sensitive information directly to the Internet.

Once you have a separate file attached to your PHP script, you have to figure out what to put in it. It is certainly possible to simply add a bunch of code that does something like setting commonly used variables or opening a log file. The script will treat that included code as if it had been written into the calling file, so the application will work. However, where you include the file will be meaningful. If you need to manipulate some variable data and you place that code in an included file, you have to make sure those variables are filled with what you need before you include the file.

For this reason (and others), it is good practice to contain your external code in functions that can be called when needed in the original script rather than run at a specific point when the file is included. If you do this, you can group the `include()` statements at the top of the script where it is easy to see what you need, and you can define multiple functions in an external file that can be used anywhere after that point in the calling script.

Defining your own function

I make sense of functions use a shopping metaphor. My includes directory, where I put the external application files, is the big mall. Each file is a wing or level of that mall, and any functions defined in it are the stores located in that wing. Stores tend to have their own structures and purposes once you cross their thresholds, and you can go back to them whenever you need the particular goods they carry.

To construct your function-store, you need to first create that threshold. You can accomplish this by creating a new block (between curly braces) that declares the function, provides a name for it, and defines any parameters it will accept. Example 3-5 shows a simple function is called `name_of_function` that takes up to two parameters. The first parameter is required—PHP will choke if at least one parameter isn't included—but the second, because I'm assigning it an empty string as the default value, is optional.

Example 3-5. A custom function returning an array

```
function name_of_function ($parameter1,$parameter2='') {
    $foo = $parameter1 + 1;
    $bar = $foo . ' was required ' . $parameter2;
    return array($foo,$bar);
}
```

Within the block of code—the inside of the function-store—are the interesting goods. For the function created in Example 3-5, we want to increment the first parameter and format a little message based on the new value and the optional text that we can pass to the function. The last statement is where we use the `return()` construct to deliver the goods—in this case, an array with the two manipulated values. In essence, this is the part where the stuff you buy gets put in a bag for you to carry home.

 PHP differentiates between constructs and functions, even though both look the same in the documentation (with parentheses added after their names). include( ) is a construct that does not require the parentheses to run. function_exists( ) is a function with a parameter and a need for parentheses to evaluate what is passed to it.

Constructs do not appear in the list of known functions when using function_exists( ) to find out if code you want to use is there.

Custom functions are invoked in the same way that built-in PHP functions are called. How you code them depends on what kind of information is being returned. If it will return a Boolean (true or false, 1 or 0) or nothing at all, the function does not usually need to be assigned to a variable. This is common for functions that are used as expressions in loops. However, if the function will return a value, you'll want to capture it in a variable when you invoke it. When multiple values are returned—as is the case in Example 3-5—the function needs to send them back contained in an array, which is then received in the original script using the list( ) function. Here are some examples from the sample applications:

```
getHeader($app_title,'css/uar.css');

$scrambled_password = scramblePassword($twitter_password);

list($thisFeed,$foo) = parseFeed($rss_feed);
```

Remember that the variables are versatile: they can be numbers, strings, list arrays, associative arrays, or even objects. Because PHP is a "loosely typed" language, you may need to use the is_*type* functions (is_int( ), is_string( ), etc.) to find out what kind of data you have. The array-to-list transfer is only needed if you need to send back different kinds of variables (a string and an array, for instance) or if you want to be able to parse the resulting data on the function side. In that case, the function can simply fill an array with the manipulated values and return that instead.

Because your code will be assembled on the fly and is intended to be reused in many ways by different applications, there is a built-in function that may add some grace to it. The function_exists( ) function checks a list of all defined functions, both those built into PHP and those defined by the programmer, and returns true if a function with the specified name is detected:

```
if (function_exists('apiRequest')) { $data = apiRequest($url); }
```

This is useful as a way to make sure the proper code is available and, if not, to allow the program to handle the problem gracefully, either by reporting it to an administrator or by simply exiting with a web page response the user can read. The alternative is an error that could kill the program and reveal some of your code in an ugly message.

SimpleXML

When it comes to sharing data, XML is the prevalent way to format information into a structure that is easily parsed. Your PHP application will need to parse XML at some point if you get data from APIs, including the API Twitter provides. Before PHP 5, you had to build your own parser, looking in the string for patterns to divide up the formatted data in a meaningful way. Now, however, PHP comes with an extension called SimpleXML that does the heavy lifting for you.

The SimpleXML extension turns XML structures into embedded objects containing the data as associative arrays. Each embedded tag in the XML becomes another link in the PHP object, as in `$xml->childnode->node['attribute']`. The sample applications use SimpleXML to parse the data received from the Twitter API and to create new XML documents with the data the applications collect. Here are the methods you'll see:

`SimpleXMLElement(well_formed_xml)`
> When you want to start building XML from scratch, `SimpleXMLElement` can help. It turns a well-formed XML string or a path to a file containing XML data into an object that can be iterated, edited, and expanded with a variety of methods. The object is a collection of tag names associated with the content the tags contain and the attributes they are assigned. Nested tags show up as objects that themselves can be parsed into tag names, attributes, and values.
>
> Example: `$xml = new SimpleXMLElement($base_xml);`

`simplexml_load_string(well_formed_xml_string)`
> For simply parsing XML data that already exists, this function takes the data in the form of a string and returns a navigable object.
>
> Example: `$xml = simplexml_load_string($data);`

`getName( )`
> The `getName( )` method returns the name of the root tag for a particular XML object. When the XML object is first created, this will be the main root of the document, but this method can be used for nested objects as well.
>
> Example: `$root = $xml->getName( );`

`children( )`
> The `children( )` method creates an iterative array of objects representing the nodes directly below the XML object calling it. Each child object can then be explored for a name, value, attributes, or any other XML objects it contains.
>
> Example: `foreach($xml->children( ) as $x) {$ids[] = $x->id;}`

`addChild(name_of_new_node,value_stored_in_new_node)`
> This method is what allows you to create your own XML documents. It accepts a text value to describe the name of the new nested tag and any value you want it to contain. It returns the new XML object, which can then be edited and expanded as if it had been part of the original XML.

Example: `$xml->channel->addChild('newchild','my text');`

asXML( )

> All of the manipulation of `addChild( )` only changes the XML object that PHP has stored in memory. To make the changes real, you need to turn the object back into a string of well-formed XML text. This can be printed or stored in a string for later use in the application. `asXML( )` will also accept a filename parameter and write the file directly to a document.
>
> Example: `echo $xml->asXML( );`

DOM

SimpleXML is great, but there are other ways to extract data from an XML document. The Document Object Model, or DOM, is a standard object model to describe markup and make it able to be manipulated by other applications. It is a required part of Java-Script, to give the scripting language the ability to access and change web pages on the fly. Some web browsers also use DOM to render web pages from HTML. DOM is particularly useful for accessing the markup out of order, navigating back and forth in the nested nodes, or jumping directly to different parts of the document.

The W3C DOM has three parts. The Core describes any structured document. There are also specific object descriptions for both XML and HTML. As of PHP 5, the DOM extension has been added to the PHP arsenal. The sample applications use DOM to parse RSS feeds. The following are the methods you'll encounter.

DOMDocument( )

> As with the `SimpleXMLElement` object, a new `DOMDocument` object can be created using this method to hold the XML data you want to explore. This gives PHP a framework for loading and parsing the structured data.
>
> Example: `$doc = new DOMDocument( );`

load(*url_to_well_formed_XML*)

> To fill the new DOM object with XML data, you have to let PHP know where to look for that data. For RSS feeds, the simplest technique is just to point to the URI for the data you are trying to parse. This path can also point to local files, returning a Boolean `true` or `false` to indicate success. The object must already exist before it can be filled.
>
> Example: `$doc->load($url);`

getElementsByTagName(*name_of_node*)

> The DOM can retrieve a specific node from the full document, returning it as an object containing all of the matching objects. The `getElementsByTagName( )` function creates a new instance of the node class, giving it access to more tools to explore the node in detail.
>
> Example: `$items = $doc->getElementsByTagName('item');`

nodeValue( )

> At the node level, the value a particular node contains within its start and end tags can be retrieved with nodeValue( ). The value can be a date, text, number, or other data type, depending on the kind of node being explored.
>
> Example: $title = $item->item(0)->nodeValue;

getAttribute( )

> Another tool at the node level is getAttribute( ), which returns the value associated with a tag attribute, such as the link stored in the href of an anchor tag. If an attribute is not found, an empty string is returned. For singleton tags, the attributes are where the node data is located.
>
> Example: $link = $node->item(0)->getAttribute('href');

cURL

PHP includes a library for retrieving URLs called *cURL*. This free software can handle a wide range of data transfers and HTTP methods. PHP includes a few tools to allow your code to access this important functionality.

> The PHP developer community typically shares code to make coding easier for everyone. One way this is done is by providing classes that can be used to extend your own installation of PHP and make the code a bit easier. You can find some cURL classes to replace the functions discussed here at *http://www.phpclasses.org/searchtag/curl/by/package/tag/curl/*.

Although cURL can do much more, the sample applications use the following cURL functions whenever they need to interact with the Twitter API:

curl_init( )

> To use cURL to access a remote file, you must first create a handle that can be used to reference the connection later in the program. curl_init( ) can be initialized as an empty shell and filled later, either by setting the CURLOPT_URL option or by passing a URL as a parameter. The new handle is returned upon success.
>
> Example: $cURL = curl_init( );

curl_setopt(*cURL_handle,name_of_option,option_value*)

> The curl_setopt( ) function allows you to configure an initialized cURL handle by setting some of its many options. The options are named with the CURLOPT_ prefix and include the following, which are used in the sample applications for this book:
>
> **CURLOPT_HTTPGET**
>
> > If set to true, this option causes the cURL handle to use the GET method for the next HTTP request. The Twitter API methods where data is queried and received all use GET. This is the default for a new cURL handle.

CURLOPT_POST

If set to true, this option causes the cURL handle to use the POST method for the next HTTP request. All of the Twitter API methods involving data changes use POST.

CURLOPT_POSTFIELDS

When the server application on the other end of the request requires an HTTP POST request, the fields containing your data must be passed as an encoded string using this option.

 If you are experiencing problems using CURLOPT_POSTFIELDS, it may be because of the default headers being passed by cURL. The Expect header may have a value like "100-continue header," which tells the server to post your data only if it responds with a status code of 100, or Continue. To get around this, you can simply clear the value in the Expect header to have cURL post without waiting:

```
curl_setopt($cURL, CURLOPT_HTTPHEADER,
    array('Expect:'));
```

CURLOPT_RETURNTRANSFER

When executing the configured HTTP request, this option should be set to true to prevent cURL from outputting the content it gets. You want to fill strings to parse.

CURLOPT_USERPWD

Twitter's API requires authentication for many of its interactions with member data. The username and password for the accessing account can be appended to the cURL request using this option and a value in the format [*username*]: [*password*].

CURLOPT_URL

This is perhaps the most important option—it tells cURL where to go to get the goods (i.e., which URL to fetch). It can be set when the handle is initialized as well.

CURLOPT_USERAGENT

When using someone's API, it is courteous to let the developers know who you are. Setting the User-Agent header in the HTTP request to something meaningful using this option will accomplish this.

The curl_setopt( ) function returns a Boolean to indicate success.

Example: curl_setopt($cURL, CURLOPT_URL, $curl_url);

curl_setopt_array(*cURL_handle,array_of_options*)

When you have to set a number of options at once, it may be easier to first create an associative array filled with the option names and values to send to cURL all at once. curl_setopt_array( ) sets multiple options for a cURL session. Specify the active cURL handle and the array of options, and the function will return a Boolean to indicate success. If any single option fails, the remainder of the array will be ignored and the function will return `false`.

Example: `curl_setopt_array($cURL, $cURL_options)`

`curl_exec(cURL_handle)`

The meat of this suite of functions is `curl_exec( )`, which actually executes the session as it is currently configured. If the `CURLOPT_RETURNTRANSFER` option has not been set to `true`, this function will output whatever it finds at the other end of its request and return a Boolean to indicate success. Otherwise, `curl_exec( )` returns the contents to save in a string.

Example: `$twitter_data = curl_exec($cURL);`

`curl_getinfo(cURL_handle,information_name)`

Each request has a meta-information channel that describes the session that was just executed. `curl_getinfo( )` gets that information and either returns it as an associative array containing all the available data or, if you include a specific variable name, returns just that variable's value. The meta-information includes `url`, `content_type`, `http_code`, `filetime`, `total_time`, `size_download`, `speed_download`, and `download_content_length`.

Example: `$status = curl_getinfo($cURL, CURLINFO_HTTP_CODE);`

`curl_close(cURL_handle)`

When you're finished, use `curl_close( )` to end the session and free up all of the application resources that were devoted to the HTTP request.

Example: `curl_close($cURL);`

 If your server does not support cURL, there are other ways to get remote content. The `file_get_contents( )` function explained in the section "File Management" on page 109 of this chapter is an option, provided PHP has been configured to turn on `allow_url_fopen`. A more complex option is `fsockopen( )`, which should work everywhere.

Debugging

Let's face it: programming involves a lot of trial and error. The first draft of an application rarely works perfectly, and the more code it contains, the more potential there is for problems that will need to be investigated and fixed. The process of debugging an application is greatly helped by good documentation and the ability to see what is happening at the points where problems are occurring.

Programming languages, including PHP, include ways for you to annotate your code without it affecting the processing that is done. Comments do come with a little extra overhead since there is more text to deal with, but the benefits greatly outweigh the trivial cost of including them. PHP comments work in a similar way to those in PHP or Perl—text that follows a special marker is interpreted as nonexecutable content and ignored when the program runs.

Comments are meant to serve as reminders for the programmer and to communicate to other programmers what is happening at various points in the code. Unlike with HTML, where anyone can look at the source behind the rendered page, the only people who will see PHP comments are programmers with an interest in and access to the script files.

There are two kinds of PHP comments. The first type is the single-line comment. By prefacing text with a double-slash character combination (//), you signal that the text between the comment character and the end of the line should be ignored during execution. For example:

```
// This is good for line-by-line annotation
```

The hash character (#) will work, too.

 I've always preferred hashes, because there is less to type and because they stand out visually in a way the slashes do not. However, most modern text editors with PHP libraries will be able to understand what comments are and display them in a different color (typically light gray) to separate them from the rest of the code.

PHP also supports a way to comment out multiple lines of text: it looks for the character combination /* to indicate the start of a comment block and the combination */ to signal the end of the block. Anything PHP encounters between these two markers, including line breaks, is considered a comment and is ignored during execution. For example:

```
/*
 *   Use Comments
 *
 *      Liberal use of comments can only help a programmer make
 *      sense of code, particularly as time passes and the
 *      reasons for using a particular function fade from memory.
 *      Except for the first and last lines to open and close the
 *      comment, the asterisks on the left are optional and are
 *      included merely for aesthetic purposes.
 */
```

Comments help a programmer remember or understand what a section of code does and maybe why certain programming decisions were made, but they don't do anything to help fix problems in the code when they arise. To do that, you need a way to peer into the inner workings of the application, from the server's perspective. Outputting variable values at different points in the program is a simple technique for debugging in PHP, to see what is changing and where.

The echo( ) construct is one way to output data: when it's executed, the variables that come after it are evaluated and displayed in the terminal or browser for all to see. For example:

```
$debug = 1;
if ($debug) { echo $div_info; }
```

You probably don't want a bunch of debugging text to show up in a production site, but for early coding and in development servers, being able to see values change is worthwhile. I sometimes build a debugging switch into the code that allows me to change one value high in the code that will tell all of my debugging output to display.

There is another command—print( )—that does the same thing. "What's the difference between echo( ) and print( )?" is a common question about PHP. The quick answer is, "Not much. Use what you want." However, there are some subtle differences that can affect your coding decisions. First, echo( ) is a little faster, since it doesn't return any value (print( ) will return a Boolean to indicate success, which might be important for logic flow). The other important difference is that echo( ) can accept multiple parameters, so you can concatenate strings together with commas. For print( ), only one string is allowed as a parameter.

For arrays, output becomes a little more complicated; all of the keys and values run together, making it very difficult to read. Fortunately, PHP has a special function for investigating array contents, called print_r( ), that will display the contents of an array in a way formatted to be readable by humans. Similarly, the var_dump( ) function will iterate through arrays and objects, displaying all of the information they contain and indenting to show how the content structure is nested:

```
print_r ($array);
var_dump ($array);
```

Finally, there is the exit( ) command, discussed earlier in the section "Controlling the Flow of Logic" on page 106. If your application does a lot of things, such as writing to a database or changing saved states that you might later need to revert, a well-placed exit( ) will save you some headaches by killing the application at the desired point. Just remember to remove it after you figure out a solution to the coding problem!

MySQL

There are a number of reasons it may become necessary to store data outside of your application in order to support what it does. We do this when we want to pre-populate web forms with saved information, and when we want to show only a part of a larger data set. The raw information is stored in a database. A database can take many forms, including a simple text file where you write the information you want to retrieve later. The dominant form of database, however, is the relational database management system (RDBMS).

MySQL is one widely distributed relational database system that is commonly installed on web hosting servers for your use. You may be limited to creating a certain number of databases. If so, don't worry; in this book we'll only use one.

 The Structured Query Language (SQL) has been around in some form for almost four decades. One of the criticisms of the language is that different servers have slightly different syntax variations, so SQL statements that run well in Microsoft SQL won't necessarily work in MySQL. This book deals specifically with MySQL syntax.

MySQL databases can be very powerful. The interaction with a typical web application, though, boils down to a handful of statements for the following tasks: creating tables, selecting data, inserting new data, updating existing data, and deleting data you no longer want.

Creating a New Table

When you first create a database, there is no *there* there. It is just an empty shell; you could use PHP to connect to it, but that's it. To make it a useful place to store and filter data, you must first create a structure to contain the data.

The CREATE TABLE statement accomplishes this by describing the fields each row, or *tuple*, of data can store. Each field is assigned a name and a data type, plus other information about its size, default value, and whether it can accept NULL values. MySQL also would like to know how you might want to access the data in the future. You can aid data retrieval by specifying which fields are going to be indexed for search. The *primary key*—the field that contains the unique identifiers to distinguish one record from the next—will always be indexed, but you can also specify that indexes be maintained for other fields. Example 3-6 shows a table called **access** with five fields.

Example 3-6. Sample CREATE TABLE statement

```
CREATE TABLE IF NOT EXISTS 'access' (
    'record_id' int(4) NOT NULL,
    'password' varchar(255) NOT NULL,
    'created_at' datetime NOT NULL,
    'date_processed' timestamp NOT NULL default CURRENT_TIMESTAMP,
    'is_enabled' tinyint(4) NOT NULL default '1',
    PRIMARY KEY  ('record_id'),
    KEY 'is_enabled' ('is_enabled')
) ENGINE=MyISAM DEFAULT CHARSET=latin1 AUTO_INCREMENT=74462 ;
```

Most database clients—including the web-based phpMyAdmin tool many web hosting companies use to allow user access to MySQL (see Figure 3-1)—provide some basic GUI or form that you can use instead of actually writing the SQL statement to create a table. The important definitions are still the same, regardless of the method of creation: you need to tell the database what kind of data you want to store and how you are likely to try to retrieve that information later.

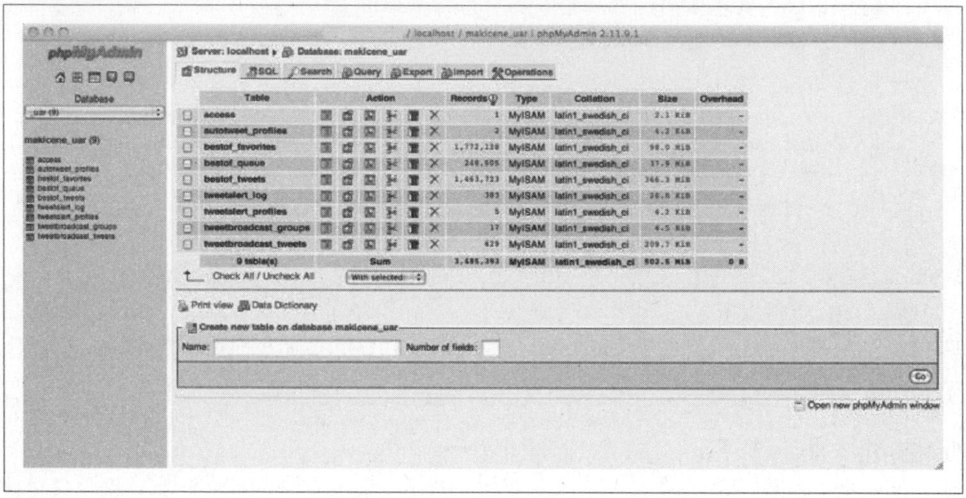

Figure 3-1. phpMyAdmin is a web-based client for MySQL databases

Retrieving Information from the Database

Most of your application's interaction with the database is likely to be in the form of SELECT statements. These SQL commands ask the database to look in the contents of its tables and return specific data that matches your criteria.

SELECT statements have a few main parts:

- SELECT names the fields you want to get.
- FROM indicates where to get the data.
- WHERE specifies some conditions to filter all the data into a useful set.
- ORDER BY allows you to sort the results on one of the returned fields.

Additionally, you can take advantage of the relational nature of MySQL by joining multiple tables together to create a new collection of data that isn't explicitly stored in the database. LEFT OUTER JOIN will connect two tables with a common field, without requiring that the second table have a matching record. If it doesn't, the fields that would have been filled by that table are returned with NULL values. An INNER JOIN requires that both tables have a common record. Example 3-7 shows a SELECT query involving two tables used by one of the sample applications, tweetbroadcast_tweets and tweetbroadcast_groups.

Example 3-7. Sample SELECT statement

```
SELECT  DISTINCT t.status_id,
        t.author_username, t.author_fullname, t.author_avatar,
```

```
          t.tweet_text, t.tweet_html, t.pub_date,
          concat(year(t.pub_date),' ',LPAD(dayofyear(t.pub_date),3,'0')) as tweet_day
FROM      tweetbroadcast_tweets t
          INNER JOIN tweetbroadcast_groups m ON m.other = t.author_username
WHERE     m.owner = 'kmakice'
ORDER BY t.pub_date desc
LIMIT 0,20
```

The `LIMIT` clause will restrict how much of the full data set is returned. It is associated with two numbers, separated by a comma: the first number reflects the record that should become the first record in the returned data (0 indicates MySQL should start at the top), and the second number is the maximum number of records that should be included with the initial record. The query in Example 3-7 will return the first 20 tweets authored by people in my broadcast group.

The last clause of interest to us is `GROUP BY`. This is an aggregation instruction that tells MySQL to return only one record for each unique group, summing, counting, or calculating the other fields over the values in all of the group's records. For example, if I had a table that stored all of my family's Twitter status updates (my wife, my son, and yes, my dog all use Twitter), I could generate some stats for each author by grouping on the `username` field and counting records. Such a query would tell us that my dog tweets more than my son. It's very sad on several levels.

Alternatively, if your goal is simply to eliminate redundancy in the data, you can use `distinct` in the `SELECT` clause to limit the data set to just one instance of any given combination of the selected fields. If I collected my son's tweet archive several times and had duplicates of the same records, without using `distinct` his aggregated statistics would be much higher than the actual count. `distinct` is handy in statements using `GROUP BY` as a way to count the number of different values in the data set, as in:

```
SELECT COUNT(distinct username)
```

The fields used in the `SELECT` list and the `WHERE` conditions for the search can be manipulated using functions in MySQL. They work in a similar fashion to functions in other languages, like PHP, in that you pass a value as a parameter and get some kind of response. For example, `DateDiff( )` will examine two dates and return the number of days that separate them. These kinds of functions become very useful when trying to compare similar data expressed in incompatible formats and for shaping the way the information is returned in the query.

Changing Information in the Database

Of course, the only way to get something out of the database is to put something in. The data doesn't appear by itself; it must be added and kept up-to-date with the help of some special editing statements that insert, change, and delete values in table fields.

Although it is possible to transfer information from one part of a database to another by combining `INSERT` and `SELECT` statements, for our purposes it is sufficient to add data one row at a time. To add data to a table, the `INSERT INTO` statement lets you specify a table and the field(s) you want to fill. You then specify the data using the `VALUES` clause, listing the new information in the same order you listed the field names. See Example 3-8.

Example 3-8. Sample SQL statements to change a database

```
/* This inserts a new row of data into 'autotweet_profiles' */
INSERT INTO autotweet_profiles
    (user_name, password, rss_url)
VALUES
    ('kmakice', 'DKFSHOIER*S(R(WE%', 'http://www.blogschmog.net/feed/')

/* This changes the values in three fields of a record in the table */
UPDATE    autotweet_profiles
SET       password = 'DKRKSIKDLER*KDOUFLIEO*',
          rss_url = 'http://www.makice.net/blogschmog/feed/',
          is_enabled = 1
WHERE     user_name = 'kmakice'

/* This removes all records for 'kmakice' from the table */
DELETE FROM autotweet_profiles
WHERE     user_name = 'kmakice'
```

`UPDATE` is a statement that works on existing records in a table, allowing you to change the stored values of specific fields. As with `SELECT`, you must first identify which table is to be targeted and which records are being changed, using the `WHERE` clause. Updates also use a `SET` clause to list the fields of interest with their new values. `UPDATE` statements can affect more than one row, based on the criteria defined in the `WHERE` clause. All of the matching records will be set with the same values specified in the `SET` clause.

Finally, there is the `DELETE FROM` statement, which removes records from data tables. To delete data, you specify the affected table and the criteria that need to be matched. Any records matching the `WHERE` clause will be removed.

A Place to Call /home

The first thing you'll need for your new web application is a home. All of your brainy ideas and masterful code won't be any more useful to other people than an email from your grandmother if your code can't be compiled and do something interesting. This section briefly looks at some of the things to consider when searching for a server from which to publish your new application.

Selecting a Host Server

There are a number of factors you will need to consider when selecting a web host to publish and protect your work. The most important one (for your bank account, at any rate) is cost.

Hosting services can have a few different kinds of configurations. These include:

Shared hosting
> Racks of machines are set up, and your account shares physical and virtual space with other accounts. If their sites go down, so do yours. If you stress the processor with a bunch of big queries, other accounts suffer the consequences, too.

Virtual Private Server (VPS)
> Your slice of the big shared hosting pie includes CPU, RAM, and disk space that are not affected by and will not affect what happens on other VPS accounts. You can have root access to your virtual machine.

Dedicated server
> You own the server, but you don't have to maintain it. This arrangement is like VPS, except that "virtual" is replaced with "physical" (your server is a real machine that no one else uses).

The best analogy I've seen is a housing analogy: dedicated hosts give you a mansion, VPS hosts give you an apartment, and shared hosts make you live in a dorm room.

Shared hosting services can offer web space and a lot of built-in support for about $10 a month. These companies try to make it very easy for people to install open source tools such as blogging and chat applications, and they will almost always support the most popular development platforms. What they won't do very well is help you with your code. If something breaks, odds are good you will have to work out your own solutions or turn to the community of web developers who share their expertise in online forums. Shared hosts frequently have slow and crowded databases, which may become problematic if your awesome new web application takes off.

The low-cost options also put limits on the amount of traffic, or *bandwidth,* you are permitted. For most small sites, this limit may seem impossibly high; it may be 10 times as large as the amount of hard drive space you are allowed, which may be a few hundred gigabytes. Text takes less bandwidth than images or movies, but if a few hundred thousand people start visiting your website, even the text adds up.

Don't underestimate the importance of bandwidth limits when it comes to a Twitter application. News of interesting tools spreads quickly among Twitter's several million accounts, and developers are often overwhelmed with the response—just ask Ryo Chijiiwa, the creator of Twitterank (see "Tools for Statistics" on page 67). It is not uncommon to have to switch web hosting to an account or a company that can better handle the traffic. It would be best to be proactive and find a hosting company that is prepared to scale with your application. Upgradable VPSs, particularly those with some allowances for bursting past your allotted limits, should meet these needs.

Before you let people know about your great new Twitter application, check with your web host about what happens if you unexpectedly exceed your bandwidth limit. In some cases, automatic charges are levied based on the amount of traffic you have. In other cases, your account—including any other websites you may be hosting—will essentially be shut down until you do something to upgrade your host configuration.

Other factors to consider include the hosting service's track record for keeping the servers up and running (99% uptime should be a minimum requirement), availability and responsiveness of tech support, domain name registration, secure FTP access, usage statistics reporting, and whether your account can support secure transactions. For the purposes of this book, the most important criteria involve common but vital functionality available on most modern web servers. The following are the primary requirements:

- MySQL database server
- PHP scripting language
- A place outside the web path to place supporting code
- *cron* jobs for scheduling tasks

The web host on which the sample code in this book was developed was a Linux server with PHP version 5.2.6 and MySQL version 5.0.67. In computing, things change quickly and incrementally, so even the most on-the-ball server administrators may lag a little behind these server application developers. If your host is reasonably close to the latest releases, you should be fine. Even if it's a bit behind, though, you should find that most of the core functionality you use works with earlier versions.

Both PHP and MySQL do add some useful functions in major new releases, such as `str_split( )` in PHP and `LOAD XML` syntax in MySQL. If you are having difficulty getting something to work, double-check the version of the server software against the version requirements of that function found on the documentation websites:

- PHP (*http://www.php.net/docs.php*)
- MySQL (*http://dev.mysql.com/doc/*)

Automation

When you build a web application, the person using the site triggers much of its functionality. There's no need to fetch data until someone shows up at the website asking for it. However, there are situations where you won't want to rely on web traffic as a catalyst for your program.

Servers do have some easy ways around this, such as using a *cron* job in Linux or the Task Manager in Windows. The latter platform also supports proprietary scheduling tools such as nnCron (*http://www.nncron.ru*) and VisualCron (*http://www.visualcron.com*), which adds a GUI and a lot of functionality to the process of automating tasks.

Traditionally, a special text file known as a *crontab* handles the work of scheduling tasks to be performed at regular intervals. A special syntax instructs the server when and where to look for scripts to run: you supply the path to the script and tell the server when to run it by specifying values for the minutes, hours, day of the month, month, and day of the week fields, with an asterisk (*) serving as a wildcard to allow any value. In this example, *script.cgi* will run at 3:30 a.m. every Saturday:

```
30 3 * * 6 /path/to/script.cgi
```

The *crontab* file is usually tucked away out of the reach of casual users. Through a web host control panel, however, scheduling a *cron* job is as easy as filling out a web form. You select the intervals for how frequently the task should run, and the *crontab* entry is generated for you.

The only tricky part is how to reference the PHP script. Some systems will accept either a URL to a web page or a server path to the *.php* file; others require just the server path. Since the server just sees the file as text and not as a powerful script, you must also tell the *crontab* to render it as PHP. This is accomplished by simply referencing the path to the PHP interpreter:

```
/path/to/php /path/to/your/cron_task.php
```

 If you can't get your *cron* job to parse the PHP, you can try to force the server to do so using a text-based browser (*/path/to/lynx*) or an HTTP request (*/path/to/wget*) instead of calling the PHP parsing engine directly (*/path/to/php*). You will have to use a URL instead of the file path to reference the PHP script.

When the *cron* job runs, the web host may have its server configured to email you the status of the script along with its output. Those notification emails can add up—scheduling a task to run once a minute will result in 1,440 emails each day.

Pseudoautomation hacks

If you don't have access to a *crontab* file, there are still ways you can simulate automation.

One way is to use a free pinging service to start your program each day. Companies such as Site24x7 (*http://site24x7.com*) will try to load a web page at regular intervals and generate a report on how successful their attempts were. Although this is useful to generate server uptime statistics, it can also have the consequence of launching a PHP page. Once launched, that script can do all sorts of things, including mining data or cleaning up files. You can also insert a call to your backend task either as part of the script generating the HTML or in the HTML itself, using `<script>` or `<img>` tags that point to the PHP file you want to run.

These tricks are not recommended, however, since they are both unreliable and can potentially get in the way of the web content you want to display. If that functionality (for example, a data-mining operation) takes a long time to run, your page load times may suffer. This is particularly problematic if the web page is heavily trafficked. There is also the risk that *no one* will visit your website on a given day. If that happens, nothing will trigger the backend task, and therefore nothing will get processed. As a result, these techniques are only really useful in situations where the jobs don't have to run regularly.

 If your web host can't support *cron* jobs, that may be a good reason to find another host. Much of the magic possible with the Twitter API comes while you are sleeping and your code is running on its own.

Further Reading

For experienced programmers and web designers, most of what was discussed in this chapter is old news. For new or casual programmers, this chapter will likely serve as a good reference for you as you create your Twitter application.

The next two chapters delve into the nitty-gritty of the Twitter API, covering the methods that let you request and change data as well as the responses those methods send back to you. I hope you got enough out of this chapter to feel confident in taking the next step. If this is your first web application (and you're trying not to feel overwhelmed), remember that you can come back and use this chapter as a reference when you code. I do want to stress, however, that this is just a sampler plate from the buffet that is Internet development. You won't need more to understand the sample code in this book, but there is more to be had.

Here are some online resources to consult to give you a more complete picture of what is possible when building web applications:

- W3C's XHTML 1.0 (*http://www.w3.org/TR/xhtml1/*)
- HTML.net's CSS tutorial (*http://www.html.net/tutorials/css/*)
- PHP code manual (*http://www.php.net/manual/en/manual.php*)
- Sun Microsystems, Inc.'s MySQL documentation (*http://dev.mysql.com/doc/*)
- CNet Review: Web Hosts (*http://reviews.cnet.com/web-hosting/*)

Additionally, here are a couple of other books worth mentioning as reference desk companions:

- *HTML & XHTML: The Definitive Guide*, Sixth Edition (*http://oreilly.com/catalog/9780596527327*), by Chuck Musciano and Bill Kennedy (O'Reilly)
- *Build Your Own Database Driven Website Using PHP and MySQL*, Third Edition, by Kevin Yank (SitePoint)
- *Essential PHP Security: A Guide to Building Secure Web Applications* (*http://oreilly.com/catalog/9780596006563*), by Chris Shiflett (O'Reilly)

CHAPTER 4

Meet the Twitter API

kmakice The ingredients for your Twitter application are found in the methods of the API. This chapter is your shopping cart.

Now that you know what Twitter is all about (Chapter 1) and have the basic skills to play in the sandbox (Chapter 3), it's time to introduce you to the building blocks for your future application. This chapter describes the specific request methods available through the Twitter API.

The section of the Twitter website that talks about the API groups the methods based on their server paths. This may be a bit confusing, for a few reasons. Some of the terminology is old and doesn't fit with the way we talk about the service today. It is also very techie language, with words like "destroy" instead of "remove" or even "delete." To help you get started, in this chapter I'll drop the tech talk and reorganize the methods into groups reflecting how you might actually use them.

In each section, I'll present one of the 40 existing API methods and explain what is needed to get data from Twitter using that method. Before we start talking about parameters and data formats, though, you need to understand how to connect to the API.

Chapters 6 through 8 provide a description of a suite of web applications used to illustrate how everything goes together. However, sometimes the best way to understand how something works is to play with the input and output. To help with this, the sample code for this book includes a */test* directory containing web forms that interface with the Twitter API. You can use these test pages to see the XML that is returned by Twitter. The sample code can be downloaded from *http://www .oreilly.com/catalog/9780596154615/*.

Accessing the API

An application programming interface, or API, is what allows an application with data to share it with the rest of the world. An API is like a no-frills website, accessed through URL requests but returning structured data instead of web pages displayed in a browser. The data returned is structured to make it easy to parse and get to the information inside. APIs also tend to separate all of the functionality of the site into single, specific actions, such as "get a list of tweets" or "change my profile picture." By combining several kinds of requests, you can use an API to power your own custom applications.

The design of the Twitter API attempts to adhere to the principles of RESTful systems. Roy Fielding conceived of REpresentational State Transfer (REST) less than a decade ago: this approach increases the ease of development as well as the scalability and flexibility of applications by making sure the data is layered, stateless, and well defined. Switching from XML to JSON, for example, is a simple matter of changing the extension on the URL used to make the request; it isn't necessary to reengineer the application or switch development platforms.

In this section, I'll present you with some basic instructions on how to access the Twitter API, select from HTTP methods, authenticate your API requests, and manage imposed limits.

 All requests in this book use HTTPS. This is the preferred way to access the Twitter API.

HTTP Requests

The Twitter API permits three kinds of HTTP requests: GET, POST, and DELETE. The default request is submitted with a GET, which passes parameters as an encoded URL query string. For API methods that change things—for example, updating or deleting status information, direct messages, or associations in the follow network—a POST is needed.

 Where indicated in the API methods, the `id` parameter is sent as part of the URL (substitute this parameter with either a user ID or a username). No form data is needed for any of these methods.

GET

The GET method accepts a URL and uses it to retrieve something from another server, after any necessary processing is done. If the URL is an *index.php* web page, for example, the GET method will capture the HTML generated by the PHP, not the PHP code itself.

Header information passed to the GET method can change its behavior. In particular, GET looks at the `If-Modified-Since` field and captures the output *only* if doing so fulfills that header condition. The purpose of this constraint is to reduce redundant network activity by avoiding unnecessary data transfers.

The following Twitter API methods are accessed with a GET:

- `https://twitter.com/account/rate_limit_status.xml`
- `https://twitter.com/account/verify_credentials.xml`
- `https://twitter.com/direct_messages.xml`
- `https://twitter.com/favorites.xml`
- `https://twitter.com/followers/ids.xml`
- `https://twitter.com/friends/ids.xml`
- `https://twitter.com/friendships/exists.xml`
- `https://twitter.com/help/test.xml`
- `https://twitter.com/statuses/followers.xml`
- `https://twitter.com/statuses/friends.xml`
- `https://twitter.com/statuses/friends_timeline.xml`
- `https://twitter.com/statuses/public_timeline.xml`
- `https://twitter.com/statuses/replies.xml`
- `https://twitter.com/statuses/show/`*id*`.xml`
- `https://twitter.com/statuses/user_timeline.xml`
- `https://twitter.com/users/show/`*id*`.xml`

Most of the methods in the API can be requested using GET. This means your parameters can be passed as a URL query string, or a series of name/value pairs following a ?.

This is great for testing, as all you need to do is type the request URL into the location bar in a regular browser. If the method requires authentication, a dialog box will pop up to get that information. This is more convenient than running early source code or using cURL, as described later in this chapter.

POST

The POST method does the same thing as GET, but it acquires its results in a different way. Whereas there is an upper limit on the size of a GET query string, a POST request encapsulates the submitted data, allowing more information to be transferred. It treats that bundle of data like an attachment to an email, something separate from and subordinate to the requested URL rather than part of it. Because the data is encapsulated and sent separately from the URL, POST data is not exposed in server logs.

 POST data should not be treated as implicitly secure. It does help guard against simple attacks such as image-based cross-site request forgeries (see *http://en.wikipedia.org/wiki/CSRF* for more details), but it is only "security by obscurity."

POST is required for API methods that actually make changes to Twitter's servers, rather than just retrieving data. This is typical of all APIs and web forms in general, and is not unique to Twitter. In the Twitter API, the following methods require POST request handling:

- `https://twitter.com/account/end_session`
- `https://twitter.com/account/update_delivery_device.xml`
- `https://twitter.com/account/update_location.xml`
- `https://twitter.com/account/update_profile.xml`
- `https://twitter.com/account/update_profile_colors.xml`
- `https://twitter.com/account/update_profile_background_image.xml`
- `https://twitter.com/account/update_profile_image.xml`
- `https://twitter.com/blocks/create/id.xml`
- `https://twitter.com/blocks/destroy/id.xml`
- `https://twitter.com/direct_messages/destroy/id.xml`
- `https://twitter.com/direct_messages/new.xml`
- `https://twitter.com/favorites/create/id.xml`
- `https://twitter.com/favorites/destroy/id.xml`

- https://twitter.com/friendships/create/*id*.xml
- https://twitter.com/friendships/destroy/*id*.xml
- https://twitter.com/notifications/follow/*id*.xml
- https://twitter.com/notifications/leave/*id*.xml
- https://twitter.com/statuses/destroy/*id*.xml
- https://twitter.com/statuses/update.xml

 POST requests to the API do not count against the rate limit.

DELETE

The Twitter API also accommodates a third protocol, the DELETE method. The purpose of this type of HTTP call is to instruct the remote server to remove the requested URL resource. There is no way for the remote client to guarantee that this has been done, however. POST requests work just as well with the API, and in this book we'll use POST instead of DELETE.

There are only a handful of API methods that will recognize a DELETE request:

- https://twitter.com/blocks/destroy/*id*.xml
- https://twitter.com/favorites/destroy/*id*.xml
- https://twitter.com/friendships/destroy/*id*.xml
- https://twitter.com/direct_messages/destroy/*id*.xml
- https://twitter.com/statuses/destroy/*id*.xml

HTTP Status Codes

One of the bits of information returned to the client in an HTTP request is the *status code*, a series of three-digit numbers used to communicate the type of success or failure encountered. The Twitter API assigns special meanings to many of these codes, which describe specific outcomes of method requests.

The following are some status codes your application may encounter, and what they likely mean in the context of the API:

200—OK
Success! The method request did what you expected it to do.

304—Not Modified
Nothing wrong, but nothing to report.

400—Bad Request

This can be caused by one of two things: either the request was formatted incorrectly (missing required parameters, unknown method, etc.), or the rate limit has been exceeded. Check the returned text for an explanation.

401—Not Authorized

The account (Twitter username or registered email address) or password you used to authenticate to the API isn't working. Check its accuracy and try again.

403—Forbidden

Twitter understood what you want to do, but won't let you do it. Check the returned text for an explanation.

404—Not Found

Probably caused by a typo or incorrect path to the API method you are requesting. You might also get this error when trying to request a nonexistent user.

500—Internal Server Error

The Twitter folks may be working under the hood. What you requested is probably OK, but the servers aren't handling it correctly. Seek counsel from engineers on the Twitter Development Talk Google Group (*http://groups.google.com/group/twitter-development-talk*).

502—Bad Gateway

Intentional Fail Whale; Twitter is probably rolling out an upgrade.

503—Service Unavailable

Unintentional Fail Whale (see "The Rise of the Fail Whale" on page 16); there are too many requests for the servers to handle right now.

Twitter will try to return any error messages in the same format being requested for the data, such as this XML version:

```
<?xml version="1.0" encoding="UTF-8"?>
<hash>
  <error>Authentication required to request your own timeline.</error>
  <request>/statuses/user_timeline.xml</request>
</hash>
```

The default format is text. Twitter will always try to return some kind of explanation, if it can.

Status codes are an easy way to direct the application logic. Parsing the returned messages will provide specifics and can be helpful for passing along interpretations of errors to the end user, but status codes are easier to access from the HTTP response. They can help direct error handling or confirm success.

 This book uses only the XML format, with one exception: the Keyword Search API method doesn't yet support XML, so I substitute Atom instead. The Twitter API does support other formats, as discussed next.

Format

Twitter currently accommodates four kinds of formatted data:

XML
> Extensible Markup Language uses semantic tags to wrap data in a structured format. It is extensible because the user can define the structure and kinds of tags; they aren't simply prescribed, as with HTML. Use of XML to structure data is an accepted way to separate the data layer from the presentation layer and make applications more versatile.

JSON
> JavaScript Object Notation is a language-independent text format used primarily to power Ajax applications. With JSON, simple text can be used to represent many different types of data and the relationships between those data types. As with XML, the data is encapsulated in a structured format; however, JSON is considered to be simpler than XML. For more information on how to use JSON, visit *http:// www.json.org*.

RSS
> Really Simple Syndication is a specific form of XML that reflects some standardized tag structures that can be read in a predictable manner. RSS feeds are widespread on blogs, news websites, and services like Twitter.

Atom
> Atom Syndication Format is an alternative to RSS that was created in part to remove the need for legacy support of older protocols. Atom uses a different date and time format than RSS and is more accommodating of modular use and international support.

We'll use XML in this book, but to switch to JSON, simply change the URL extension from `.xml` to `.json` in the HTTP request. That's what RESTful design principles do for you!

RSS and Atom

Only a few Twitter API methods make use of the RSS and Atom formats. The following are used on the official Twitter website, allowing people to subscribe to information streams:

- `https://twitter.com/direct_messages.rss`
- `https://twitter.com/favorites.rss`
- `https://twitter.com/statuses/friends_timeline.rss`
- `https://twitter.com/statuses/public_timeline.rss`
- `https://twitter.com/statuses/replies.rss`
- `https://twitter.com/statuses/user_timeline.rss`

Authentication

Most API requests require a valid username and password. Authentication is necessary for two reasons. First, some of the information available through the API is specific to the authenticated user, so the user context determines what data is returned. Second, authentication is the most reliable way to facilitate limiting the rate of access to the API. Imposing rate limits was necessary to ensure the success of Twitter, in terms of both cultivating members and encouraging third-party application development.

 Asking for authentication information from users is difficult to avoid for some of the functions and data available through the Twitter API. For further discussion on some of the issues involved with asking end users to provide their username and passwords, see "Gone Phishing: A Word About Passwords" on page 182.

Although Twitter does have plans to improve the scheme to use OAuth,[*] as of this writing authentication is done through HTTP Basic Authentication, referred to as Basic Auth. Twitter asks for either an account username or the email address used to create the account, along with a password, before doing any of the heavy lifting in terms of data retrieval or modification. Any future changes are likely to become optional improvements, with the current system remaining fully supported.

 Be aware that the user account information passed as plain text in cURL is only slightly obfuscated; it will be fully readable to anyone monitoring the network. cURL facilitates HTTPS requests, and Twitter recommends using encryption to interact with the API.

If a method is requested without a valid username and password, the data response will be XML containing the following error statement:

```
<hash>
  <error>Could not authenticate you.</error>
  <request>/account/verify_credentials.xml</request>
</hash>
```

If you are not interested in the specifics of the error message (which can easily change), examine the HTTP status code as a quicker and more reliable indication of success or failure (see "HTTP Status Codes" on page 137).

There are a few API methods that return data without authentication. Here's the complete list:

---

[*] The private beta of Twitter's implementation of OAuth launched in early 2009. It is expected to be tested throughout the first half of the year and incorporated into the next release of the API. The current HTTP Basic Auth will be deprecated six months after OAuth becomes fully supported.

View the Public Timeline
```
https://twitter.com/statuses/public_timeline.xml
```
View an Individual Timeline (public accounts only)
```
https://twitter.com/statuses/user_timeline/14067832.xml
```
Show a Tweet
```
https://twitter.com/statuses/show/937878916.xml
```
Show Member Profile
```
https://twitter.com/users/show/id.xml
```
Keyword Search
```
https://search.twitter.com/search.atom
```
Test
```
https://twitter.com/help/test.xml
```

All of these unauthenticated methods require a GET request, and some (such as Member Profile) will provide more information if the user context is known when the information is retrieved.

 At press time, Twitter's OAuth was in beta, being tested by the developer community. One of the testers, Abraham Williams, quickly published some sample code at *http://github.com/poseurtech/twitteroauth*. See the next section for more on OAuth.

A Peak at OAuth

In February 2009, Twitter released its first implementation of OAuth as a closed beta to developers on the Google discussion group (*http://groups.google.com/group/twitter-development-talk*). A few hours after this release, Inuda (*http://inuda.com*), a web application design firm, quickly showed a proof of concept with Twitter's code.[†] Within a week, successful tests and sample code existed for PHP, Python, and Ruby. A growing list of OAuth resources is available on the Twitter API wiki (*http://apiwiki.twitter.com/OAuth-Examples*).

Among those efforts was a sample script from Abraham Williams (*@poseurtech*).[‡] Williams' solution follows a straightforward process to authenticate with Twitter's OAuth. OAuth functions by managing multiple pairs of tokens: the tokens for the specific user request, and the ones used to allow the application to later access parts of that user's Twitter account. There is also an initial pair used to register the application.

[†] From the February 12, 2009 blog article, "Never Share Your Twitter Password Again," published on the Inuda blog (*http://blog.inuda.com/2009/02/12/never-share-your-twitter-password-again/*).

[‡] Abraham Williams' sample PHP code can be downloaded at *http://github.com/poseurtech/twitteroauth*.

Each application will first need to be registered with Twitter. Developers in the beta test were given a new tab in the Settings section of the Twitter website that allowed them to make this request. Twitter returns the key/secret tokens for the application to build a `TwitterOAuth` object from the registered URI. With the key and secret strings, the application requests tokens for the user with a new OAuth method. These tokens become part of a request link that the end user can click on to grant the application access to her Twitter account.

In Basic Auth, Twitter isn't involved with this handoff of account access. Users share their screen names and passwords with the third-party application, which then uses them to access the API on their behalf. Not only is this an all-or-nothing level of access, but it is the same access that would be shared with other third-party applications. The result is a network of systems reliant on the same authentication information.

With OAuth, Twitter becomes the middleman in the negotiation between the application and the user. The application uses its identifying tokens—acquired through the initial registration—to request access to the user's account in the form of a request link. This link is presented to the user on the third-party application, sort of like how a parking receipt is given to a conference attendee to take to the information desk to be validated. When the user clicks on this link, he is taken to the Twitter website, along with the tokens that identify which application will need the account access. At this point, the application is no longer involved; it is a dialogue between the user and Twitter. If the former approves access, he is taken back to the third-party application site with the token pair needed to make future API requests.

This only gets us halfway there. These request tokens are saved locally by the third-party application and used whenever more API interaction is required. The request tokens don't grant access, but they do authorize future requests for data without the user being present. Assuming the user hasn't revoked access in the interim, the application can present the request tokens to get access to the user's data—sort of like giving a special pass to a bouncer to get backstage at a concert.

The big benefit of OAuth is that it avoids password-sharing behavior. Instead of asking the user to provide her actual username and password, the OAuth process results in a new form of the user authentication that can only be used by this particular application. For third-party applications, there is more accountability, since the tokens are unique. For users, there is more control, since you can revoke or deny access rights to one application while granting it to another.

 OAuth is still a work in progress, not just for Twitter but also as a method and movement. By mid-2009, Twitter will be releasing its OAuth to production applications, but that doesn't mean every application will be inclined or able to use it.

Parameters

The information returned by Twitter can be refined during the HTTP request. Most API methods accept one or more parameters, most of which are optional but some of which are required. Not all parameters are available to every method.

The Twitter API relies on UTF-8 encoding of all parameter values, which means you can't send some special characters as plain text without confusing the machines that have to deal with that information. This is particularly important in differentiating between parameter string connectors, such as & and =, and the actual values contained within each parameter. Encoding gives the API a means to distinguish between the two. Fortunately, most programming languages—including PHP—have some functions that make encoding parameter values simple.

 Angle brackets (< and >), double quotes ("), and the ampersand (&) are converted to entities as a security precaution against attacks from web applications. The resulting encoded characters count toward the 140-character limit for Twitter messages.

I have gathered together all of the possible parameters, both required and optional, into one place to give you a convenient reference. Not every API method will accept all of these, but the parameters work the same way for the methods that do recognize them.

Parameters that may be required

For several of the Twitter API methods, it is not enough to just send the URL; the request also requires that some parameter value be included to let Twitter work its magic. The following are descriptions of parameters that may be required for some API methods:

id/user_a *and* user_b/user
: A Twitter user can be referenced using either an integer ID or the username associated with that account. For status or direct messages, the ID must reflect an existing record number. The id (or similar) parameter is passed as part of the URL request.

status/text
: The text for a status update or direct message is limited to 140 characters after URL encoding.

location
: The location of the user is not standardized in any way. Any encoded text can be published to the location field in the user's profile.

device
: The device must be one of the two valid options supported by Twitter, namely sms or im. To turn off device notifications, the value should be none.

Although this parameter allows for future expansion, in practice it can only be used to turn cell phone messages on or off—Twitter officially discontinued IM support in 2008.

q

(Search only.) Although the Keyword Search method will return header information if you don't include a query string, any API requests without this parameter are almost meaningless. The q string must be URL-encoded.

Other parameters that may be useful

The power and efficiency of the API are increased when you send additional instructions to Twitter to shape what information is returned. In addition to any parameters that a given method may require, there are usually additional options that can be set to filter data before it is returned to you. The following list describes parameters that may be optional for some API methods:

id, in_reply_to_status_id

Even when it isn't required, the value of id will still be either an integer ID or the username associated with the account when referring to a person (for user methods), or an existing record number when referencing a message (for status methods). The id parameter is passed as part of the URL itself, not as a separate query string or POST field value.

The in_reply_to_status_id parameter references the specific status update by another user with which a tweet is associated.

email

A user's email address can be used if you do not know the user ID or username. This parameter is also used to edit the member profile and change which email address is associated with a given account.

user_id

This parameter overrides id (which can contain either a user ID or screen name) with the ID of the specified member account. It was added to prevent ambiguities when the screen name is a number.

screen_name

This parameter overrides id (which can contain either a user ID or screen name) with the screen name of the specified member account. It was added to prevent ambiguities when the screen name is a number.

since

This parameter can be used to limit results to the most recent activity, performing the same function as the If-Modified-Since header in an HTTP request. This filter ignores information older than the specified time (which must be within the last

24 hours). The value must be encoded to be in the form **Tue%2C+20+Jan +2009+11%3A30%3A00+GMT**.

since_id

This parameter functions similarly to since, except that it filters based on the ID of a specific status update or direct message instead of a date. Twitter returns only the records with IDs greater than the specified value (i.e., records that postdate the message with the specified ID).

count

For timeline requests, count limits the results to the *n* most recent status updates, where *n* is the integer value specified in the request. The maximum allowed count value is 200.

rpp

(Search only.) This parameter (results per page) specifies the number of status messages to return on each page, given a specified search term. The maximum allowed rpp value is 100.

page

This integer value paginates the Twitter results for status updates, direct messages, and members of a follow network. For status updates, each page contains up to 20 items. For followers and people you follow, each page holds up to 100 authors. The Keyword Search method also uses this parameter, but it allows the application to dictate (with rpp) how many of the 1,500 matching tweets are displayed at a time (and therefore how many pages are needed to browse the full corpus).

 The page parameter always begins at 1, which is the default, not 0.

follow

This is a Boolean value that indicates whether you want to be notified on your cell phone or some other device when the user indicated by the id parameter posts a status update. This parameter is used to enable notifications at the same time that you begin following a new person.

name

The full name of a member is often more readable and meaningful than the user account handle. This option allows you to change the full name listed on a member account. The maximum length is 40 characters.

url

Each member can associate her account with a single link to a website. This parameter allows you to change the URL listed for a member account. The maximum length is 40 characters.

location

The location of the user is not standardized in any way: any encoded text not longer than 30 characters can be published to the location field in the profile. This parameter allows you to change the location listed for a given member account.

description

This parameter specifies the text (maximum 160 characters) describing a member or organization using Twitter. This description shows up on the member's Twitter profile web page.

image

The background image to display or tile behind your Twitter member profile web page can be controlled with this parameter. The image must be a GIF, JPG, or PNG and cannot exceed 2,048 pixels or 800 KB. For the profile picture associated with all of your tweets, the maximum values are 500 pixels and 700 KB.

profile_background_color, profile_text_color, profile_link_color, profile_side bar_fill_color, profile_sidebar_border_color

These parameters control the web page color scheme for a user's Twitter member profile. Each option must be specified using a valid hexadecimal code (as in "#f09" or "#ff0099"). The colors are set through the update_profile_colors method (see "Update Profile Colors" on page 170) and dictate how most of the text, links, borders, and shading are displayed.

show_user

(Search only.) When set to true, this parameter tags the beginning of each tweet that is returned in the search results with a username and a colon (e.g., "kmakice:Writing").

geocode

(Search only.) This parameter filters the search results by location, using the self-disclosed location information in the author profiles. The geocode parameter has three parts: latitude, longitude, and radius of interest. The resulting comma-delimited string must be URL-encoded, as in 39.123456%2C-86.345678%2C10km. The radius must be specified in units of either mi (miles) or km (kilometers).

 Twitter members use the location field in different ways. Most of the time, the information is accurate—thanks in part to the propagation of smart phones, like the iPhone, among Twitter users—but it can also be out-of-date or nonsensical (e.g., "Space").

lang

(Search only.) This parameter filters the search results by language, using an accepted ISO 639-1 code such as en, es, or fr.

callback

(Search and JSON only.) A callback allows a program to pass a reference to a dynamic function on the application side. Because we are focusing on XML in this book, we won't use callbacks.

Rate Limiting

In late 2007, use of Twitter's API reached a sufficient level that some throttling of requests had to be instituted. Clients are now permitted only so many requests every 60 minutes, measured from the time the first request is made. The current level is 100 requests each hour, but the limit fell as low as 30 during the worst of the server strains in the summer of 2008.

Two kinds of rate limits are being tracked: authenticated and unauthenticated accesses. When you authenticate with a valid Twitter username and password, the API starts tallying when you use the API and charges requests against the rate limit for that account. When you are able to get data without authentication, requests are tracked for the IP address you're using.

 In theory, this might allow you to double your rate limit to 200 GET requests per hour, provided no authentication is needed for the data you are interested in getting. If you really have need for that many accesses, however, I suggest requesting whitelisting from Twitter, as discussed later in this section.

In general, any method using POST is exempt from rate limiting. This includes any request where the server data is changed, such as requests related to adding or deleting status updates, direct messages, or associations in the follow network.

When a request is made that exceeds an account or IP address's rate limit, a data response is sent that indicates the error:

```
<hash>
  <request>/statuses/user_timeline.xml</request>
  <error>Rate limit exceeded. Clients may not make more than 100 requests
    per hour.</error>
</hash>
```

Until an hour has passed since the first of those 100 requests, no more data will be accessible. A status code of 400 is also returned, providing another indicator that a problem has occurred without it being necessary to parse the XML, JSON, or plain text containing the specific error message.

The search API is currently handled a little differently than the rest of the Twitter API, due to its history as a third-party application (Summize). Future versions of the Keyword Search method may be similarly limited, but for the time being, Twitter simply monitors for abuse and acts on a case-by-case basis. Any rate limits for the search API are "a bit fuzzier" than the main Twitter API and are based entirely on IP address.

Checking the rate limit status

To help developers manage their access to the API, Twitter created a special method to return information about the rate limit status of the authenticating account:

```
https://twitter.com/account/rate_limit_status.xml
```

Requesting this method does not count against the rate limit and can provide useful information about the current maximum, the number of hits remaining in the current hour, and when the clock will be reset (both in absolute clock time and elapsed seconds). The Check Rate Limit Status method is discussed in "API Administration" on page 174.

Whitelisting

For most uses of the API, developers can work within the rate limit. However, in some cases, an application will require more than 100 requests at a time in order to provide its functionality. Twitter sometimes makes allowances for this by adding user accounts to a whitelist, where limits are raised or eliminated.

If you are developing an application that requires a lot of requests to the API, you can submit a web form (*https://twitter.com/help/request_whitelisting*) and ask Twitter to be considered for addition to the whitelist of high-volume screen names. This will raise your upper limit from 100 to 20,000 API requests per hour.

Keeping Development Light

In the past, Twitter engineers have taken a beating in the blogosphere about their ability (or rather, inability) to keep the service running under stress. Although much of the traffic to Twitter comes from the API, outages have rarely been attributed to API traffic. One of the reasons for that may be the developer community's willingness to play nice with the servers.

 At a gathering of regional API providers, Twitter's Alex Payne hinted that Ph.D. students grabbing data is the biggest problem APIs face.[§]

[§] From a December 19, 2008 tweet (*https://twitter.com/al3x/status/1068021673*).

In addition to working within the restrictions the company puts on accessing its data, Twitter advises adopting a few other strategies:

Load the minimum
Get more data only when the action is triggered by user interaction.

Maintain a local archive
If you will need to request the same kind of information again, look to your local copy first to avoid repeatedly asking for the same content.

Paginate
Make use of the page parameter rather than count. If you use count, combine it with the since_id parameter to retrieve only new information.

Identify yourself
Set the User-Agent header in the HTTP request to help engineers troubleshoot your applications.

Finally, give credit where credit is due. A simple "Powered by Twitter" link to the service ties your application back to the larger community. Look at the Terms of Service section in the Twitter API wiki (*http://apiwiki.twitter.com/Search+API+Documentation*) for more information.

 The Twitter API wiki organizes the methods differently from the way I do in this chapter. If you want to see a simpler list of methods in structural order, including a summary of parameters you can use, check out the Appendix.

Play Along at Home

The best way to learn the Twitter API methods is to try them out as you read through the material in this chapter. One way to test how the API methods work is through the computer command line, using cURL commands:

curl
Invoke the cURL connection.

-u *username:password*
Authenticate with your Twitter username or ID and password. The username can be substituted with an email address, as only one account is associated with each address.

-d status=*your+message+here*
For methods that require a POST, this option is needed to get a valid response from Twitter. The text used in conjunction with the POST option sends parameter data to the API to be processed with the request.

https://twitter.com/category/methodname.format
Provide the method URI requested from the Twitter API.

If cURL returns an error when you use an HTTPS request (specifically, "certificate verify failed"), you can disable the verification of the secured certificate by using the -k option.

This is not an ideal solution, though; I include it here only for convenience. Turning off verification of secure certificates can defeat the purpose of HTTPS encryption. It is better to adjust the certificate bundle to include what you need. Visit *http://curl.haxx.se/docs/sslcerts.html* for more information on how to do this.

These commands can be strung together to produce a new status message in the public timeline, as in:

```
curl -u username:password -d 'status=test' https://twitter.com/statuses/update.xml
```

If cURL is not installed on your system, you can download it from *http://curl.haxx.se/download.html* for almost any OS. For more information on using cURL, see "cURL" on page 118.

If you are hesitant about using command-line cURL to test your Twitter API method requests, there are other options to help you see the HTTP status codes and content passing between your machine and the rest of the world.

Charles (*http://www.charlesproxy.com*) is a debugging proxy ideal for investigating HTTPS traffic and XML interactions that travel to and from your machine. You can download the software for a free 30-day trial and then pay $50 for the full license. The simplest way to look at the Twitter API responses, though, is probably through a regular browser. Simply type the method request into the browser's location field. If authentication is needed, the browser will ask for it.

Most of the methods in the API can be requested using GET, but not all of them. The methods that make changes to Twitter data, such as posting a new status update or deleting a message, won't work with GET. They require POST and won't be usable through a browser.

The API Methods

You may find it easier to navigate the API if we focus on which part of Twitter each method affects. The 38 API methods currently maintained by Twitter can be organized into the following operational groups based on what they're used for:

Publishing
Changing the content published to Twitter

The Information Stream
Retrieving and managing the content published to Twitter

The Follow Network
Managing the people whom you follow and who follow you

Communication
> Exchanging direct messages with other members

Member Account
> Dealing with your Twitter account

Administration
> Negotiating access to the Twitter API

Search
> Looking for keywords in the tweet archives

The sections that follow explore each group, describing how to format requests with each of the API methods and showing some examples of XML output.

> Remember that successful requests return an HTTP status code of 200. You can use this to check how you did if you don't want or need to parse the data response from Twitter.

Publishing

Twitter is nothing without its 140-character posts, or tweets. The API methods in this category manage the creation and removal of tweets. Quite simply, you can use these methods to publish content to or remove it from the Twitter information stream.

> When successful, the publishing methods return status objects. See "Status Objects" on page 198 for more details about the data that is returned.

Post a Tweet

This method adds a tweet to the information stream for the authenticated user. In Twitter terminology, this is an update of the current member's status:

```
https://twitter.com/statuses/update.xml
```

To make this URL request function, authentication is required (so that the new status message can be assigned to the correct account). Since it involves a change to the service database and not simply a data grab, the POST method is required to encapsulate the parameter data in this request.

The Post a Tweet method requires one parameter, **status**, filled with encoded text of no longer than 140 characters. Omitting the message results in no status being published and subsequently no content being returned. When successful, Twitter returns XML containing information about the new status update (see "Status Objects" on page 198).

To identify which tool published the tweet—as in "from the web" or "from twitterrific"—there is an optional parameter, source, that can contain the short identifying string registered with Twitter upon request. There is also an optional parameter, in_reply_to_status_id, that can attach this tweet to another specific status update by another user. This will associate the message with the author specified in the in_reply_to_user_id attribute in the status data object. If the reply status ID is not valid, the parameter will be ignored.

Many older Twitter applications assume that a new message sent as a reply is a response to the most recent status update by the targeted author. For active accounts, this can cause replies to be attached to more recent updates than are intended, causing some issues in the integrity of threaded conversation.

Twitter has added elements to support better threading for replies, but the association to the replied-to author's last tweet is still programmed into many third-party Twitter tools.

Delete a Tweet

After a status update has been published, it can be deleted. However, this can only be done if the authenticated user is also the author of the update to be removed:

```
https://twitter.com/statuses/destroy/id.xml
```

The id parameter is required to identify which existing status update is to be deleted—information that is included by referencing the status ID in the request URL (replacing id in the preceding link). If the request is successful, Twitter returns the status object information. This is the same response posting a new tweet will produce (see the previous section). If the status ID is not provided or is invalid, the XML returns an error: "No status found with that ID" (see "Hash Objects" on page 209).

Deleting a tweet is a practice that should be discouraged. Part of the value of Twitter is that it provides a long-term record of the little things we do and say, including the mistakes. Although there will almost certainly be times when you will need to remove a tweet you've posted, it is important to realize that your timeline is not an inbox. Leave your footprints for posterity.

There are some known issues with deleted status updates still appearing in Twitter searches. This problem should be resolved with the next upgrade to the Twitter API, expected in 2009.

The Information Stream

The collection of published tweets creates a flow of information in Twitter. There is a public timeline of updates, fed by all accounts that are not configured to be private streams and are therefore available for anyone to view. Individual members also have their own streams, which they craft by deciding which members to follow.

This section describes the methods used to access different kinds of streams, display details about specific status updates, and manage the bookmarks—called *favorites*— that mark content of interest.

When successful, the Information Stream methods return status objects. See "Status Objects" on page 198 for more details.

Show a Tweet

This method was created to enable us to view the details for a single status update:

```
https://twitter.com/statuses/show/id.xml
```

This type of request returns XML structured in the same way as that returned by the publishing methods described earlier, including a description of the update author as well as the message itself (see "Status Objects" on page 198). If the status ID is not provided or is invalid, the XML returns an error.

Remember, you can easily change the format to JSON by editing the extension used in the URL to request the method, from .xml to .json.

Authentication is not needed, provided the tweet is public. To view protected status updates made by private authors who have authorized you to do so, you must provide a valid username and password.

View the Public Timeline

This method returns the 20 most recent status updates from public accounts in Twitter:

```
https://twitter.com/statuses/public_timeline.xml
```

Authentication is not required and thus retrieval from the public timeline does not count against the API rate limit, even if you do authenticate.

A successful request returns information about the recent status updates, following the same format and structure as that returned by the publishing methods, but with multiple status data objects contained within a `<statuses type="array"></statuses>` XML wrapper (see "Status Objects" on page 198).

The public timeline is cached once per minute, so there is no reason to request public tweets more often than that. This means that, with over a million updates posted to Twitter every day, most tweets will slip through the cracks. Twitter has grown too big to capture everything through the main API.

Twitter does offer two other options: a data mining feed that returns 600 tweets per request, and the "firehose" that gives researchers everything coming across the timeline. See "Other Data Options" on page 181 for more information.

The public timeline is not a complete picture of all Twitter traffic. An estimated 10% of all user accounts are private accounts;[‖] those users' status updates are available only to approved people and are not included in the public timeline. Additionally, Twitter requires that an account be minimally configured to include a custom user icon for it to be part of the public timeline.

View a Friends Timeline

Similar to the one for the public timeline, there is a method in the API to retrieve recent tweets from the perspective of a specific user. Calling the View a Friends Timeline method returns the 20 most recent status updates posted by the authenticated user and the authors that user follows:

```
https://twitter.com/statuses/friends_timeline.xml
```

This data is the same stuff you'll see on the home page after logging into the Twitter website. A successful request returns XML structurally identical to that of the data returned by the View the Public Timeline method.

There are several optional parameters that can be used to filter the data that is returned. Three of them—since, since_id, and count—change the number of status updates returned by truncating older tweets. The since parameter gives the API a certain point in time to use as the cutoff, whereas the since_id parameter identifies a specific status ID (presumably the last one your application successfully captured). The count parameter specifies the number of recent tweets to return. When creating applications that monitor the activity of an account, these are great parameters to use to avoid redundancy.

The page parameter allows the application to navigate further back than just the 20 tweets available on the first page of the friends timeline. Current restrictions maximize the archive at 200 tweets, which translates to 10 pages of timeline content.

‖ Bruno Peeters estimated in 2008 that 10–15% of all accounts were protected, based on his work tracking TwitDir membership numbers (*http://twitterfacts.blogspot.com/2008/03/1-million-twitter-users.html*), but growth in the Twitter membership base is diluting those estimates. My own research suggests that figure is between 3 and 9%.

View an Individual Timeline

A third view of the Twitter timeline is the user archive. This stream contains just the tweets published by a single author. The View an Individual Timeline method returns the 20 most recent status updates posted by the authenticated user:

```
https://twitter.com/statuses/user_timeline.xml
```

It's also possible to request another user's timeline by adding another level to the URL path and identifying that user, as in:

```
https://twitter.com/statuses/user_timeline/id.xml
```

The id parameter is replaced with the user's ID or username. This is the same content one would see by visiting a member's Twitter profile page.

 If the requested user has a public account, authentication isn't necessary; simply reference the user ID or username in the request.

Without authentication or inclusion of a public user ID, this method returns a variation of the standard error message: "Authentication required to request your own timeline" (see "Hash Objects" on page 209).

Successful requests respond with an array of status data objects (see "Status Objects" on page 198), as is the case with other timeline methods. The results can be filtered in the same way as those for the friends timeline, using since, since_id, count, and page.

View Replies

Replies are status updates that reference another Twitter member. The convention, culled from the old days of Instant Relay Chat (IRC), is to precede the username with the @ symbol. Although Twitter wasn't originally meant for conversation, many people post status updates as replies to direct conversation to particular users.

These replies can be viewed as a separate timeline by using a special API method:

```
https://twitter.com/statuses/replies.xml
```

This method returns the 20 most recent @ replies addressing the authenticated user. These will include status updates posted by people the user is not following if the account configuration is set to include replies from all users.

 Replies are recognized in Twitter only if the reply indicator appears at the beginning of a tweet. Any @*username* references within the body of the status update will not be included in the replies timeline. However, any reference to a particular user can be found using the search API (see "Content searches" on page 177).

Twitter currently allows retrieval of up to 40 pages, or 800 replies, by using the optional `page` parameter. This method also facilitates retrieval of the freshest replies by recognizing the `since` and `since_id` parameters.

Successful requests return the standard status data object array, as with the timeline methods discussed previously.

View Favorites

In Twitter, you can create a bookmark (called a "favorite") to mark a status update you want to remember. There is a separate view of the timeline that returns the 20 most recent "favorited" statuses for the authenticated user:

```
https://twitter.com/favorites.xml
```

As with the regular user timeline, you can specify an `id` in the request URL to get a list of favorites for a user other than the one whose credentials were used to authenticate to the API:

```
https://twitter.com/favorites/kmakice.xml
```

If that user has a public account, the information can be retrieved without authenticating. Pagination through the `page` parameter is the only option available to let the application navigate back to see the full list of all favorited tweets.

Create a Favorite

To create a new bookmark, you must specify the ID of the status update to be favorited in the request URL:

```
https://twitter.com/favorites/create/id.xml
```

This command returns a single status data object for the favorite message when successful, and a "Not found" error if the status message doesn't exist or is inaccessible to the authenticated user. The new favorite will be associated with the authenticated user.

Delete a Favorite

Deleting a bookmark doesn't delete the status message (how could it, if you've marked other people's tweets as favorites?), but it does remove the flag you have previously set to remind you how much you liked the content. Times change, and you may need to distance yourself from the memory of a particular update. By using this method, you can un-favorite a specified status message:

```
https://twitter.com/favorites/destroy/id.xml
```

The `id` of an existing message must be included in the request URL to indicate the message you now want to forget. If you try to un-favorite a message that doesn't exist or isn't currently a favorite of the authenticated user, a "Not found" error message will be returned (see "Hash Objects" on page 209). Success brings one last reminder in the form of a single status data object that describes the message and its author.

The Follow Network

Twitter isn't just about posting updates when you go to lunch. The magic happens when you grow your network of authors to the point where you start benefiting from the collective wisdom of your tweeps. Those you follow and those who follow you together make up your *follow network*. This section looks at methods that show you who is in your network, how to expand or contract it, and how to protect it from spammers.

When successful, the follow network methods return information about particular Twitter members. See "User Objects" on page 192 for more details about the data Twitter makes available.

The notable exception is Confirm a Follow, which returns a response object indicating whether or not one person is following another.

Show Member Profile

People are the main unit of currency in a follow network. Each member contributes to the collective wisdom, by talking about what is important to them at a given moment and also by identifying other people of interest. When you encounter a new person on Twitter, looking at her profile is one way you can decide whether you want to follow her.

The Show Member Profile method gives you all the basic profile information you have already seen attached to the status data objects, plus a lot of new information about the specified user. Most importantly, this is the method you need to use to find out statistics such as the number of updates a user has posted and how many people that member is following:

```
https://twitter.com/users/show/id.xml
```

Even to access your own profile information, the `id` needs to reflect your username or user ID and be included in the request URL.

The /show part of the URL isn't needed. These two URLs return the same results:

```
https://twitter.com/users/show/id.xml
https://twitter.com/users/id.xml
```

Alternatively, you can use the `email` parameter to get profile data, as in:

```
https://twitter.com/users/show.xml?email=kmakice@gmail.com
```

Doing so allows you to look up a Twitter member's account information by referencing the email address used to register that account (for public accounts, authentication is not required). Private accounts are protected from this search, unless the authenticating user has been granted access to those accounts. Twitter also added two other parameters—`user_id` and `screen_name`—that can identify which member account you want returned. Either can be used as a query string variable (e.g., `https://twitter.com/users/show.xml?user_id=415`) to help disambiguate between user IDs and screen names that are composed entirely of numbers. `id` assumes a number is a user ID and returns that, which made it impossible to view some profiles. The two newer parameters were added to give you more control and in fact take precedence over use of `id`.

> Accounts are sometimes disabled. When that happens, the Twitter API will return a status code of 404, rather than showing any profile information for that account.

The detail in the XML gives you a lot of information about the design of the specified member's profile page, including the style scheme used on the page and whether it has a background tile. Although you may not be too interested in what the member's profile page looks like, you also get details on the user's time zone setting, the number of status messages that user has bookmarked (favorites), the total number of updates he has posted, and the number of other people he is following. The profile data also includes information about the member's latest update (see "User Objects" on page 192).

If the request is sent with authentication, a couple of extra fields are available in the XML:

```
<following>false</following>
<notifications>false</notifications>
```

This information has to do with the relationship between the two Twitter users (the authenticated user and the user identified by the `id` parameter). In this example, the authenticated user is not following the requested user. This information will appear for unauthenticated requests as well, defaulting to a `following` value of `true` and a `notifications` value of `false`.

> For protected accounts, these fields and the embedded short-form status object are not included. This was a bug fix to improve security for twitterers with private accounts. It was revealed when someone used the short-form status object to identify the "billionth tweet," which was published by a member with a protected account.#

On November 11, 2008, Blair Bends used this security hole in the API to track down the identity of the person who had posted status update 1,000,000,000. Nathan Reed had launched a countdown site several weeks prior to that date, anticipating the moment when Twitter served up ID number one billion. Although this almost certainly was not the actual billionth tweet, the milestone did attract some attention in the Twitter community. For more information on this milestone, read my blog account at *http://www.blogschmog.net/2008/11/11/a-billion-served/*.

View Members Being Followed

The more important half of the follow network is the list of people you follow. Although it is great to have a throng of devoted fans hanging on every word you tweet, your experience with Twitter will be affected much more by the content you see than by how many people read your own tweets.

The API provides a method to show who is contributing to your personal information stream:

```
https://twitter.com/statuses/friends.xml
```

The following lists are available for any public account. Simply including the id parameter in the request URL (username or user ID) without authenticating will allow you to look at how another member's information stream is composed:

```
https://twitter.com/statuses/friends/kmakice.xml
```

Accessing this information for a private account, however, requires not only authentication but also the permission of the account holder, which you gain by virtue of being allowed to follow that user's status updates.

The View Members Being Followed method returns a list of up to 100 Twitter members that the authenticating or identified user is following, with the members who have updated most recently appearing first. If the user is following more than 100 members, you can access the full list by using the page parameter to navigate to less active authors. Each successive page will include the next 100 users, until the list of followed authors is exhausted.

This method also allows use of the since parameter, which is quite useful for keeping tabs on just the latest changes to a following list. You can specify a URL-encoded date and time (no more than 24 hours old) and have Twitter return only the latest additions. A successful request returns an array of user data objects (see "User Objects" on page 192).

 One shortcoming of the API is that you can't easily track changes in the network over time. Daily monitoring of an account using the since option will let you see how a member's following list grows over time, but not how it shrinks.

Each user's Twitter profile information can be found in the structured data, including a flag that indicates whether the account is private (`<protected>false</protected>`) and how many followers that person boasts.

View Followers

The other half of your follow network consists of the people who find the minutiae of your life so interesting that they decide to hang on every word you tweet. Followers are people who include your content in their information streams, and there is a nice method in the API to request the list of followers:

```
https://twitter.com/statuses/followers.xml
```

A successful request again gets the array of user profile data, but the ordering is different from that of the following list: Twitter currently lists followers according to when they signed up for Twitter, with the newest members appearing at the top of the list.

 The sort order for such lists is subject to change. Pay attention to the Twitter API Change Log (*http://apiwiki.twitter.com/REST-API-Change log*) for information about adjustments or new parameters, especially if the order is factored into your code.

If you have a large number of followers, it's likely that while a lot of information about your new followers will be on the first page of results, not all of it will be. Any time an established Twitter user follows you, that information will be buried deep in the pagination; to find it, you'll have to use the **page** parameter.

The list of people who follow you is a much more guarded secret than the list of those you follow. For starters, you must be authenticated in order to view anyone else's list. If you are not, or if the person whose information you are trying to get has a protected account and is not someone you follow, an authorization error will result:

```
<hash>
  <error>Not authorized</error>
  <request>/statuses/followers/cmakice.xml</request>
</hash>
```

About half of the members of the Twitterverse will have more followers than people being followed. The latter is in one's control, but the former is not. For that reason, exploring someone else's following list—where everyone has been vetted in some minimal fashion—is probably more useful than looking at their followers.

Get All Followers

One of the big obstacles facing developers interested in social graphs of Twitter activity is how to identify all the members of a follow network. Until recently, the only way to get a list of everyone following a given member was to loop through multiple requests of the View Followers method. Now, there is an easier way to do this:

```
https://twitter.com/followers/ids.xml
```

This method returns a simple XML list of the user IDs of all of the authenticating user's followers. No other information is included, such as those members' latest tweets or even their usernames. This method makes it much easier to keep tabs on social relationships, but the trade-off is you don't get any extraneous information.

User IDs are the preferred way to keep track of Twitter members. Members can change their usernames via the Settings on the main website, but their user IDs will never change.

The Get All Followers method requires authentication. To get a list of followers for someone other than the authenticating user, add that member's username or ID to the request:

```
https://twitter.com/followers/ids/id.xml
```

If you don't authenticate with the API request, you'll get a message like, "Could not authenticate you."

Get All Friends

The same kind of method is available for the other half of the follow network, too. You can get a simple XML list of the user IDs of all the people you choose to follow by making a single API request:

```
https://twitter.com/friends/ids.xml
```

This method does not require authentication, unless the person whose list you want to access has a protected account.

 A good way to make use of these two social graph methods is to conduct separate lookups for user profile information for only those members your application doesn't already know about.

Follow a Member

To build your follow network, you need a method for adding a friend. This method allows you to do that, as well as to optionally add this person to your notifications list to receive their tweets on your cell phone.

 Back in the olden days of Twitter, those you followed were called "friends." That's why the API methods use the terminology "create friendships," even though on the website and elsewhere this action is now referred to as "following." The next version of the Twitter API will correct this, but thanks to backward compatibility, friends are likely to be a permanent part of Twitter programming.

To follow another user, you need to create a relationship between the authenticated user and some other user, identified with the id parameter:

```
https://twitter.com/friendships/create/id.xml
```

What comes back when this request is successful is the short-form profile information for the new friend. The request will only be successful, though, if the relationship doesn't already exist. If you try to follow someone already on your list, Twitter returns an error: "Could not follow user: id is already on your list" (see "Hash Objects" on page 209).

There is an optional parameter—follow—that lets you have a two-for-one by automatically adding your new friend to your notifications list. If this parameter is present and set to a value of true, this member will have notifications enabled so you can immediately start receiving her tweets on your cell phone. This is the same action performed by the Turn On Notification method described in "Member Account" on page 168.

There is often confusion about the difference between the Follow a Member method and the one dealing with devices (Turn On Notification). The Follow a Member method establishes the network relationship but does not by default enable notifications. Members for whom notifications are enabled (via either the follow parameter to this method or the Turn On Notification method) form a subgroup of the people you follow whose content is sent directly to your registered device (usually a cell phone).

Notifications are useful for having status updates from close friends or family members sent directly to your phone; you can stay in close contact with a select few people and follow many more users casually through the Web or third-party desktop tools.

Following another account has a few side effects. First, that person's content is included in your information stream. This happens immediately if the account is public, but only after approval if the account is protected.

If you follow a protected account, the response will be nearly identical to the one you get when following a public account. The only hint you will get that you have to wait for approval is the presence of <protected>true</protected> in the XML output.

Users with private accounts who have not approved you will still appear in your following list, even if you cannot yet see their content.

Second, most accounts are configured to send a notification when a new follower is added. This is an effective way to expand your follow network, because odds are good that someone interested in what you are tweeting will be interesting to you. Conversely, it is possible that the act of following someone will result in that person following you.

Unfollow a Member

Does your new friend tweet too much about Barney the Dinosaur? No problem. Simply unfollow that person to remove his content from your personal information stream:

```
https://twitter.com/friendships/destroy/id.xml
```

The format and response are the same as for the follow request, except you are removing rather than adding a tweep. If you are not already following that member, then Twitter sends an error: "You are not friends with the specified user" (see "Hash Objects" on page 209).

Unfollowing is one of the basic rights of a Twitter member and one of the things that makes the experience so rich. The sharing of information on Twitter is technically decoupled, so you can choose to follow someone who doesn't follow you. Although reciprocation happens frequently, it isn't a requirement in Twitter as it is in Facebook and other social networks.

> You do not get a notification when someone unfollows you. Your first clue that this has happened may be if that user then follows you again, resulting in an alert notification. For a third-party solution to this problem, read about Qwitter (*http://usequitter.com*) in "Tools for the Follow Network" on page 74.

No two information streams are alike, and the same goes for users. What might seem to you a paltry rate of tweeting could be overwhelming to someone else. Use the Unfollow a Member method to adjust your flow of status updates, and try not to take it personally when someone chooses not to follow you.

Confirm a Follow

Wading through all of the pages of your follow network lists, or even requesting profile information for another member to find out whether you're following that person, is an awkward way to investigate the connections in your follow network. Fortunately, Twitter provides a simple method that can be used to check whether one user is following another:

```
https://twitter.com/friendships/exists.xml
```

This method requires two variables —user_a and user_b—that contain the user IDs or screen names for the two Twitter members whose relationship you want to confirm. For example:

```
https://twitter.com/friendships/exists.xml?user_a=amakice&user_b=kmakice
```

If the check is successful, Twitter responds with simple output (see "Response Objects" on page 209).

If the first user is not following the second—because either the relationship or one of the users does not exist—the value of the returned field will be `false`. If the users are not included in the request, Twitter will return an error: "Two user ids or screen_names must be supplied" (see "Hash Objects" on page 209).

Since the follower relationship is not coupled (i.e., you can follow someone who doesn't follow you), the order of these two IDs is very important. In an asymmetrical relationship, you will get opposite results depending on which member is listed first as `user_a`.

Block a Member

The great thing about Twitter is that you can choose to unfollow anyone you find too annoying, too noisy, or too obsessed with the sweet, sweet taste of Edwardo's Pizza in Chicago. Sigh. Those aren't necessarily reasons to block someone, however. A block is a more serious way to distance yourself from another user.

When you block a user, you aren't blocking her from seeing your updates. A public account is still a public account. Your status updates, the list of people you follow, and your profile information all remain readily accessible to that user. However, blocking does make it impossible for that person to follow you and keeps your Twitter icon off her profile page.

 Twitter reportedly monitors blocking, so if a user receives enough blocks, that user's account will be flagged for investigation.

Blocks should not be used lightly. They are appropriate for the worst account spammers and those who may be personally harassing you. For anything else, you're only an unfollow away from peace of mind.

The API method to create a block requires authentication and inclusion of the dissed user's `id` in the request URL:

```
https://twitter.com/blocks/create/id.xml
```

If this action is successful, the short-form profile data object for the blocked user is returned.

If you block another user, that user will not be notified. Twitter is intentionally subtle in how it conveys the action back to the victim of a block: if that person tries to follow you, he will get an ambiguous error on your profile page. However, the API is much more straightforward about what has happened, providing this message: "Could not follow user: You have been blocked from following this account at the request of the user" (see "Hash Objects" on page 209).

For private accounts, of course, the de facto state is that everyone is effectively blocked. You can only include a private member's status updates in your information stream if the private account holder gives you the OK.

Remove a Block

All good things must come to an end. This, too, shall pass. What goes around comes around. Pick your colloquialism, but what I'm trying to say is: blocks aren't permanent.

You can remove a previous block on another user by using a different method in the API:

```
https://twitter.com/blocks/destroy/id.xml
```

This authenticated POST request will find the user account specified in the URL (`id`) and remove the block that prevents that person from following your status update stream. When successful, it returns the short-form profile for the specified user.

Imposing a block removes any follower relationships between the authenticated user and the victim of the block, so removing a block on someone you used to follow will not reinstate that relationship—the user will remain out of your stream until you follow her (or she tries to follow you) again. The user will not be informed that the block has been removed; she will only realize this if she's told or if she tries to follow you again and succeeds.

If you choose to follow someone whom you currently have blocked, the block will be removed automatically. You do not have to explicitly remove the block in order to follow the victim; that happens automatically with a follow request.

Communication

Twitter is not a chat client. Although the culture and the technology recognize replies, the contextual nature of each individual information stream makes it somewhat rude to carry on extended 1:1 conversations with another user whose messages may or may not be included in your other followers' information streams. For such personal communications, the direct message is your friend.

In addition to the public status update channel, Twitter provides a back channel messaging system that allows you to communicate directly with another member. This can be useful for extended exchanges, for personal questions not meant for public consumption, and to facilitate third-party applications without mucking up the information stream.

 To send messages directly to and receive messages directly from another user, you must be following each other. So, although status updates are decoupled (even for private accounts), direct messages require a mutual handshake.

This section covers the creation of new messages, the listing of sent and received messages, and the deletion of existing messages.

When successful, the communication methods return information about the Twitter messages. See "Message Objects" on page 202 for more details about the data Twitter makes available.

List Received Messages

A separate tab in the Twitter interface handles the flow of direct messages, which will occur at a much slower rate than status updates. You can set your account to send you direct message notifications via text or email, and clients such as Twitterrific use the API to bring the messages into a single information stream.

There is an API method to list all of the messages the authenticated user has received, which are returned in groups of 20:

```
https://twitter.com/direct_messages.xml
```

This method recognizes some navigation and filtering parameters to control which page you retrieve (`page`) and to look for only the most recent messages (`since`, `since_id`).

The returned list is an array of direct message data objects, each with three distinct parts. The information about the message has some overlap with the information for a status update, in that it provides a record ID, the message text, and the creation date. In addition to describing the author, though, it must also report who the recipient is. Embedded in the direct message object is the familiar short-form profile information about both the sender and the receiver of the direct message (see "Message Objects" on page 202).

Since direct messages are not as common as status updates, it is not unusual for an account to have no record of direct messages being received. In that case, the API returns an empty object in the XML (see "Response Objects" on page 209).

List Sent Messages

Twitter also lets you keep track of the direct messages you have sent. A second messaging method lets you access your outgoing message archive:

```
https://twitter.com/direct_messages/sent.xml
```

Similar to the method for listing received messages, this method returns the 20 most recent direct messages *sent* by the authenticated user. The same optional parameters (`since`, `since_id`, and `page`) are available to adjust which part of the full list of messages is pulled out of the API.

Create a Message

You can create a new direct message using a special method provided by Twitter:

```
https://twitter.com/direct_messages/new.xml
```

This method requires two parameters: the user parameter identifies who will receive your private bit of wisdom, and the text parameter *is* your private bit of wisdom. The message must be URL-encoded and is limited to the signature 140 characters. Like all requests to change the Twitter database, this method requires a POST.

If successful, Twitter returns a single direct message data object containing the same information described in the communication methods discussed earlier. Mistakes in the format of the request will result in an "Invalid request" error. Because the sender and the receiver of the message must be following each other, Twitter will return an error if that is not the case: "Can't send direct messages to users who aren't your friend" (see "Hash Objects" on page 209).

You can also send direct messages using the Post a Tweet method:

```
https://twitter.com/statuses/update.xml
```

You must start the status text with d *username* to direct the message to the person you want. This is the same function the text-based commands perform in Twitter clients.

Delete a Message

Not everyone likes to keep a permanent archive of all of the little messages they send and receive. There is no search mechanism for these messages, so it is sometimes helpful to prune out the ones you don't want to keep (assuming you want to keep any at all).

Deleting an existing direct message is as easy as using another API method:

```
https://twitter.com/direct_messages/destroy/id.xml
```

This method follows more or less the same procedures as that of a status update removal: you identify the ID of the message to be removed and authenticate using the account credentials of either the sender or the receiver. If successful, you will get the message information as a data object.

Until recently, only the receiver of a message had the power to delete it. However, you are now also able to delete messages that you yourself sent—the recipients are no longer the only ones with the power to remove your missives from the face of the Twitosphere.

 If you do decide to delete a message, understand that it will disappear from both the sender's sent message list and the receiver's received message list. There is only one copy of each direct message, and either person involved in the exchange can remove it.

You can only destroy what has first been created. If you send a request to delete a received message using an invalid ID, Twitter will let you know it can't do it: "No direct message with that ID found" (see "Hash Objects" on page 209).

Show a Message

Surprisingly, there is no method that allows you to retrieve a single direct message. One might expect something like this to work:

```
https://twitter.com/statuses/show/id.xml
https://twitter.com/direct-messages/show/id.xml
```

Attempting such a request, however, results in the following response from the API:

```
<html><body>You are being <a href="https://twitter.com/direct_messages">
    redirected</a>.</body></html>
```

That means if you want to get information on a particular message, you have to either page through the full list until you find it, or delete it and get the single direct-message data object one last time.

 The lack of functionality in this part of the API may be one reason why more applications haven't developed tools to manage direct messages.

Member Account

One area where third-party development has helped change the API is in making changes to a member's profile. Twitter added the Update Member Location method, for example, after a need for it materialized with the iPhone: developers wanted to be able to leverage the geocode information to pinpoint a user's location at any given moment, and a method was needed to facilitate this update. The creation of that method changed the value of that open text field, in turn, since it now reflected where certain users were at a particular moment in time, rather than where they chose to call home.

This section covers all the functions available through the Twitter API to help manage a Twitter member's account.

Update Member Location

For a long time, one of the few profile changes you could make through the API was to set your location. Prior to this method being added to the arsenal, the only way to change this text was to log into the Twitter website and manually edit your account settings there. That was before the iPhone, BrightKite, and other location-aware systems started integrating with Twitter.

The Update Member Location method allows you to change the location field in the authenticated user's profile through the API:

```
https://twitter.com/account/update_location.xml
```

This method has one required parameter, `location`, which contains the new text you want to place on your user profile, replacing whatever is currently in the location field.

 At the time of this writing, the location is simply text. Twitter makes no attempt to normalize the content or turn everything into geocodes or latitude and longitude values. The applications that use this method likely pass valid geocode data, but there is nothing to validate or verify it in the API.

Omitting the `location` parameter will result in the current location being reset to an empty string, rather than generating an error. The short-form user profile data object returned by the API indicates success.

 This method has been deprecated in favor of the Update Member Profile method, which contains an optional parameter for location. To keep your application from breaking in the future, you should avoid using `update_location`.

Update Member Profile

Many other bits of information are displayed on the member profile pages on the Twitter website. This method allows you to change some of that information through the API:

    https://twitter.com/account/update_profile.xml

All of the parameters for this method are related to fields found under the "Account" tab of the Settings page on the Twitter website. Only specified parameters will result in updates to the profile. A user object is returned with the new information to indicate success (see "User Objects" on page 192).

 You are supposed to include at least one parameter. However, even if you fail to do so, you will still get a user object, making the request act like an authenticated `users/show` method.

This method allows for several parameters, including `location` (to update the user's location, which used to be handled through the deprecated method discussed in the preceding section). You can also adjust the full name of the account holder (`name`), the URL pointing to a company or personal web page (`url`), the email address associated with the account (`email`), and the short text statement about the account holder (`description`). Length limits of between 40 and 160 characters are imposed, depending on the parameter.

In addition to being valid, the email address must also be unique. You cannot assign an email address to an account if it is already being used by another account.

Update Profile Colors

Although the number of tweets posted from the Twitter website has decreased to under 50% of the full archive, most active users visit the main website on a regular (perhaps even daily) basis to check out the profiles of new followers. Not surprisingly, an eye for design is on the rise. The trend began in 2008 with a Photoshop template that was virally distributed to extend the profile information by using a background image. Later that year, Twitter added themes to allow members to differentiate their web pages' appearances, even if they didn't want to go as far as designing a custom look. Every day, the visuals matter a little more.

The Update Profile Colors method lets you make changes to the color scheme used on your member page. The five available parameters are the same ones you would find under the "Design" tab on the Settings page of the main website. The "change design colors" link at the bottom of that page reveals fields to control the color of the profile background (`profile_background_color`), text (`profile_text_color`), links (`profile_link_color`), sidebar shading (`profile_sidebar_fill_color`), and border (`profile_sidebar_border_color`). This method accepts parameters to change the values of each of those fields:

```
https://twitter.com/account/update_profile_colors.xml
```

All values have to be sent as hexadecimal, either the short (fff) or long (ffffff) form. Because this method deals with changing things on the Twitter server, it requires a POST and is not charged against your rate limit. The method returns a user object with the new information (see "User Objects" on page 192).

Use the hexadecimal values only, not the hash (#) used on the website. If you include the hash, you will get an "Invalid hex color" error.

Changing the background color will not necessarily lead to that color being seen. If the account already has a background image in place, the web page will use that instead; the background image has to be removed before a change to the background color will be visible.

Twitter themes take precedence when you are editing the appearance of the profile page. Even if the API shows the account with white text, the web page may still show the theme's text color in the web form. This behavior goes away when the background image is removed.

Update Background Image

One of the early e-business ventures dealing with advertising on Twitter was Twit-tads (*http://twittads.com*). This company allows individuals to set a price for how much their Twitter profiles are worth and sell ads to display as their background images for a given period of time. This method can be used to automate that process, switching the advertising for you to make sure it gets done.

This method accepts a required `image` parameter to set the authenticating member's theme with a new background graphic:

```
https://twitter.com/account/update_profile_background_image.xml
```

The `image` parameter expects the raw multipart data as its value, not simply a URL linking to an existing file—even though that is what you get from Twitter in the user object XML that is returned (see "User Objects" on page 192). The graphic can be in GIF, JPG, or PNG format. The background image can have a maximum of 2,048 pixels and the file must be smaller than 800 KB. The file size is a firm limit, but larger pixel sizes will be scaled down to fit.

> Some initial problems with GIF formats were reported in Twitter Developers Talk discussions. You may get better results by using PNG and specifying the mime type.

The background image on a member's profile page can be displayed as a fixed image attached to the upper left corner of the browser window, or it can be tiled, which means the image is repeated again and again to fill the entire window. You currently have to go back to the website to check a box for tiling, and unless you replace it with another file through the API, visiting the site is also the only way to remove a background image. At the time of this writing, Twitter doesn't provide a way through the API to either remove a background picture or have the site tile it.

> It may be a good programming strategy for your application if you keep a local copy of the default image used by Twitter, as well as check the existing profile configurations. That way, you can easily use the API to restore the profile to its previous state.

In late 2008, Twitter Patterns (*http://twitterpatterns.com*)—a site by designer Natalie Jost of *olivemanna*—launched with a gallery of high-quality downloadable background images for users to upload to Twitter. Although as of this writing no tools are available to create custom themes, it isn't much of a leap to believe that these newest API methods that facilitate changing the design of Twitter profile pages will lead to support for such tools in 2009.

This book's sample applications don't cover interacting with the image methods (that coverage may come in the next edition), but here is a quick command-line request using cURL that might give you a hint about how to make the `update_profile_background_image` and `update_profile_image` methods work:

```
curl -k -F 'image=@filename.jpg;type=image/jpeg' -u
yourusername:yourpassword -H 'Expect:'
https://twitter.com/account/update_profile_image.xml
```

The important part here is -F section, which allows the raw data to be sucked out of a graphics file (*@filename*.jpg) and POSTed to the Twitter method. For more information about using cURL from the command line, see "Play Along at Home" on page 149.

Update Profile Image

Twitter also provides a method to change your profile image (the picture shown with your tweets). As is the case with the Update Background Image method, this method requires an `image` parameter:

```
https://twitter.com/account/update_profile_image.xml
```

The profile picture is usually quite a bit smaller than the background image for the member profile page, and thus it has smaller maximum values: the GIF, JPG, or PNG file can have a maximum of 500 pixels and must be smaller than 700 KB. Larger pixel dimensions will be scaled down, but bigger files are rejected. Twitter typically stores three versions of every profile picture: the full-sized picture uploaded by the user; the big version used on the profile page (with a `_bigger` suffix); and the regular version (with a `_normal` suffix) for display with each tweet.

Most errors are trapped and explained with a vague message: "There was a problem with your picture. Probably too big." (See "Hash Objects" on page 209.) Look for a status code of 200 to let you know whether you were successful. You can also check the website; the image changes are immediate, if successful.

Even before another Twitter member reads your status update, chances are he's looking at your Twitter avatar. This visual reminder of who you are is helpful when your readers are scanning through dozens of tweets at a time looking for something you wrote. The ability to create new programs to manage changes to this important part of your profile is a huge advancement for developers and for the people who will use their new tools. In my opinion, this particular addition to the Twitter API has the greatest potential to have an impact on Twitter culture and behavior.

Update the Delivery Device

Another configuration setting handled through the API is where you want status updates from the people you follow to be sent:

```
https://twitter.com/account/update_delivery_device.xml
```

This method requires one parameter, `device`, which can contain one of only three possible options: once set, the authenticated user will be configured to receive status updates as text messages on a cell phone (`sms`), via a chat client (`im`), or neither (`none`).

 In 2008, Twitter officially discontinued support of IM, which had been disabled for several months prior to the decision. It is not expected back in the foreseeable future, rendering the `im` value meaningless.

Routing your Twitter information stream through your mobile phone is an acquired taste. For some people, this is the only interface they use. For others, phone notifications provide a way to filter down the larger following list to just a handful of closely watched friends (as described in the next section).

The API response for a successful edit of the delivery device is the short-form profile data object for the authenticating user (see "User Objects" on page 192). If you omit the required parameters or pass along a value that isn't one of the approved devices (say, `device=cow`), an error will be returned: "You must specify a parameter named 'device' with a value of one of: sms, im, none" (see "Hash Objects" on page 209).

Turn On/Off Notification

If you decide you do want your information streamed to your cell phone, Twitter lets you customize which members of your following list are included:

```
https://twitter.com/notifications/follow/id.xml
```

This method will enable the notification setting for the *individual* user identified in `id` and will start sending that user's status updates to the device set with the Update the Delivery Device method.

 Obviously, if the device setting is not `sms`, these individual notification settings are ignored.

Success is once again signified with XML containing the specified user's short-form profile. If you attempt to add notifications for a user you do not follow, or one for whom you have already enabled them, an error will be reported: "There was a problem following the specified user" (see "Hash Objects" on page 209).

The evil twin to this method is Turn Off Notification, which disables notifications for the user identified in the request URL:

```
https://twitter.com/notifications/leave/id.xml
```

Device notification toggles can cover receipt of direct messages, too. There are two criteria for receiving direct messages from a specific user on your phone: you must have included that user in your notifications list by turning on notification, *and* direct messages must be selected in the Devices tab in the Settings section of the Twitter website. This latter control is buried in a pull-down menu that appears only after you successfully register your cell phone number with your Twitter account.

 Enabling and disabling notifications for a user is not the same as following or unfollowing that user. Rather, by setting up notifications you can essentially designate a subgroup of the larger list of people you follow (unless you include everyone) whose content you specifically want delivered to your phone as SMS messages.

API Administration

Yes, sending updates and messages to your many followers is fun, but sometimes you need to deal with "the meta," or the info about the info. This section covers all the administrative and technical functions available through the Twitter API to help manage the application you are trying to debug.

Test

Sometimes coding is a nightmare. Things don't work, and you don't know why. When that happens, it helps to step back and check whether all your equipment is properly connected. Twitter helps you do this with a simple API method to ping the system:

```
https://twitter.com/help/test.xml
```

This method does nothing except return a simple string—an appropriate HTTP status code along with a Boolean (see "Response Objects" on page 209).

If you get a status code of 200, the problem is likely buried somewhere in your code. If you get an HTTP error, stop deconstructing your programming skills and figure out what's keeping you from the API.

Verify Credentials

One of the more helpful methods to incorporate into your application is the credentials check:

```
https://twitter.com/account/verify_credentials.xml
```

This method returns a 200 status code if the username and password you plan to use with other methods is valid. The XML response is a user object for the authenticating user (see "User Objects" on page 192).

This is a prime example of why checking the HTTP status code is a good idea. At the end of 2008, Twitter changed the output from a simple response object (`<authorized>true</authorized>`) to a full user profile. If your code was looking for that text at the time, the program probably started acting like the account didn't verify.

If your authentication doesn't work, for whatever reason, Twitter will let you know with an error message: "Could not authenticate you" (see "Hash Objects" on page 209).

Although you could figure out whether your username and password work simply by trying any method that requires authentication, this method is the preferred way of verifying credentials. It has less overhead than most of the other methods and is easier to use in the code logic.

Check Rate Limit Status

One of the other obstacles your application may encounter—especially if you expect to perform many data requests in rapid succession—is the error that says you have been cut off:

```
Rate limit exceeded. Clients may not make more than
    100 requests per hour
```

When that happens, you are at the mercy of the clock. The API won't give you the things you want until the hour is up, leaving you and your users hanging.

Twitter created a method specifically to check on the status of your rate limit, providing a great tool to help you anticipate the problem and manage how your application will deal with the bad news:

```
https://twitter.com/account/rate_limit_status.xml
```

This method returns a short data object filled with numbers and dates (see "Hash Objects" on page 209) that will tell you how long you have to wait until you can start making API requests again. A common coding strategy is to check the rate limit status once at the beginning of the application run, and then keep a counter going to let PHP know when to stop bugging the API for data. This approach enables you to gracefully pause or halt the application before bumping into the error from Twitter.

This method doesn't require authentication, but even if you do authenticate the request it does *not* count against the rate limit for the account you are checking. If you don't provide user credentials, it returns the tally for the requesting IP address.

Remember, yours is not likely to be the only application making use of a given user account. Clients such as Twitterrific, TweetDeck, and Twhirl function by hitting the API with each individual account.

It is good practice to follow a credentials check (Verify Credentials) with an initial rate limit check. If the account is already spent for the hour, you can gracefully exit the program and ask the user to try again later. Otherwise, you can count down the remaining hits to the API and let the user know, once the limit is hit, that the processing will take a while.

Heavy request applications can use a direct message to send a new URL to the user as the last action when a long-running job has finished processing.

End a Member Session

For applications that manage user sessions—which are typical of publishing clients—Twitter created a method to clean up the access and make sure the authenticated user is logged out:

```
https://twitter.com/account/end_session.xml
```

Success is reported with the following XML message: "Logged out" (see "Hash Objects" on page 209).

Search

One of the more successful third-party development projects to make use of the Twitter API was Summize. This company, which began collecting data in spring 2008, created a search engine specifically for exploring the millions of tweets passing through Twitter each week. Summize also created its own API, which in turn spawned a few interesting new applications that tried to make sense of the Twitter content.

Summize was so good at what it did that Twitter acquired the company a few months after its launch. Now, Summize's search API is being integrated into the original Twitter API as part of an overhaul of the system. At present, the Twitter search API is still effectively separate from the original Twitter API, as it was created under different rules. There are a number of nuanced differences that should go away with the next version of the Twitter API.

The methods described in this book are expected to continue to function for at minimum six months after the release of the next version of the API, sometime in mid-2009.

The Twitter search API does not support XML. For the purposes of this book, we will use Atom as a substitute format.

This section deals with the Twitter Keyword Search method and the many optional parameters used to shape the results. We'll also take a look at the Monitor Trends method.

Keyword Search

Ignoring for the moment the means by which you make the request, searching with the API is very similar to conducting any search through a website. You need to know what keywords you want to find and how you want the results returned to you.

 Twitter doesn't limit use of the search API. It does monitor for abuse, however, and reacts to unusual activity on a case-by-case basis. If you encounter errors you can't explain, contact Twitter to investigate.

The request method for tweet searches uses a slightly different URL, with the required q parameter added to the end as an encoded string:

```
http://search.twitter.com/search.atom?q=query
```

That q parameter is very powerful. Depending on what you put into it, it can be a great filter for the tweet corpus. Each query string has to be encoded for travel in the GET request.

Content searches. The query string can contain multiple keywords and symbols that are matched against tweet content. The most general of these is a standard keyword search. For example, if I want to find all of the many, many fans of the Chicago Bears during a big game, I can search for "Go Bears":

```
http://search.twitter.com/search.atom?q=Go+Bears
```

The query string can also look for the special formatting patterns Twitter uses to interpret tweets as replies. Any authors referencing the user "aboy" will likely use the convention "@aboy" in the body of the tweet content, and all other messages can be filtered out with this query:

```
http://search.twitter.com/search.atom?q=%40aboy
```

 Even though the servers have no problem doing so, URL encoding of special characters can be difficult for humans to read. Here are a few symbols used in Twitter searches, with their encoded forms:

- @ is encoded as %40
- # is encoded as %23
- ? is encoded as %3F
- : is encoded as %3A

There is no special handling of a hash (#) in the way that @ signifies a reply, but Twitter does recognize the tagging convention in its advanced searches. The hashtag (#) is a convention imported from IRC and other Twitter ancestors to group content with other messages on the same topic. Its whole reason for being is to facilitate searching, tying similar content together. When the Bears again return to the Super Bowl, I can create a stream of tweets by searching for #superbowl:

```
http://search.twitter.com/search.atom?q=%23superbowl
```

It is certain to be a very long list...next year.

 #Hashtags tend to make #reading #tweets difficult and consume precious characters. Fortunately for my eyes, not everyone uses them. There is no #meta #channel, however, that would allow #you to #tag your tweets. #necessaryevil #hate #rant

Another common structure of interest to searchers is whether or not the tweet contains a question. Twitter will scan tweets for the presence of a ?, returning only status updates that contain that character. For example, this search looks for instances of Twitter members questioning existence:

```
http://search.twitter.com/search.atom?q=existence+%3F
```

One of the more innovative searches is for emoticons, such as :) and :(, that are often included in status updates to reflect the author's mood. Including emoticons in the search request causes the API to return an interesting collection of statements that share an emotional state:

```
http://search.twitter.com/search.atom?q=sometimes+%3A)
http://search.twitter.com/search.atom?q=sometimes+%3A(
```

Meta filters.   Content searches like these look only at what is in the tweet, not at the meta descriptions of the status updates. The advanced search in Twitter interprets several special formats of the query string to examine the network, location, composition, and creation date.

Every Twitter author updates her status from some location in the world. This reported location may be very accurate—smart phones can update geographic information as the user travels—or it may just be wherever the user initially set for her account location. A location is assigned to every tweet and can be leveraged in web search with the `near:` and `within:` filters to pinpoint tweets originating from a particular area:

```
http://search.twitter.com/search?q=slouching+near%3Abethlehem
http://search.twitter.com/search?q=pizza+near%3ABloomington%2C+Indiana+within%3A1mi
```

The Search API no longer recognizes these location filters, requiring the `geocode` parameter instead. Twitter searches also easily identify tweets containing links, which make up a sizeable chunk of the corpus. Sometimes the published links are intentional, placed there purposely to direct readers to some interesting resource on the Web. In many cases, they are added automatically as part of integration with some other system, such as BrightKite. Using `filter:links`, you can filter a keyword search to return only the tweets containing links:

```
http://search.twitter.com/search.atom?q=fluffy+kitten+filter%3Alinks
```

The time and date a link was published are also search fodder. You've already seen how to use the `since:` filter as a parameter (`since`) in the original Twitter API methods. This filter identifies a specific point in time and asks the search API to return only matching tweets published after that date. Although there is no matching Twitter API parameter, searches can also look on the other side of that date using the `until:` filter. That will cause only the relevant tweets published before the specified date to be returned:

```
http://search.twitter.com/search.atom?q=Fail+Whale+since%3A2008-09-01
http://search.twitter.com/search.atom?q=olympics+until%3A2008-08-08
```

 The date filters accept the yyyy-mm-dd format.

Twitter makes an attempt to thread some tweets together using the @ reply convention. By virtue of this network of replies, the average twitterer can be connected to many individual tweets. You can get a list of those tweets by using `from:` and `to:` to identify a username:

```
http://search.twitter.com/search.atom?q=from%3Ahere
http://search.twitter.com/search.atom?q=to%3Aeternity
```

 Replies retrieved by a `from:`*username* search will not include any such user references occurring later in the tweet. Twitter recognizes the @*username* convention as signaling a reply only if it appears at the start of the message. For example, "@tilla rampages across the plain" is a reply, but "You are so rampaging across the plain, @tilla" is not.

This behavior will likely change as more people make use of the `in_reply_to_status_id` field Twitter added to the API in 2008.

Operators. Twitter searches accept more traditional operators, too. The default for a multikeyword search is to look for tweets containing instances of all the keywords listed, but the keywords don't have to appear next to each other or in the order given. This probably isn't a problem if the keywords are unusual, but for more common words the proximity may be important. Fortunately, it's also possible to specify an exact phrase to search for. These two searches return different results because of the exclusion and inclusion of wrapping quotes:

```
http://search.twitter.com/search.atom?q=Fail+Whale
http://search.twitter.com/search.atom?q="Fail+Whale"
```

To be more inclusive and look for tweets containing either "Fail" or "Whale," include the Boolean operator OR between the keywords as part of the query string. This will expand on the first search and probably include tweets about failing a test and tweets about Greenpeace:

```
http://search.twitter.com/search.atom?q=Fail+OR+Whale
```

Sometimes a search word is too ambiguous; the tweets returned may match the same word, but used in different contexts. If for some reason you wanted to search for status updates involving bears, but not the great professional football team from Chicago, you could do so by specifying which additional terms to ignore in combination with "bears." You would do this by using the - sign as a prefix to the offending words:

```
http://search.twitter.com/search.atom?q=Bears+-Chicago
```

Details on all of these content searches, meta filters, and operators can be found in the advanced search interface on the Twitter Search site.

Incidentally, if the q parameter is empty, the search API will still return content—albeit just the header information (see "Search Objects" on page 205).

Optional parameters. In addition to the query string, the Keyword Search method accepts a number of optional parameters to help refine the search or adjust the way the results are returned. Some of these will be familiar to you from previous methods or from our examination of query string variations, and others will be new.

The standard Twitter parameters for navigation (page) and for pruning tweets to include only the most recent ones (since_id) operate in the same way as described earlier for other methods. The page size, however, is set by the rpp parameter, which indicates how many tweets should be returned per page. The maximum number allowed is 100, and the default is 16. You can change the size of this parameter depending on whether you want to display matches (smaller pages) or mine the corpus and save the results into a database (bigger pages).

Of growing use and importance is the geocode parameter. As iPhones propagate and location-centric tools grow in popularity, searches of Twitter content by location will increase. This optional parameter accepts specified values of latitude, longitude, and the radius of interest (in mi or km), and returns only the tweets written by authors whose locations match:

```
http://search.twitter.com/search.atom?geocode=31.12345%2C-88.98765%2C1km
```

This can no longer be done with the near: filter described earlier for web search. The Search API requires the geocode parameter to indicate location. It is often easier to post these search options as separate parameters rather than dealing with encoded multi-parameter query strings.

The lang parameter accepts standard ISO 639-1 codes to indicate which languages should be included in the search results. This can be helpful, for example, to conduct English (en) or Spanish (es) language searches separately.

The content itself can be adjusted, too. When set to **true**, the `show_user` parameter will add *username:* to the start of every tweet. The reason for doing this is primarily a need to display who published what when, giving these results to the end user.

 There is also a `callback` option intended for JSON development with JavaScript programming. The callback is a development feature that allows better integration with client-side applications. Since this book doesn't work with JSON, we won't go into details; just know that the search API does accommodate JavaScript developers.

When the search API returns results in the Atom format, the list of entries is wrapped in a feed object that provides information about the conditions of the search, including when it was done and links to duplicate it. Details about each matched tweet are encapsulated in an entry element (see "Search Objects" on page 205).

Monitor Trends

Finally, the Twitter API includes a method that returns the top 10 descriptive keywords that are currently being used on Twitter. The response includes the time of the request, the name of each trending topic, and the URL to the Twitter search results page for that topic. Currently, the only supported format for this method is JSON. The `callback` parameter is supported, however.

The request URL for this method is:

```
http://search.twitter.com/trends.json
```

 Twitter continues to evolve. New methods will be added to the API in the future, some of which will be created as replacements for some of the functions discussed in this chapter. Since an API provider's work is never done, these methods will continue to evolve. It is a good idea to routinely check the Twitter API wiki (*http://apiwiki.twitter.com*) for new information. In the next chapter, we'll take a closer look at the information that comes from making these requests to the API.

Other Data Options

There are a few other ways to get data out of Twitter, when the data flow coming out of the regular API is not fast enough.

The first option is to use the data mining feed, established specifically to help academics collect a large chunk of data more quickly than was possible with the View the Public Timeline method (see "The Information Stream" on page 152). The data mining feed caches 600 tweets every minute, expanding on what the public feed already provides.

There is no cost involved, but access to the feed is available only upon request. Researchers have to first provide a description of their projects and specify the IP addresses (you can submit more than one) where the API requests will originate. This information is sent in an email to *api@twitter.com*.

The shortcoming of the data mining feed is that it just provides more data, not a complete list of everything being published. For that, Twitter will begin offering the "firehose," a stream of all public status updates on Twitter. Starting in 2009, this HTTP-push option will be made available to a select group of trusted projects, to test how it affects the stability of the service. Partners will be added on a case-by-case basis. Eventually, the firehose should support streams generated by a group of users; for example, you could connect to get near real-time tweets published by local members living in your hometown.

 Neither of these options—the data mining feed or the firehose—include the private tweets published by authors with protected accounts. Authentication and permission from the author (in the form of acceptance of your follow request) is the only way to get this protected data out of the API.

One more way to get high-volume tweet data is through Gnip (*http://gnipcentral.com*), a paid service that powers data streams for sites like MyBlogLog and Plaxo on the consumer end. Gnip is a pinging service, which means it contacts your application whenever the data you are interested in shows up in the stream. Twitter provides its public stream to Gnip, which means you can pay Gnip to get access to that data.

Gone Phishing: A Word About Passwords

One weakness of the Twitter API is its reliance on individual usernames and passwords to be able to access the gooey caramel center of Twitter data. In the winter of 2008–2009, a couple of incidents generated a lot of conversation about how authentication is used with the API.

In November 2008, Twitterank (*http://twitterank.com*) launched, jumping into a sea of existing Twitter applications. Like some other projects at the time, its purpose was to try to quantify Twitter members, this time by applying the PageRank algorithm (the Twitterank developer worked at Google). Twitterank's reach spread quickly in the form of self-promoting tweets published by the web application as each new member looked up her ratings. It didn't do anything more than show you a number, though (your Twitter rank); there was no explanation, attribution, or much effort put into inspiring confidence through design.

The backlash was quick and angry. People started complaining about the viral posts, not realizing they had granted permission to tweet by default. Fueled by Oliver Marks's article about user gullibility on ZDNet (see "Twitterank" on page 72), a witch hunt began, 140 characters at a time. Passwords were changed. The programmer responded[*] by devoting much of the next few days to quickly iterating the site to regain some credibility. In the end, Twitterank proved not to be a phishing site; it was just a fumbled launch to another Twitter development project.

Fast-forward about two months to the start of the new year. One day after launch, another startup application, twply (*http://www.twply.com*), was quickly auctioned on SitePoint for about $1,200. This came about after some 800 people had willingly entered their usernames and passwords into the new site, which promised to turn @*username* replies into emails.[†] Within days, a phishing scam propagated through the Twitosphere in the form of direct messages suggesting that friends follow a link to a site. This site was a replica of the Twitter login page, inviting users to submit their Twitter access information. Many speculated that this was all related, although the DNS address of the Twitter phishing site was registered to a location in China.[‡] Throw in a separate incident involving hacking of some celebrity accounts, and the Twitter community was a bit shaken.

Blogger Louis Gray posted a great reflection about the Twitterank panic, speculating on some worst-case scenarios for a successful phishing expedition on Twitter:

> The downsides of somebody hacking into my Twitter account and getting my credentials are low to begin with. In theory, if my account were compromised, they could Tweet on my behalf and make me look like a fool for some time, until I managed to get to Twitter support. In the meantime, you'd be sure to hear about it, and I assume others would be vocal in my favor. Another concern would be if you or I used the same login and password combination on other services. The perpetrator could then guess your ID on other services, or even access your financial records or anything else sensitive. But again, given the other Twitter developers' comments in regards to OAuth, I tend to believe this is something the coders are working around, and I don't think this is a mass account grab.[§]

I bring up all of this because it is vital that you, as a budding Twitter developer, be aware of both the cultural and technical implications of asking for someone's Twitter credentials to use your application.

Due to the way the API was developed during its first few years, there is sometimes a functional need to have individual users provide their usernames and passwords. Authentication in the API is currently used for two purposes:

---

[*] From the November 13, 2008 blog article "Some follow up...", by Ryo Chijiiwa, published on the Twitterank blog (*http://twitterank.wordpress.com/2008/11/13/some-follow-up/*).

[†] From the January 9, 2009 blog article "The Curious Case of Twitter and Twply," by Joshua Porter, published on Bokardo (*http://bokardo.com/archives/the-curious-case-of-twply-and-twitter/*).

[‡] From the January 3, 2009 blog article "Phishing Scam Spreading on Twitter," by Chris Pirillo (*http://chris.pirillo.com/phishing-scam-spreading-on-twitter/*).

[§] From the November 12, 2008 blog article "Twitterank Can Have My Password, No Questions Asked," by Louis Gray (*http://www.louisgray.com/live/2008/11/twitterank-can-have-my-password-no.html*).

- To impose rate limits on a given account (something that is also handled through IP addresses, in the absence of authentication to some of the more open methods)
- To grant access to data that is otherwise not open to the public, namely changes to the content or settings of the account and viewing private member status updates

Although the *twishing* (Twitter phishing) meme lit a fire under the debate, the fact remains that hundreds of applications built using the API have had to deal with this issue of users providing their credentials (sometimes referred to as an "anti-pattern"). This isn't something new, nor does it have to be crippling. However, what's at stake does need to be understood.

Is Twishing Worth the Effort?

The list of things you can do with someone's Twitter account information seems long. In practice, however, it is quite limited. Most of the content you can see when you log into the website is already available through the API without authenticating, and the things an imposter might change are mostly harmless. A hacker with stolen authentication could certainly annoy, and assuming the darkest intent, there are some security holes that might be attractive.

 Several of the changes that can be made to your account can be done through the Twitter API, at the same time that your username and password are being compromised. That means that a strategy of changing your password immediately after testing a new web application won't necessarily prevent damage from being done. It's always a matter of trust.

The things one can do to a compromised Twitter account fall into a number of categories: I'll call them Controlling, Invading, Stealthing, Screaming, Damaging, Annoying, and Deceiving. In the lists in the following sections, I've indicated the functionality that is available only through the Twitter website, not through the API.

Controlling

The most obvious thing a hacker can do is deny you access to your own Twitter account. There are failsafes, however, in the form of Twitter's great customer service and a historical willingness to help people reclaim their identities. Twitter keeps backups of your data, so even if you are blocked out for a day, there is nothing irreparable about it. Also, Twitter allows only one user account per email address, making this an unattractive target.

Malicious actions in this category include:

- Changing your Twitter password [web-only]

- Changing the email address associated with your account (the same address cannot be used for another account)

 A caveat: the reality is that many people use the same username and password for all of their various logins. If you do this, a phisher could use your Twitter account details to access whatever funds are in your bank account. It's always a good idea to use very different credentials for each of your more sensitive online accounts.

Invading

Some information isn't available without your Twitter authentication. For example, if your account is compromised, people who protect their accounts and trust you enough to allow you to follow what they post will be vulnerable to the imposter coming in and capturing their tweets.

 This might be a good argument to eliminate the "protected" account option altogether. Technically, nothing shared is ever private.

Among the account settings, the most appealing bit of information is probably the phone number you use for your mobile updates. This could be a personal number that might not be widely distributed or even published elsewhere. A hacker could also access all of the private messages you have exchanged with others in your group. If you aren't in the practice of deleting them, those messages might contain sensitive information about you or those with whom you converse.

Malicious actions in this category include:

- Viewing direct messages you've sent and received
- Viewing the timelines of protected account holders you follow
- Viewing the mobile phone number you use for updates (if configured) [web-only]

Stealthing

Other changes a hacker could make are hidden from view. In mass, compromised accounts could be scanned for blocks on a spammer account, which could then be removed to force the users to follow that account. Not many people use favorites on Twitter, nor do these bookmarks have much value yet for third-party developers. However, if that changes, a hacker could target a few preferred tweets with marketing links and make sure they appear on everyone's favorites list.

These actions are difficult to monitor, especially since they can all take place through API interactions, without the account holder knowing what is happening.

Actions in this category include:

- Removing a block on another member
- Favoriting a tweet
- Removing a favorited tweet

Screaming

Of course, some attacks can be quite visible, such as the January 2009 hacks that posted prank status updates to the timelines of a couple of dozen Twitter celebrities.[||]

Less obvious but equally visible would be gaining access to the compromised member's profile page to upload a new avatar or background image. The hacker could also make changes to the web link or description stored in the member profile, or even change your profile picture (although that is much more likely to be noticed, and thus quickly corrected). Unless you visit your own profile web page regularly, you might not notice other changes to your page.

Malicious actions in this category include:

- Changing user profile info, such as your description, web link, and full name
- Posting a status update
- Uploading a different avatar picture
- Mucking with the theme design, color scheme, or background image of your Twitter profile web page
- Changing your location

Damaging

An authenticated user can remove content. Deleting a recent public tweet may or may not be noticed, but odds are much greater that direct messages and old tweets won't be reviewed as frequently. There isn't much incentive for a phisher to do this—it's the electronic equivalent of knocking down someone's mailbox as you drive by. Presumably, Twitter could restore everything to an earlier state and fix the damage.

What might be more difficult to restore is damage to a reputation. For example, a specific member could be targeted with a massive blocking campaign using a number of stolen accounts, causing some reputation problems or damaging relationships.

Malicious actions in this category include:

- Deleting a published tweet

[||] This particular hack was not the result of phishing. The celebrity accounts were compromised thanks to a Twitter employee's poorly chosen password, cracked in a dictionary attack. More information can be found in the January 6, 2009 blog article "Weak Password Brings 'Happiness' to Twitter Hacker" by Kim Zetter, published in *Wired* (*http://blog.wired.com/27bstroke6/2009/01/professed-twitt.html*).

- Blocking another member
- Deleting an existing direct message
- Changing your follow network by following or unfollowing people

Annoying

If you targeted a specific user, an action such as turning off device notifications—or scheduling them to only show up at 2 a.m.—might be disruptive enough to cost that person sleep or make him miss a big meeting. Most of the changes in this category, however, are merely annoyances that would probably damage Twitter's reputation more than the individual.

Malicious actions in this category include:

- Toggling on or off the private status of the account [web-only]
- Changing the device used for notifications
- Changing whether direct messages are the only messages sent to the device [web-only]
- Changing the sleep settings that temporarily disable device notifications during certain hours (e.g., at night while you're sleeping) [web-only]
- Adjusting the notification settings, which include when you get email, what kinds of replies you see, and whether you want to be "nudged" after a period of inactivity [web-only]

Deceiving

If there is one truly scary thing about a compromised Twitter account, it probably isn't to do with posting to the public timeline or messing with account settings. The biggest weapon available to a hacker in a compromised account is trust.

The New Year's phishing problems in early 2009 are a prime example of what can happen when someone communicates with your friends through direct messages. The probability that someone you know will click on a link because they think the recommendation is coming from you is quite high. A direct message is dripping with trust by definition, since the victim has chosen to follow you, and direct messages are comparatively rare and therefore stand out.

There's only one malicious action in this category, but it's a biggie:

- Sending a direct message

OAuth Can Help

The API team has been working for a while on ways to improve the authentication scheme used to access Twitter data. The protocol talked about most often is OAuth, a way to secure API authorization with simple methods called by desktop and web applications.

 Twitter is expected to fully implement and support OAuth by the middle of 2009. The current system (HTTP Basic Auth) will go away in 2010.

OAuth is the product of a collaboration between former Twitter architect Blaine Cook (*@blaine*) and Chris Messina (*@chrismessina*), who spent the first part of 2007 trying to implement OpenID in the Twitter API. Others got involved as the group moved on to a review of industry authentication practices in systems such as Flickr, Amazon, and AOL. Finding no standard, they collaborated to write one. OAuth Core 1.0 was drafted in October 2007.

OAuth is a safer way for users to give applications access to the data and tools accessible via an API. User passwords don't have to be spread around the Web, and developers can request only the access they need. This creates greater transparency about what each web application might do, and it also leads to less recklessness by users now in a position to be deliberate with the permissions they share.

The best analogy for this authentication scheme is the valet key:

> Many luxury cars today come with a valet key. It is a special key you give the parking attendant and unlike your regular key, will not allow the car to drive more than a mile or two. Some valet keys will not open the trunk, while others will block access to your onboard cell phone address book. Regardless of what restrictions the valet key imposes, the idea is very clever. You give someone limited access to your car with a special key, while using your regular key to unlock everything.#

The user has control over that key, granting access on Twitter to the other third-party sites requesting specific kinds of allowable actions. With OAuth, you don't share your identity; you only share some of your content or details. For more information about OAuth, visit *http://oauth.net*.

What OAuth *won't* do is protect people from themselves. It isn't a cure-all. Phishing wasn't invented on Twitter in 2009, after all. A phishing attack is an intentional, widespread attack that uses trust and carelessness as its weapons. I don't want to downplay Twitter's role in its phishing issues, but the worst thing that happened to people's Twitter accounts was that some messages were delivered on their behalf by impersonators. Human nature did the rest.

From "What is it for?" on *http://oauth.net/about*.

That said, the popularity of Twitter web applications, coupled with a growing acceptance that giving away your account credentials is normal practice, makes phishing on Twitter that much easier. We are being trained to share our access details, and ultimately that is what disturbs some people most.

 OAuth *will not stop phishing attacks*. Attempts to gain usernames and passwords through deception are problems that plague any popular system, from Facebook to PayPal to your local bank. OAuth can give access away to malicious systems; it just does so with more granularity over which parts of the account someone else can access.

Twitter will help improve the situation by taking steps to reduce the need for such authentication. In fact, that's already happening. Third-party developers can help, too, by working their code away from situations where they need to ask for users' passwords. Developers can also help the greater Twitter community by assuming some responsibility for the quality of the tools they release into the world.

 The suite of sample applications described in this book *does* ask for passwords. The code is meant to be "instructional, not productional." As you use it to help you build your own web applications, keep these issues of security and trust in mind.

CHAPTER 5

Meet the Output

 kmakice You give and give and give. Let Twitter return the favor.

In the previous chapter, we looked at all the wonderful ways you can send commands to the Twitter API. Now, what are those commands going to do for you? For starters, Twitter will give you lots of useful data. In this chapter, we'll take a closer look at the stuff Twitter sends back to you in answer to your requests for data.

The Twitter API supports different formats (*.xml*, *.json*, *.rss*, and *.atom*), but for this book I will use the custom XML format provided by Twitter (*.xml*). You could use *.json* instead, and it would work just as well. One format isn't appreciably better than the other; they're just different. It's a matter of personal choice, and I chose XML.

 One exception is with applications using the Search method. The search API returns results using Atom, a particular variation of XML.

XML uses semantic tags to wrap up the data in a way that is easy to extract. The format is useful in separating the data layer from the presentation layer, so the same information can be rendered on a computer or cell phone screen in whatever way works best for that device.

 Unless you are specifically looking for the data returned by Twitter, it is better practice to look at the HTTP status code returned from the request. A code of 200 always indicates success. Response objects can and *will* change, but the status codes are less likely to fluctuate.

User Objects

Despite all the interest in the content being generated in the timeline, Twitter is primarily about people. Those with small, undeveloped networks tend to tweet less on average than those who follow more people. Every time someone posts a status update, it is an act of connection. Knowing something about who is at the other end of that ping helps people build stronger relationships.

The API returns two variations of the *user data object*, which consists of a series of XML elements containing information about a given Twitter member. The first variation is the *short-form* user object. This nested set of elements contains the core information provided by Twitter to describe an individual user. Some methods will return only one member profile, whereas other methods return lists of many people, wrapped in a **users** array element (see Example 5-1). The short-form user object is also embedded in each status object, so when you request a status update you can get the same basic information about the author of a tweet without needing to make a separate request for that data.

Example 5-1. Short-form profiles for multiple users

```
<users type="array">
<user>
  <id>15916583</id>
  <name>Soxblagforaday</name>
  <screen_name>Soxblagforaday</screen_name>
  <location></location>
  <description></description>
  <profile_image_url>http://static.twitter.com/images/default_profile_normal.png
    </profile_image_url>
  <url></url>
  <protected>false</protected>
  <followers_count>3</followers_count>
  <status>
    <created_at>Wed Aug 20 20:37:33 +0000 2008</created_at>
    <id>893662791</id>
    <text>Russell stikes out LaHair to end the game and complete the 3-game sweep.
      Ten homers in the series as we outscore the M's 33-8.</text>
    <source>web</source>
    <truncated>false</truncated>
    <in_reply_to_status_id></in_reply_to_status_id>
    <in_reply_to_user_id></in_reply_to_user_id>
    <in_reply_to_screen_name></in_reply_to_screen_name>
    <favorited>false</favorited>
  </status>
</user>
<user>
  <id>17545521</id>
  <name>John Newfry</name>
  <screen_name>jnewfry</screen_name>
  <location>Chicago</location>
  <description>IT Project Manager, baseball fan, poker player and
    Chicagoan</description>
```

```
<profile_image_url>http://s3.amazonaws.com/twitter_production/
   profile_images/67248323/3094417045_995c3bf288_normal.jpg</profile_image_url>
<url></url>
<protected>false</protected>
<followers_count>13</followers_count>
<status>
  <created_at>Tue Feb 03 16:34:05 +0000 2009</created_at>
  <id>1173367898</id>
  <text>I'm attending Chicago Startup Weekend -- http://tinyurl.com/7ztjjc</text>
  <source>web</source>
  <truncated>false</truncated>
  <in_reply_to_status_id></in_reply_to_status_id>
  <in_reply_to_user_id></in_reply_to_user_id>
  <favorited>false</favorited>
  <in_reply_to_screen_name></in_reply_to_screen_name>
</status>
</user>
</users>
```

The second variation is the *detailed* user object. This is what is returned when you use the API to request a member's full profile: the short-form information is augmented with more statistics, account configuration settings, and details on customization of the user's web profile (see Example 5-2). It is important to note that although you can get the number of followers a person has from a short-form user object, in order to get the other key profile statistics—e.g., the number of status updates posted, the count of people that author is following, or the number of bookmarked tweets—you have to request the full profile.

Example 5-2. Detailed user profile

```
<user>
  <id>14067832</id>
  <name>anonymous</name>
  <screen_name>anonymous_</screen_name>
  <location>Nowhere</location>
  <description>Academic R and D</description>
  <profile_image_url>http://static.twitter.com/images/default_profile_normal.png
    </profile_image_url>
  <url></url>
  <protected>false</protected>
  <followers_count>2</followers_count>
  <profile_background_color>8B542B</profile_background_color>
  <profile_text_color>333333</profile_text_color>
  <profile_link_color>9D582E</profile_link_color>
  <profile_sidebar_fill_color>EADEAA</profile_sidebar_fill_color>
  <profile_sidebar_border_color>D9B17E</profile_sidebar_border_color>
  <friends_count>2</friends_count>
  <created_at>Sun Mar 02 06:29:16 +0000 2008</created_at>
  <favourites_count>0</favourites_count>
  <utc_offset>-18000</utc_offset>
  <time_zone>Eastern Time (US &amp; Canada)</time_zone>
  <profile_background_image_url>
    http://static.twitter.com/images/themes/theme8/bg.gif
  </profile_background_image_url>
```

```
<profile_background_tile>false</profile_background_tile>
<following>false</following>
<notifications>false</notifications>
<statuses_count>2</statuses_count>
<status>
   <created_at>Tue Jan 20 15:28:14 +0000 2009</created_at>
   <id>1133385028</id>
   <text>testing</text>
   <source>web</source>
   <truncated>false</truncated>
   <in_reply_to_status_id></in_reply_to_status_id>
   <in_reply_to_user_id></in_reply_to_user_id>
   <favorited>false</favorited>
   <in_reply_to_screen_name></in_reply_to_screen_name>
</status>
</user>
```

Most of the methods that deal with Twitter member profile data will return a single
user object (see Table 5-1), but some include profile data for several users (see Table 5-2). All of the user objects, though, will include each author's latest status update
nested in the user element. This means you don't have to waste an API hit from your
rate limit in order to see some content (see "Status Objects" on page 198).

Table 5-1. Twitter API methods returning a single user data object

Function	Path
Show Member Profile	/users/show/*id*.xml
Follow a Member	/friendships/create/*id*.xml
Unfollow a Member	/friendships/destroy/*id*.xml
Block a Member	/blocks/create/*id*.xml
Remove a Block	/blocks/destroy/*id*.xml
Update Member Profile	/account/update_profile.xml
Update Profile Colors	/account/update_profile_colors.xml
Update Background Image	/account/update_profile_background_image.xml
Update Profile Image	/account/update_profile_image.xml
Update Member Location	/account/update_location.xml
Update the Delivery Device	/account/update_delivery_device.xml
Turn On Notification	/notifications/follow/*id*.xml
Turn Off Notification	/notifications/leave/*id*.xml

Table 5-2. Twitter API methods returning multiple user data objects

Function	Path
View Members Being Followed	/statuses/friends.xml
View Followers	/statuses/followers.xml

User Elements

Each user object contains several XML elements that can be used to identify and describe a particular Twitter member. The following elements are included in every user object:

id

> Each user has a unique ID assigned by Twitter. These IDs are not sequential, but they are incremental, meaning higher ID values reflect newer registrations. Twitter appears to alternate between incrementing by 1 and by 10, which gives the ID values an unpredictable look.

screen_name

> Although the account ID never changes, the screen name (or username) each account holder uses to access Twitter is not fixed. Twitter allows a registered user to log into the main website and change his screen name at any point, which can create some issues with finding people you know are part of the community. However, changing usernames does not affect the follow network, because the relationships are maintained with the account ID, not the screen name. You can use the current screen name or the account ID to reference a particular user in API methods.

name

> Each user can select a name to display that is different from that user's screen name. This feature is often used to get past the constraints of the user naming convention (for example, no spaces) when registering with Twitter. The member name can be any text, but most commonly it is set to the full name of the user. This name is not meant to be used as a reference to an account when accessing the API.

location

> Like the display name, the location value is just text and is not constrained to any existing format to describe the actual location of the user. The arrival of iPhones, which can fairly accurately determine where in the world they are currently located, prompted API support to let applications change this location text automatically.

A handful of common formats accurately reflect the geographical location of the user (e.g., "Bloomington, Indiana"), but sometimes the location text is vague ("Midwest") or joking ("Trapped near the seventh circle of Hell"). Location-aware devices (such as the iPhone) and software (such as BrightKite) are changing the meaning of the field, from hometown to actual current location.

Despite being an open text field, location data is usually a fairly accurate indication of where in the world a member lives. You can trust what you see in this field, but your application shouldn't rely on this information.

description

Another open profile field is the one provided for users to supply short descriptions of themselves. This field may contain anything from a job title to a philosophical statement and can include links to other websites.

url

Each user is invited to include a link to one primary website (often a personal blog, a related company or project site, or a LinkedIn résumé).

profile_image_url

Twitter doesn't maintain a library of user avatars on its own servers; instead, it stores these small iconic pictures on the Amazon Simple Storage Service (S3). When a member uploads an image, it is stored on S3, and a link to that image is associated with the user's Twitter account. To be included in the public timeline, a user must have a public account *and* upload a custom profile image.

 Like all things on the Web, the location of the actual files may change in the future. Regardless of whether Twitter continues to use S3 for storage, it will continue to provide absolute URLs to point to the profile images.

profile_background_image_url

This field contains a link to the image file to be used as the background of the user's member profile web page on the Twitter website. The maximum size of this file is 2048 pixels and 800 KB. The byte size is a hard limit, but larger pixel dimensions will be scaled down to an appropriate size.

profile_background_tile

The background image, if used, can be displayed on the member profile web page in one of two ways, dictated by the value stored in this field. If the value is true, the image will be repeated horizontally and vertically until it fills the entire browser window (this is called *tiling*). If the value is false, the image will be fixed in the upper-left corner of the browser window, maintaining its stored size.

protected

It is estimated that between 7 and 12% of all Twitter accounts are set up as private accounts. The only people who can see private account holders' content and profile details are the people whom they allow to follow them. When accessing the API, an error will be returned if you try to access a protected account without authenticating with an account granted permission to do so. This element will contain a simple true or false to indicate whether or not this user has a private account.

followers_count

The only statistics you get about a user in the short-form user object, regardless of access rights, is the number of followers that person has acquired. This information is found on the user's Twitter web profile, along with the three other stats (followed members, number of updates, and favorites) that you can get by requesting the full profile from the API.

status

The status element actually contains a nested set of elements that describe the most recent status update made by this user. The information you get in the status object is the same you would get by using the Show a Tweet API method. By including it with the user object, Twitter saves you a hit that would be charged against your rate limit. The status subelements include:

- created_at
- id
- text
- source
- in_reply_to_status_id
- in_reply_to_user_id
- in_reply_to_screen_name
- truncated
- favorited

More information about these data elements can be found in the next section of this chapter, "Status Objects" on page 198.

Sometimes that basic information is not enough. Although you may not have much use for a user's Twitter web page customization details, included in the full profile data are other elements containing useful statistics and the time zone preferred by the user. Here's the full list of what you'll find in addition to the short-form data:

profile_background_color, profile_text_color, profile_link_color, profile_side
bar_fill_color, profile_sidebar_border_color

These five XML elements contain the hex code to determine the color scheme of the web page for this user's Twitter profile. You can edit the appropriate Settings form on the website to change the color of the background, sidebar, sidebar border, links, and text.

 It is becoming more popular to upload a background graphic containing additional profile information, such as contact information and a short statement. When an image is used, the background color is not seen.

created_at

The date the account was created is returned as text in GMT time (as in "Tue Mar 27 10:05:07 +0000 2007"). The relative age of an account can also be estimated by looking at the user's account ID, as lower numbers equate to older accounts.

friends_count

The number of Twitter members this user is following is contained in the `friends_count` element. "Friends" is the original terminology used by Twitter. Authors who are followed contribute their status updates to the information streams of their followers.

statuses_count

Twitter keeps track of the total number of status updates published by each user. The cumulative count is included in the member profile and as an element in the detailed user object. Deleting a tweet will lower this count.

favourites_count

Although this feature is used by less than 1% of all users, it's possible to bookmark a given status update for later reference. Tweets can also be marked as a means of endorsing a particularly clever or useful update. If the number of favorites (spelled in the API using British English) is more than zero, this user has bookmarked published status updates.

utc_offset

The offset is the number of seconds to add to GMT time to calculate the local time of this user. This value is set when the time zone is changed in the member profile on the Twitter website.

time_zone

The time zone is the text label displayed to identify the offset amount (as in, "Eastern Time (US & Canada)").

following

If the account used to authenticate the API request is following this user, the content of the `following` element is `true`. If no authentication is used, this element will not be included in the detailed user object.

notifications

This value is set to `true` if the authenticating user is receiving notifications of this user's status updates on her device of choice. Again, if no authentication is used to access the API, this element is not included in the response.

Status Objects

Many applications focus on content and how to aggregate it to reveal twitterers' collective wisdom. Tools such as Twist (*http://twist.flaptor.com*) and Twitscoop (*http://twitscoop.com*), for example, do a great job of identifying and extracting the interesting topics being discussed on Twitter at any given moment. To create tools like these, you have to be able to access the content of each post.

The API methods that deal with the information stream (see "Publishing" on page 151 and "The Information Stream" on page 152) all return status data objects. The status object includes elements that describe the content of the status update as well as elements that contain meta-information about how and when it was published. Each object also has a nested **user** element containing the short-form information about the author of the status update (see Example 5-3), as described earlier in this chapter As is the case with user objects including status information, the inclusion of author data eliminates the need to make a separate call to the API for that data.

Example 5-3. A status update object

```
<statuses type="array">
  <status>
    <created_at>Sat Sep 27 14:06:55 +0000 2008</created_at>
    <id>937108231</id>
    <text>FYI... On October 4, the electro-rock cacophony known as Brother Eye,
      will bring its brand of audio terror to The Crossroads in Garwood, NJ</text>
    <source>web</source>
    <truncated>false</truncated>
    <in_reply_to_status_id />
    <in_reply_to_user_id />
    <favorited>false</favorited>
    <user>
    <id>16402306</id>
    <name>Tico</name>
    <screen_name>tontino</screen_name>
    <description>Avid student of human folly</description>
    <location>USA</location>
    <profile_image_url>http://s3.amazonaws.com/twitter_production/profile_images/
      60501541/somatic sm normal.jpg</profile_image_url>
    <url></url>
    <protected>false</protected>
    <followers_count>3</followers_count>
  </user>
  </status>
  <status>
    <created_at>Mon Feb 02 20:24:45 +0000 2009</created_at>
    <id>1170872081</id>
    <text>Critical mass of tweets has been reached: It is now impossible for me to
      avoid watching Groundhog Day tonight.</text>
    <source>&lt;a href=&quot;http://iconfactory.com/software/
      twitterrific&quot;&gt;twitterrific&lt;/a&gt;</source>
    <truncated>false</truncated>
    <in_reply_to_status_id></in_reply_to_status_id>
    <in_reply_to_user_id></in_reply_to_user_id>
    <favorited>false</favorited>
    <in_reply_to_screen_name></in_reply_to_screen_name>
    <user>
      <id>808824</id>
      <name>Kevin Makice</name>
      <screen_name>kmakice</screen_name>
      <location>Bloomington, Indiana</location>
      <description>Impoverished Ph.D. student at the Indiana University School of
        Informatics</description>
      <profile_image_url>http://s3.amazonaws.com/twitter_production/
        profile_images/72512210/2009avatar_normal.jpg</profile_image_url>
      <url>http://www.blogschmog.net</url>
```

```
      <protected>false</protected>
      <followers_count>686</followers_count>
    </user>
  </status>
</statuses>
```

Methods that deal with Twitter status update data will return either a single status object (see Table 5-3) or multiple statuses listed in the same result set (see Table 5-4). When multiple status updates are included, they are wrapped in a `statuses` element tag, as in Example 5-3.

Table 5-3. Twitter API methods returning a single status data object

Function	Path
Post a Tweet	/statuses/update.xml
Show a Tweet	/statuses/show/*id*.xml
Delete a Tweet	/statuses/destroy/*id*.xml
Create a Favorite	/favorites/create/*id*.xml
Delete a Favorite	/favorites/destroy/*id*.xml

Table 5-4. Twitter API methods returning multiple status data objects

Function	Path
View the Public Timeline	/statuses/public_timeline.xml
View a Friends Timeline	/statuses/friends_timeline.xml
View an Individual Timeline	/statuses/user_timeline.xml
View Replies	/statuses/replies.xml
View Favorites	/favorites.xml

Status Elements

There are fewer status elements than those created for user information, but what Twitter does provide goes beyond just the content displayed on the website. Each status update is also associated with meta-information about how it was published to Twitter:

text
> The most important element is the one that contains the visible content. This text is processed for publication, including encoding some characters and transforming long links into short ones with TinyURL.

created_at
> The date and time the status was updated is stored in GMT (as in, "Sat Sep 27 14:06:55 +0000 2008").

id

Each status update has its own unique record ID. This is the value to use when referencing a status update in the Twitter API.

source

This value indicates the tool used to update the status. By default the value is `web`, but each application can provide an approved code that will customize it to identity the specific tool, such as `twitterrific`. As of fall 2008, the Web remained the most common source of tweets, responsible for almost half of all publications. Other popular means of updating include Twitterfeed, SMS, Twitterrific, Twhirl, and Twitterfox.

 The resource code is available upon request and after review by Twitter. You will need to visit *http://twitter.com/help/request _source* and provide the name of your application, the application URL, and a brief description of the tool. Unapproved codes will default to `web`.

truncated

Twitter accepts strings longer than 140 characters (the longest string of text that all forms of SMS have in common), but it doesn't display that extra text. A true value here indicates that the tweet was chopped off at the end to fit the 140-character convention. (Twitter also lets the author and his followers know that something has been snipped when the tweet is sent.)

in_reply_to_user_id

Twitter wasn't built to be a conversational medium. In fact, Twitter developers had to be persuaded to add support for the old IRC convention of using @ to direct a message to a specific user. For active users, the lack of early support for threading caused some unusual associations between messages, since several updates might have been published in the interim, before another user's reply arrived. Author replies on Twitter are also limited to tweets beginning with *@username*, ignoring any other username references in the body of the message.

The best use of this element, which contains a user ID, seems to be to extract networks of conversation rather than specific conversation threads.

in_reply_to_screen_name

Like `in_reply_to_user_id`, this element associates a tweet with the author of the user who inspired it. Unlike the user ID, however, each member can change her screen name without losing any data in the network or archive. This is a distinctive feature of Twitter, as it gives people the flexibility to be creative or adjust to changes in their lives (e.g., getting a new job, getting married) without being tied to some outdated identity. This field maintains the username of the author to whom the reply is directed at the time of the post; the username is not updated if that author subsequently changes it.

`in_reply_to_status_id`

This newer field attaches this status update directly to another status update, facilitating the threading of tweeted discussion. This field is not incorporated into many older applications but will likely become heavily utilized in the future by developers who create conversational Twitter tools. Before it becomes really useful, though, many of those older applications will need to upgrade.

`favorited`

If the authenticating user has bookmarked this status update, the value of this element will be `true`. This element will be present even if no authentication is used, but the value will default to `false`.

> Be aware that there is sometimes a lag between actions taken through the website and the information retrieved through the API. Marking a status as a favorite on the Twitter website doesn't instantly trigger a change in the `favorited` element value.

`user`

Just as the user data object includes "extra" information pertaining to the specified user's last status update, the status data object contains some information specific to the update's author. Nested elements wrapped in the `user` tag mimic the short-form version of the user data object. These include `id`, `name`, `screen_name`, `description`, `location`, `profile_image_url`, `url`, `protected`, and `followers_count`. More information about these data elements can be found earlier in this chapter in "User Objects" on page 192.

Message Objects

Twitter may not be ideal for private, one-to-one communication, but the service does facilitate the delivery from one user to another of messages that don't appear in any timelines. The *direct message* is a kind of back channel you can use to send a short tweet to a specific person in your follower list. You don't have to be able to read the recipient's information stream in order to message him, but you will have to follow that user if you expect him to be able to reply to you.

> Not everyone uses or appreciates direct messages in the same way. Some third-party Twitter tools allow you to automatically greet new followers with a short direct message. A user's human BS detector, though, can sense when a machine is doing the sending and may discount it as spam.

Message data objects are similar to status data objects except that they have to include information for *two* users—the sender and the receiver (see Example 5-4). The order is important because only the receiver will have the right to delete the message after the sender posts it to Twitter. Doing so removes it for both users.

 The restriction preventing the deletion of sent messages only applies to the Twitter API. If you try to delete a message you have sent using the Delete a Tweet API method, Twitter returns an error: "Users may only delete messages that they have received." Through the main website, however, the message author may delete it as well.

Example 5-4. Direct message object

```
<direct-messages type="array">
<direct_message>
  <id>37377295</id>
  <sender_id>14462589</sender_id>
  <text>having lunch with jeff on th  Thanks for the intro</text>
  <recipient_id>808824</recipient_id>
  <created_at>Tue Sep 30 14:31:59 +0000 2008</created_at>
  <sender_screen_name>iuksb_talbott</sender_screen_name>
  <recipient_screen_name>kmakice</recipient_screen_name>
  <sender>
    <id>14462589</id>
    <name>John Talbott</name>
    <screen_name>iuksb_talbott</screen_name>
    <location>Bloomington, Indiana</location>
    <description>Visiting Lecturer at Indiana University, Dad, Runner,
      Cyclist</description>
    <profile_image_url>http://s3.amazonaws.com/twitter_production/profile_images/
      59293512/darwin_normal.jpg</profile_image_url>
    <url>http://marketfarkus.com</url>
    <protected>false</protected>
    <followers_count>121</followers_count>
  </sender>
  <recipient>
    <id>808824</id>
    <name>Kevin Makice</name>
    <screen_name>kmakice</screen_name>
    <location>Indiana University: School of Library &amp; Information Science
      </location>
    <description>Impoverished Ph.D. student at the Indiana University School of
      Informatics</description>
    <profile_image_url>http://s3.amazonaws.com/twitter_production/profile_images/
      60374185/2008avatar150_normal.jpg</profile_image_url>
    <url>http://www.blogschmog.net</url>
    <protected>false</protected>
    <followers_count>499</followers_count>
  </recipient>
</direct_message>
</direct-messages>
```

There are four API methods that return message data objects. Two of them return only a single direct message (see Table 5-5), and the other two return lists of multiple direct message objects in the same result set (see Table 5-6). For more information about these methods, see "Communication" on page 165.

Table 5-5. Twitter API methods returning a single message data object

Function	Path
Post a Tweet	/direct_messages/new.xml
Delete a Tweet	/direct_messages/destroy/*id*.xml

Table 5-6. Twitter API methods returning multiple message data objects

Function	Path
List Received Messages	/direct_messages.xml
List Sent Messages	/direct_messages/sent.xml

Direct Message Elements

The data returned for each message falls into one of three groups: information about the sender, information about the receiver, and information about the message itself. Many of these elements will seem familiar if you have read "User Objects" on page 192 and "Status Objects" on page 198:

id
> The record IDs for direct messages are kept separately from those of status updates, whose numbers passed the 1 billion mark on November 10, 2008. Direct message counts are more modest, only totaling around 40 million at the same point in time. To reference an existing message to delete it—the only time a reference is needed— you use the ID value in this element.

created_at, text
> These two values—the creation date and the content of the message—operate in the same way as in the status element (see "Status Objects" on page 198).

sender_id, recipient_id
> The sender and recipient each have their own user IDs. Twitter differentiates between the two with XML elements so you can do so in your programming.

sender_screen_name, recipient_screen_name
> The sender and recipient also have screen names that can be used to reference their information with additional requests to other API methods.

sender, recipient
> Included with each message data object are nested elements containing the short-form user data objects for both the sender and the recipient. Wrapped in their respective XML tags, this data includes the usual suspects: id, name, screen_name, description, location, profile_image_url, url, protected, and followers_count.

More information about these data elements can be found in "User Objects" on page 192.

Search Objects

If you paid attention to the earlier examples, you will quickly notice that something is different in the search data object. The search API is a separate beast, at the moment, from the main Twitter API. It was created by Summize, a startup that Twitter acquired in the summer of 2008, just a few months after it launched its search engine for tweets. Although Summize's search engine was quickly integrated into Twitter's website, the structure, naming conventions, and format of the response is not yet in line with what Twitter uses elsewhere in the API.

Search data objects are returned in the Atom format (they're also available in JSON, but not XML). This means that the structure of the elements is a bit different (see Example 5-5). Once you extract the information from the tags, though, you get a description of the search just performed and a list of status updates that matched the search query.

Example 5-5. Search query results object

```
<feed xmlns:google="http://base.google.com/ns/1.0" xml:lang="en-US"
  xmlns:openSearch="http://a9.com/-/spec/opensearch/1.1/"
  xmlns="http://www.w3.org/2005/Atom" xmlns:twitter="http://api.twitter.com/">
  <id>tag:search.twitter.com,2005:search/informatics</id>
  <link type="text/html" href="http://search.twitter.com/search?q=informatics"
    rel="alternate"/>
  <link type="application/atom+xml"
    href="http://search.twitter.com/search.atom?q=informatics" rel="self"/>
  <title>informatics - Twitter Search</title>
  <link type="application/opensearchdescription+xml"
    href="http://search.twitter.com/opensearch.xml" rel="search"/>
  <link type="application/atom+xml"
    href="http://search.twitter.com/search.atom?q=informatics&amp;since_
    id=937058928" rel="refresh"/>
  <updated>2008-09-26T22:28:54Z</updated>
  <openSearch:itemsPerPage>15</openSearch:itemsPerPage>
  <link type="application/atom+xml"
    href="http://search.twitter.com/search.atom?max_id=937058928&amp;page=2&amp;q=
    informatics" rel="next"/>
  <entry>
    <id>tag:search.twitter.com,2005:936325004</id>
    <published>2008-09-26T22:28:54Z</published>
    <link type="text/html" href="http://twitter.com/naufal/statuses/936325004"
      rel="alternate"/>
    <title>@shinejikids &#3611;.&#3605;&#3619;&#3637;&#3617;&#3637;&#3626;&#3629;
      &#3609;&#3604;&#3657;&#3623;&#3618;&#3611;&#3656;&#3634;&#3623; Bio
      Informatics</title>
    <content type="html">&lt;a
      href="http://twitter.com/shinejikids"&gt;@shinejikids&lt;/a&gt;&#3611;
      .&#3605;&#3619;&#3637;&#3617;&#3637;&#3626;&#3629;&#3609;&#3604;&#3657;
```

```
      &#3623;&#3618;&#3611;&#3656;&#3634;&#3623;  Bio&lt;b&gt;Informatics&lt;
      /b&gt;</content>
    <updated>2008-09-26T22:28:54Z</updated>
    <link type="image/png"
      href="http://s3.amazonaws.com/twitter_production/profile_images/
      56581453/arrow_nau_normal.png" rel="image"/>
    <twitter:source>&lt;a href="http://www.tweetdeck.com/"
      &gt;TweetDeck&lt;/a&gt;</twitter:source>
    <author>
      <name>naufal (naufal)</name>
      <uri>http://twitter.com/naufal</uri>
    </author>
  </entry>
</feed>
```

There is currently only one API method that returns a search data object (see Table 5-7); it belongs to the search API, not the main Twitter API. The other method available in the search API returns a list of the top 10 keywords members are tweeting about, listed only in JSON format. For more information, see "Search" on page 176.

Table 5-7. Twitter API methods returning multiple search data objects

Function	Path
Keyword Search	search.twitter.com/search.atom?q=*query*

Feed Elements

The first group of elements in the search object deals with the search itself. This information is wrapped in the `feed` tags and provides links and descriptions of the search, to allow it to be repeated or navigated:

id
: Unlike in the user, status, and message objects, the `id` element in a search object does not contain an integer ID; instead, it contains a text string to identify the search in more general terms. Unless your application is tracking and managing search queries, this information probably won't be very useful.

link
: Several `link` elements are included in the `feed` tags. These are empty elements, which means they contain their own end tags (as in `<link />`). Each contains type, URL, and label attributes to describe a different kind of link. These include pointers to an HTML page, navigation links for paginated search results, and XML for OpenSearch, which facilitates syndication of search results.

title
: Each search has a reader-friendly title that contains the keyword used in the search and the "Twitter Search" label. This might be useful to save you the trouble of constructing one yourself.

openSearch:itemsPerPage

> This element contains the number of search results included in the data set. The default is 15, but this number can be raised up to 200 using the `rss` parameter in the search (see "Search" on page 176).

entry

> Each matching status update is contained in a nested set of tag elements wrapped in `entry` tags. These elements (discussed next) include `id`, `published`, `link`, `title`, `content`, `updated`, and `author`.

Entry Elements

Each item matching the search query is encapsulated in its own `entry` tags. Contained within those tags are some elements that describe the matching status update. This data is not quite as complete or easy to parse as the information returned by the main Twitter API, but it still contains the basics—text, reference ID, and author—that your application can use to display or send another API request to fill in the gaps. The elements include:

id

> As is the case with the feed ID, this is a text code to identify this particular item in the search results. There is no integer record ID included as a separate search element, but this text probably gives you the best chance to extract it by parsing the string. The record ID is also embedded in some of the `link` elements.

published, updated

> These values are identical and translate to the creation date in the status data object. The published date is still given in GMT but is presented in a slightly different format (e.g., "2008-09-26T22:28:54Z").

link

> These empty elements contain type, URL, and label information in their attributes. Each search result item includes a link to the HTML web page for this status update, a link to the author's profile image stored on Amazon S3, and a link to any threaded responses created by other users replying to this status update.

title, content

> The content of the message is contained in the `title` element. The text is partially encoded but still readable with the naked eye. The `content` element also contains the status update text, but it additionally includes the HTML needed to create a link to the update on a web page. If you are looking to analyze the readable text, use `title`.

twitter:source

> This element contains the encoded HTML link to the publishing source application (e.g., "<a href="http://www.tweetdeck.com/">TweetDeck</a>").

author

In yet another set of nested elements, the author tags wrap two bits of information about the user who published the tweet. The name element contains a short string with both the full name and screen name of the user, whereas the uri element points to the author's Twitter profile on the Web.

ID Objects

The most recent addition to the API is small in function but huge in stature. Before these social graph methods were added in February 2009, developers had to loop through pages and pages of user lists to get a full sense of someone's follow network. Now, Twitter lets you grab everything at once in the form of a list of user IDs. The social graph methods (Table 5-8) each contain one element specific to the request.

Table 5-8. Twitter API methods returning an ID object

Function	Path
Get All Friends	/friends/ids/*id*.xml
Get All Followers	/followers/ids/*id*.xml

ID Elements

The trade-off between the newer Get All Followers and Get All Friends methods and the original View Followers and View Friends methods (see "The Follow Network" on page 157) is one of brevity for completeness. Twitter gives you the full list of all your followers or all the people you follow, but it only provides the user ID to help you identify each one. To get more information, you have to use those IDs to request full member profiles. The list that is returned consists of a set of simple id elements (see Example 5-6) wrapped in <ids></ids> tags.

Example 5-6. ID object for complete list of followers

```
<ids>
  <id>808824</id>
  <id>14986286</id>
</ids>
```

The lone element included is:

id

This element contains the user ID of someone in your follow network (either a follower or someone you follow). The ID is more reliable than a username, which can change over time, as the member wishes.

Response Objects

In some instances, you aren't looking for lists of content or users; you just want to know whether or not something is true. There are a few methods in the API just for this purpose (see Table 5-9). The XML they return is the simplest response: one element, as shown in Example 5-7.

Example 5-7. Simple response object

```
<friends>true</friends>
```

Table 5-9. Twitter API methods returning a single response data object

Function	Path
Confirm a Follow	/friendships/exists.xml
Verify Credentials	/account/verify_credentials.xml
Test	/help/test.xml

In some cases, such as Verify Credentials, it is sufficient to examine the HTTP status code rather than going to the trouble of parsing the XML Twitter returns (see "Accessing the API" on page 134). A status code of 200 is an indication that no problems exist. Anything else will throw an error message.

Response Elements

Twitter uses five kinds of response elements, but they fall nicely into two groups—a Boolean response and a null response:

friends, authorized, ok
> In the Boolean group, the only element values are `true` and `false` (see Example 5-7). The name of the tag element wrapping that value doesn't really mean anything. When confirming a Twitter follow relationship between two users, the tag name is `friends`. For verifying authentication credentials, the element is named `authorized`. For the basic test method, it's `ok`. What really matters is the info inside the wrapper.

Hash Objects

The final group of XML data objects are the hash objects. There are only three methods in the Twitter API that intentionally return hash data objects as a sign of success. The rate limit status check method (see Table 5-10) contains four XML elements specific to this request. Two others (see Table 5-11) return an error when everything goes smoothly.

Table 5-10. Twitter API methods returning a single hash data object

Function	Path
Check Rate Limit Status	/account/rate_limit_status.xml

Table 5-11. Twitter API methods returning success as an error

Function	Path
End a Member Session	/account/end_session.xml
Delete a Tweet	/direct_messages/destroy/*id*.xml

Hash Elements

Checking the rate limit status is a free method request that gives you the number of remaining hits you have and the exact time when the clock will be reset (see "API Administration" on page 174). This is a very useful method to incorporate into any application where the rate limit may become an issue, as you can use this information to pause your application gracefully until it is time to resume mining data (see Example 5-8). This is the only nonerror hash data object.

Example 5-8. Hashed feedback object for rate limit status

```
<hash>
  <reset-time type="datetime">2008-09-27T15:08:32+00:00</reset-time>
  <remaining-hits type="integer">99</remaining-hits>
  <hourly-limit type="integer">100</hourly-limit>
  <reset-time-in-seconds type="integer">1222528112</reset-time-in-seconds>
</hash>
```

The elements included are:

reset-time

This GMT datetime indicates when the rate limit will be restored to the maximum number of hits per hour (e.g., "2008-09-27T15:08:32+00:00"). This clock starts with the first hit on the API.

reset-time-in-seconds

This integer value represents the Unix timestamp version of the time when the rate limit will be reset. This is measured in seconds since the beginning of 1970 and represents a date and time in the immediate future. When translated, it is the same datetime listed in reset-time. To calculate the number of seconds remaining on your reset clock, subtract the current Unix timestamp.

remaining-hits

This integer value represents the number of remaining hits on the API until the clock is reset. This value is always smaller than or equal to the maximum number of hits allowed for a given account. When the number of remaining hits gets down to zero, an error will result (see Example 5-8 earlier).

`hourly-limit`
>Back in fall 2007, Twitter started imposing a limit on how many times per hour each account can access certain methods in the API. This number fell to as low as 20 during the worst of the company's technical problems, in late spring 2008. Currently, the maximum is 100 hits per hour.

Errors

When something goes wrong, Twitter has to have a way to let you know. All of the methods have the potential to return hash data objects because all of them can error for any number of reasons.

 The only reason to investigate the XML content of an error hash object is if you want to get the text Twitter associates with the problem. If you are only looking to find out whether the method request was successful, check for an HTTP status code of 200.

Twitter's error reporting is handled through a `hash` element (see Example 5-9).

Example 5-9. Hashed feedback object for error reporting

```
<hash>
  <error>This method requires authentication.</error>
  <request>/favorites.xml?</request>
</hash>
```

The hash element contains two nested XML elements, `error` and `request`:

`error`
>This text describes the nature of the error. Some of the messages you may encounter include:
>
> • This method requires authentication.
>
> • Not found.
>
> • Not authorized.
>
> • Could not authenticate you.
>
> • Two user ids or screen_names must be supplied.
>
> • No direct message with that ID found.
>
> • Users may only delete messages that they have received.

`request`
>The requested path is returned as the value of this element, confirming which method was used that resulted in an error.

This is a very versatile structure, as it can respond to a range of problematic API requests. The errors listed here were encountered when testing the system. Others may crop up, but they will all use this same format.

CHAPTER 6
Application Setup

 kmakice Get ready to run your applications by putting all the parts on the server. Don't forget to stretch.

Back in Chapter 2, I introduced you to some examples of existing web applications using the Twitter API. Now it's time to see what you might find under the hood of those tools by building one of your own.

The Twitter community is very generous with the code it generates. A number of premade libraries help simplify interaction between the Twitter API and a variety of languages. For PHP, there are several options that will let you download some code and access the API with fewer lines of code than programming it from scratch. Some of these libraries include:

Arc90_Service_Twitter, by Matt Williams
   http://lab.arc90.com/2008/06/php_twitter_api_client.php

PEAR Services_Twitter, by Joe Stump and David Jean Louis
   http://pear.php.net/package/Services_Twitter/

PHP Twitter, by Tijs Verkoyen
   http://classes.verkoyen.eu/twitter/

TwitterLibPHP, by Justin Poliey
   http://github.com/jdp/twitterlibphp/

PHP Twitter, by David Billingham and Aaron Brazell
   http://emmense.com/php-twitter/

Other programming languages with similar libraries include ActionScript/Flash, C++, C#/.NET, Java, Objective-C/Cocoa, Perl, PL/SQL, Python, and Ruby. Visit the Twitter API wiki (*http://apiwiki.twitter.com/Libraries*) for links to other libraries that you can download and use in your code.

If you have questions about programming for Twitter, the developer community is filled with knowledgable and generous people. A list of developers is maintained at *http://apiwiki.twitter.com/Developers*, most of whom are also active on the Google group (*http://groups.google.com/group/twitter-development-talk*). You should also follow *@twitterapi*, which is manned by someone in the API group dedicated to supporting developers.

The strategy for this book is to present you with a few working applications that are built from the ground up. Use this book as a starting point, and indulge your inquisitiveness by exploring ways to improve the code.

 As developers sometimes say, "Good code is working code." All of the sample applications in this book are "good" in that they work, but there are certainly many different ways to program the same features.

In this chapter, you'll see how to prepare your web environment to run a suite of sample web applications built to illustrate different interactions with the API. The setup includes establishing a Twitter account, creating tables in a MySQL database, and making a directory for included files. Chapters 7 and 8 contain descriptions of the applications and automated tasks.

 A reminder that this sample application code can be downloaded from this book's website (*http://www.oreilly.com/catalog/9780596154615*). It is open and available for anyone to use.

Establishing Your Twitter Account

Whether you have purchased this book or are just browsing through it in your local bookstore, odds are good that you already have a Twitter account. If so, there's nothing to see here; move along to the next section ("Creating Your Database" on page 222). If you do not yet have an account—maybe you've heard people talking about Twitter or seen it mentioned in the news and are curious about microblogging—stick around. You will need to become a member of the Twitter community to make full use of its API.

Having a valid Twitter account is an important part of your application work, both as a developer and for customer engagement. Not only will it give you access to data in the API that cannot be acquired with an unauthenticated request, but your member account will also serve as your identity in this community. Your Twitter account is a way to cultivate relationships with the people who use your application. You can solicit feedback on your work and thank people for helping you develop your web tools.

This section will take you through the new member registration process and get your Twitter account up and running.

Registering a New Twitter Member Account

Registering for a new Twitter account takes about five minutes. To get started, load the Twitter home page (*http://twitter.com*) into your browser. Right below the beautiful graphic image of a bird on a limb is a big green "Get Started Now" button (Figure 6-1). Click this button, and you're five minutes away from a new account.

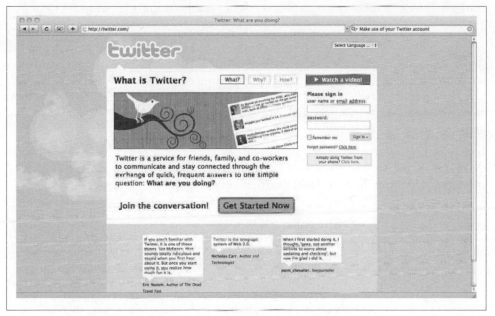

Figure 6-1. Creating a new Twitter member account to access the API

The next page you'll see is a simple registration form. It asks you for just a few key bits of information:

- Your preferred username
- Your preferred password
- A valid email address

Twitter recently added a nice bit of client-side programming to check whether the username you enter is available. Usernames are limited to just 15 characters (numbers, letters, and underscores only). The site also reserves use of "twitter," preventing new account holders from having that as part of their usernames.

The email address you use must be unique to Twitter, meaning each email address can have no more than one member account associated with it. The username is actually just a convenient handle for the user ID, which is automatically assigned to each new email address upon registration. Unlike many other social networks, it is easy to change your Twitter username after registering—your handle has to be unique, but it does not have to be permanent. Select something you like now; if you want, you can change it later without affecting your account.

You will also be asked to complete a reCAPTCHA form to prove you are a human being. CAPTCHA forms are tests some sites use to prevent automated programs from creating accounts automatically, usually to spam other members. CAPTCHAs ask you to complete a task that is easy for a human but difficult for a computer: you have to read a distorted graphic and type the text (letters and/or numbers) you see in it.

reCAPTCHA is an altruistic variant created by researchers at Carnegie Mellon University that adds a bit of distributed cognition to the task. In addition to performing the traditional CAPTCHA task to prove you are human, you are also asked to decipher a second word, thereby taking part in a long-term project to digitize old books. Computer scanners perform much of that work, but they can't always accurately digitize the text, and words they can't handle must be read by a human and converted manually. You help out when you register for Twitter.

If you want to receive newsletter updates from Twitter, click the box next to "I want the inside scoop." Twitter is a very transparent company that has made good use of this email service in the past, and I recommend subscribing.

Read the Terms of Service, and then click "I accept. Create my account." Congratulations, you now have a Twitter account!

 Twitter gives you an opportunity to go viral by leveraging your own contact lists on web-based mail services such as Gmail, Hotmail, and Yahoo!. If you want, you can ask Twitter to retrieve your email contacts from those services and select which contacts you want to inform that you now have a Twitter account. Otherwise, skip the invite and rave about Twitter later.

A new Twitter account page looks empty (Figure 6-2). You have no followers, you aren't following anyone, and you've made no status updates. You can take care of the last thing by typing in the big box that asks the core question, "What are you doing?" Once you hit the "update" button below the text area, your page should refresh with a couple of key changes. First, your message will be displayed in your timeline, along with some meta-information (the relative time at which it was created and the tool you used to publish it—here, "the web"). Second, your update count in the profile area in the upper-right corner will increment.

If you mouse over the "RSS" link toward the bottom of the page, in the status bar of your browser you should see the URI to the feed for your status updates. Every time you tweet, anyone subscribing to your timeline will see it in her RSS reader. At the end of the URI, you'll also see your Twitter user ID:

```
http://twitter.com/statuses/friends_timeline/18220846.rss
```

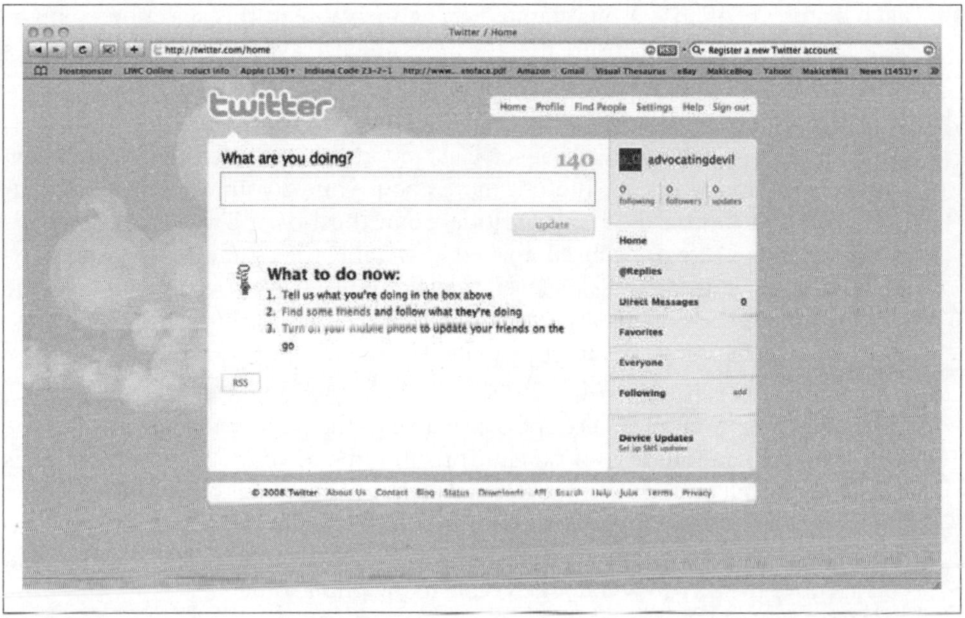

Figure 6-2. A new Twitter account, fresh from the oven

The right column of the page contains information about your account and some navigation links. At the top is a short-form version of your profile statistics, with links to the full lists of your followers and those you are following. Those pages are empty when you first register but will become web views of the same data you might request from the API. Below the profile section is a series of vertical tabs that allow you to see different views of your timeline and messages. The "Everyone" tab links to the public timeline, which consists of all the updates published by active users with nonprotected member accounts who have replaced the default avatar with some other graphic. Since you have not yet changed your profile picture, at the moment that does *not* include you, Newbie.

Configuring Your New Account

At the very top right of the web page, above your profile information, is a set of control links. One of these links is "Settings." Clicking on the Settings link will give you access to the forms that you can use to further customize your member account and do things such as upload a picture.

Account tab

The "Account" tab is the default view for the Settings. This is where you can describe yourself and customize your new online identity. Here are a few key items to notice:

Confirm your time zone
> Each status update has a timestamp. Setting the value in this selection menu to your local time zone will ensure that the times are displayed in a way that matches the clock in your living room or on your desktop.

Add information about yourself
> There are three fields of note that serve as opportunities for letting people know who you are and where to find out more about you or your organization: your URL, your one-line bio, and your location. Some third-party Twitter ranking tools put value on these fields being completed, preferably with some accuracy. Reportedly, links added to these fields (even the URL one) won't count toward Google rankings or even be spidered by search engines anymore. For human visitors, however, providing accurate details about who you are can increase follows.

Review your account privacy
> By default, a new member account is available to the public. That means anyone who wants to can follow your timeline or subscribe to your RSS feed; the things you tweet are put out into the world for all to see. Twitter does offer you the option to protect your updates by checking a box in the Account tab of the Settings controls on the website. Doing so means that other people can see your tweets only if you approve them. You will not be visible in the public timeline.

> In practice, "protected" is not the same as private. Keep in mind that your approved tweeps can not only read your super-secret tweets about how you *really* feel about your boss, they can also retweet them, add them to their blogs, or talk about them with whomever they choose. Sharing information in any social context means you are ultimately giving that information to the world. Don't be afraid of public accounts, but tweet authentically as if everyone is listening.

Although Twitter has routinely disabled this functionality (it is taxing on its servers), you can completely delete your account. However, this is not advised. If you are done with Twitter, just stop using it. You may change your mind down the road, and those old tweets and your identity may be valuable.

You can use this form to change your Twitter username at any point without affecting your follow network, replies, direct messages, or anything in your archive. The associations between you and your content or others are based on user IDs, not usernames. The only consequence of changing your username is a social one: it may be more difficult for people to find you if they knew you under a previous Twitter handle.

Picture tab

Use of avatars and profile pictures seems to have greater meaning in Twitter than in most other social networks, probably because the size of the textual content is so small. A picture is worth a thousand words, which (assuming an average of six characters per word) gives you 976 more words than you are allowed in any given tweet.

To change your profile picture from the default image to something special, click on the "Picture" tab under Settings. You will see an input box where you can tell Twitter where to find the image file you want to use. Click the "Choose file" button to open up a file explorer dialog box that allows you to browse your desktop and locate that file. Once you select the image file you want, click "Choose" and then click "Save" on the web page. The picture displayed on the reloaded page should be the one you uploaded.

Picture files can be no larger than 700 K and must be in one of the three standard graphic file formats (JPG, GIF, or PNG). If you upload a square graphic, you will have an opportunity to make some minor cropping adjustments, but it is advisable to do that kind of image editing offline. Faces are recommended—either human or avatar—since the thumbnail used with your tweets is small. The more image detail you include, the less likely it is that other users will be able to decipher the picture.

 Twitter honors requests by individuals and organizations to control their own identities, and will transfer usernames to their rightful owners upon request (e.g., Steven Wright, the *Mad Men* characters). So take caution if you choose a trademarked username or image. You may be forced to change it.

Other settings

You can do a few other things with the settings available on the Twitter website. These things affect your access to your tweet stream and the outward appearance of your profile page:

Change your password
    You can change your password on the "Password" tab in the Settings controls. You can't do this through the API. If you change your password, be aware that the new password will not automatically propagate to third-party applications such as Twitterrific. If you change your password via the website, you'll also need to change it in any other tools you use to help augment and manage your Twitter experience; otherwise, they'll cease to work.

Get updates on your phone
    One of the cool things about Twitter is that you don't have to constantly visit the official website to read and post content. From the beginning, Twitter has been built with other channels in mind. In particular, SMS allows people already familiar and comfortable with text messaging to use their mobile phones to access Twitter.

On the "Devices" tab under Settings, you will find two controls. The first allows you to decide whether or not you want to have status updates or direct messages sent to your mobile phone as SMS messages. If this option is off, it won't matter what is configured for your notification device—you won't get any notifications sent in that way. The second control allows you to create a blackout period, such as during the night when you are asleep, when tweets won't be sent to your phone.

In mid-2008, Twitter changed its support of SMS in some countries, such as the U.K. Make sure you know whether and how much your cell phone carrier charges for each text message before enabling this method of delivery.

Although Twitter doesn't have a grouping function for the people you follow, it does have a filter that allows you to determine which updates are sent to your chosen device. This means you can separate your general follow network from those you want to follow on your phone. The controls are set from your following directory. Next to each member profile picture is a radio button, set to "Off" by default. Click on the "On" button to add a member to your inner circle.

Determine how you want to be notified

On the "Notices" tab under Settings you will find the controls to expand your conversational awareness beyond your network and get emails about activity involving your account. By default, only the *@username* replies posted to people you follow will be included in your timeline. I recommend changing that to show all replies posted by the people you follow, even if they are directed to people outside your current follow network. Doing so is a way to help expand your own network by paying attention to the conversations your friends are having with others. This is such an important part of the Twitter culture that I'm not sure why the default is to exclude these external conversations.

This is a confusing setting. Many (including me) have interpreted the @replies setting as a filter that prevents people you don't follow from reaching out to you with a reply tweet. For more detailed information on how this filter really works, see the Twitter Support article on the subject at *http://help.twitter.com/forums/23786/en tries/14595*.

The Notices tab also includes toggles for being sent an email when someone starts following you, when you receive a direct message, and when Twitter publishes a newsletter update. If your notification device is enabled, you can also ask Twitter to "nudge" you if it has been 24 hours since your last update. Someone else will have to tell you if that function works, because with 6,600 tweets in about two years, I have never had that situation arise.

Customize your profile page

You can shape the way your profile page looks to other people by clicking on the "Design" tab in the Settings controls. In mid-2008, Twitter added a number of canned themes you can easily select to change the default look into something a little more fanciful. Simply click on the theme you want, and the background image and colors will change. You can also change these things individually, by uploading your own background file and editing the hexadecimal color codes for the background, text, links, sidebar, and sidebar border.

Many members take advantage of the custom background to create an "extended" profile page by putting additional resume or contact information in the left side of a tiled image. One company, Twittad, helps members sell this background image space to advertisers.

Remember to click "Save changes" to keep your handiwork; the design changes will show up instantly when you make them, but they will go away if you forget to save. Figure 6-3 shows what a user profile page might look like after a bit of customization.

Figure 6-3. A new Twitter account, after some basic configuration

Creating Your Database

Now that you have your Twitter membership under your belt, you need to make sure you have a place to store any data you may collect when using it to access the Twitter API. You can accomplish this by executing some SQL statements to create a few database tables.

A variety of database platforms are commonly used to power the backend of Internet applications, MySQL being one of them. Most web hosting companies will offer MySQL as an option, which is why I am using it to handle the data storage and retrieval chores for the sample applications in this book. For more information on databases and selecting a web host, see Chapter 3.

I developed these applications on a shared hosting service. For about $10 a month, I can do quite a bit, including hosting a number of WordPress blogs and managing many MySQL databases. Such hosting services often provide a control panel to let you access all of the things you need to keep your sites running, including backup services, canned applications, email, and FTP access (see Figure 6-4).

Figure 6-4. A sample control panel for a hosted web account

Among the many iconic links on this page is one for configuring MySQL. Since every host will be a little different, I'll just explain the things you need to do to get your database installed. Consult your web host's documentation or check with your server administrator for specific instructions on how to install your database.

Making Sure There Is a There There

PHP will need to have a way to access your database. The required information includes the name of the database, the server on which it is located, and the username and password to use to access its rich, gooey center, where your information will be stored. Your first step is to set up all of these things.

The server location will almost certainly be "local," which means that PHP doesn't have to look on some other remote server to find the database. The database name, though, will be determined when you make your new database. Naming a new database might involve something as simple as submitting a web form, but there is always some SQL statement backing up that action. For our sample database, that statement might look something like this:

```
CREATE DATABASE 'database_name'
DEFAULT CHARACTER SET utf8 COLLATE utf8 bin;
USE 'database_name';
```

PHP will also need a user account and password to be able to access the database. Without a web interface for this, some administrative access to the MySQL server is needed to allow you to create a new user account and grant it proper access. Because this is meant to be an account used with a web application, you won't want to give the new user account permission to do everything. It should be able to do only as much as is needed. For the sample applications, the basics should be sufficient:

- SELECT
- INSERT
- UPDATE
- DELETE

With permissions set up this way, if someone used your new user account to try something malicious, at least they would only be able to act within the constraints of the tables you create. There is a minor risk to your data, but at least the database schema can't be affected.

Giving the Database Some Structure

Once you've created the database, you need a way to start adding tables. Although there are some nice GUI desktop applications, such as SQLyog, that give you a rich way to muck with your data, the simplest and most common way to interact with MySQL is via a web-based interface called phpMyAdmin (*http://www.phpmyadmin .net*). This tool allows you to create database objects, such as tables and data columns, using a web form rather than SQL. The export option generates the SQL statements automatically. (We'll look at those statements momentarily.)

Let's look briefly at how those tables are built. Every table has a unique `record_id` to point to each record it contains. With each new insertion of data, the ID automatically increments; you don't have to manage those values. The tables each have different names and numbers of data columns, but all of them fall into one of three basic data types:

- Integer (int and the smaller tinyint)
- Variable character (varchar)
- Date and time (datetime and timestamp)

In some instances, the kind of data you capture with the API will be interchangeable with more than one format (dates, for example, can be expressed as date and time, number, or text values), but you will get a database error if MySQL encounters data values that cannot be converted to the proper format.

If the data column is created to allow it, the value can also be a NULL or empty value. NULLs are treated as something different than a zero or an empty string and are often disallowed in the database schema to force the programmer to commit to putting something meaningful into the column. Sometimes you don't have all of the information a record may require at the time you create it. Database designers can anticipate that situation by declaring a valid default value to put in the column to allow the rest of the record to be inserted. All this is defined in the table-creation statements in Example 6-1.

Example 6-1. SQL script to create database tables

```
-- Table structure for table 'access'
CREATE TABLE IF NOT EXISTS 'access' (
  'record_id' int(4) NOT NULL,
  'password' varchar(255) NOT NULL,
  PRIMARY KEY ('record_id')
) ENGINE=InnoDB  DEFAULT CHARSET=utf8 COLLATE=utf8_bin;

-- Table structure for table 'autotweet_profiles'
CREATE TABLE IF NOT EXISTS 'autotweet_profiles' (
  'record_id' int(11) NOT NULL auto_increment,
  'user_name' varchar(50) NOT NULL,
  'password' varchar(255) NOT NULL,
  'rss_url' varchar(255) NOT NULL,
  'date_processed' timestamp NOT NULL default CURRENT_TIMESTAMP,
  'is_enabled' tinyint(4) NOT NULL default '1',
  PRIMARY KEY ('record_id'),
  KEY 'is_enabled' ('is_enabled'),
  KEY 'user_name' ('user_name')
) ENGINE=InnoDB  DEFAULT CHARSET=utf8 COLLATE=utf8_bin AUTO_INCREMENT=1 ;

-- Table structure for table 'bestof_favorites'
CREATE TABLE IF NOT EXISTS 'bestof_favorites' (
  'record_id' int(11) NOT NULL auto_increment,
  'status_id' int(11) NOT NULL,
  'user_id' int(11) NOT NULL,
  'created_at' datetime NOT NULL,
  PRIMARY KEY ('record_id'),
```

```
  KEY 'status_id' ('status_id','user_id','created_at')
) ENGINE=InnoDB  DEFAULT CHARSET=utf8 COLLATE=utf8_bin AUTO_INCREMENT=1 ;

-- Table structure for table 'bestof_queue'
CREATE TABLE IF NOT EXISTS 'bestof_queue' (
  'record_id' int(11) NOT NULL auto_increment,
  'user_id' int(11) NOT NULL,
  'user_name' varchar(50) NOT NULL,
  'user_avatar' varchar(255) NOT NULL,
  'last_status_id' int(11) NOT NULL,
  'last_checked_date' datetime NOT NULL,
  'queue_date' timestamp NOT NULL default CURRENT_TIMESTAMP,
  PRIMARY KEY  ('record_id'),
  KEY 'user_id' ('user_id','last_status_id','last_checked_date'),
  KEY 'queue_date' ('queue_date')
) ENGINE=InnoDB  DEFAULT CHARSET=utf8 COLLATE=utf8_bin AUTO_INCREMENT=1 ;

-- Table structure for table 'bestof_tweets'
CREATE TABLE IF NOT EXISTS 'bestof_tweets' (
  'record_id' int(11) NOT NULL auto_increment,
  'status_id' int(11) NOT NULL,
  'author_user_name' varchar(50) NOT NULL,
  'author_user_id' int(11) NOT NULL,
  'author_avatar' varchar(255) NOT NULL,
  'tweet' varchar(160) NOT NULL,
  'favorited' int(11) NOT NULL default '1',
  'created_at' datetime NOT NULL,
  PRIMARY KEY  ('record_id'),
  KEY 'status_id' ('status_id','author_user_id','favorited','created_at')
) ENGINE=InnoDB  DEFAULT CHARSET=utf8 COLLATE=utf8_bin AUTO_INCREMENT=1 ;

-- Table structure for table 'tweetalert_log'
CREATE TABLE IF NOT EXISTS 'tweetalert_log' (
  'record_id' int(11) NOT NULL auto_increment,
  'status_id' int(11) NOT NULL,
  'scan_datetime' datetime NOT NULL,
  'keywords' int(11) NOT NULL default '0',
  'matches' int(11) NOT NULL default '0',
  'messages' int(11) NOT NULL default '0',
  PRIMARY KEY  ('record_id'),
  KEY 'status_id' ('status_id'),
  KEY 'keywords' ('keywords')
) ENGINE=InnoDB  DEFAULT CHARSET=utf8 COLLATE=utf8_bin AUTO_INCREMENT=1 ;

-- Table structure for table 'tweetalert_profiles'
CREATE TABLE IF NOT EXISTS 'tweetalert_profiles' (
  'record_id' int(11) NOT NULL auto_increment,
  'user_name' varchar(50) NOT NULL,
  'keyword' varchar(140) NOT NULL,
  PRIMARY KEY  ('record_id'),
  KEY 'user_name' ('user_name'),
  KEY 'keyword' ('keyword')
) ENGINE=InnoDB  DEFAULT CHARSET=utf8 COLLATE=utf8_bin AUTO_INCREMENT=1 ;

-- Table structure for table 'tweetbroadcast_groups'
```

```
CREATE TABLE IF NOT EXISTS 'tweetbroadcast_groups' (
  'record_id' int(11) NOT NULL auto_increment,
  'owner' varchar(50) NOT NULL,
  'other' varchar(50) NOT NULL,
  PRIMARY KEY ('record_id'),
  KEY 'owner' ('owner'),
  KEY 'other' ('other')
) ENGINE=InnoDB  DEFAULT CHARSET=utf8 COLLATE=utf8_bin AUTO_INCREMENT=1 ;

-- Table structure for table 'tweetbroadcast_tweets'
CREATE TABLE IF NOT EXISTS 'tweetbroadcast_tweets' (
  'record_id' int(11) NOT NULL auto_increment,
  'status_id' int(11) NOT NULL,
  'author_username' varchar(50) NOT NULL,
  'author_fullname' varchar(50) NOT NULL,
  'author_avatar' varchar(255) NOT NULL,
  'tweet_text' varchar(160) NOT NULL,
  'tweet_html' varchar(255) NOT NULL,
  'pub_date' timestamp NOT NULL default '0000-00-00 00:00:00',
  PRIMARY KEY ('record_id'),
  KEY 'author_username' ('author_username'),
  KEY 'pub_date' ('pub_date')
) ENGINE=InnoDB  DEFAULT CHARSET=utf8 COLLATE=utf8_bin AUTO_INCREMENT=1 ;
```

In phpMyAdmin, there are two ways to get these statements into the MySQL database: by cutting and pasting, or by loading the *.sql* file directly. However you finally manage to execute the SQL, you should get nine tables when the dust settles (see Figure 6-5).

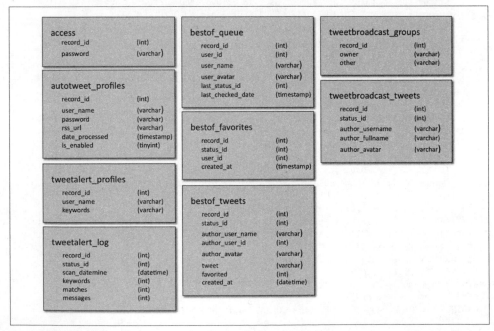

Figure 6-5. The database tables used by the sample applications

At this point, your database should be ready to roll. You have access, and you have a place for the sample applications to store the new data. What you need now is a place to put all the code you are going to write.

Included Functions

As described earlier in "PHP" on page 96, includes are files that contain additional code not native to your main program. Including external code helps combat redundancy and makes maintenance of your code more efficient. In this section, we will look at how to get your files to a more secure place outside of the web path and investigate what each external function is supposed to do to support the sample web applications.

 The code for the sample applications relies heavily on built-in functions that come with PHP. I constructed the custom functions described in this chapter to help centralize some key parts of the code, provide a little extra security in places, and make the code easier to maintain. However, there are a number of popular component libraries and frameworks (PEAR, CodeIgniter, Cake, etc.) that do this work for you.

Understanding how the core commands and functions of PHP work will help you with future customization, but you are *strongly* encouraged to familiarize yourself with PHP frameworks (*http://www.phpframeworks .com*) to help you build applications quickly and cleanly.

Creating Your Includes Directory

Ideally, you want the place where you put your external code—in particular, any hard-coded database or Twitter access information—to reside outside of the web path. If you place your PHP files in the web path—perhaps in a subdirectory under your application interface files—people will have an opportunity to call those pages directly or find other ways to interact with that code in ways you didn't anticipate and may not desire. There are ways to prevent this with additional lines of code or clever use of directory permissions, but the easiest method is to not put the included files in the web path.

In most web hosting accounts, you are given access to your files on the remote server through the Secure File Transfer Protocol (SFTP). You can use desktop clients to transfer your code from your local computer to the web server. Alternatively, some web page editing tools, such as Dreamweaver, can be configured to automatically update the server whenever you save your work. I like using desktop clients because publishing to the Web feels deliberate, but whatever means you use to get your files to the web hosting server space is OK.

There are many FTP clients—such as CuteFTP (*http://www.cuteftp .com*) or FileZilla (*http://filezilla-project.org*) for Windows, and Fetch (*http://fetchsoftworks.com*) or Cyberduck (*http://cyberduck.ch*) for Mac OS X—that offer secure protocol options.

If you cannot navigate up the directory path to get to a level higher than your website root (the place where the main index page of your website typically lives), you may not have any choice but to create your included files directory in the web path. If you can go up a level in the directory structure, you will likely see a *public_html* or *www* directory. This is the directory housing your web pages; anything not in this folder is not directly accessible by the Web. This is where you might consider creating a new directory to house the external files you want to include.

Twelve included files containing over three dozen functions support this book's sample applications. In brief, here are the files and what they're used for:

environment.php
> Figuring out where files live on the remote server

api_config.php
> Connecting to the Twitter API

database.php
> Connecting to the MySQL database

sql_queries.php
> Generating the specific database queries needed to get data

parse_data.php
> Turning XML files into useful array data for PHP, and vice versa

pw_manage.php
> Scrambling and unscrambling the stored passwords

validate_data.php
> Performing some basic checks of user input data

sort_data.php
> Ordering the Twitter data in a meaningful way

calculate_stats.php
> Computing some stats for the network groups

log_manage.php
> Opening and closing files to document activity and outcomes

status_messages.php
> Turning integer error codes into text for feedback to the user

html_template.php
> Generating the web page parts

Not all applications will need to include all of these files, but together they provide the functions to handle much of the redundant logic. The code for every function—shown throughout this chapter in Examples 6-2 through 6-37—should be copied into a text editor and saved to create these dozen PHP files. When they are uploaded to the *includes* directory, the list should look like Figure 6-6.

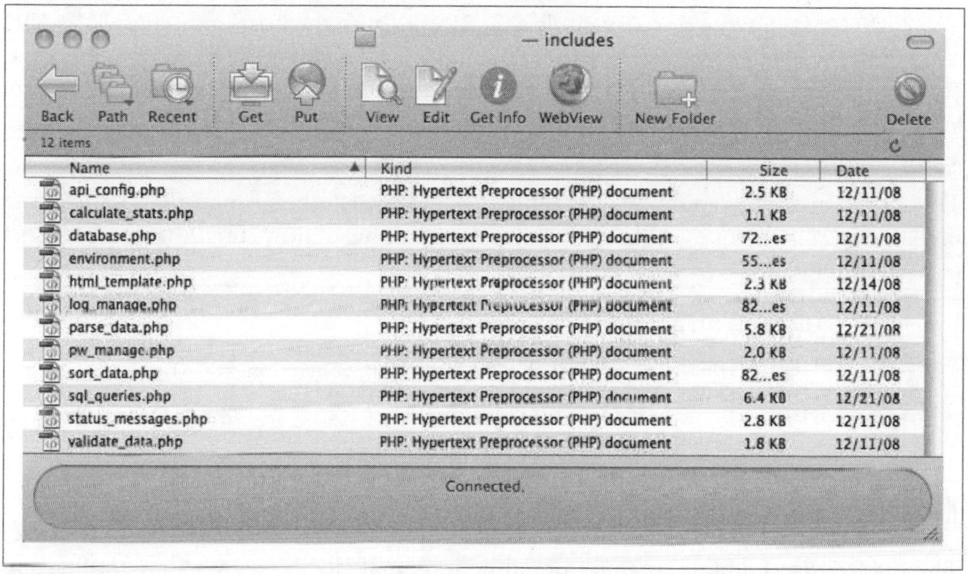

Figure 6-6. The files containing included functions to support the sample apps

Environment Functions

The first file, *environment.php*, contains two functions that find where the calling page is situated within the web server's directory structure. These functions prevent you from having to hardcode strings for your web domain or file path.

getServerPath( )

The getServerPath( ) function (Example 6-2) accepts the URI used in the web page request and returns the server path to the directory where the calling file resides. For example, if the file that included and called this function was http://makice.net/uar/ test.php, the function would return /uar/ as the server path, or the part added to the root of the domain.

The basename( ) function is the key. It separates the filename from the rest of the request URI and then removes that text from the end of the full path.

Example 6-2. Function getServerPath( )

```
function getServerPath ($request_uri) {
    if (strpos($request_uri, basename($request_uri)) !== false) {
```

```
    $request_uri = reset(explode(basename($request_uri), $request_uri));
    }
    return $request_uri;
}
```

getHTTPpath( )

The getHTTPpath( ) function (Example 6-3) accepts both the host domain and the URI used in the web page request, returning the full HTTP URL to the directory where the calling file resides. For example, if the file that included and called this function was http://makice.net/uar/test.php, the function would return http://makice.net/uar/ as the home page of this file's directory.

This saves on a little typing by leveraging the getServerPath( ) function to remove the filename from the request URI. This code is an example of how functions can build off of each other.

Example 6-3. Function getHTTPpath( )

```
function getHTTPpath ($http_host,$request_uri) {
    $url = 'http://'. $http_host . getServerPath($request_uri);
    return $url;
}
```

API Configuration Functions

The *api_config.php* file contains three functions that do the legwork in configuring PHP's connection to the Twitter API. As the API changes, this is the place to make the corresponding changes to method paths and names so they'll propagate across all of your applications instantly.

 These functions rely on the cURL extension being configured by the web host. cURL is a useful way to grab data remotely, but it is not part of the default PHP build. You'll need to confirm with your web host that it is supported.

prepAPI( )

The prepAPI( ) function (Example 6-4) doesn't take any parameters: it is merely an encapsulation of all the configuration settings that define how PHP will be able to talk to the Twitter API through cURL. It returns the master account username and an associative array filled with simple method references and the URL needed to request it. Some of the method URLs also include a placeholder—[id]—that can be substituted for a Twitter member's username or user ID in the application.

This function is set up to allow you to change the format, domain or method calls to match whatever Twitter allows in the future. Since the associative array references the key and not the URL stored in its value, this should limit edits outside of this function.

Example 6-4. Function prepAPI( )

```
function prepAPI () {

    # This is the Twitter account to use to run these applications
    $master_username    = 'your_twitter_username';

    # Define how to access Twitter API
    $api_domain         = 'https://twitter.com';
    $api_format         = 'xml';
    $search_domain      = 'http://search.twitter.com';
    $search_format      = 'atom';

    # Define method paths ... [id] is a placeholder
    $api_method = array(
        'end_session"            => '/account/end_session',
        'rate_limit'             => '/account/rate_limit_status',
        'delivery_device'        => '/account/update_delivery_device',
        'location'               -> '/account/update_location',
        'profile'                => '/account/update_profile',
        'profile_background'     => '/account/update_profile_background_image',
        'profile_colors'         -> '/account/update_profile_colors',
        'profile_image'          => '/account/update_profile_image',
        'credentials'            => '/account/verify_credentials',

        'block'                  => '/blocks/create/[id]',
        'remove_block'           => '/blocks/destroy/[id]',

        'messages_received'      => '/direct_messages',
        'delete_message'         => '/direct_messages/destroy/[id]',
        'post_message'           => '/direct_messages/new',
        'messages_sent'          => '/direct_messages/sent',

        'bookmarks'              => '/favorites/[id]',
        'create_bookmark'        => '/favorites/create/[id]',
        'remove_bookmark'        => '/favorites/destroy/[id]',

        'followers_ids'          => '/followers/ids/[id]',

        'following_ids'          => '/friends/ids/[id]',

        'follow'                 => '/friendships/create/[id]',
        'unfollow'               => '/friendships/destroy/[id]',
        'confirm_follow'         => '/friendships/exists',

        'downtime_schedule'      => '/help/downtime_schedule',
        'test'                   => '/help/test',

        'turn_on_notification'   => '/notifications/follow/[id]',
        'turn_off_notification'  => '/notifications/leave/[id]',

        'delete_tweet'           => '/statuses/destroy/[id]',
        'followers'              => '/statuses/followers/[id]',
        'following'              => '/statuses/friends/[id]',
        'friends_timeline'       => '/statuses/friends_timeline',
        'public_timeline'        => '/statuses/public_timeline',
```

```
                'replies'                => '/statuses/replies',
                'show_tweet'             => '/statuses/show/[id]',
                'post_tweet'             => '/statuses/update',
                'user_timeline'          => '/statuses/user_timeline/[id]',

                'show_user'              => '/users/show/[id]',
    );

        # Construct cURL sources
        foreach ($api_method as $key => $value){
            $urls[$key]      = $api_domain . $value . '.' . $api_format;
        }
        $urls['search']       = $search_domain . '/search.' . $search_format;
        $urls['search_web']   = $search_domain . '/search';
        $urls['trends']       = $search_domain . '/trends.json';

        return array($master_username,$urls);
}
```

prepRequest( )

The prepRequest( ) function (Example 6-5) accepts up to three parameters and uses them to initialize the cURL object. cURL (see "cURL" on page 118) is the mechanism by which PHP will be able to communicate with the API. For that dialogue to begin, the application has to open up a channel. It does this with curl_init( ), assigning the object to $cURL for convenient referencing while it is needed. The handle variable the custom function returns can be used to make remote requests from the main web application.

A number of tools are available to help with configuration and execution of the cURL handle. One such function is curl_setopt_array( ), which sets several configuration options for the connection at once:

CURLOPT_USERAGENT

Setting the User-Agent header in the HTTP request to something meaningful will tell the API developers who you are (a courtesy that can help both parties be proactive in troubleshooting potential problems). To customize the signature for each of the sample applications, a $title parameter is appended onto the name of the entire suite.

CURLOPT_USERPWD

For most applications, the person submitting the web form will provide the $username and $password. However, in this administrative tool the account used is the one powering the whole suite. These two parameters are passed to cURL as a single string, separated by a colon (:).

CURLOPT_RETURNTRANSFER

cURL can output the data it receives as it arrives, which can be useful when you want to include remote content verbatim. This application, however, will work best if that content can be examined before it's shown to the end user. Setting this value to true, or 1, will allow the response from the API to be stored in variables for PHP to manipulate.

CURLOPT_SSL_VERIFYPEER

When set to false, this serves the same function as -k in the command-line cURL request (see "Play Along at Home" on page 149): namely, it disables the verification of the secured certificate to allow the secure method to be requested.

 Again, this is not an ideal solution. Turning off verification of secure certificates can defeat the purpose of HTTPS encryption. A better option would be to fix the certificate bundle to include what you need using the CURLOPT_CAPATH and CURLOPT_CAINFO options. Visit *http://php.net/curl_setopt* for more information.

CURLOPT_HTTPHEADER

When performing a POST operation, cURL will automatically add an "Expect: 100-continue" header. That is an instruction to wait for an HTTP response of 100 before continuing. Not all web servers support this, however, and errors are sometimes returned. You can fix this problem by suppressing the Expect header, filling its array value with an empty string.

These values are defined in a $cURL_options associative array using the option names as keys. The array is then passed along with the cURL object as its parameter to set those options in one swoop. Alternatively, you can use curl_setopt( ) to set each option individually.

Example 6-5. Function prepAPI( )

```
function prepRequest ($title='',$username='',$password='') {
$options = array(
        CURLOPT_USERAGENT       => 'Twitter Up and Running - '.$title,
        CURLOPT_RETURNTRANSFER  => 1,
        CURLOPT_SSL_VERIFYPEER  => false,
        CURLOPT_HTTPHEADER      => array('Expect:')
    );
    if ($username != '') {
        $options[CURLOPT_USERPWD] = "$username:$password";
    }
    $cURL = curl_init();
    curl_setopt_array($cURL, $options);
    return $cURL;
}
```

apiRequest( )

The apiRequest( ) function (Example 6-6) accepts two parameters: the cURL handle and the URL for a specific API method, as built previously using the prepAPI( ) function. After setting the method URL as an option, the cURL request is executed and the results are returned as an array of two values: the HTTP status code response (see "Accessing the API" on page 134) and the XML response from Twitter.

A few untested assumptions are at work with this function. First, it is presumed that the cURL handle exists and is valid. Second, it is presumed that all other options—such as the username and password, or HTTP POST method—are set prior to calling this function. You can adapt this function to add checks on the parameter values being passed, but this version doesn't bother with that level of graceful error handling.

Example 6-6. Function apiRequest( )

```
function apiRequest ($cURL,$url) {
    curl_setopt($cURL, CURLOPT_URL, $url);
    $foo            = curl_exec($cURL);
    $status         = curl_getinfo($cURL, CURLINFO_HTTP_CODE);
    return array($status,$foo);
}
```

Database Functions

The *database.php* file contains three functions that connect PHP to the MySQL database. This file is where your user access information (including a database password) is stored. This is the biggest reason why your include files should not reside in your web path.

getDBconfiguration( )

The getDBconfiguration( ) function (Example 6-7) accepts no parameters; it is an encapsulation of code to set some important array values (the host, the database name, and the username and password of an account that can access that database).

This function is not called directly by the web applications, but instead is called by the openDB( ) function as part of the process of establishing a database connection.

Example 6-7. Function getDBconfiguration( )

```
function getDBconfiguration () {
    $db['host']     = 'localhost';
    $db['name']     = '<name of database>';
    $db['username'] = '<database username>';
    $db['password'] = '<database password>';
    return $db;
}
```

Remember from earlier in this chapter that what you can do with your database connection will be determined by the access rights granted to the user account you use to connect. If you are attempting to program in ways to change the schema, for instance, you will have to adjust the user rights on the database side.

openDB()

The openDB() function (Example 6-8) also accepts no parameters. It is invoked by any application that needs to access the database you created earlier in this chapter. This function relies on the getDBconfiguration() function to retrieve the database access information and then connects to MySQL through special PHP functions. It returns the handle for an open database connection.

Example 6-8. Function openDB()

```
function openDB () {
    $db = getDBconfiguration();
    $db_connection = mysql_connect($db['host'], $db['username'], $db['password']);
    mysql_select_db($db['name']);
    return $db_connection;
}
```

closeDB()

The closeDB() function (Example 6-9) takes a handle for an active database connection and closes that connection. It returns a Boolean to indicate whether or not it was successful in doing so.

A function like this may not seem to do much, but it does present a structure that will make the code expandable in the future. Not only is the new function reference more compact than the actual MySQL function, but setting up closeDB() allows you to easily piggyback other actions with the close database action, such as writing to a log file or performing other cleanup actions.

Example 6-9. Function closeDB()

```
function closeDB ($db_connection) {
    return mysql_close($db_connection);
}
```

SQL Queries

The *sql_queries.php* file contains one function that stores all of the SQL statements needed for each calling application. Not every SQL query used in the applications is included here, since some are rewritten dynamically when looping over a data set. What this function does handle are the query statements that do not change during the course of a particular application.

getQueries()

The getQueries() function (Example 6-10) will populate an associative array with query names and corresponding SQL statements, returning that array back to the calling program. The function accepts an associative array, $stuff, that contains key/value pairs of required variables to complete those queries.

To avoid SQL injection attacks, the values in the `$stuff` associative array must be passed through the `mysql_real_escape_string( )` function to be parameterized. This is where using the improved `mysqli` extension for database access would help automatically.

Since each application will need a different set of queries, this function leverages switch logic to keep each set separate. The cases are based on the `basename( )` of the `$_SERVER['SCRIPT_NAME']`, which should be the filename of the requested web page. For the automated tasks, however, there is no web page request; the applications are invoked by a *crontab* by the host server. Since the case will fall through to the default, there is a second nested `switch` statement that looks for a variable to identify the page (`$stuff['file_id']`).

Example 6-10. Function getQueries( )

```
function getQueries ($stuff) {
    foreach($stuff as $key => $value) {
        $stuff[$key] = mysql_real_escape_string($value);
    }
    $sql = array();
    switch (basename($_SERVER['SCRIPT_NAME'])) {

        case 'uar_auto_tweet.php':
            # stuff => twitter_username, scrambled_password, rss_feed
            $sql = array (
                'Retrieve_Stored_RSS' =>    "
SELECT   rss_url
FROM     autotweet_profiles
WHERE    user_name = '{$stuff['twitter_username']}'
                ",
                'Create_Profile'      =>    "
INSERT INTO autotweet_profiles
        (user_name, password, rss_url)
VALUES
        ('{$stuff['twitter_username']}',
        '{$stuff['scrambled_password']}',
        '{$stuff['rss_feed']}')
                ",
                'Update_Profile'      =>    "
UPDATE   autotweet_profiles
SET      password = '{$stuff['scrambled_password']}',
         rss_url = '{$stuff['rss_feed']}',
         is_enabled = 1
WHERE    user_name = '{$stuff['twitter_username']}'
                ",
                'Disable_Profile'     =>    "
UPDATE   autotweet_profiles
SET      is_enabled = 0
WHERE    user_name = '{$stuff['twitter_username']}'
                ",
                'Remove_Profile'      =>    "
DELETE FROM autotweet_profiles
```

```
WHERE    user_name = '{$stuff['twitter_username']}'
             "
         );
         break;

    case 'uar_broadcast.php':
         # stuff => twitter_username
         $sql = array (
             'Retrieve_Recent_Tweets' =>    "
SELECT  DISTINCT t.status_id,
        t.author_username, t.author_fullname, t.author_avatar,
        t.tweet_text, t.tweet_html, t.pub_date,
        concat(year(t.pub_date),' ',LPAD(dayofyear(t.pub_date),3,'0')) as
            tweet_day
FROM    tweetbroadcast_tweets t
        INNER JOIN tweetbroadcast_groups m ON m.other = t.author_username
WHERE   m.owner = '{$stuff['twitter_username']}'
ORDER BY t.pub_date desc
             ",
             'Retrieve_Publish_Date'  =>    "
SELECT  max(t.pub_date) as last_update
FROM    tweetbroadcast_tweets t
        INNER JOIN tweetbroadcast_groups m ON m.other = t.author_username
WHERE   m.owner = '{$stuff['twitter_username']}'
             "
         );
         break;

    case 'uar_tweet_alert.php':
         # stuff => twitter_username
         $sql = array (
             'Retrieve_Stored_Alerts' =>    "
SELECT  keyword
FROM    tweetalert_profiles
WHERE   user_name = '{$stuff['twitter_username']}'
             ",
             'Remove_Alerts'          =>    "
DELETE FROM tweetalert_profiles
WHERE   user_name = '{$stuff['twitter_username']}'
             "
         );
         break;

    case 'uar_tweet_broadcast.php':
         # stuff => twitter_username
         $sql = array (
             'Retrieve_Stored_Group' => "
SELECT  distinct other
FROM    tweetbroadcast_groups
WHERE   owner = '{$stuff['twitter_username']}'
ORDER BY other
             ",
             'Retrieve_Stored_Memberships' => "
SELECT  distinct owner
FROM    tweetbroadcast_groups
```

```
WHERE    other = '{$stuff['twitter_username']}'
         and owner <> '{$stuff['twitter_username']}'
ORDER BY owner
             ",
             'Remove_Group'          => "
DELETE FROM tweetbroadcast_groups
WHERE    owner = '{$stuff['twitter_username']}'
             "
         );
         break;

     case 'uar_store_master_pw.php':
         # stuff => scrambled_password
         $sql = array (
             'Update_Password'       => "
UPDATE   access
SET      password = '{$stuff['scrambled_password']}'
             "
         );
         break;

   case 'all_time.php':
         # stuff => id, since
         $id_conditional = "lower(t.author_user_name) = '{$stuff['id']}'";
         if (is_int($stuff['id']+0)) {
             $id_conditional = "{$stuff['id']} in (0,t.author_user_id)";
         }
         $sql = array (
             'Retrieve_Favorites'    => "
SELECT   t.status_id, t.author_user_name, t.author_user_id, t.author_avatar,
         t.tweet, t.favorited, t.created_at
FROM     bestof_tweets t
WHERE    $id_conditional
         AND t.created_at > FROM_UNIXTIME({$stuff['since']})
ORDER BY t.favorited desc
LIMIT 0,20
             "
         );
         break;

   default:
         # Presumably, this is an automated script out of the web path
         switch ($stuff['file_id']) {

             case 'uar_rss_to_tweet.php':
                 # stuff => [none]
                 $sql = array (
                     'Retrieve_Stored_RSS' => "
SELECT   record_id, user_name, password, rss_url, date_processed
FROM     autotweet_profiles
WHERE    is_enabled = 1
                     "
                 );
                 break;
```

```php
                case 'uar_collect_broadcast.php':
                    # stuff => [none]
                    $sql = array (
                        'Retrieve_Stored_Group' => "
SELECT   m.other,
         CASE WHEN max(t.status_id) is NULL THEN 0
              ELSE max(t.status_id) END last_status_id
FROM     tweetbroadcast_groups m
         LEFT OUTER JOIN tweetbroadcast_tweets t ON t.author_username = m.other
GROUP BY m.other
ORDER BY m.other
                        ",
                        'Remove_Old_Tweets'    => "
DELETE FROM tweetbroadcast_tweets
WHERE    Datediff(current_date,pub_date) > 20
                        "
                    );
                    break;

                case 'uar_collect_favorites.php':
                    # stuff => [none]
                    $sql = array (
                        'Retrieve_Queue'       => "
SELECT   user_id, user_name, last_status_id
FROM     bestof_queue
WHERE    DateDiff(current_date,last_checked_date) > 1
         or DateDiff(current_date,last_checked_date) IS NULL
ORDER BY last_checked_date
LIMIT 0,5
                        ",
                        'Retrieve_Master_Password' => "
SELECT   password
FROM     access
LIMIT 0,1
                        ",
                        'Retrieve_Default_ID'      => "
SELECT   case when min(last_status_id) is null then 0
         else min(last_status_id) end default_status_id
FROM     bestof_queue
WHERE    DateDiff(current_date,last_checked_date) > 0
                        "
                    );
                    break;

                case 'uar_scan_tweets.php':
                    # stuff => [none]
                    $sql = array (
                        'Retrieve_Stored_Alerts'  => "
SELECT   distinct keyword
FROM     tweetalert_profiles
                        ",
                        'Retrieve_Master_Password' => "
SELECT   password
FROM     access
LIMIT 0,1
```

```
                            ",
                    'Retrieve_Last_Status'        => "
    SELECT  CASE WHEN max(status_id) is null THEN 0
            ELSE max(status_id) END last_status_id
    FROM    tweetalert_log
                            ",
                    'Prune_Log'                   => "
    DELETE FROM tweetalert_log
    WHERE   Datediff(current_date,scan_datetime) > 30
                            "
                    );
                    break;

                default:
                    break;

            }
            break;
    }

    return $sql;
}
```

Data Parsing Functions

The *parse_data.php* file contains eight functions that extract information from RSS files or use RSS writers to create new files. This file incorporates two different ways of parsing data: with a DOM document, and with SimpleXML.

parseFeed( )

The parseFeed( ) function (Example 6-11) accepts two parameters: the URL of the RSS feed to parse (required), and an optional date to use as a filter. It returns an array containing an associative array and a string. The associative array is filled with details about each article found in the feed, and the string contains the title of the feed.

 Only a very rudimentary check is performed to make sure the URL entered begins with "http". Better validation is warranted.

This function relies on the DOM document methods to perform the parsing, looking for a very particular XML structure. Each new article in the RSS feed is nested in <item> tags, which contain standard elements that hold details (title, article URL, article ID, and publication date) that will be useful in creating a tweet.

The optional date parameter acts as a filter to identify the new material. Any encountered items whose publication dates are more recent than the date parameter value will be included, and others will be discarded.

Example 6-11. Function parseFeed( )

```php
function parseFeed ($url,$date=0) {
    $thisFeed       = array();
    $feed_title     = '';
    if(preg_match("/^http/", $url)) {
    try {

        $doc        = createDOMfromURL($url);
        $feed_title = $doc->getElementsByTagName('title')->item(0)->nodeValue;
        $item       = $doc->getElementsByTagName('item');
        foreach ($item as $item) {
            $articleInfo = array (
                'title'    => $item->getElementsByTagName('title')->item(0)->
                              nodeValue,
                'link'     => $item->getElementsByTagName('link')->item(0)->
                              nodeValue,
                'id'       => $item->getElementsByTagName('id')->item(0)->
                              nodeValue,
                'pubDate'  => $item->getElementsByTagName('pubDate')->item(0)->
                              nodeValue
            );
            if (($date == 0)
            || (strtotime($articleInfo['pubDate']) > strtotime($date))) {
                array_push($thisFeed, $articleInfo);
            }
        }

        $entry      = $doc->getElementsByTagName('entry');
        foreach ($entry as $entry) {
            $articleInfo = array (
                'title'     => $entry->getElementsByTagName('title')->item(0)->
                               nodeValue,
                'link'      => $entry->getElementsByTagName('link')->item(0)->
                               getAttribute('href'),
                'id'        => $entry->getElementsByTagName('id')->item(0)->
                               nodeValue,
                'pubDate'   => $entry->getElementsByTagName('pubDate')->item(0)->
                               nodeValue,
                'published' => $entry->getElementsByTagName('published')->item(0)->
                               nodeValue
            );
            foreach($articleInfo as $key => $value) {
                $articleInfo[$key] = htmlspecialchars($value, ENT_QUOTES, 'UTF-8');
            }
            if (($date == 0)
            || (strtotime($articleInfo['pubDate']) > strtotime($date))
            || (strtotime($articleInfo['published']) > strtotime($date))) {
                array_push($thisFeed, $articleInfo);
            }
        }
    } catch (Exception $e)                    { $form_error = 15; }
    }
    foreach($thisFeed as &$value) {
        $value = htmlspecialchars($value, ENT_QUOTES, 'UTF-8');
    }
```

```
    $feed_title = htmlspecialchars($feed_title, ENT_QUOTES, 'UTF-8');
    return array($thisFeed,$feed_title);
}
```

parseXML( )

The parseXML( ) function (Example 6-12) accepts a string containing XML data that has already been retrieved from elsewhere in the application. Using SimpleXML parsing methods, the function fills an array with the information for each record found in the parsed string.

The Twitter API returns several different XML structures (see Chapter 5) that require different nomenclature to parse properly. The important switch logic in this function uses the name of the root node for its cases, returning an array filled with information parsed in a manner suitable for the particular structure. This code is able to parse single and multiple users and status updates.

Example 6-12. Function parseXML( )

```
function parseXML ($data) {
    $thisFeed      = array();

    try {
        $xml       = createParserFromString(utf8_encode($data));
        $root      = $xml->getName();
        switch ($root) {

            case 'user':
                $thisFeed[] = array(
                    'user_id'             => $xml->user->id,
                    'user_name'           => $xml->screen_name,
                    'full_name'           => $xml->name,
                    'avatar'              => $xml->profile_image_url,
                    'location'            => $xml->location,
                    'description'         => $xml->description,
                    'url'                 => $xml->url,
                    'is_protected'        => $xml->protected,
                    'followers'           => $xml->followers_count,
                    'following'           => $xml->friends_count,
                    'tweets'              => $xml->statuses_count
                );
                break;

            case 'status':
                $thisFeed[] = array(
                    'status_id'           => $xml->id
                );
                break;

            case 'users':
                foreach($xml->children() as $item) {
                    $thisFeed[] = array(
                        'status_id'           => $item->status->id,
                        'user_id'             => $item->id,
```

```
                    'user_name'        => $item->screen_name,
                    'full_name'        => $item->name,
                    'avatar'           => $item->profile_image_url,
                    'location'         => $item->location,
                    'description'      => $item->description,
                    'url'              => $item->url,
                    'is_protected'     => $item->protected,
                    'followers'        => $item->followers_count,
                    'tweet_text'       => $item->status->text,
                    'tweet_html'       => $item->status->text,
                    'pub_date'         => gmdate("Y-m-d H:i:s",strToTime($item->
                                          status->created_at)),
                    'favorites_count' => $item->favorites_count
            );
        }
        break;

    case 'statuses':
        foreach($xml->children() as $item) {
            $thisFeed[] = array(
                    'status_id'        => $item->id,
                    'user_id'          => $item->user->id,
                    'user_name'        => $item->user->screen_name,
                    'full_name'        => $item->user->name,
                    'avatar'           => $item->user->profile_image_url,
                    'location'         => $item->user->location,
                    'description'      => $item->user->description,
                    'url'              => $item->user->url,
                    'is_protected'     => $item->user->protected,
                    'followers'        => $item->user->followers_count,
                    'tweet_text'       => $item->text,
                    'tweet_html'       => $1tem->text,
                    'pub_date'         => gmdate("Y-m-d H:i:s",strToTime($item->
                                          created_at)),
                    'favorites_count' => $item->favorites_count
            );
        }
        break;

    default:
        break;
    }
} catch (Exception $e) {  }

return $thisFeed;
}
```

createDOMfromURL( )

The createDOMfromURL( ) function (Example 6-13) accepts a URL to a web document, presumably one that can be parsed as an RSS feed. If it is able to load the page content, this function will return the handle for a new DOM document. This function is not called directly by the web application, but rather is referenced as part of the RSS parsing function (parseFeed( )).

Example 6-13. Function createDOMfromURL( )

```
function createDOMfromURL ($url) {
    $doc          = new DOMDocument();
    $doc->load($url);
    return $doc;
}
```

createParserFromString( )

The createParserFromString( ) function (Example 6-14) accepts a string containing valid XML and returns the handle for a new XML object. This function is not called directly by the web application, but rather is referenced as part of the XML parsing function (parseXML( )).

Example 6-14. Function createParserFromString( )

```
function createParserFromString ($data) {
    $xml = simplexml_load_string($data);
    return $xml;
}
```

createXMLshell( )

The createXMLshell( ) function (Example 6-15) initiates a new SimpleXML document with a string containing an empty `<statuses></statuses>` shell. This function does not ask for any parameters, returning the XML object that can be filled with new status items.

Example 6-15. Function createXMLshell( )

```
function createXMLshell () {
    $base_xml = <<<BASE_XML
<?xml version="1.0" encoding="UTF-8"?>
<statuses type="array">
</statuses>
BASE_XML;
    $xml = new SimpleXMLElement($base_xml);
    return $xml;
}
```

createRSSshell( )

Similar to createXMLshell( ), the createRSSshell( ) function (Example 6-16) creates a new XML object filled with the initial elements needed to build an RSS feed. Unlike that other function, however, a parameter is expected and is used to populate the title, link, and current publication date for the feed.

The RSS structure differs from the XML used by Twitter in that it is a more defined standard with an initial tag element devoted to describing the entire feed, not just the list of articles. The RSS object can be populated using the addChild( ) function, an example of which is included in this function to create a `<generator>` element.

Although my code is very trusting of the data Twitter provides through the API, it might be considered more correct to escape all data that comes from outside the program (including from the database).

Example 6-16. Function createRSSshell( )

```
function createRSSshell ($data) {
$base_rss = <<<BASE_RSS
<?xml version="1.0" encoding="UTF-8"?>
<rss version="2.0">
    <channel>
        <title>{$data['title']}</title>
        <link>{$data['link']}</link>
        <description>This is a sample application from the O'Reilly book, "Twitter:
            Up and Running"</description>
        <language>en</language>
        <pubDate>{$data['last_update']}</pubDate>
    </channel>
</rss>
BASE_RSS;
    $xml = new SimpleXMLElement($base_rss);
    $xml->channel->addChild('generator',$data['generator']);
    return $xml;
}
```

formatTweetAsXHTML( )

The formatTweetAsXHTML( ) function (Example 6-17) accepts an associative array as a parameter and returns a string containing the XHTML for a single tweet. This function is used to help aggregate several tweets into a single RSS article for use in the Tweet Broadcast tool (see "Tweet Broadcast" on page 291).

Example 6-17. Function formatTweetAsXML( )

```
function formatTweetAsXHTML ($data) {
    $xhtml = <<<RSS_TWEET
<div id='{$data['status_id']}'>
    <div class='tweet'>
        <p>
            {$data['tweet_html']}
        </p>
        <div class='meta'>
            <span>
                <a href='{$data['status_url']}'>{$data['pub_date']}</a>
            </span>
        </div>
    </div>
    <div class='attribution'>
        <div class='avatar'>
            <a href='{$data['author_url']}'><img
                alt='{$data['author_username']} avatar'
                src='{$data['author_avatar']}' /></a>
        </div>
```

```
        <div class='username'>
            <a href='{$data['author_url']}'>{$data['author_username']}</a>
        </div>
        <div class='author'>
            {$data['author_fullname']}
        </div>
    </div>
</div>
RSS_TWEET;
    return $xhtml;
}
```

addItem( )

The addItem( ) function (Example 6-18) returns a new child element as an XML object after filling it with data. The function accepts three parameters: the XML object that will serve as the parent of this new item, the name of the new nested tag structure, and an associative array containing the names and values of each child element.

This information is used to add content to an initial XML shell.

Example 6-18. Function addItem( )

```
function addItem ($xml,$child,$data) {
    $item = $xml->addChild($child);
    foreach($data as $key => $value){
        $value = htmlspecialchars($value, ENT_QUOTES, 'UTF-8');
        $item->addChild($key, $value);
    }
    return $item;
}
```

> It isn't a problem for this code, but it might be a good improvement to make sure the $key value is not numeric. XML doesn't like that.

Password Management Functions

The *pw_manage.php* file contains four functions that convert sensitive passwords into strings that can be stored in a database, and vice versa. Passwords should never be saved as plain text, if they are kept at all. Encrypting a password and then duplicating that process later to verify user access is highly secure. Scrambling a password in a way that can be unscrambled back to the plain-text version is less secure, but it is still preferable to just storing a readable version of the password.

Asking your users for their passwords and saving them to your server is unavoidable if you want to perform some of the functions that make the Twitter API so powerful, such as posting content to the timeline. Be sensitive to the issues that come along with this request (see "Gone Phishing: A Word About Passwords" on page 182) and avoid asking for credentials when possible.

securePassword( )

The securePassword( ) function (Example 6-19) takes a plain-text password and returns an encrypted version that can safely be stored in a database. The secured version relies on a random "salt" text string to increase the complexity of the encryption. Because the salt is appended to the hashed password, it can also be extracted for later use in comparing the stored hash to a new one created from user data.

This kind of encryption is a one-way process. You can't undo the hashing process, which means you shouldn't save the password in this form with the expectation that you will be able to use it later. This method of encryption is good for comparison only, by using the same salt to recreate the string and compare the result to what is already stored in the database. If they are the same, the user's password is correct.

Because the purpose of saving a Twitter member's password is to reuse it to access the Twitter API for functions such as automatically posting from an RSS feed, this function is not one that is used in the sample applications. I have included it only as an example of how to encrypt a plain-text password.

Example 6-19. Function securePassword( )

```
function securePassword ($password) {
    $salt = substr(str_pad(dechex(mt_rand()),8,'0',STR_PAD_LEFT),-8);
    $secured = $salt . hash('sha256',$password.$salt);
    return $secured;
}
```

comparePassword( )

The companion to securePassword( ) is the comparePassword( ) function (Example 6-20). This function accepts a plain-text password, provided by the end user, and the encrypted string stored in the database, returning a Boolean indicating whether the two are equivalent.

To do this, the salt text is first separated from the full stored string. It is then used to duplicate the hashing process. Since this echoes the securePassword( ) function, the same plain-text password with the same salt should result in the same encryption string.

This function is not used in the sample applications because the passwords you would need to store would need to be retrieved for reuse with the Twitter API, not simply compared against a new login.

Example 6-20. Function comparePassword( )

```
function comparePassword($password,$stored_password) {
    $salt = substr($stored_password,0,8);
    $secured = $salt . hash('sha256',$password.$salt);
    return $stored_password == $secured;
}
```

scramblePassword( )

The `scramblePassword( )` function (Example 6-21) accepts a plain-text password and returns a scrambled and salted version that can be stored in a database. Unlike hashing, this is a two-way reversible process; you can retrieve the plain-text version again using the companion `unscramblePassword( )` function.

Since your application may need to save the password with which the user authenticates to Twitter—a necessity for features like automatically posting a tweet to someone else's timeline—the password must be saved in a way that is encoded but still accessible. Hashing is a one-way conversion and is no good for reestablishing Twitter access at a later date. For that, you must construct a two-way encoder that allows you to get back your original information.

All of this string manipulation may be overkill for the sample applications, but the string functions used in `scramblePassword( )` are included to provide an example of the kinds of reversible changes that are possible with PHP.

Example 6-21. Function scramblePassword( )

```
function scramblePassword ($password) {
    $salt = substr(str_pad(dechex(mt_rand()),8,'0',STR_PAD_LEFT),-8);
    $modified = $password.$salt;
    $secured = $salt . base64_encode(bin2hex(strrev(str_rot13($modified))));
    return $secured;
}
```

unscramblePassword( )

The `unscramblePassword( )` function (Example 6-22) accepts a string encoded with the companion `scramblePassword( )` function and returns a plain-text version of the string. The salt is extracted from the scrambled string and used to separate the real password from the noise added to make the process more secure.

For this to work correctly, the functions must be used in a first-in-last-out order, reversing the treatment performed in `scramblePassword( )`. It is advisable to edit these two functions to make the algorithm your own, but be aware that any edits must be performed simultaneously on both functions.

Example 6-22. Function unscramblePassword( )

```
function unscramblePassword ($stored_password) {
    $salt = substr($stored_password,0,8);
    $modified = substr($stored_password,8,strlen($stored_password)-8);
```

```
$modified = str_rot13(strrev(pack("H*",base64_decode($modified))));
$password = substr($modified,0,strlen($modified)-8);
return $password;
}
```

 Rolling your own encryption scheme is better than nothing, but it's not ideal. If your web host can install the mcrypt extension for use in PHP, it is better to go with a known and tested cipher. For more information, visit *http://us.php.net/mcrypt/*.

Data Validation Functions

The *validate_data.php* file contains five functions that perform some cursory checks on the quality of the user-provided data. These checks can easily be augmented to incorporate other or more detailed validation of what the user types into your forms.

checkInput( )

The checkInput( ) function (Example 6-23) accepts an associative array containing the user input data that needs to be checked for valid values. This function also requires two other parameters: an active cURL handle, and an associative array containing the Twitter method to verify access credentials. Depending on which web application calls the function, a series of checks are performed using other functions in this included file, with a nonzero error code being returned if a problem is encountered.

Rather than using a series of nested if...elseif...else statements, the validation checks rely on nested calls to other functions that perform the checks. The resulting code is a bit more difficult for a human to parse, but it leaves a smaller footprint. For example, isSubmitted(isValidTweet(hasCredentials( ))) would first check to see whether the username and password were provided before checking for the presence of something to post as a tweet and if the form was submitted from the correct place.

Example 6-23. Function checkInput( )

```
function checkInput ($input,$cURL,$url) {
    $code = 0;
    switch (basename($_SERVER['SCRIPT_NAME'])) {

        case 'uar_auto_tweet.php':
        case 'uar_network_viewer.php':
        case 'uar_tweet_alert.php':
        case 'uar_tweet_broadcast.php':
        case 'uar_store_master_pw.php':
            # input  => twitter_username, twitter_password, submit_button
            $code = isSubmitted(
                hasCredentials($code,
                    $input['twitter_username'],$input['twitter_password']),
                $input['submit_button']
                );
```

```
            break;

        case 'uar_tweet_publisher.php':
            # input  => twitter_username, twitter_password, submit_button, $tweet
            $code = isSubmitted( isValidTweet(
                hasCredentials($code,
                    $input['twitter_username'],$input['twitter_password']),
                $input['tweet']), $input['submit_button']
                );
            break;

        default:
            $code = 100;
            break;
    }
    if ($code)                            { return $code; }
    elseif (!(hasAccess($cURL,$url)))     { return 4; }
    return 0;
}
```

isSubmitted( )

The isSubmitted( ) function (Example 6-24) accepts the current error status code and
a string. If the string is blank, the error code is changed to -1, indicating that the calling
application was not submitted with the correct web form.

This is a very rudimentary check that assumes that the submit button will be detected
only if the user submitted the web form (i.e., not if it was submitted by a bot or through
some automated process). There are better, more accurate ways to prevent form submissions from external sources; this is just a simple check.

Note that this function doesn't know or care where the value in the $foo string origi-
nates. This function could be called with other values, and the error code would be
changed to a value of -1 any time that string is blank. It doesn't have any knowledge
about the web form.

Example 6-24. Function isSubmitted()

```
function isSubmitted ($code,$foo) {
    if ($foo == '') { $code = -1; }
    return $code;
}
```

isValidTweet( )

The isValidTweet( ) function (Example 6-25) accepts the current error status code and
a string. If the string doesn't have a valid length (something between 1 and 140 characters), the error code is changed to a specific nonzero value.

This function doesn't care where the $foo string value originates; it is concerned only
with its length. The intended purpose of this function is to make sure that the size of
the tweet entered by the end user is something that makes sense to post to Twitter.

Technically, the upper limit of 140 for the size of a text message is not a character limit, but rather a byte size limit. Ligatures (like æ) and Unicode characters may take up 2 or more bytes each, lowering the readable character length allowed by SMS. Since `strlen( )` counts bytes, not characters, this function works well for Twitter.

You will see different responses from different systems, however. The Twitter API measures in characters. The Twitter website measures in bytes, but it posts the longer message anyway. If you want to count characters and not bytes, use `mb_strlen( )`.

Example 6-25. Function isValidTweet( )

```
function isValidTweet ($code,$foo) {
    if (strlen($foo) < 1)           { $code = 1; }
    elseif (strlen($foo) > 140)     { $code = 2; }
    return $code;
}
```

hasCredentials( )

The `hasCredentials( )` function (Example 6-26) accepts the current error status code and two strings. If the string lengths aren't both nonzero—meaning something was entered for both fields—the error code is changed to a value of 3.

The error code means something only in the context of the greater suite of applications, not within the function itself. `hasCredentials( )` doesn't care where the strings originate; it's only concerned with their lengths. The `if` conditional is a shorter way of performing both string length checks at once. The logic is that if either string is empty, the calculation will trigger an error (anything multiplied by zero is zero).

Example 6-26. Function hasCredentials( )

```
function hasCredentials ($code,$foo,$bar) {
    if ((strlen($foo)*strlen($bar)) < 1) { $code = 3; }
    return $code;
}
```

hasAccess( )

The `hasAccess( )` function (Example 6-27) accepts an active cURL handle and an associative array containing all of the Twitter API method calls. It returns `true` or `false` to indicate whether the current username and password represent a valid Twitter member account.

This function assumes that the `CURLOPT_USERPWD` option for cURL has already been set to include the Twitter username and password. The code might be improved to make sure the `apiRequest( )` function has set that value properly.

Example 6-27. Function hasAccess( )

```php
function hasAccess ($cURL,$url) {
    if (function_exists('apiRequest')) {
        list($status,$foo) = apiRequest($cURL,$url['credentials']);
        if ($status == 200) { return true; }
    }
    return false;
}
```

Data Sorting Functions

The *sort_data.php* file contains two functions that sort a multidimensional associative array on several dimensions. These functions support a specific application (see "Network Viewer" on page 313), but the technique can be expanded to help other applications where sorted data is part of the functionality.

sortData( )

The **sortData( )** function (Example 6-28) accepts an associative array and the name of a sorting function, returning the same array ordered according to that comparison algorithm. **usort( )** is a PHP function that facilitates custom sorting methods; in this case, it is used in conjunction with another function, **compareFollowNet( )**.

Example 6-28. Function sortData( )

```php
function sortData ($array, $sort_type='compareFollowNet') {
    usort($array, $sort_type);
    return $array;
}
```

 You can make function parameters optional by initializing them with default values. In this case, **sortData($array)** would not choke.

compareFollowNet( )

The **compareFollowNet( )** function (Example 6-29) is a custom sorting algorithm that compares multiple dimensions of an associative array. It accepts two array items and returns one of three values (**-1**, **0**, or **1**) to indicate whether the first item should be ordered before the second.

This function is used in conjunction with the **usort( )** function to order an entire array, iterating over the entire data set contained in the array by repeatedly calling the **compareFollowNet( )** function. Specifically, this sorting function compares two items on several dimensions: follow net group, account protection, location string, number of followers, and username. As soon as a comparison is found that is nonzero (indicating one item should be placed before the other), it returns that result.

Example 6-29. Function compareFollowNet( )

```
function compareFollowNet ($a, $b) {
    $x = strnatcmp($a['follow_net'], $b['follow_net']);
    if (!$x) {
        $x = strnatcmp($b['is_protected'], $a['is_protected']);
        if (!$x) {
            $x = strnatcmp($a['author_location'], $b['author_location']);
            if (!$x) {
                $x = strnatcmp($b['total_followers'], $a['total_followers']);
                if (!$x) {
                    return strnatcmp($b['author_username'], $a['author_username']);
                } else { return $x; }
            } else { return $x; }
        } else { return $x; }
    } else { return $x; }
}
```

Statistics Functions

The *calculate_stats.php* file contains one function that calculates some specific metrics for a group of Twitter members, returning them as descriptive text. This function supports a specific application (see "Network Viewer" on page 313), but these statistics could be handy to reuse for your own custom programming.

groupStats( )

The groupStats( ) function (Example 6-30) accepts two associative arrays, one filled with cumulative statistics about a group of Twitter members, and the second containing all of the locations self-disclosed by that group with the count of the number of members at each location. The function returns a formatted description containing the values calculated from this data. The returned string is used in the title attribute of headers in the XHTML display to provide some mouseover information about the composition of the group.

Example 6-30. Function groupStats( )

```
function groupStats ($stats, $locations) {
    if ($locations) {
        arsort($locations);
        list($city, $count) = each($locations);
        $location_pct  = number_format(100*$count/$stats['count'],0);
        $location_txt  = "$location_pct% of this group"
                        ." list $city as their location.";
    }
    else {
        $location_txt  = "No locations were provided.";
    }
    if ($stats['count'] > 0) {
        $private_pct  = number_format(100*$stats['private']/$stats['count'],0);
        $avatar_pct   = number_format(100*$stats['avatars']/$stats['count'],0);
        $avg_followers = ceil($stats['followers']/$stats['count']);
```

```
    }
    else {
        $private_pct  = 0;
        $avatar_pct   = 0;
        $avg_followers = 0;
    }

    $description = <<<GROUP_STATS
Of these {$stats[0]['count']} people, $private_pct% are private accounts
and $avatar_pct% are using the default Twitter avatar. $location_txt

Each member has has attracted an average of $avg_followers followers.
GROUP_STATS;

    return $description;
}
```

Log Management Functions

The *log_manage.php* file contains four functions that manage use of files within applications. There is much more that can be done with files (including reading previously stored data), but this set of functions assumes that the intention is to generate output, primarily supporting the logging mechanisms in the automated tasks of Chapter 8.

openFile( )

The openFile( ) function (Example 6-31) accepts a string containing the name of the file to open and a code indicating how that file should be opened. It returns the handle for the opened file.

The values for the second parameter are restricted in this function to either 'a' for append (keep whatever data is already in the file and add the new stuff at the end) or 'w' for write (overwrite any data that is found in an existing file), which is the default. The fopen( ) function in PHP has several other, more nuanced types, but they aren't necessary for the sample applications.

Example 6-31. Function openFile( )

```
function openFile ($filename,$type) {
    if (array_search($type,array('w','a')) < 0) { $type = 'w'; }
    $filehandle = fopen($filename,$type) or die("can't open file $filename");
    return $filehandle;
}
```

writeFile( )

The writeFile( ) function (Example 6-32) requires an open file handle and the message to write to that file. It returns a Boolean indicating the success or failure of the fwrite( ) command, appending a newline character to the end of the message written to the file.

Example 6-32. Function writeFile( )

```
function writeFile ($filehandle,$message) {
    return fwrite($filehandle, $message . "\n");
}
```

closeFile( )

The closeFile( ) function (Example 6-33) requires an open file handle; it returns true if the fclose( ) command has succeeded in closing the file so that data can no longer be written to it. The file will automatically be closed when the calling PHP application exits, but it is cleaner and is appropriate practice to formally destroy the active file handle.

Example 6-33. Function closeFile( )

```
function closeFile ($filehandle) {
    return fclose($filehandle);
}
```

> You can also use file_put_contents( ) to replace the file open, write, and close functions. This function does the same thing as calling fopen( ), fwrite( ), and fclose( ) in succession.

deleteFile( )

The deleteFile( ) function (Example 6-34) requires the name of an existing file; it returns true if the unlink( ) command has succeeded in deleting the file from the server. It is presumed that the file named in the parameter is situated relative to the calling application. If the file lives in higher in the directory structure or along a different file path, the full server path to the file must be specified. The calling application must also have the proper server permissions to be able to remove the file.

This function isn't used in the sample applications, but it can be handy when temporary files are used to store data for use online during the running of the applications. It is included here as an example of how to delete a file.

Example 6-34. Function deleteFile( )

```
function deleteFile ($filename) {
    return unlink($filename);
}
```

Status Messages

The *status_messages.php* file contains one function that translates a numeric status code into the text to display to the user or include in report logs. This information could easily be stored in a database table and retrieved through a SQL query; however, not every application will require database support, and that approach would create a lot of overhead for something that could be handled just as well by an included function.

getResponse( )

The getResponse( ) function (Example 6-35) accepts an integer error code and an optional default message to display; it returns a short feedback message to present to the end user. The possible responses include:

  –1 - Form wasn't submitted, or improperly submitted
  1 - Missing tweet
  2 - Tweet is too long (140 character limit)
  3 - Missing authentication
  4 - Authentication to API failed
  5 - Could not post message to Twitter
  6 - Existing RSS feed deleted; automation is turned off
  7 - Deletion requested, but there was nothing in the database
  8 - The RSS feed may be inactive or invalid
  9 - This RSS feed is already automated
  10 - No changes to the group detected
  11 - Group has been removed
  12 - No changes to your list of keywords were detected
  13 - Alert has been removed
  14 - Could not retrieve user profile information
  15 - Could not parse user profile information
  16 - Could not retrieve follow network
  17 - Could not parse follow network.
  100 - This page is not yet defined in the programming.

You'll notice that there are no **break** commands after each case, unlike in other **switch** statements in the included functions. This is because the **return** statement acts as a **break** by terminating the function as it gives a value back to the calling application. Once a condition value is satisfied, there is no way to perform additional checks within the function.

Example 6-35. Function getResponse( )

```
function getResponse ($error_code,$message='') {
    switch ($error_code) {
        case -1:
            return 'Greetings.';
        case 1:
            return 'Where is your message? Please type your tweet and try again.';
        case 2:
            return 'Your post is too long. Please edit and try again.';
        case 3:
            return 'You need to enter a valid Twitter username and password.';
        case 4:
            return 'Could not authenticate to Twitter. Please re-enter your
```

```
            username and password.';
        case 5:
            return 'Could not post to Twitter.';
        case 6:
            return 'RSS feed has been removed. There will be no more automated
            tweets for this account.';
        case 7:
            return 'Deletion was requested, but there was nothing in the database
            to delete.';
        case 8:
            return 'This may be an invalid or inactive RSS feed. We could not parse
            this data.';
        case 9:
            return 'This feed is already being automated to post tweets to this
            member account.';
        case 10:
            return 'No changes to the group were detected.';
        case 11:
            return 'Your group has been removed. No more aggregation will be done
            for this account.';
        case 12:
            return 'No changes to your list of keywords were detected.';
        case 13:
            return 'Your alert has been removed. No more keyword tracking will be
            done for this account.';
        case 14:
            return 'There was a problem trying to get your user profile
            information.';
        case 15:
            return 'There was a problem trying to parse your user profile
            information.';
        case 16:
            return 'There was a problem trying to get your follow network.';
        case 17:
            return 'There was a problem trying to parse your follow network.';
        case 100:
            return 'This page has not been defined in the data validation function.
            See the programmer.';
        default:
            return $message;
    }
}
```

HTML Template Functions

The *html_template.php* file contains three functions that output parts of the web page template. Putting the HTML in one place makes it easier to make changes to design and functionality that affect the entire suite of applications. For instance, adding a simple navigation bar with links to each tool would have involved several edits instead of one, had this include not been created.

getHeader( )

The getHeader( ) function (Example 6-36) accepts two parameters: the string used as the web page title, and the location of the CSS stylesheet file that the browser should call to help with the web page rendering. This function will output the formatted XHTML rather than returning it as a string to save as a variable in the calling application.

The XHTML generated by this function is what is needed to begin a valid web page. Any changes to expand the header information or add a standard header visible in the body can be added to this function once, and it will appear in all of the web applications that call it.

Example 6-36. Function getHeader()

```
function getHeader ($title,$css) {
    $xhtml    = <<<FORMAT_HTML_HEADER
<!DOCTYPE html PUBLIC "-//W3C//DTD XHTML 1.0 Strict//EN"
    "http://www.w3.org/TR/xhtml1/DTD/xhtml1-strict.dtd">
<html xmlns="http://www.w3.org/1999/xhtml" xml:lang="en" lang="en">
<head>
    <meta http-equiv="Content-Type" content="text/html; charset=utf-8"/>
    <style type="text/css" media="all">@import url($css);</style>
    <title>Twitter Up and Running | $title</title>
</head>

<body>

FORMAT_HTML_HEADER;
    echo $xhtml;
    return;
}
```

getInterface( )

The getInterface( ) function (Example 6-37) accepts one associative array that contains the data needed to populate the XHTML it outputs to the end user.

This interface markup contains placeholders for content that may or may not have values associated with the calling application. It is meant to be versatile, a one-size-fits-all approach to the web pages displayed in the suite of sample web applications.

Example 6-37. Function getInterface()

```
function getInterface ($data) {
    $xhtml = <<<FORMAT_HTML_HEADER
<div id="uar_interface">
    <form action="" method="post">
        <div id="uar_navigation"> |
            <a href="{$data['url']}index.php">About</a> |
            <a href="{$data['url']}uar_tweet_publisher.php">Publisher</a> |
            <a href="{$data['url']}uar_auto_tweet.php">Auto Tweet</a> |
            <a href="{$data['url']}uar_tweet_broadcast.php">Broadcast</a> |
```

```
            <a href="{$data['url']}uar_tweet_alert.php">Alert</a> |
            <a href="{$data['url']}uar_network_viewer.php">Network Viewer</a> |
            <a href="{$data['url']}admin/uar_store_master_pw.php">Admin</a> |
        </div>
        <div id="uar_title">
            <strong>{$data['title']}</strong>
        </div>
        <div id="uar_authentication">
            <fieldset>
                <legend>
                    Authenticate:
                </legend>
                <div id="uar_username"{$data['hide_username']}>
                    Twitter Username:<br />
                    <input type="text" name="twitter_username" size="25"
                        value="{$data['username']}" />
                </div>
                <div id="uar_password">
                    Twitter Password:<br />
                    <input type="password" name="twitter_password" size="25"
                        value="" />
                </div>
                <div id="uar_new"$show_alerts>
                    {$data['reset']}
                    <a href="{$data['url']}passwords.php">Why are you asking for my
                        password?</a>
                </div>
            </fieldset>
        </div>
        {$data['info']}
        <div id="uar_submit">
            <input type="submit" name="submit_button" value="{$data['label']}" />
        </div>
        <div id="uar_feedback"{$data['show_message']}>
            {$data['message']}
        </div>
        {$data['supplemental']}
    </form>
</div>
{$data['columns']}
FORMAT_HTML_HEADER;
    echo $xhtml;
    return;
}
```

 This function assumes that the user-entered data has been escaped to
prevent cross-site scripting (XSS) attacks before it is submitted in the
$data array.

getFooter( )

The getFooter( ) function (Example 6-38) outputs the XHTML needed to close an open web page. If you wanted to create a footer that would appear on all pages in the site, this would be the place to add that code.

Example 6-38. Function getFooter( )

```
function getFooter () {
    $xhtml = <<<FORMAT_HTML_HEADER

</body>
</html>
FORMAT_HTML_HEADER;
    echo $xhtml;
    return;
}
```

CSS

The sample applications are coded to manage the presentation of data through an external stylesheet. Unlike the included PHP files, this must be in the web path, since it is the browser (not the PHP application) that is responsible for pulling it into the rendering process. This file—*uar.css*—is located in a subdirectory called *css*, located in the same directory as the main web application files.

The styles in the suite of sample applications are intended to be clean and simple. Feel free to edit them to include background images, more complicated layouts, and vivid colors. More information on the stylesheet properties used in this code (see Example 6-39) can be found in "CSS" on page 90.

Example 6-39. uar.css stylesheet for the sample applications

```
*{margin:0;padding:0;}
body {text-align:center;font-family:Helvetica,Arial,sans-serif;
font-size:.9em;color:#666666;}

#uar_interface {text-align:left;width:500px;margin:10% auto;padding:
10px;background-color:#eeeeee;}

#uar_title {margin-bottom:20px;}
#uar_info {margin-bottom:20px;}
#uar_info textarea {font-family:Courier,serif;font-size:.9em;margin-top:5px;}
#uar_authentication {margin-bottom:20px;padding:2px;}
#uar_authentication fieldset {background-color:#ffffff;}
#uar_authentication fieldset legend {padding-left:5px;}
#uar_new {padding:2px;float:right;font-size:.8em;}

#uar_username {width:46%;margin:2%;float:left;font-size:.9em;}
#uar_username input {background-color:#eeeeee;}
#uar_password {width:46%;margin:2%;float:right;font-size:.9em;}
#uar_password input {background-color:#eeeeee;}
```

```
#uar_submit {text-align:right;}

#uar_feedback {background-color:#eeddcc;margin-top:20px;padding:10px;}
#uar_supplemental {margin-top:20px;margin-bottom:20px;padding:2px;}
#uar_supplemental ol {margin:5px;margin-left:20px;}

#uar_columns {text-align:left;width:700px;margin:1% auto;padding:
0px;background-color:#ffffff;}
#uar_left {padding:10px;width:210px;float:left;}
#uar_center {padding:10px;width:210px;float:left;}
#uar_right {padding:10px;width:210px;float:right;}
h4 {margin-bottom:10px;font-size:1.1em;}
p {margin-bottom:10px;font-size:.8em;}

#uar_avatar {padding:10px;width:80px;float:left;}
#uar_detail {padding:10px;width:380px;}

#uar_navigation {font-size:.8em;color:#666666;text-align:center;
background-color:#ffffff;padding:2px;margin-bottom:15px;}
#uar_navigation a {text-decoration:none;color:#000000;}

#uar_about {background-color:#ffffff;padding:20px;margin-top:20px;}
#uar_about ol, #uar_about ul {margin:5px;margin-left:20px;}
#uar_about ol li, #uar_about ul li {margin-top:10px;margin-bottom:10px;}
```

Once all of the files are installed on your web server, you're ready to work on the applications they support. Chapter 7 describes the web applications, and Chapter 8 describes the automated tasks.

CHAPTER 7

Sample Applications

 kmakice No more walking. Time to run.

The stage is set. You understand the Twitter culture and have seen examples of web applications developed by your peers. You have at least a basic understanding of how to work with PHP, MySQL, and other languages. You understand how to access the API and what you should expect to get as a response. In Chapter 6, you set up your web hosting environment to give your web application a happy home. Now it's time to meet the sample web applications that will serve as a base for your own programming adventure.

Meet the Sample Apps

This small suite of sample web applications is offered to you as a way to illustrate use of the Twitter API, the collection of web service methods that bring Twitter data into third-party programming. These applications explore some common reasons to access the API:

Administration Tool

A master account is needed to do things like send direct messages and conduct data mining on the backend. Unlike most of the user-driven tools, the master account must be available even when the account holder (you) isn't around to log in. This simple tool allows the master account's password to be saved to the database in a safe way. Only you will use this tool. In fact, without knowing the password attached to the master Twitter account, others shouldn't be able to do anything with this application.

Tweet Publisher

This application is a straightforward status updater. To publish to your own timeline, enter your Twitter account information and a short 140-character message. After doing so, you will see a link to the new tweet.

Auto Tweet

Each member account can be associated with a single RSS or Atom feed, from which a new tweet will be automatically generated. There is an automated task associated with this application that checks each registered feed for new content in six-hour cycles and posts the most recent article.

Tweet Broadcast

This is an aggregation tool, where you can collect daily tweets from a handful of other Twitter members into a single RSS item. An RSS feed is generated that contains information for up to 20 days of activity, collected by an automated task that checks for new tweets once a day. Each member account can have one aggregation feed, accessible at *uar_broadcast.php?username*.

Tweet Alert

Tracking tweets based on keywords is made easy with the Twitter search API. Each member can list a few keywords in Tweet Alert and receive a notification when any of those terms appears in a public tweet. The content scans are performed every 15 minutes. If a match is found—and the member is following your master Twitter account—a direct message is sent to that member with a link to the search results.

Network Viewer

Probably the most useful among the suite of tools, this web application allows Twitter members to see the profile images of all the people they're following. Private accounts are outlined in red, and (in most modern browsers) mousing over each picture reveals additional detail about that member.

 Although the *@the_api_book* account has been whitelisted (thanks, Twitter!), rate limits or issues with the web host may surface that could affect performance of some or all of these sample applications. The functionality of the Network Viewer is also tied to your own account, so larger follow networks may not be displayed in full.

Best of Twitter API

Only a small percentage of Twitter users (many of whom are Japanese) "favorite," or bookmark, other members' tweets. One of the reasons may be that the current API makes it difficult to access data about favorites. We'll create two automated tasks that work together to try to address this problem by looking in the public timeline for active users and retrieving each member's archive of favorite tweets. There is no frontend viewer to look at the aggregated data, but a rudimentary second-generation API is available to allow others to make use of this data as it accumulates.

These tools are meant to be a bare-bones foundation for something better; a template or working illustration of ways you might be able to come up with interesting and useful tools of your own. Use your imagination. Make the Twitosphere a better place.

As you adapt this code to make your own applications, remember to consider issues of server load, data security, and error handling in greater detail than you will find in this book. For more information on these topics, check out *High Performance MySQL*, Second Edition (*http://oreilly.com/catalog/9780596101718*) by Baron Schwartz et al. (O'Reilly).

The specific PHP code needed to run these applications is presented throughout this chapter in the form of Examples 7-1 through 7-8. This code can be copied into a text editor and saved using the file path and name given in each Example header. Together with the *css/uar.css* file from the section "CSS" on page 90, these files should be uploaded to your site root. You should wind up with a list that looks like Figure 7-1.

Name ▲	Kind	Size	Date
admin	Folder	–	12/12/08
css	Folder	–	12/12/08
favorites	Folder	–	12/12/08
index.php	PHP: Hypertext Preprocessor (PHP) document	7.4 KB	12/12/08
uar_auto_tweet.php	PHP: Hypertext Preprocessor (PHP) document	8.5 KB	17/17/08
uar_broadcast.php	PHP: Hypertext Preprocessor (PHP) document	4.7 KB	12/11/08
uar_network_viewer.php	PHP: Hypertext Preprocessor (PHP) document	12.2 KB	12/12/08
uar_tweet_alert.php	PHP: Hypertext Preprocessor (PHP) document	10.1 KB	12/12/08
uar_tweet_broadcast.php	PHP: Hypertext Preprocessor (PHP) document	9.6 KB	12/12/08
uar_tweet_publisher.php	PHP: Hypertext Preprocessor (PHP) document	5.7 KB	12/12/08

Figure 7-1. The web root directory for the suite of sample applications

Why Are You Asking for My Password?

The current version of the Twitter API requires users to authenticate in order to gain access to protected data and account actions. In order to function, the sample applications must ask users to submit their credentials. Twitter has announced plans to implement OAuth, an improved way of granting permission for applications to access parts of users' accounts, but it is not expected to be fully supported until the summer of 2009. In the meantime, we're stuck with the "anti-pattern" (see "Gone Phishing: A Word About Passwords" on page 182 for more information on security and third-party applications).

Yes, the sample applications ask for your Twitter password. If you are uncomfortable providing this information, don't. However, the apps won't work without this access.

Following is a description of why each tool asks for authentication and what it does with the access it's granted:

Administration Tool
    The password requested by this tool must be the valid password for the main account. No other password will work.

Tweet Publisher
    The primary reason for authentication is to permit this application to publish a status update to your timeline. Your information is verified and then used once to post your message. The access information is discarded by the time the submitted page reloads.

Auto Tweet
    This tool also needs your Twitter access to publish a tweet on your behalf, but unlike with Tweet Publisher where you provide the content at the same time you authenticate, the status update comes at a later time, when you may not be around. As a result, not only does this application need to validate and use your password to post, *it also has to save it to a database for later use*. The password is not saved in plain text; it is encrypted before storage.

Tweet Broadcast
    Your password is not needed to perform the broadcast task, but it is needed to validate that you are a current Twitter user. Only one broadcast feed is allowed for each account holder. To prevent someone from creating a custom RSS feed using someone else's account, this tool verifies that you are the owner of the account.

Tweet Alert
    As with Tweet Broadcast, the reason for asking for your password is to verify that you are a Twitter member and that you own the username you provide. Authentication is slightly more important for this tool, since submitting search terms will result in direct messages being sent when status updates containing those terms are published. For direct messages to be sent, the recipient must follow the main account, but this interface merely verifies that that relationship exists; it does not add the follow relationship automatically. All direct messages are sent using the master account credentials, through an automated task.

Network Viewer
    One reason for an application like this to require authentication is to share the API rate limit load. For larger networks, searching for all of your followers and friends can eat up a lot of requests. If the main account handled that without help, the application could serve very few people before being rendered useless for an hour. In this case, the bigger concern is not rate limits but rather access to information.

You have to authenticate to allow the tool to request protected information about your follow network on your behalf. The application requests all of your followers and friends, as well as your user profile.

Best of Twitter API

This tool does not have a user interface and therefore does not ask for your password.

Administration Tool

Let's start with the sample application with no appeal to anyone but you. The administration tool only does one thing—it saves the password of your master Twitter account to the database—but without it, several of the other applications would not be able to work.

A master account is needed to do things like sending direct messages and mining data on the backend (see "Establishing Your Twitter Account" on page 214 for more details on creating a master account for this purpose). The username or ID for this account is hardcoded into the applications for use where needed, but the password will be stored in the database for safekeeping.

This simple tool first confirms that your password works with the master account you hardcoded into your application, and then it scrambles the password into a form suitable to be saved in the database. Without knowing the password attached to the master account, this application is useless, even for this simple function. Hooray for that!

Take the App for a Spin

You can access this no-frills application by clicking on the "Admin" link at the far end of the header on any of the sample application pages. You can also reach it directly by loading the *admin/uar_store_master_pw.php* file into your browser from wherever you uploaded your application files (e.g., *http://makice.net/uar/admin/uar_store_master _pw.php* was my development environment). Doing so should get you a web page display that looks something like Figure 7-2.

Once the page is loaded, the form is simple to complete:

1. Enter the password.

   Type the valid password for the hardcoded main user account into the box labeled "Twitter Password."

2. Click "Save Password."

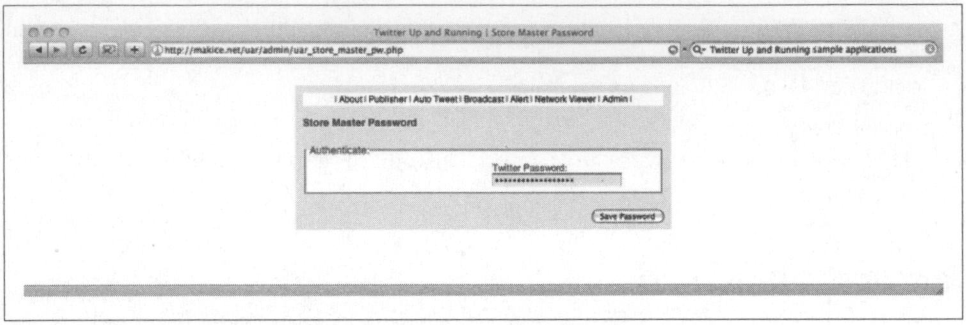

Figure 7-2. Store a valid password for your master Twitter account

Yep, that's it. The ground probably didn't shake underneath your feet, but even this simple form relied on the Twitter API to do its thing. That's because this administration tool will check with Twitter to make sure that the password works with your master account. If Twitter reports back that the credentials work, the application will return this message:

```
The password for the master account is saved in the database.
```

If the password is not valid—which could mean you made a typo, entered an incorrect password, or entered the right password for some other account—the Twitter API will know and will tell the application. If this happens, you will instead get the following message:

```
Could not authenticate to Twitter.
Please re-enter your username and password.
```

This means no one will be able to overwrite your master password with this tool. This is simply a means to save an encoded version of your Twitter password to the database, for later use by other applications.

Check Under the Hood

The code for all of the sample applications will follow a similar structure. Here are the steps for the code that makes saving your password possible:

1. Include required custom functions.
2. Initialize values, particularly those needed for web page display.
3. Parse and validate any input data, making the user values available to the application.
4. Initialize connections to the Twitter API and your database, as needed.
5. ***Do stuff.***
6. Formulate a feedback response.
7. Clean up the open connections.

8. Render the web page.

For the code in this first administration tool (see Example 7-1), I'll belabor my description. The structure of the other sample applications will look very familiar.

Example 7-1. PHP to change the master password

```php
/* Include External Functions */
$root_path = str_replace('/public_html', '/uar', $_SERVER['DOCUMENT_ROOT'])
                          ./'/includes/';
include $root_path.'environment.php';
include $root_path.'status_messages.php';
include $root_path.'validate_data.php';
include $root_path.'api_config.php';
include $root_path.'pw_manage.php';
include $root_path.'database.php';
include $root_path.'sql_queries.php';
include $root_path.'html_template.php';

/* Initialize Values */
$app_title           = 'Store Master Password';
$twitter_password    = '';
$form_response       = '';
$submit_button_label = '';
$show_message        = '';
$form_error          = 0;

/* Parse Input */
$twitter_password    = $_POST['twitter_password'];
$submit_button       = $_POST['submit_button'];
$scrambled_password  = scramblePassword($twitter_password);
$this_dir            = getHTTPpath($_SERVER['HTTP_HOST'],$_SERVER['REQUEST_URI']);
$root_dir            = str_replace('/admin/','/',$this_dir);

/* Configure API Requests */
$cURL_source         = prepAPI();

/* Initiate cURL */
$cURL                = prepRequest($app_title,$master_username,$twitter_password);

/* Prepare Database Interaction */
$db_connection       = openDB();
$sql_variables       = array (
   'scrambled_password'   => $scrambled_password
   );
$sql_query           = getQueries($sql_variables);

/* Validate Access */
$submit_button_label = ' Save Password ';
$form_error          = checkInput(array(
    'submit_button'        => $submit_button,
    'twitter_username'     => $master_username,
    'twitter_password'     => $twitter_password
   ),$cURL,$cURL_source);
```

```
/* Save Data */
if ($form_error == 0) {
    mysql_query($sql_query['Update_Password'])
        or die('Error, update query failed');
}

/* Determine Feedback Response */
if ($form_error < 0) { $show_message = ' style="display:none;"'; }
else {
    $default_response = <<<DEFAULT_MESSAGE
     The password for the master account is saved in the database.
DEFAULT_MESSAGE;
    $form_response    = getResponse($form_error,$default_response);
}

/* Clean Up */
apiRequest($cURL,$cURL_source['end_session']);
curl_close($cURL);
closeDB($db_connection);

/* Render Interface */
getHeader($app_title,'../css/uar.css');
$html_info          = array(
        'title'             => $app_title,
        'url'               => $root_dir,
        'hide_username'     => ' style="display:none;"',
        'username'          => $master_username,
        'reset'             => '',
        'info'              => '',
        'label'             => $submit_button_label,
        'show_message'      => $show_message,
        'message'           => $form_response,
        'supplemental'      => '',
        'columns'           => ''
);
getInterface($html_info);
getFooter();
```

Now let's take a look at each of those steps.

Include external functions

First, PHP needs to know which nonstandard functions are going to be called for this application. Many of the custom functions described in Chapter 6 will be needed here. In fact, eight of the dozen include files will become part of this application: *environment.php*, *status_messages.php*, *validate_data.php*, *api_config.php*, *pw_manage.php*, *database.php*, *sql_queries.php*, and *html_template.php*. The include files you can ignore are *parse_data.php*, *sort_data.php*, *calculate_stats.php*, and *log_manage.php*.

To get this external functionality into the hands of the application, PHP has to know where to look for the files. This information could be hardcoded, but that would mean if you moved your application to a new location on your server, you would have to change the path to the files. Instead of typing it manually, you can have PHP figure out the location itself by parsing the $_SERVER['DOCUMENT_ROOT']) environment variable.

> Environment variables are filled at the discretion of the web servers. A good way to see what information is available to you is to create a simple PHP script that will output the $_SERVER array. You may need to find a different way let PHP figure out where a file lives.

In this case, I created a place to put my application files (*uar*) outside of the web path (*public_html*). Within that non-web path is a folder (*includes*) that contains my included files. Knowing this much of the mystery, I was able to instruct PHP to use one of its own functions—str_replace—to figure out the server path to my included files and store it in a new variable, $root_path:

```
$root_path = str_replace('/public_html', '/uar',
                         $_SERVER['DOCUMENT_ROOT']) . '/includes/';
```

This variable can now be used to point PHP to the specific files containing the custom functions, as in:

```
include $root_path.'environment.php';
```

> Not every web host will start you out with a root directory called *public_html*. Substitute your own nomenclature in the code.

Initialize values

PHP doesn't require explicit initialization of a variable or a declaration of its type. The scripting language will try to figure that out on its own through the context of the code. However, you can sometimes generate unintended results if you don't let PHP know ahead of time what variables are going to be used. In some cases—such as with the variable $form_error—the initial value serves as the default state for the application. I am assuming that everything is going to execute without a hitch and will look for specific places of failure before changing the value of the error flag.

In some programming circles, it is considered good form to define the variables you use for other programmers' sake. This lets any future programmers know which variables are needed for the display of the web page at the end of executing the application. Placing these declarations at the top of the page also makes it easier to change the values, as you don't have to search through the code for the first mention of a variable. In certain PHP configurations, this also acts as a safety measure: initializing all of your variables before using them may help thwart some malicious users.

Parse input

For the application to be interactive, PHP has to have a way to communicate with the person submitting the form. This is handled through the special variables `$_POST['twitter_password']` and `$_POST['submit_button']`, which contain the values posted by the user. The application also creates a scrambled version of the password, preparing it to save in the database once Twitter says it's valid. Here, the application also fills a couple of variables—`$this_dir` and `$root_dir`—that will be used later in the web page to link this application form to the rest of the suite of sample applications.

Configure API requests

Since all of the work is being done in a custom function, all this application has to do is invoke it. The `prepAPI()` function retrieves the master account username—so you only have to set it in one place should you change it—and an array filled with all of the API method URLs. See "API Configuration Functions" on page 230 for more details on how this custom function works.

Initiate cURL

This is where the application starts paving the way to make a request of the Twitter API. This is done with cURL, which is configured in a custom function, `prepRequest()`. Three parameters are passed to this function: the `$app_title` identifies the specific program (in this case, "Store Master Password"), and the authentication credentials for the master password are then passed as the next two parameters. If no username is provided, the API request will be unauthenticated.

The function returns `$cURL`, a handle representing the cURL configuration that is used later when validating the password entered by the user.

 The sample code requires a little editing in places for it to work with your Twitter and database accounts. See "API Configuration Functions" on page 230 and "Database Functions" on page 234 for the places in the custom functions to put your access information.

Prepare database interaction

Any time an application is planning to persistently store or retrieve information, PHP has to be able to communicate with the database where the information will live. There are some built-in functions for that purpose (see "Connecting to the Database" on page 111) that the application can use here. Again, because we took the time to create some custom functions, the code that initiates that connection is short.

There are two parts to preparing PHP to communicate with MySQL. First, the application needs some queries (the instructions it plans to send to the database to store or retrieve data). One of the custom functions—`getQueries()`—already has the statements this application needs. The variables required to format those queries are passed as a parameter ($sql_variables) to return an associative array ($sql_query) containing query names and SQL statements. Next, PHP has to create an object that allows it to talk to the database. This is accomplished with another custom function, openDB( ). That function takes care of figuring out the name and account access needed to open the connection to MySQL. Any future database actions can be performed on the variable $db_connection.

 See the sections "Database Functions" on page 234 and "SQL Queries" on page 235 for more details about how these two custom functions work.

Validate access

Users can enter any data they like when submitting the web form, including stuff that's not useful or possibly even harmful to your application. JavaScript and other client-side options can be used to validate what a user submits, but the application should also handle this on the server side.

The checkInput( ) custom function was built for this purpose (see "Data Validation Functions" on page 249): it contains a single call that returns an integer value to indicate whether there are any problems with the input data. Each application in our suite of tools has its own data-validation needs, requiring different parameters to allow those checks to be done. Passing it an associative array of these values with the cURL handle and array of API methods enables checkInput( ) to set a specific $form_error value if a problem is detected. The default assumption is that the data is fine, in which case $form_error will return with a value of zero.

Save data

This is where the administration tool becomes distinct from the other applications: it's the "Do Stuff" part of the code. In this case, the task is to simply store in the MySQL database a scrambled version of the password the user enters. Because the data will have been validated using checkInput( ), the application can assume that if $form_error has a value of zero, it is OK to save the scrambled password to the database.

The application can perform the save by referencing a specific SQL statement (retrieved earlier with getQueries( )) that already contains the scrambled password and the destination table column. This variable value is passed to a built-in PHP function—mysql_query( )—that uses the opened database connection to send the commands to MySQL:

```
mysql_query($sql_query['Update_Password'])
    or die('Error, update query failed');
```

The die( ) function will trap any error that occurs during that process and kill the application on the spot if a problem occurs; the only thing displayed will be the error message passed as a parameter. You could also trap this error in other ways that might allow the application to continue and render a prettier page to the user.

Determine feedback response

The result of all those checks and functions trying to get the password stored in the database now needs to be interpreted. The application only has a variable value, stored in $form_error, to give it a hint as to whether that operation was successful. If the value is greater than zero, it means there was some problem that requires a special message to be displayed to the end user. If it is zero, everything went off without a hitch and the application should render a message of success. To do this translation, the application passes that value and the default message as parameters to a custom function, getResponse( ). The feedback message that should be displayed when the web page is finally rendered is returned and stored in $form_response.

 For more detail on how this function works, see "Status Messages" on page 255.

There is one other state that $form_error might represent. If this is the first time you're loading the page, you won't want to see an error telling you to fill in a form field you haven't seen yet. These sample applications use a negative value (-1) to indicate this state. Instead of looking up a canned message or displaying nothing, the application will use CSS styles to hide the message box completely:

```
if ($form_error < 0) { $show_message = ' style="display:none;"'; }
```

Clean up

The hard work for PHP is done at this point, and it is time to clean up some connections. First, the application tells Twitter that it's done with the API by sending a final request to a special method to end the session. Next, it lets PHP know it is through using the cURL connection, closing it with the built-in function curl_close( ). Finally, the application closes the database connection by passing its object variable to a custom function, closeDB( ).

The reality is that none of these actions are required—PHP should get the hint to close these connections when the script is through processing. However, it is good practice to explicitly close the files and connections you have open.

Render interface

All this work won't mean a thing if you don't share it with your end user. Because all of the sample applications use the same template, the application just needs to pass along the new data and configuration settings to the custom functions responsible for generating the XHTML.

There are three parts to the web page: the header, the interface, and the footer. getHeader( ) takes two parameters: the application title and the path to the CSS stylesheet. This function outputs everything up to the part the user will see in the body of the web page. The closing tags are outputted by getFooter( ). If the application did nothing more, you would see a valid but completely empty web page. To fill the page with the interesting parts, we use getInterface( ) and a parameter ($html_info) containing all of the relevant information accumulated by the application earlier in the code.

 If you want to adjust any of the XHTML used in this application, see "HTML Template Functions" on page 257 for more details about how these functions work.

Shifting Gears

Although this administrative tool does only one task—saving a master password—the mind does not have to stretch very far to see that other functionality could be added. If you plan to support your application, building some tools to monitor activity and/or provide user support is recommended. This sample administration tool might provide some structure for you to add additional pages.

Here are a few ways you could make changes to this sample application:

Protect the administration directory
> The simplest way to restrict access to a web page is to force the user to log into the server with a username and password. Web servers commonly use two files—*.htpasswd* and *.htaccess*—to control this behavior. A simple Google search for "protecting a web directory" will yield a number of tutorials on how this can be achieved. In a nutshell, one file contains the username and encrypted password to compare, and the other resides in the directory and contains the instructions for how to protect that part of the website.
>
> Alternatively, you could leverage two functions—securePassword( ) and comparePassword( )—to create a PHP-based authentication scheme. See "Password Management Functions" on page 246 for more information on how these functions work.

Improve the web page presentation

The XHTML for this application is largely contained in the three custom functions to render the web page (see "HTML Template Functions" on page 257). Any changes to the markup there will affect all pages, depending on what information is passed to the functions. For style changes, edit the *uar.css* file located in the *css* directory (see "CSS" on page 90).

Change the feedback messages

The feedback messages represent the different problems that the sample applications might encounter. They are all contained in a single custom function, `getResponse( )` (see "Status Messages" on page 255). The default message displayed when there are no errors is created in the main code and stored in the `$default_response` variable. You could change the wording and add additional instructions to make the user experience more enjoyable.

Adjust the algorithm to scramble your password

The custom functions to scramble and unscramble passwords stored in the database (see "Password Management Functions" on page 246) make use of four kinds of reversible string operations. By changing the order of these functions, you can alter the algorithm used to create a more secure password string. It is recommended that you make some kind of adjustment and test it before putting this code into production.

Change the application signature sent to the Twitter API

The `CURLOPT_USERAGENT` option in cURL is one way Twitter will be able to identify who you are and what you are doing with the API. The `$app_title` variable is set when the display variables are initialized in the main code. That value is appended onto the suite title when the user agent option is set during initialization of the cURL connection. Change these values to create your own signature.

Many of these changes apply to all of the sample applications, since they involve making adjustments to shared custom functions in the included files. If you want these changes to affect only a particular application, you can add additional parameters to trigger new behavior, or simply create new functions that will be called only by the affected application.

 Descriptions of the other sample applications will focus on what is unique to each tool. Please refer back to the detailed explanation in this section when looking under the hood of the rest of the PHP code. All of the applications are built along similar lines, so most of the comments apply.

Tweet Publisher

The most basic Twitter tool is one that enables you to answer the defining question, "What are you doing?" To get their answers onto the Twitter timeline, members need a form to submit their status updates to the API.

Tweet Publisher is a straightforward tool to update a member's status. To add to your own timeline, you enter your Twitter account username, your password, and a short message (up to 140 characters) into the form. When you submit this information, your tweet is published.

There are dozens of Twitter applications that duplicate this core function. I offer this one here not to set the Twitosphere ablaze with excitement, but as an example of an important interaction with the API.

The Twitter API currently requires individual usernames and passwords in order to make changes to accounts or retrieve protected information. Please note that some users will be hesitant to provide this information. See "Gone Phishing: A Word About Passwords" on page 182 for more detail on the issues that arise with shared authentication.

Adding disclaimers that include your contact information and other evidence of accountability is an important part of gaining the trust needed to entice someone to provide this access. Be clear, too, whether you need to save this data and how you will go about using your borrowed access.

Take the App for a Spin

To access the Tweet Publisher application, click on the "Publisher" link near the right side of the header included on all of the sample application pages. You can also reach it directly by loading the *uar_tweet_publisher.php* file into your browser from wherever you uploaded your application files (e.g., *http://makice.net/uar/uar_tweet_publisher .php* in my development environment). Doing so should get you a web page display that looks something like Figure 7-3.

To publish a new status update, you have to give the application some information:

1. Enter your Twitter username.

   Type your username into the text box labeled "Twitter Username." You can also enter your Twitter ID, if you know it, as the ID and username are interchangeable.

2. Enter your Twitter password.

   Type your current Twitter password into the text box labeled "Twitter Password." The content of the password input field is masked (i.e., your input is displayed as bullet characters instead of what you actually type), to give you some protection against people nearby who may see your password as you enter it.

3. Compose your status update.

   Type your answer to the Twitter question in the text area labeled "What are you doing?" There is a 140-character limit on what you can publish to your timeline. If you type too much (or leave this field empty), the application will return an error message without publishing anything.

4. Click the "Tweet!" button to submit the form.

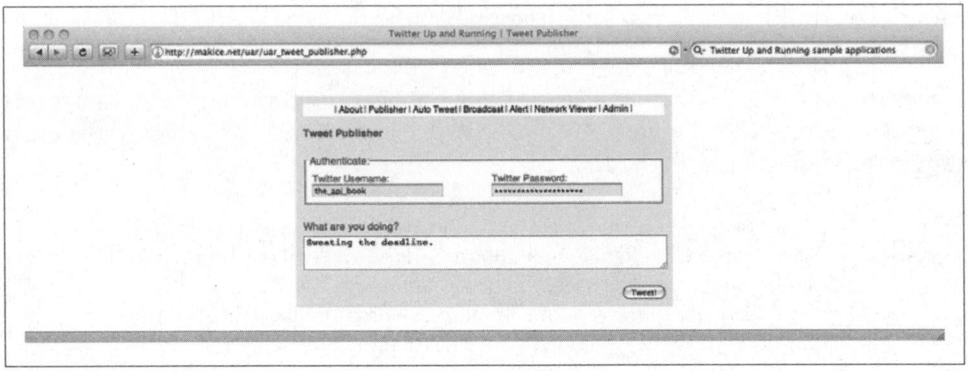

Figure 7-3. Tweet Publisher

When you submit this form successfully, Tweet Publisher will return a message ("Your tweet has been posted.") and include a link to view the new status update. If an error occurs, the feedback message will let you know what went wrong that needs correction on your next attempt to publish your tweet.

Check Under the Hood

The basic structure of this code (see Example 7-2) is the same as that for the administration tool, with two notable exceptions. First, there is no need for a database connection; the user input will go straight to Twitter and will not be stored locally in a database table. Second, different "stuff" will be done in the middle. Specifically, the application will publish a new tweet using the Twitter API rather than saving something to the application's database. I'll focus on the new logic here. If you need a refresher explanation on the rest of the code, please refer to the discussion of the administration tool in the preceding section.

Example 7-2. PHP to publish a status update to Twitter

```
/* Include External Functions */
$root_path = str_replace('/public_html', '/uar', $_SERVER['DOCUMENT_ROOT'])
                        .'/includes/';
include $root_path.'environment.php';
include $root_path.'status_messages.php';
include $root_path.'validate_data.php';
include $root_path.'api_config.php';
```

```php
include $root_path.'parse_data.php';
include $root_path.'html_template.php';

/* Initialize Values */
$app_title          = 'Tweet Publisher';
$twitter_username   = '';
$twitter_password   = '';
$tweet              = '';
$form_response      = '';
$submit_button_label = '';
$show_message       = '';

/* Parse Input */
$form_error         = 0;
$post_ok            = 0;
$twitter_username   = $_POST['twitter_username'];
$twitter_password   = $_POST['twitter_password'];
$tweet              = $_POST['tweet'];
$submit_button      = $_POST['submit_button'];
$tweet_encoded      = urlencode(stripslashes(urldecode($tweet)));
$API_query          = 'status='.$tweet_encoded;
$this_dir           = getHTTPpath($_SERVER['HTTP_HOST'],$_SERVER['REQUEST_URI']);

/* Configure API Requests */
list($master_username,$cURL_source) = prepAPI();

/* Initiate cURL */
$cURL               = prepRequest($app_title,$twitter_username,$twitter_password);

/*  Validate Access */
$submit_button_label = ' Tweet! ';
$form_error         = checkInput(array(
    'submit_button'     => $submit_button,
    'twitter_username'  => $twitter_username,
    'twitter_password'  => $twitter_password,
    'tweet'             => $tweet
    ),$cURL,$cURL_source);

/* Post Message */
if ($form_error == 0) {
    curl_setopt ($cURL, CURLOPT_POST, true);
    curl_setopt ($cURL, CURLOPT_POSTFIELDS, $API_query);
    list($cURL_status,$twitter_data) =
                                apiRequest($cURL,$cURL_source['post_tweet']);
    if ($cURL_status == 200)    {
        $post_ok        = 1;
        $tweet          = parseXML($twitter_data);
        $new_status_id = $tweet[0]['status_id'];
    }
    else                    { $form_error = 5; }
}

/* Determine Feedback Response */
$default_response   = '';
if ($form_error < 0) { $show_message = ' style="display:none;"'; }
```

```
if ($post_ok) {
    $tweet = '';
    $default_response = <<<DEFAULT_MESSAGE
    Your tweet has been posted.
    <a href="http://twitter.com/$twitter_username/statuses/$new_status_id">View</a>
DEFAULT_MESSAGE;
}
$form_response          = getResponse($form_error,$default_response);

/* Clean Up */
apiRequest($cURL,$cURL_source['end_session']);
curl_close($cURL);

/* Render Interface */
getHeader($app_title,'css/uar.css');
$tweet = htmlspecialchars($tweet, ENT_QUOTES, 'UTF-8');
$div_info               = <<<DIV_INFO
        <div id="uar_info">
            What are you doing?<br />
            <textarea name="tweet" rows="3" cols="60">$tweet</textarea>
        </div>
DIV_INFO;
$html_info              = array(
    'title'                 => $app_title,
    'url'                   => $this_dir,
    'hide_username'         => '',
    'username'
                            => htmlspecialchars($twitter_username, ENT_QUOTES, 'UTF-8'),
    'reset'                 => '',
    'info'                  => $div_info,
    'label'                 => $submit_button_label,
    'show_message'          => $show_message,
    'message'               => $form_response,
    'supplemental'          => '',
    'columns'               => ''
);
getInterface($html_info);
getFooter();
```

Let's take a look at the important sections of code for this application.

Parse input

The only new wrinkle for retrieving user-submitted data in Tweet Publisher is the need to make the tweet safe to send to Twitter. This is done by encoding the text entered into the web form, to make it easier for the Twitter API to differentiate between special characters and the text intended for display. The application sets a variable ($API_query) to hold the query string containing the member's new status update.

Post message

The main function of this application is to update the user's status with new content she has provided. After first doing all of the standard opening of API connections and data validation, the application can safely proceed. The main code relies on both built-in and custom functions to get the new text to the Twitter API.

Each API method has slightly different requirements for which HTTP method to use (see "Accessing the API" on page 134). To publish a new tweet, the POST method is needed. This means that the initiated cURL connection—referenced with the $cURL variable—must be configured to make this kind of request. Individual options for cURL are set with the curl_setopt( ) function by passing the connection handle with the option name and desired value. Tweet Publisher prepares for its next API request by setting CURLOPT_POST to true and filling CURLOPT_POSTFIELDS with the $API_query value formatted earlier in the script.

Once properly configured, the application calls the custom function apiRequest( ) to make the API method request to post the tweet using the open cURL object. This function returns both an HTTP status code and the actual response from the API, which should be XML. The most important indicator of success is the HTTP status code. A status code of 200 indicates that the message was posted.

Tweet Publisher could have stopped there, but I wanted to add a link pointing to the new tweet. To do this, the application needs to parse the API response and retrieve the status ID for the tweet. Thanks to work done in the previous chapter to create some reusable functions, this can be accomplished easily by passing the string containing the XML response ($twitter_data) to parseXML( ). This function returns a nested array filled with the contents of the XML object (see "Data Parsing Functions" on page 240). By referencing the first (and only) status element and the name of the specific element we need—status_id—we can store the new tweet ID in a variable for later use, as in:

```
$new_status_id = $tweet[0]['status_id'];
```

Render interface

With this application, the data the user enters in the text area to be published has the potential to be displayed back to the form. Usually, this won't happen; success will reset the $tweet variable to an empty string. However, if there is a problem, the previous text will be returned to the user to edit and resubmit.

This causes problems if not handled properly, as an attacker could try to take advantage of unescaped content and submit the HTML needed to load some malicious script (this is called an XSS attack). The browser will only see valid markup to render and will do what it is told, as if you planned to have some hacker script as part of your page. You can prevent this kind of behavior by escaping the user-provided text with the built-in function htmlspecialchars( ), as in:

```
$tweet = htmlspecialchars($tweet, ENT_QUOTES, 'UTF-8');
```

This will make replacements to any characters reserved for rendering web pages and make it possible for the browser to skip the part you didn't provide. For more information on XSS, see *http://en.wikipedia.org/wiki/Cross-site_scripting*.

Shifting Gears

In addition to the general improvements to the code suggested in the section on the Administrative Tool, there is a lot you could do with this simple Tweet Publisher application. Here are a few changes you could make to this sample application:

Make the use of passwords more secure
> The simplest change that could improve security in this application is not to prepopulate the password field, preventing the password from being included as plain text in the XHTML source. Another option might be to encrypt the password and save it in a browser cookie. There are even better ways to allow the user the convenience of logging in once without putting his authentication information at risk with each new page load. The rub here is that, unlike with authentication schemes you can control, in the end Twitter has to get the password that works in its own API.

Add templates that become tweet starting points
> Even the simple question "What are you doing?" can sometimes be difficult to answer. A drop-down selection menu that uses JavaScript to populate the main text area field might get those slow starters going with a prompted structure.

Invite a response to a random tweet
> Another way to prompt a user is to give her something to talk about. The public timeline is continuously streaming such prompts in the form of recent tweets. Grab one at random, and ask your user what she thinks of it. This might be a fresh and effective way to encourage connections with new people.

Show a list of similar status updates
> One way to add value is to have your application respond to user input with something unexpected but useful. On any given day, a few hundred thousand people will post some kind of message to the public timeline. Turn your next tweet into a search for other authors writing about similar things by using the text of the status update as keywords to match.

Auto Tweet

Whereas Tweet Publisher is a tool to let you compose a new tweet from scratch, Auto Tweet will compose a status update for you using the latest material from a designated news feed.

With this sample application, every member account can be associated with a single RSS or Atom feed, from which a new tweet will be automatically generated. This web interface collects only the information needed to accomplish this. A separate automated task is associated with this application that checks each feed registered in the database in six-hour cycles and posts the most recent article as a tweet (see "RSS to Tweet" on page 332).

There are other tools, including the very effective and popular Twitterfeed (*http://twit terfeed.com*), that perform this service. As with Tweet Publisher, there is nothing earth-shattering about another application that turns RSS into a Twitter update, but it is a useful power trick.

Take the App for a Spin

You can access the Auto Tweet application by clicking on the "Auto Tweet" link in the header included on all of the sample application pages. You can also reach it directly by loading the *uar_auto_tweet.php* file into your browser from wherever you uploaded your application files (for example, *http://makice.net/uar/uar_auto_tweet.php* in my development environment). Doing so should get you a web page display that looks something like Figure 7-4.

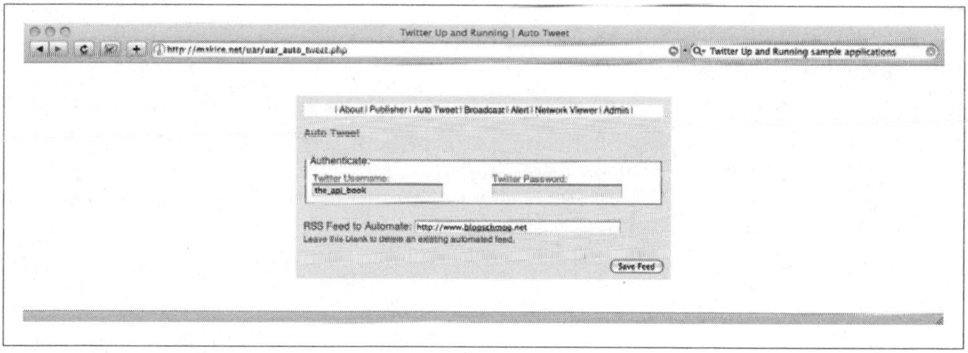

Figure 7-4. Auto Tweet

To configure your account to start publishing new tweets automatically, the application needs some information:

1. Enter your Twitter username.

   Type your username into the text box labeled "Twitter Username." You can also provide your Twitter ID, if you know it, since the ID and username are interchangeable.

2. Enter your Twitter password.

   Type your current Twitter password into the text box labeled "Twitter Password." The text will be displayed using bullet characters instead of showing what you are actually typing. This is to give you some protection against people nearby who may see your password as you enter it.

3. Enter the URI for your news feed.

   In the text field labeled "RSS Feed to Automate," enter the URI of the RSS or Atom news feed you want to use to populate your timeline. This should include the *http://* part of the link address. Leaving this field blank will either result in an error asking you to include a feed link or, if you have previously configured a feed, remove that feed.

4. Click the "Save Feed" button to submit the form.

Successful registration of a news feed will result in the message, "Your feed has been added to the queue." As a way of verifying the content, the application will also scan your feed and return an example of a tweet using the most recent article, as in:

```
'Congressional Tweets http://tinyurl.com/675e9e'
```

This tweet is composed of the article title and a TinyURL link to the full article.

If any problems occur, appropriate messages will be returned to you to let you know what happened after you submitted the form. To remove your registered feed and stop the automation, submit the form again, leaving the "RSS Feed to Automate" text field blank.

Check Under the Hood

In this sample application, the database is a big part of the picture. This tool both adds and edits data, as well as possibly deleting a record entirely. It also needs to deal with RSS parsing. The "Do Stuff" part of this code does a lot:

- Disables profile
- Retrieves stored data
- Processes deletion request
- Checks feed
- Saves profile

Otherwise, the basic structure of this code (see Example 7-3) is the same as for the administration tool. If you need a refresher on the rest of the code, please refer to the section on that tool earlier in this chapter.

Example 7-3. PHP to register an RSS feed for automatic tweets

```
/* Include External Functions */
$root_path = str_replace('/public_html', '/uar', $_SERVER['DOCUMENT_ROOT'])
                        .'/includes/';
include $root_path.'environment.php';
include $root_path.'status_messages.php';
include $root_path.'validate_data.php';
include $root_path.'api_config.php';
include $root_path.'pw_manage.php';
include $root_path.'database.php';
```

```php
include $root_path.'sql_queries.php';
include $root_path.'parse_data.php';
include $root_path.'html_template.php';

/* Initialize Values */
$app_title           = 'Auto Tweet';
$twitter_username    = '';
$twitter_password    = '';
$rss_feed            = '';
$form_response       = '';
$submit_button_label = '';
$show_message        = '';

/* Parse Input */
$form_error          = 0;
$post_ok             = 0;
$twitter_username    = $_POST['twitter_username'];
$twitter_password    = $_POST['twitter_password'];
$rss_feed            = $_POST['rss_feed'];
$submit_button       = $_POST['submit_button'];
$twitter_username    = strtolower($twitter_username);
$scrambled_password  = scramblePassword($twitter_password);
$this_dir            = getHTTPpath($_SERVER['HTTP_HOST'],$_SERVER['REQUEST_URI']);

/* Configure API Requests */
list($master_username,$cURL_source) = prepAPI();

/* Initiate cURL */
$cURL                = prepRequest($app_title,$twitter_username,$twitter_password);

/* Prepare Database Interaction */
$db_connection       = openDB();
$sql_variables = array (
    'twitter_username'       => $twitter_username,
    'scrambled_password'     => $scrambled_password,
    'rss_feed'               => $rss_feed,
    );
$sql_query           = getQueries($sql_variables);

/* Validate Access */
$submit_button_label = ' Save Feed ';
$form_error          = checkInput(array(
    'submit_button'          => $submit_button,
    'twitter_username'       => $twitter_username,
    'twitter_password'       => $twitter_password
    ),$cURL,$cURL_source);

/* Disable Profile */
if ($form_error == 4) {
    mysql_query($sql_query['Disable_Profile'])
        or die('Error, disable query failed');
}
elseif ($form_error == 0) {

/* Retrieve Stored Data */
```

```
    $sql_result = mysql_query($sql_query['Retrieve_Stored_RSS'])
        or die('Error, selection query failed');
    while ($row = mysql_fetch_assoc($sql_result)) {
        $rss_feed_stored = $row['rss_url'];
        break;
    }
    mysql_free_result($sql_result);

/* Process Deletion Request */
    if (strlen($rss_feed) < 1) {
        $form_error   = 7;
        if (strlen($rss_feed_stored) > 0) {
            $form_error = 6;
            $sql_result = mysql_query($sql_query['Remove_Profile']);
        }
    }

/* Check Feed */
    elseif ($rss_feed == $rss_feed_stored)          {
        $form_error   = 9;
    }
    else {
        list($thisFeed,$foo) = parseFeed($rss_feed);
        $sample_tweet = $thisFeed[0]['title'];
        $sample_link  = file_get_contents(
                'http://tinyurl.com/api-create.php?url='.$thisFeed[0]['link']);
        if (strlen($sample_link) > 0)  { $sample_tweet .= " $sample_link"; }
        if (strlen($sample_tweet) < 1) { $form_error = 8; }

/* Save Profile */
        else {
            if (strlen($rss_feed_stored) > 0) {
                mysql_query($sql_query['Update_Profile'])
                    or die('Error, update query failed');
            }
            else {
                mysql_query($sql_query['Create_Profile'])
                    or die('Error, insert query failed');
            }
        }
    }
}

/* Determine Feedback Response */
if ($form_error < 0) { $show_message = ' style="display:none;"'; }
$default_response     = <<<DEFAULT_MESSAGE
    Your feed has been added to the queue.
    You should see an automated post within the hour:
    <br /><div style='padding:20px;'>'$sample_tweet'</div>
DEFAULT_MESSAGE;
$form_response        = getResponse($form_error,$default_response);

/* Clean Up */
apiRequest($cURL,$cURL_source['end_session']);
curl_close($cURL);
```

```
closeDB($db_connection);

/* Render Interface */
getHeader($app_title,'css/uar.css');
$div_reset     = "<a href='$this_url'$show_message>Another user broadcast</a> | ";
$rss_feed = htmlspecialchars($rss_feed, ENT_QUOTES, 'UTF-8');
$div_info                = <<<DIV_INFO
        <div id="uar_info">
            RSS Feed to Automate:
            <input type="text" name="rss_feed" size="40" value="$rss_feed" /><br />
            <small>Leave this blank to delete an existing automated feed.</small>
        </div>
DIV_INFO;
$html_info            = array(
    'title'               => $app_title,
    'url'                 => $this_dir,
    'hide_username'       => '',
    'username'
            => htmlspecialchars($twitter_username, ENT_QUOTES, 'UTF-8'),
    'reset'               => $div_reset,
    'info'                => $div_info,
    'label'               => $submit_button_label,
    'show_message'        => $show_message,
    'message'             => $form_response,
    'supplemental'        => '',
    'columns'             => ''
),
getInterface($html_info);
getFooter();
```

Let's look at the work this code performs.

Parse input

Because it needs to make regular changes to the member's Twitter account by posting links to the new articles in the desired news feed, this application has to save the user's password in the database for later use. It also has to protect that data in some way. The code leverages the scramblePassword( ) function (see "Password Management Functions" on page 246) to turn the password the user enters into a long string of characters. Later, an automated task will use a complementary function—unscramblePassword( ) —to turn that stored string back into a useful password to send to the Twitter API (see "RSS to Tweet" on page 332).

Disable profile

As members start to register different feeds to be automatically published in their timelines, the list of accounts to manage can become quite long. There is no way around processing the queue if you want the tool you built to work for everyone. However, it's a good idea to drop whatever dead weight you can from that to-do list so your server isn't wasting bandwidth and processor time on accounts that don't work.

If the application encounters a stored account that no longer verifies with Twitter—this will happen as soon as a member changes his password on the Twitter site—there is no need to make further attempts to publish a new tweet. Without working access to that account, all posts will be rejected by the API. Rather than spinning its wheels, the application will use this failure as an opportunity to update a data flag in the profile record stored in the database to show that this registered user can be ignored:

```
mysql_query($sql_query['Disable_Profile'])
    or die('Error, disable query failed');
```

No further action is taken, and the application displays an error message to the end user.

Retrieve stored data

If the submitted username validates with Twitter, the application takes the next step of checking the database for an existing record. This is done so the application can compare the entered URI to whatever is already stored in the database. A SQL statement already retrieved from getQueries( ) can be passed to the open database connection with a built-in function, mysql_query( ), which returns all of the matching data rows and columns specified in the system.

An easy way to get the query result data into a usable form is to tell PHP to loop through each of the rows. Each row is an associative array containing the name of the database column as the key and whatever is stored inside as the value:

```
while ($row = mysql_fetch_assoc($sql_result)) {
    $rss_feed_stored = $row['rss_url'];
    break;
}
```

For this particular query, the application expects only one row. It takes whatever it finds in the rss_url column of the first row of data and then follows with a break to exit the loop. The same could also be written as:

```
$row = mysql_fetch_assoc($sql_result);
$rss_feed_stored = $row['rss_url'];
```

However, this may throw a warning if the result set is empty. Using the while loop prevents $row['rss_url'] from being referenced unless the query returns at least one record.

Once PHP has retrieved the stored link to the RSS feed (if one exists), the script is finished with this particular data set. For the sake of tidiness, we then use another built-in MySQL function in PHP—mysql_free_result( )—to free up the memory allocated to the data in $sql_result.

As with other closure operations, the script likely will work just fine without explicitly releasing the data from memory; however, it's good practice to do this. Freeing the query results also prevents data from persisting when you don't want it to. By taking this extra step, you may prevent coding errors where the wrong data is being used.

Process deletion request

Auto Tweet does not have a delete button. As a way of simplifying the code, I opted for including fewer form objects. The trade-off is that deleting an existing RSS feed is not intuitive (maybe that's something you can work on). Deletions are handled by combining two states: having an existing feed and submitting a blank RSS form field. The application interprets that situation as a request to stop automating tweets.

The first condition that must be met is that the value in the RSS feed field (`$rss_feed`) must be empty. There are a few different ways to find out whether the submitted field was empty; I prefer to examine the length of the string rather than the content. The second condition that must be met is that the database must have something in it. Earlier, PHP put whatever it found in the database into `$rss_feed_stored`, so the length of that value can also be tested.

Only if there was a stored URL feed but the user provided no RSS link will the application ask MySQL to remove that record from the database. When the link vanishes, so does any chance that the automated task that runs every six hours will publish anything to this user's timeline.

Check feed

The main function of this web interface is to verify the information that will be stored for later processing. One of the criteria for "valid" is that the RSS link leads to something that can be understood.

Most of the work is done by a custom function, `parseFeed()`, which turns the URI into usable data. It fills a variable (`$thisFeed`) with a nested array of information about the articles it finds in the RSS feed (see "Data Parsing Functions" on page 240). Taking the first article in that list, the application formats its title and web link as a tweet. If this doesn't work, an error is returned to the end user to indicate that there is a problem.

Part of the process of formatting a new tweet includes shortening the potentially long URI for the latest article into something more likely to fit along with a title in 140 characters. TinyURL, a link-shortening service, has a handy API method that allows this to be done on the fly. I use the built-in PHP function `file_get_contents()` to send this request, capturing the returned TinyURL in a variable (`$sample_link`) that can be inserted into the status update:

```
$sample_link = file_get_contents(
        'http://tinyurl.com/api-create.php?url='.$thisFeed[0]['link']);
```

If there is no difference between what was entered and what was already stored, the application will skip this step and instead return a feedback message indicating that no changes need to be made.

Save profile

Finally, the application is at the point where it can store the new information in the database and thus add it to the list of accounts to process during the next run of the automated task. By now, the application has declared the RSS feed to be valid, and we know whether this member has already saved a link. It is an easy matter to decide whether to create or update the database record.

Shifting Gears

In addition to the general improvements to the code suggested in the sections on the Administrative Tool and Tweet Publisher, here are a few more ways you could make changes Auto Tweet to make it better:

Accommodate more formats
> For this sample application, only two kinds of feeds were included: RSS and Atom. Although those kinds of documents are easy to parse because of their standard formats, any web page has the potential to be mined for new data. Some creative parsing might make this tool more versatile.

Provide template options for tweet structure
> Displaying just a title and a link to an article reeks of automation. People following your timeline may want something more personal, or possibly just some variety. Design a few options using the data in the RSS feed you are mining, and let the user decide how to compose the automated tweet.

Perform more checks on the validity of the tweet
> All this tool is currently doing is grabbing whatever is in the title and tacking on a TinyURL, if possible. If that title is extra long, the end of the tweet may get truncated. Adding a check to better understand what is coming out of the pipe would be a plus.

Use a different URL shortening service
> TinyURL is convenient and pretty reliable, but it is not the only service you can use to turn a long URI into a short one. Metamark (*http://metamark.net*), notlong (*http://notlong.com*), and SnipURL (*http://snipurl.com*) also have API support. If either you or the user has a preference on which service to use, TinyURL could be replaced. Heck, you could even create your own service by assigning a unique code to each link and keeping track of that list in a new table.

Facilitate multiple feed management
> Right now, this application lets you update from only one feed at a time. That's convenient for the code, but it may not be enough for the end user. Adjust the SQL

queries and processing of stored data to allow more than one feed to be used at a time. You might be forced to replace the deletion method with a click-to-remove function, too.

Control how often and how much the feed gets mined

Every six hours (four times a day), the automated task associated with this web interface will examine each of the feeds used by the account and pick the most recent new article to turn into a tweet. If the RSS feed produces content more regularly than that, there may be a need to let the user dictate the timing of the automation or how many tweets to allow at once.

Tweet Broadcast

Whereas Auto Tweet turns aggregated information into a single tweet, Tweet Broadcast goes in the other direction, turning multiple tweets into a news feed. This application aggregates tweets from different authors to create a daily synopsis of what each of those members were doing each day.

By specifying a handful of user accounts, you can use this sample application to generate an RSS feed that contains information for up to 20 days of timeline activity. This interface only collects the names of members to include, saving them in the database.

Two other PHP applications are associated with this tool. One is an automated task that checks for new tweets once a day and maintains a local store of recent status updates (see "Aggregate Broadcast" on page 338). The second associated application is the feed itself. Each member account can have one aggregation feed, accessible at *uar_broadcast.php?username*. This dynamic RSS page will gather and group recent status updates published by the Twitter members you want to follow.

Twitter Digest (*http://twitter-digest.appspot.com*) is an early third-party Twitter application that does this beautifully. It even includes some threading of messages. There is lot of functional power in knowing how to aggregate individual tweets in a useful way.

Take the App for a Spin

You can access the Tweet Broadcast application by clicking on the "Broadcast" link, in the middle of the header links included on the sample application pages. You can also reach it directly by loading the *uar_tweet_broadcast.php* file into your browser from wherever you uploaded your application files (for example, *http://makice.net/uar/uar _tweet_broadcast.php* in my development environment).

To configure your account to start aggregating the tweets of your friends, the application first needs to know who you are:

1. Enter your Twitter username.

Type your username into the text box labeled "Twitter Username." You can also use your Twitter ID, if you know it, as the ID and username are interchangeable.

2. Enter your Twitter password.

   Type your current Twitter password into the text box labeled "Twitter Password." The text will be displayed using bullet characters instead of showing what you are actually typing. This is to give you some protection against people nearby who may see your password as you enter it.

3. Click the "Identify yourself" button to submit the form.

If your access information checks out with Twitter, the application will reload the page, adding a new text area box (see Figure 7-5). If you have previously configured your custom RSS feed, the usernames of the other member accounts you are aggregating each day will be displayed in the box. Otherwise, the box will empty and waiting for your input.

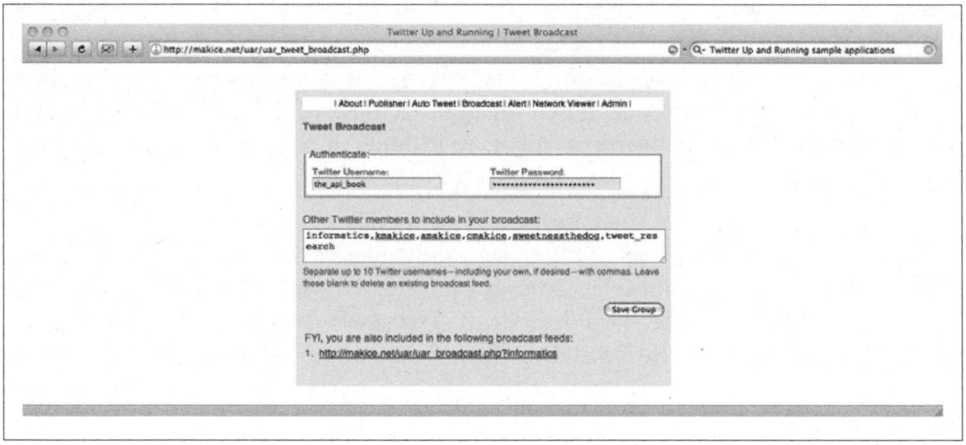

Figure 7-5. Tweet Broadcast

 The username and password fields are pre-populated so you don't have to type them more than once. Even though the web browser renders the password as a string of bullet characters, the actual password remains in plain text as that field's default value. Although this adds some convenience for the user, it is not ideal from a security standpoint.

To customize the content in your feed:

1. List the usernames to aggregate.

   Type the names of the other Twitter accounts you want to aggregate in the text box labeled "Other Twitter members to include in your broadcast." The usernames should be separated with commas. Be sure to include your own username if you want to be a part of the broadcast feed; it is not added automatically. To delete an existing broadcast feed, simply remove any text that already appears in the text area.

2. Click the "Save Group" button to submit the form.

If successful, the page will reload with a feedback message ("Your group has been saved") and a link to the customized RSS feed. Any problems will be displayed as error messages without any changes being made to the database.

 Tweet Broadcast uses a lazy constraint on the number of members that can be included in a single feed—the limit of 10 Twitter usernames is suggested on the submission form but not enforced in the code. This is one area where you can improve this code by adding some checks on the server side.

One other feature of this sample application is that after you authenticate the first time, you may see a few links listed below the web form. These links point to other broadcast feeds generated by this tool that include your tweets. This kind of added value is a trade-off between privacy and discovery.

Check Under the Hood

Tweet Broadcast works a lot like Auto Tweet, in that it simply collects a little user input to help create a to-do list for an automated task that runs separately. The primary differences have to do with the nature of the information being collected—in this case, a list instead of a simple URL.

Because lists are involved, the data needs to be checked and saved in a slightly different way, by looping through each item in the list and dealing with it individually. The rest of the code (see Example 7-4) will look very similar to that of the other sample applications. If you need a deeper explanation of part of the code not covered in this section, please refer to the discussions earlier in this chapter.

Example 7-4. PHP to save a list of members to aggregate

```
/* Include External Functions */
$root_path = str_replace('/public_html', '/uar', $_SERVER['DOCUMENT_ROOT'])
                        .'/includes/';
include $root_path.'environment.php';
include $root_path.'status_messages.php';
include $root_path.'validate_data.php';
include $root_path.'api_config.php';
include $root_path.'database.php';
include $root_path.'sql_queries.php';
include $root_path.'html_template.php';

/* Initialize Values */

$app_title          = 'Tweet Broadcast';
```

```php
$twitter_username     = '';
$twitter_password     = '';
$group_members        = '';
$group_list           = '';
$group_stored         = array();
$membership_stored    = array();
$form_response        = '';
$submit_button_label  = 'Please identify yourself';
$show_message         = '';
$show_supplement      = ' style="display:none;"';
$show_group           = ' style="display:none;"';

/* Parse Input */
$form_error           = 0;
$twitter_username     = $_POST['twitter_username'];
$twitter_password     = $_POST['twitter_password'];
$group_members        = $_POST['group_members'];
$submit_button        = $_POST['submit_button'];
$group_members        = trim($group_members);
$twitter_username     = strtolower($twitter_username);
$this_dir             = getHTTPpath($_SERVER['HTTP_HOST'],$_SERVER['REQUEST_URI']);

/* Configure API Requests */
list($master_username,$cURL_source) = prepAPI();

/* Initiate cURL */
$cURL                 = prepRequest($app_title,$twitter_username,$twitter_password);

/* Validate Access */
$form_error           = checkInput(array(
    'submit_button'       => $submit_button,
    'twitter_username'    => $twitter_username,
    'twitter_password'    => $twitter_password
    ),$cURL,$cURL_source);

if ($form_error == 0) {
    $show_group          = '';
    $submit_button_label = ' Save Group ';

/* Prepare Database Interaction */
    $db_connection   = openDB();
    $sql_variables   = array (
        'twitter_username' => $twitter_username
        );
    $sql_query       = getQueries($sql_variables);

/* Retrieve Stored Data */
    $sql_result = mysql_query($sql_query['Retrieve_Stored_Group'])
        or die('Error, selection query failed');
    while ($row = mysql_fetch_assoc($sql_result)) {
        array_push($group_stored, $row['other']);
    }
    mysql_free_result($sql_result);
    $group_list = implode(",", $group_stored);
```

```php
    $sql_result = mysql_query($sql_query['Retrieve_Stored_Memberships'])
        or die('Error, selection query failed');
    while ($row = mysql_fetch_assoc($sql_result)) {
        array_push($membership_stored, $row['owner']);
    }
    mysql_free_result($sql_result);
    if (sizeof($membership_stored) > 0) { $show_supplement = '';}

/* Process Deletion Request */
    if ($submit_button != 'Please identify yourself') {
        if (strlen($group_members) < 1) {
            $form_error = 7;
            if (sizeof($group_stored) > 0) {
                $form_error = 11;
                $sql_result = mysql_query($sql_query['Remove_Group']);
            }
        }
        else {

/* Compare Groups */
            $group_member_check = array();
            foreach ($group_stored as $this_member) {
                $group_member_check[$this_member] = FALSE;
            }
            $group_member_array = explode(",",$group_members);
            foreach ($group_member_array as $this_member) {
                if (in_array(trim($this_member), $group_stored)) {
                    $group_member_check[$this_member] = TRUE;
                }
                else {
                    $group_member_check[$this_member] = FALSE;
                    break;
                }
            }
            $group_list = implode(",", $group_member_array);
            if (in_array(FALSE, array_values($group_member_check))) {

/* Save Group */
                if (sizeof($group_stored) > 0)          {
                    mysql_query($sql_query['Remove_Group'])
                        or die('Error, deletion query failed');
                }
                $twitter_username = mysql_real_escape_string($twitter_username);
                foreach ($group_member_array as $this_member) {
                    $this_member = mysql_real_escape_string($this_member);
                    $sql_query['Create_Group'] = "
                        INSERT INTO tweetbroadcast_groups (owner, other)
                        VALUES ('$twitter_username', '$this_member')
                        ";
                    mysql_query($sql_query['Create_Group'])
                        or die('Error, insert query failed');
                }
            }
            else {
                $form_error = 10;
```

```php
                }
            }
        }
        closeDB($db_connection);
}

/* Determine Feedback Response */
$default_response       = '';
if (($form_error < 0) || (($form_error == 0)
        && ($submit_button == 'Please identify yourself')) )
        { $show_message      = ' style="display:none;"'; }
else {
        $broadcast          = "uar_broadcast.php?$twitter_username";
        $broadcast_visible = $this_dir . $broadcast;
$default_response       = <<<DEFAULT_MESSAGE
        Your group has been saved.
        Aggregation will begin soon, and your custom broadcast feed will be available
        at:
        <br />
        <div style='padding:20px;'><a href='$broadcast'>$broadcast_visible</a></div>
DEFAULT_MESSAGE;
}
$form_response          = getResponse($form_error,$default_response);

/* Clean Up */
apiRequest($cURL,$cURL_source['end_session']);
curl_close($cURL);

/* Render Interface */
getHeader($app_title,'css/uar.css');
$div_reset  = "<a href='$this_url'$show_group>Another user broadcast</a> | ";
$group_list = htmlspecialchars($group_list, ENT_QUOTES, 'UTF-8');
$div_info               = <<<DIV_INFO
        <div id="uar_info"$show_group>
                Other Twitter members to include in your broadcast:
                <textarea name="group_members" rows="3" cols="60">$group_list
                </textarea>
                <br />
                <small>Separate up to 10 Twitter usernames&mdash;including your own, if
                        desired&mdash;with commas. Leave these blank to delete an existing
                        broadcast feed.</small>
        </div>
DIV_INFO;
$div_supplemental       = <<<DIV_SUPPLEMENTAL_START
        <div id="uar_supplemental"$show_supplement>
                FYI, you are also included in the following broadcast feeds:
                <ol>
DIV_SUPPLEMENTAL_START;
foreach ($membership_stored as $broadcast) {
        $broadcast_url = "uar_broadcast.php?$broadcast";
        $broadcast_visible = $this_dir . $broadcast_url;
        $div_supplemental .= "<li><a href='$broadcast_url'>$broadcast_visible</a>
                </li>\n";
}
$div_supplemental       .= <<<DIV_SUPPLEMENTAL_END
```

```
            </ol>
        </div>
DIV_SUPPLEMENTAL_END;
$html_info        = array(
    'title'             => $app_title,
    'url'               => $this_dir,
    'hide_username'     => '',
    'username'          => htmlspecialchars($twitter_username, ENT_QUOTES, 'UTF-8'),
    'reset'             => $div_reset,
    'info'              => $div_info,
    'label'             => $submit_button_label,
    'show_message'      => $show_message,
    'message'           => $form_response,
    'supplemental'      => $div_supplemental,
    'columns'           => ''
);
getInterface($html_info);
getFooter();
```

Let's take a look at the new elements in this code.

Retrieve stored data

The data retrieval code here looks a lot like the code used in Auto Tweet, with a couple of twists. First, there are two data sets to make available to PHP. Second, the SQL statements are expected to return more than one record.

The first query (`Retrieve_Stored_Group`) fetches all of the other authors this member is already including to create her daily tweet feed. These usernames will have previously been processed and stored in the database. If this is a first-time user of the Tweet Broadcast tool, the data set will be empty. Whatever information is found is stored in an array (`$group_stored`) using the `array_push( )` PHP function, which tacks a new value onto the end of an existing array. Since you'll also display this list in the web form as a pre-populated field the next time the user authenticates, the application creates a second version of the same data as a comma-delimited list of values (`$group_list`). This is achieved using the `implode( )` function.

The second query (`Retrieve_Stored_Memberships`) is structurally identical to the first. This time, however, the application is interested in figuring out which other members are incorporating this user's tweets into their own aggregation feeds. Again, an array is created to store all of the usernames returned by the SQL query (`$membership_stored`). However, this time there is no need to make a comma-delimited list. If the query returns any results, the usernames will become part of a supplemental list of links to other broadcast feeds.

Process deletion request

As in the Auto Tweet application, Tweet Broadcast has no button to click to turn off a broadcast. Instead, the user has to submit a blank field, essentially setting the group membership to nothing. With nothing to process, there is no aggregation.

The two conditions that have to be satisfied in order to remove an existing group from the database are the same as those that must be satisfied to remove an RSS feed in the Auto Tweet application. First, the user must submit a blank field (`$group_members` has no length). Second, there has to be something in the database to delete (`$group_stored` has a length). If both of those conditions are met, you can tell PHP to send the deletion SQL statement to the database.

Compare groups

There is no need to bother the nice database if you have nothing to change. This section of code uses a new associative array—`$group_member_check`—to compare the list of usernames stored in the database (`$group_stored`) with the list of usernames just submitted by the user (`$group_members`). Unfortunately, it isn't as easy as just comparing strings of text. "Bears, Defeat, Packers" is not the same as "Packers, Defeat, Bears", even if the two lists contain the same three items. For this application, order doesn't matter; we just want to check whether each array contains the same items. That's where `$group_member_check` comes in.

First, PHP loops through the array of usernames stored in the database. On each iteration, the username becomes the key and a value of FALSE is assigned to that item. This approach assumes that none of these stored members will be in the list submitted by the user.

Next, the application moves on to the user-submitted list. To perform the same looping maneuver, the data has to be converted from a comma-delimited list to an array. PHP has a great built-in function for this, called `explode( )`:

```
$group_member_array = explode(",",$group_members);
```

This time, when PHP looks at each value in `$group_member_array`, it will check to see whether the username is also in `$group_stored` (whose members are already registered with the associative array `$group_member_check`). If the `in_array( )` check is positive, the application will flip the value flag for that member from FALSE to TRUE. If not, the script will add a FALSE value for the current username and break out of the loop.

If at the end of all this looping even one value is still FALSE, the application will know that something is different and needs to be saved to the database.

Save group

If something in the aggregation group has changed, we need to reflect those changes in the database. The group, however, isn't contained in a single profile. In the database schema, each member is associated with the authenticated user individually. The easiest way to resolve all of the differences is to wipe the slate clean and start over.

Fortunately, the application has already done the required legwork to figure out whether there is anything in the database to remove. Checking the size of the array `$group_stored` will let the application know if it needs to send the Remove_Group SQL statement to the database (a size greater than zero means something is in the database). The slate is now clean, one way or the other.

Because each username in the group needs its own record to put it in the queue for the automated task to process, another loop is required. The application uses **foreach** to examine each item in the **$group_member_array**. Generally speaking, the sample applications have been designed to move all of the SQL statement syntax to a custom function, **getQueries( )**. In this case, however, the application can't know ahead of time what the user might type, so I opted to create the needed query on the fly and send that SQL statement to the database for each item.

 If possible, move your SQL statements out of the web path and into a more protected area still accessible by PHP. Doing so lowers the chance that some unscrupulous person will be able to mess with your database.

For example, $sql_query['Create_Group'] could easily be filled from a new custom function that accepts $twitter_username and $this_member as parameters.

Render interface

Creating the XHTML output works the same in this application as in the others. In Tweet Broadcast, however, we make use of a supplemental display area below the web form. This is where the links to other broadcast feeds are listed. Whether this part of the page is displayed or not is dictated by a variable—$show_supplement—that either is empty, indicating that the content should be shown, or contains an inline style to hide the <div> content.

Shifting Gears

Here are a few suggestions of ways you could make changes to the Tweet Broadcast interface to improve on this starter code:

Validate the data being submitted
> When entering a list of Twitter members to aggregate, the user can type a comma-delimited list or recreate the Gettysburg address. The application currently only looks at whether there is content (because a lack of content has meaning); it doesn't examine the quality of what is included. Each item in the list could be checked to see whether it is a valid username for a public account.

Allow more members to be included in the feed
> The lazy constraint displayed in this application's interface suggests that no more than 10 member accounts may be used to populate a daily aggregator. Although there are some reasons (scalability, server load) for setting a cap on the number of usernames in a given group, that limit is both arbitrary and unenforced. Being deliberate about the maximum group size will add clarity to the tool.

Create broadcast feeds based on other factors, like keywords or location
> The API method powering Tweet Broadcast returns content from a member's personal timeline. However, this approach could be adapted to look at the search API to find matches based on other criteria, such as keywords, hashtags, or location. Adding an option to check content or location instead of the author might give this tool more utility.

Broadcast Feed

A companion to Tweet Broadcast is Broadcast Feed, which generates a dynamic RSS feed from the profile information each member stores in the database. The broadcast feed is a PHP application that queries a local repository of recent tweets, grouping them by day.

Take the App for a Spin

The Broadcast Feed application is not included in the header links in the sample application pages, but a link is provided in Tweet Broadcast after you use that application to update your list of aggregated Twitter members. You can also reach it directly by loading the *uar_broadcast.php* file into your browser from wherever you uploaded your application files and including your Twitter username as the query string (e.g., *http://makice.net/uar/uar_broadcast.php?the_api_book* in my development environment).

What happens when you load this page depends entirely on what you are using to view it. The output is valid RSS, as you would find attached to a WordPress blog. The Safari browser will render it as a news feed and show the contents. Firefox may try to load it into Google Reader or some other feed manager. Using cURL and the command line will show you the raw tag structure. The beauty of RSS is that many different clients can read and manipulate the encapsulated content.

Check Under the Hood

Although the setup for this special part of the Tweet Broadcast application will look very familiar, there are some key differences between this and the other code already explored in this chapter. The biggest wrinkle is that no HTML is generated; the application generates an RSS document disguised as a PHP page.

The second half of the code for this application (see Example 7-5) diverges sharply from the earlier programs. The following tasks are performed:

- Retrieve update timestamp
- Initiate XML

- Add daily updates
- Render RSS feed

If you need a deeper explanation of the code not covered in this section, please refer to the discussions earlier in this chapter.

Example 7-5. PHP to display the RSS for an aggregated feed

```php
/* Include External Functions */
$root_path = str_replace('/public_html', '/uar', $_SERVER['DOCUMENT_ROOT'])
                        .'/includes/';
include $root_path.'environment.php';
include $root_path.'database.php';
include $root_path.'sql_queries.php';
include $root_path.'parse_data.php';

/* Parse Input */
$app_title          = 'Tweet Broadcast';
$twitter_username   = $_SERVER['QUERY_STRING'];
$this_url           = "http://". $_SERVER['HTTP_HOST'] . $_SERVER['REQUEST_URI'];
$this_dir           = getHTTPpath($_SERVER['HTTP_HOST'],$_SERVER['REQUEST_URI']);

/* Prepare Database Interaction */
$db_connection      = openDB();
$twitter_username   = strtolower($twitter_username);
$sql_variables      = array (
    'twitter_username'      => $twitter_username
    );
$sql_query          = getQueries($sql_variables);

/* Retrieve Stored Data */
$tweets_stored      = array();
$sql_result = mysql_query($sql_query['Retrieve_Recent_Tweets'])
    or die('Error, selection 1 query failed');
while ($row = mysql_fetch_assoc($sql_result)) { $tweets_stored[] = $row; }
mysql_free_result($sql_result);

/* Retrieve Update Timestamp */
$sql_result = mysql_query($sql_query['Retrieve_Publish_Date'])
    or die('Error, selection 2 query failed');
$row = mysql_fetch_assoc($sql_result);
$last_update = $row['last_update'];
mysql_free_result($sql_result);

closeDB($db_connection);

/* Initiate XML */
$xml_variables      = array (
    'title'                 => 'Twitter Up and Running - '.$app_title,
    'link'                  => $this_url,
    'pubDate'               => $last_update,
    'generator'             => $this_dir.'uar_tweet_broadcast.php'
    );
$xml                = createRSSshell($xml_variables);
```

```
/* Add Daily Updates */
$this_day              = '';
$this_tweet_format     = '';
$this_tweet_authors    = array();
foreach ($tweets_stored as $this_tweet) {
    if (($this_day != '') && ($this_day != $this_tweet['tweet_day'])) {
        $this_tweet_format  = preg_replace('/&(?!\w+;)/',
                                '&amp;', $this_tweet_format);
        $item               = array (
            'link'              => $this_tweet['status_url'],
            'pubDate'           => $this_tweet_date,
            'generator'         => $this_dir.'uar_tweet_broadcast.php',
            'dc:creator'        => implode(', ',array_keys($this_tweet_authors)),
            'category'          => '<![CDATA[Twitter Up and Running]]>',
            'description'       => $this_tweet_format,
            'content:encoded'   => '<![CDATA['.$this_tweet_format.']]>',
            'guid'              => $this_tweet['status_url']
        );
        $tweet              = addItem($xml->channel,'item',$item);
        $this_tweet_format  = '';
        $this_tweet_authors = array();
    }
    # Process this tweet for the next aggregation
    $this_tweet['author_url'] =
                        'http://twitter.com/'.$this_tweet['author_username'];
    $this_tweet['status_url'] =
                $this_tweet['author_url'].'/status/'.$this_tweet['status_id'];
    $this_tweet_authors[$this_tweet['author_fullname']] = 1;
    $this_tweet_date    = $this_tweet['pub_date'];
    $this_title         = date("l, F dS, Y",strtotime($this_tweet['pub_date']));
    $this_tweet_format .= formatTweetAsXHTML($this_tweet);
    $this_day           = $this_tweet['tweet_day'];
}

/* Render RSS feed */
echo $xml->asXML();
```

Let's see what this code does under the hood.

Parse input

When variables are passed to this script using the GET method, the names and values for each are paired in one long, encoded query string attached to the URI. PHP will automatically parse that information into a special associative array: _GET. This application also uses the query string as an identifier, as in *http://makice.net/uar/uar _broadcast.php?kmakice*, where *kmakice* is the query string. PHP accommodates this by offering another special array to retrieve the username:

```
$twitter_username = $_SERVER['QUERY_STRING'];
```

Retrieve update timestamp

To let RSS readers know when the information in this feed was last updated, the script will ask the database for the most recent tweet in the data set and return its date. This helps readers avoid unnecessary parsing or redistribution of the same content.

Initiate XML

Even if there is no content to include in the output, it is important to at least provide the XML elements expected by RSS readers to describe the feed itself. The application sends an array—$xml_variables—as a parameter to the custom function createRSSshell( ). This function uses that information to create and return an XML object containing all of the essential parts to describe the feed. For more details on what this shell looks like, see "Data Parsing Functions" on page 240.

Add daily updates

What is missing at this point is the content for each article in the feed. If there is nothing to include—i.e., if the selected group of authors hasn't published anything, or there are no authors in the group— all that will be output is the shell. However, if there is something to aggregate, that data needs to be added to the XML object, $xml.

The content used to populate the XML object is found in $tweets_stored, an array of arrays created earlier in the application code by querying the database for relevant tweets. The SQL query that returned these results also sorted them in a way that helps us aggregate the group's contributions into daily snapshots of their tweets.

When looping through this array, the application must keep track of when the timestamp included with each status update changes to a new day. That moment acts as a trigger, telling PHP it is time to transfer whatever it has aggregated into the XML object as a new item, and then start over. The $this_day variable is used as a trigger for this purpose; its value is compared to the value in the tweet_day column for each tweet.

For each new day, the tweet data is used to set the variables that will be added to $xml. The most important one is $this_tweet_format, which contains a growing string of tweets formatted for inclusion in each daily snapshot item. The formatting is done by a custom function—formatTweetAsXHTML( )—and tweets are appended to whatever has already been processed.

When a new day is detected, an associative array ($item) is created using the values to be added as RSS elements in the new article. The array is then passed as a parameter to the custom function addItem( ), along with the specific location in the XML object hierarchy where the new elements should be placed:

```
$tweet = addItem($xml->channel,'item',$item);
```

Once the aggregated tweets are safely tucked away in the XML object, the application clears the aggregation variables to start collecting content for the next RSS article.

For more information about the formatting of the tweets or about adding items to the XML object, see "Data Parsing Functions" on page 240.

Render RSS feed

Of course, no one is going to see all this handiwork unless PHP turns the object into formatted text. With SimpleXML functions (see "PHP" on page 96), this is...well, simple:

```
echo $xml->asXML();
```

All of the necessary headers and tag formatting is done for me, yielding content any RSS reader will love.

Shifting Gears

Although this script may function correctly, that doesn't mean there isn't a lot of room for improvement. Here are a few ways you could make changes to this application to make it better:

Cache the feed

Broadcast Feed currently has to check with the database every time someone requests information. With the tweets stored in the database changing only once each day, the result will be a lot of redundant querying that could unduly tax the database. MySQL has some caching support when the system variable have_query_cache is set to YES. As long as the SQL statement is exactly the same and the database tables used in the query have not changed, this setting will reduce the load on the server.

PHP also has a function called serialize( ) that can help with caching by converting the data set type and structure into a form that can be written to a file. Later queries can recall the content of that file and use unserialize( ) to return the data to its original, just-queried state without bothering the database.

Save the feed as a static file, updated daily

Alternatively, you can adjust the Broadcast Feed script to output the RSS content to a static file, and then reference that file instead. When new content is available, you can regenerate the data and overwrite the static file. This will eliminate the redundant use of SQL queries.

Include threaded conversations

Each status object comes with a couple of interesting elements: in_reply_to_user_id and in_reply_to_status_id (see "Status Objects" on page 198). The values in these XML elements point to other authors or tweets that have prompted a Twitter reply. Paying attention to these fields gives you the option of performing extra API method requests to include relevant status updates in the daily snapshots. Providing context to a reply preserves a sense of meaning not present in the isolated tweets.

Tweet Alert

In the early days of Twitter—before the tech problems in the summer of 2008—one of the best features of the microblogging service was keyword tracking. Each member could designate terms, and Twitter would monitor the public timeline for instances of those terms. Best of all, the results were delivered via an IM client. Sadly, Twitter no longer supports keyword tracking. The good news, though, is that the search API is chock full of hooks to allow developers to recreate this cool tool for discovery.

Twitter's search API allows an application to regularly scan the latest tweets for relevant content, picking up where it left off the last time. Tweet Alert is a simple application that sends a direct message to members whenever new tweets are found that match their desired keywords.

This application allows a member to specify a list of terms to track, but the real work is performed by a separate automated task (see "Scan Tweets" on page 342) that checks the search API every 15 minutes. If matches to a term are found—and the member is following your master Twitter account—a direct message is sent to that member with a link to the search results.

A few third-party applications, such as Tweet Scan (*http://tweetscan.com*) and Tweet-Beep (*http://tweetbeep.com*), will email a member whenever tweets matching their specified keywords are found. Those tools aggregate all of the matches since the last check into one communication, providing some additional controls to allow users to customize when and how the information is delivered. Discovery applications like these are very useful for building communities around topics or locations, as well as for monitoring chatter about a business or product.

Take the App for a Spin

You can access the Tweet Alert application by clicking on the "Alert" link in the header of any of the sample application pages. You can also reach it directly by loading the *uar_tweet_alert.php* file into your browser from wherever you uploaded your application files (for example, *http://makice.net/uar/uar_tweet_alert.php* in my development environment). Doing so should get you a web page display that looks like a simpler version of Figure 7-6.

To configure your account to start checking the corpus of tweets for content of interest, the application first needs to know who you are:

1. Enter your Twitter username.

   Type your username into the text box labeled "Twitter Username." You can also enter your Twitter ID, if you know it, as the ID and username are interchangeable.

2. Enter your Twitter password.

   Type your current Twitter password into the text box labeled "Twitter Password."
   Password input fields display bullet characters instead of showing what you are
   actually typing, to give you some protection against people nearby who may see
   your password as you enter it.

3. Click the "Please identify yourself" button to submit the form.

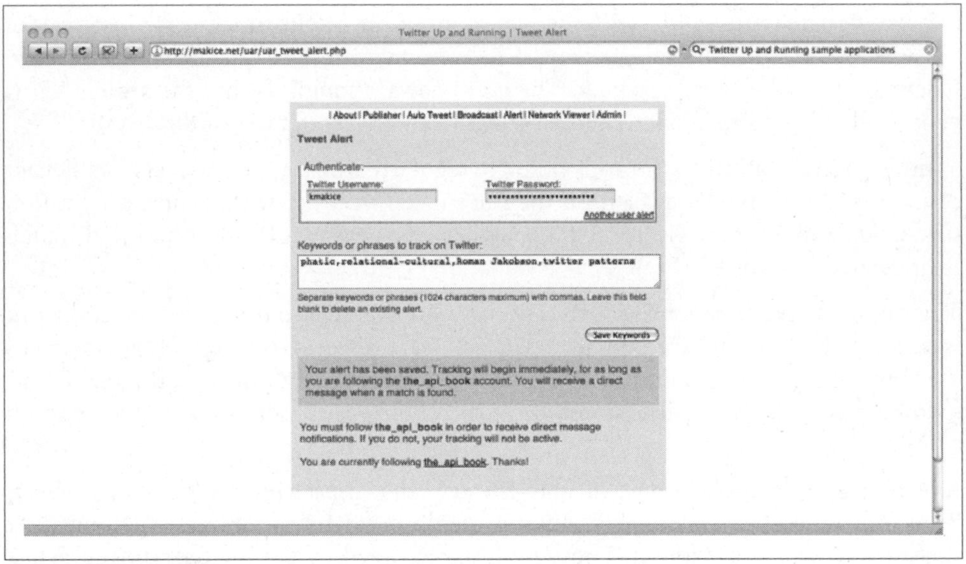

Figure 7-6. Tweet Alert

As with Tweet Broadcast, if your access information checks out with Twitter, the application will reload the page, revealing a new text area box. If you have previously
saved your keyword list, the terms you are tracking will be displayed in the box.
Otherwise, the box will be empty, indicating that no tracking is taking place.

To initiate Twitter keyword tracking:

1. List the terms to track.

   Type the words or phrases that interest you in the text area box labeled "Keywords
   or phrases to track on Twitter." These search terms should be separated with commas. To delete existing keywords that you are tracking, simply remove them from
   the text area.

2. Click the "Save Keywords" button to submit the form.

If successful, the page will reload with a feedback message, "Your alert has been saved."
Tracking begins immediately, with the next run of the automated task to check the
Twitter timeline. Any problems will be displayed as error messages without any changes
being made to the database.

Like Tweet Broadcast, this sample application uses a lazy constraint to limit the number of search terms. The text on the page says you can enter a maximum of 1,024 characters, but this limit is not enforced in the code. That limit is imposed by the database schema, however, so a database error will occur if the string you enter is too long. Adding better validation is suggested.

Unlike existing tracking tools offered by third-party developers, this application does not send notifications of matching content via email. I chose to use direct messages mainly to show how the API can be used as a private channel to distribute information. In testing this application, though, I have found the direct message notification very reminiscent of Twitter's old tracking messages on IM.

 Some search terms are more useful than others. Including "Twitter" as one of your alerts would be pointless; you might as well just keep refreshing an open web page in Twitter's advanced search. For more rare or more specific terms, such as "informatics," the direct messages arrive at a nice pace to keep you aware without being overwhelmed.

The catch to using direct messages as the means to communicate is that the member has to be following the sender account (in this case, *@the_api_book*). With that in mind, a check is performed on the authenticated username to see if it is already following the master account for the application. Below the web form, Tweet Alert will display a message to let you know whether or not it can send you direct messages.

Be aware that competing dynamics are at work when you require someone to follow you in order to reap the benefits of your application. On the one hand, users may want to be notified with the sought-after information; on the other hand, they may be reluctant to expose themselves to a potential flood of traffic. Each user will have her own threshold as to where communication becomes a nuisance.

 If you are too noisy, conversational, or frequent with the tweets from your master account, you may create a barrier that keeps people from using your application.

Check Under the Hood

This application's code (see Example 7-6) is almost a mirror of the code for Tweet Broadcast. It follows the same basic structure and logic as it swaps and saves configuration profiles for the users of this tool. However, instead of working with a list of usernames to include in an aggregated daily broadcast feed, Tweet Alert deals with keywords each user wants to track through direct messages. The one new element that distinguishes the two programs is the addition of a call to the Twitter API to check whether the user is following the main Twitter account for the application; this is a requirement in order for the tool to send notices through the Twitter back channel. If you need an explanation of the rest of the code, please refer to the discussions of other sample applications—in particular, Tweet Broadcast—earlier in this chapter.

Example 7-6. PHP to save a list of keywords to track

```php
/* Include External Functions */
$root_path = str_replace('/public_html', '/uar', $_SERVER['DOCUMENT_ROOT'])
                       .'/includes/';
include $root_path.'environment.php';
include $root_path.'status_messages.php';
include $root_path.'validate_data.php';
include $root_path.'api_config.php';
include $root_path.'database.php';
include $root_path.'sql_queries.php';
include $root_path.'parse_data.php';
include $root_path.'html_template.php';

/* Initialize Values */
$app_title            = 'Tweet Alert';
$twitter_username     = '';
$twitter_password     = '';
$alert_keywords       = '';
$keyword_stored       = array();
$keyword_stored_list  = '';
$form_response        = '';
$submit_button_label  = 'Please identify yourself';
$is_following         = '';
$show_message         = '';
$show_supplement      = ' style="display:none;"';
$show_alerts          = ' style="display:none;"';

/* Parse Input */
$form_error           = 0;
$twitter_username     = $_POST['twitter_username'];
$twitter_password     = $_POST['twitter_password'];
$alert_keywords       = $_POST['alert_keywords'];
$submit_button        = $_POST['submit_button'];
$alert_keywords       = trim($alert_keywords);
$twitter_username     = strtolower($twitter_username);
$this_url             = "http://". $_SERVER['HTTP_HOST'].$_SERVER['REQUEST_URI'];
$this_dir             =
                       getHTTPpath($_SERVER['HTTP_HOST'],$_SERVER['REQUEST_URI']);

/* Configure API Requests */
list($master_username,$cURL_source) = prepAPI();

/* Initiate cURL */
$cURL                 = prepRequest($app_title,$twitter_username,$twitter_password);

/* Validate Access */
$form_error           = checkInput(array(
    'submit_button'        => $submit_button,
    'twitter_username'     => $twitter_username,
    'twitter_password'     => $twitter_password
```

```
    ),$cURL,$cURL_source);

if ($form_error == 0) {
    $show_alerts            = '';
    $show_supplement        = '';
    $submit_button_label    = ' Save Keywords ';

/* Prepare Database Interaction */
    $db_connection          = openDB();
    $sql_variables          = array (
        'twitter_username'      => $twitter_username
        );
    $sql_query              = getQueries($sql_variables);

/* Retrieve Stored Data */
$sql_result = mysql_query($sql_query['Retrieve_Stored_Alerts'])
        or die('Error, selection query failed');
    while ($row = mysql_fetch_assoc($sql_result)) {
        $keyword_stored[] = $row['keyword'];
    }
    $keyword_stored_list    = implode(",",$keyword_stored);
    mysql_free_result($sql_result);

/* Confirm Follower Status */
    $follower_status        = 0;
    $is_following           = 'You are currently not following <a
        href="http://twitter.com/'.$master_username.'">'.$master_username.'</a>.
        Please do.';
    $cURL_query             = "?user_a=$twitter_username&user_b=$master_username";
    list($cURL_status,$confirmation) =
                    apiRequest($cURL,$cURL_source['confirm_follow'].$cURL_query);
    if ($confirmation == '<friends>true</friends>') {
        $follower_status        = 1;
        $is_following           = 'You are currently following <a
            href="http://twitter.com/'.$master_username.'">'.$master_username.'</a>.
            Thanks!';
    }

/* Process Deletion Request */
    if ($submit_button != 'Please identify yourself') {
        if (strlen($alert_keywords) < 1)        {
            $form_error = 7;
            if (sizeof($keyword_stored) > 0) {
                $form_error = 13;
                $sql_result = mysql_query($sql_query['Remove_Alerts']);
            }
            $keyword_stored_list = '';
        }
        else {

/* Compare Keywords */
            $keyword_check = array();
            foreach ($keyword_stored as $this_term) {
                $keyword_check[$this_term] = FALSE;
            }
```

```php
            $alert_keywords_array = explode(",",$alert_keywords);
            foreach ($alert_keywords_array as $this_term) {
                if (in_array(trim($this_term), $keyword_stored)) {
                    $keyword_check[$this_term] = TRUE;
                }
                else {
                    $keyword_check[$this_term] = FALSE;
                    break;
                }
            }
            if (in_array(FALSE, array_values($keyword_check))) {

/* Save Alert */
                if (sizeof($keyword_stored) > 0)        {
                    mysql_query($sql_query['Remove_Alerts'])
                        or die('Error, deletion query failed');
                }
                $twitter_username = mysql_real_escape_string($twitter_username);
                foreach ($alert_keywords_array as $this_term) {
                    $this_term = mysql_real_escape_string($this_term);
                    $sql_query['Create_Alert'] = "
                        INSERT INTO tweetalert_profiles (user_name, keyword)
                        VALUES ('$twitter_username', '$this_term')
                        ";
                    mysql_query($sql_query['Create_Alert'])
                        or die('Error, insert query failed');
                }
                $keyword_stored_list = implode(",",$alert_keywords_array);
            }
            else {
                $form_error = 12;
            }
        }
    }
    closeDB($db_connection);
}

/* Determine Feedback Response */
$default_response    = '';
if (($form_error < 0) || (($form_error == 0)
    && ($submit_button == 'Please identify yourself')) )
    { $show_message    = ' style="display:none;"'; }
else {
$default_response    = <<<DEFAULT_MESSAGE
    Your alert has been saved.
    Tracking will begin immediately, for as long as you are following the
    <strong>$master_username</strong> account.
    You will receive a direct message when a match is found.
DEFAULT_MESSAGE;
}
$form_response           = getResponse($form_error,$default_response);

/* Clean Up */
apiRequest($cURL,$cURL_source['end_session']);
curl_close($cURL);
```

```
/* Render Interface */
getHeader($app_title,'css/uar.css');
$div_reset          = <<<DIV_RESET
            <div id="uar_new"$show_alerts>
                <a href="$this_url">Another user alert</a>
            </div>
DIV_RESET;
$div_reset = "<a href='$this_url'$show_alerts>Another user alert</a> | ";
$keyword_stored_list = htmlspecialchars($keyword_stored_list, ENT_QUOTES, 'UTF-8');
$div_info           = <<<DIV_INFO
        <div id="uar_info"$show_alerts ?>
            Keywords or phrases to track on Twitter:
            <textarea name="alert_keywords" rows="3" cols="60">$keyword_stored_list
            </textarea>
            <br />
            <small>Separate keywords or phrases (1024 characters maximum) with
                commas. Leave this field blank to delete an existing alert.</small>
        </div>
DIV_INFO;
$div_supplemental    = <<<DIV_SUPPLEMENTAL
        <div id="uar_supplemental"$show_supplement>
            You must follow <strong>$master_username</strong> in order to receive
            direct message notifications. If you do not, your tracking will not be
            active.
            <br /><br />
            $is_following
        </div>
DIV_SUPPLEMENTAL;
$html_info         = array(
    'title'             =>   $app_title,
    'url'               => $this_dir,
    'hide_username'     => '',
    'username'          => htmlspecialchars($twitter_username, ENT_QUOTES, 'UTF-8'),
    'reset'             => $div_reset,
    'info'              => $div_info,
    'label'             => $submit_button_label,
    'show_message'      => $show_message,
    'message'           => $form_response,
    'supplemental'      => $div_supplemental,
    'columns'           => ''
);
getInterface($html_info);
getFooter();
```

Let's explore the important parts of this code.

Confirm follower status

For this tool to work, the user has to follow the main account ($master_username) that is set in the prepAPI( ) custom function. The main account doesn't have to reciprocate, but if the Twitter member hoping to track terms appearing in the public timeline does not follow that account, no notifications will ever arrive.

The purpose of this Tweet Alert interface is merely to collect and queue the keywords and phrases to be tracked, not to issue the alerts. However, it is helpful to let the users know when they enter their search terms whether they are ready to receive those notifications.

The application starts this check by assuming the member is not yet following the main account and setting the value of `$follower_status` to zero (or "false" in binary). Tweet Alert even composes the default message to say, "You are currently not following. Please do." Then, the application uses the open cURL connection to ask the Twitter API whether that assumption is correct.

With the Confirm a Follow API method (see "The Follow Network" on page 157), the order of the two member usernames in the query string is important. As far as this web form is concerned, it doesn't matter if the main account is following the user; all that matters is that that user is following the main account. The username for the main account is therefore assigned to `user_b`, with the value for `user_a` representing the member submitting the form:

```
$cURL_query = "?user_a=$twitter_username&user_b=$master_username";
```

This query string is appended to the URI for the confirmation method and passed with the cURL handle to the custom function `apiRequest( )`. If the XML returns an indication of "true," the follow relationship exists and direct messaging is enabled. The feedback to the end user is adjusted to give the happy news.

Shifting Gears

Here are a few suggestions for how you could improve the Tweet Alert sample application:

Incorporate support for email notification
> Not everyone wants to follow a Twitter account that is managing an automated tool, and some will not find direct messages to be an ideal way of receiving alerts. Email is more universal and familiar. Mail clients also allow rules to be added to route incoming messages in specific ways. Giving the end user an option for the method of delivery improves the user experience.

Aggregate all terms into a single message
> I track a few different keywords with Tweet Alert. Each term is processed separately, so if during the same run of the automated task performing the searches someone has tweeted about all of them, I get more than one direct message with the same link. This doesn't happen often enough for me to be annoyed, but it still might be preferable to receive only one message containing all of the links.

Let users control how often the checks are performed
> Tracking a popular word (such as "Twitter") will get you an alert in almost every 15-minute cycle, and the resulting noise in the back channel might be a disincentive

to using Tweet Alert. The user might want to receive notifications once every hour or once per day, rather than being subjected to a steady stream of alerts.

Network Viewer

If third-party Twitter development in the latter half of 2008 could be summed up in one word, it would be "networks." From September through December, several high-profile third-party applications—Twitter Grader, Twinfluence, and Mr. Tweet, to name a few—emerged with the promise of revealing the hidden meaning of our personal networks. They assigned values, ranked connections, and suggested who might be good additions for individual members' timelines.

Network Viewer doesn't reach for those heights, but it is probably the most useful sample application among this suite of tools. It allows a Twitter member to see in iconic form his full follow network—that is, you can see both the people you follow and those who follow you.

After you enter your Twitter username and password, the application retrieves your full list of followers and the list of members you follow for some simple analysis. It sorts each of these members into one of three groups: followers you don't follow, followers you do follow, and people you are following who aren't reciprocating. Private accounts are outlined in red, and mousing over each picture reveals additional detail about that member or group.

 For very large follow networks, the individual rate limit constraints will likely prevent the full sets from being calculated and displayed. You probably won't notice any issues unless you follow or are followed by upwards of 4,000–5,000 people, or if you have recently used other similar tools that require your account to access the API.

This tool has proven to be a very useful way to quickly scan my Twitter network and make adjustments. With the mouseover summaries that include profile information such as location, it is easy for me to add local people who are following me to my follow network.

Take the App for a Spin

You can access the Network Viewer application by clicking on the "Network Viewer" link near the right side of the list of header links in the sample application pages. You can also reach it directly by loading the *uar_network_viewer.php* file into your browser from wherever you uploaded your application files (for example, *http://makice.net/uar/uar_network_viewer.php* in my development environment). Doing so should get you a web page form asking for your Twitter credentials, which should look very familiar by now.

Since all this application does is retrieve information, Network Viewer just needs to know who you are so it can start examining your network:

1. Enter your Twitter username.

   Type your username into the text box labeled "Twitter Username." You can also enter your Twitter ID, if you know it, as the ID and username are interchangeable.

2. Enter your Twitter password.

   Type your current Twitter password into the text box labeled "Twitter Password." Password input fields display bullet characters instead of showing what you are actually typing. This is to give you some protection against people nearby who may see your password as you enter it.

3. Click the "Please identify yourself" button to submit the form.

When you submit valid account credentials, the magic begins. Of course, the magic may take a little while to finish, depending on the size of your network. In the end, you will get a page like the one shown in Figure 7-7.

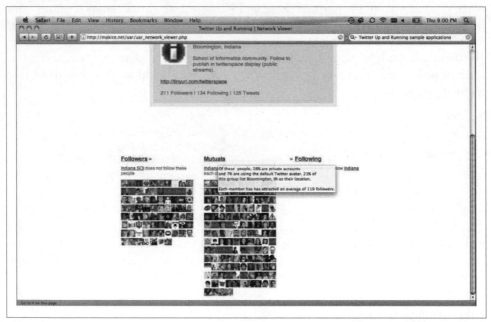

Figure 7-7. Network Viewer

The full network is divided into three columns of small member profile pictures. The first column contains only followers who you do not follow in return. These are people you may want to review and add to your timeline. The second column contains the mutuals, or the followers who you do follow. The third column shows all of the people you follow who aren't giving you the time of day (at least in tweet form). If you are looking to prune your network, some of these folks may be good candidates.

There are a few other features of note in the display that provide added value. First, the profile pictures of members with private accounts are outlined with a red border and grouped at the top of each column. Second, moving your mouse over any icon will (in most modern browsers) show some profile information about that member. Finally, you can find out more about each of the three groups of people in your network by mousing over the column titles, where some statistics are calculated for the members in that column.

Check Under the Hood

The previous few sample applications have been configuration tools, designed to gather preferences from individual members and put that information in a place where other scripts can do the heavy lifting. In contrast, Network Viewer does all of the work itself.

Although the basic structure of the code (see Example 7-7) does echo that of the other applications, Network Viewer moves into the world of followers, friends, and member profiles. In order to show your entire follow network as three columns of icons, this application has to do a few new tricks:

- Get user profile
- Get follow network
- Sort follow network
- Format follow network

Network Viewer can be an expensive tool to use, in terms of time and API hits. However, it's a great way to begin exploring what you can do with the personal networks that evolve on Twitter. We'll look at the new aspects of this code momentarily. For a refresher on what the rest of the code does (and how), please see the explanations of the other applications earlier in this chapter.

Example 7-7. PHP to display a follow network

```
/* Include External Functions */
$root_path = str_replace('/public_html', '/uar', $_SERVER['DOCUMENT_ROOT'])
                        .'/includes/';
include $root_path.'environment.php';
include $root_path.'status_messages.php';
include $root_path.'validate_data.php';
include $root_path.'api_config.php';
include $root_path.'parse_data.php';
include $root_path.'sort_data.php';
include $root_path.'calculate_stats.php';
include $root_path.'html_template.php';

/* Initialize Values */
$app_title          = 'Network Viewer';
$twitter_username   = '';
$twitter_password   = '';
$form_response      = '';
```

```
$submit_button_label     = 'Please identify yourself';
$show_message            = '';
$show_info               = ' style="display:none;"';
$followers               = '';
$mutuals                 = '';
$following               = '';

/* Parse Input */
$form_error              = 0;
$twitter_username        = $_POST['twitter_username'];
$twitter_password        = $_POST['twitter_password'];
$submit_button           = $_POST['submit_button'];

$this_dir                = getHTTPpath($_SERVER['HTTP_HOST'],$_SERVER['REQUEST_URI']);

/* Configure API Requests */
list($master_username,$cURL_source) = prepAPI();

/* Initiate cURL */
$cURL              = prepRequest($app_title,$twitter_username,$twitter_password);

/* Validate Access */
$form_error              = checkInput(array(
    'submit_button'         => $submit_button,
    'twitter_username'      => $twitter_username,
    'twitter_password'      => $twitter_password
    ),$cURL,$cURL_source);
if ($form_error == 0) {
    $show_info              = '';
    $submit_button_label = ' Refresh Network ';

/* Get User Profile */
    $user_detail            =
                    str_replace("[id]",$twitter_username,$cURL_source['show_user']);
    list($cURL_status,$twitter_data) = apiRequest($cURL,$user_detail);
    if ($cURL_status > 200)      { $form_error = 14; }
    else {
        # Parse the XML file
        try {
            $authors = parseXML($twitter_data);
            foreach ($authors as $author) {
                $author_id            = $author['user_id'];
                $author_username      = $author['user_name'];
                $author_fullname      = $author['full_name'];
                $author_avatar        = $author['avatar'];
                $author_location      = $author['location'];
                $author_description   = $author['description'];
                $author_url           = $author['url'];
                $is_protected         = $author['is_private'];
                $total_followers      = $author['followers'];
                $total_following      = $author['following'];
                $total_tweets         = $author['tweets'];
                break;
            }
            $author_profile       =
```

```php
                "<a href='http://twitter.com/$author_username'>$author_fullname</a>";
            # Estimate API calls needed to retrieve follow network
            $followers_pages    = ceil($total_followers/100);
            $following_pages    = ceil($total_following/100);
        } catch (Exception $e)   { $form_error = 15; }
    }


/* Get Follow Network */
    if ($form_error == 0) {
        $follow_net             = array();
        for ($i=1; $i <= $followers_pages; $i += 1) {
            $follower_net    =
                    str_replace("[id]",$twitter_username,$cURL_source['followers']);
            $follower_net    .= "?page=$i&count=100";
            list($cURL_status,$twitter_data) = apiRequest($cURL,$follower_net);
            if ($cURL_status > 200) { $form_error = 16; }
            else {
                # Parse the XML file
                try {
                    $followers = parseXML($twitter_data);
                    $x = -1;
                    foreach ($followers as $follower) {
                        $follow_net[$follower['user_name'] . ''] = array(
                            'follow_net'            => $x,
                            'author_username'       => $follower['user_name'],
                            'author_fullname'       => $follower['full_name'],
                            'author_avatar'         => $follower['avatar'],
                            'author_location'       => $follower['location'],
                            'author_description'    => $follower['description'],
                            'author_url'            => $follower['url'],
                            'is_protected'          => $follower['is_protected'],
                            'total_followers'       => $follower['followers']
                        );
                    }
                } catch (Exception $e) { $form_error = 17; }
            }
        }
        for ($i=1; $i <= $following_pages; $i += 1) {
            $following_net    =
                    str_replace("[id]",$twitter_username,$cURL_source['following']);
            $following_net    .= "?page=$i&count=100";
            list($cURL_status,$twitter_data) = apiRequest($cURL,$following_net);
            if ($cURL_status > 200) { $form_error = 16; }
            else {
                # Parse the XML file
                try {
                    $following = parseXML($twitter_data);
                    foreach ($following as $followed) {
                        if (in_array($followed['user_name'].'',
                            array_keys($follow_net))) { $x = 0; }
                        else { $x = 1; }
                        $follow_net[$followed['user_name'] . ''] = array(
                            'follow_net'            => $x,
                            'author_username'       => $followed['user_name'],
                            'author_fullname'       => $followed['full_name'],
```

```
                          'author_avatar'           => $followed['avatar'],
                          'author_location'         => $followed['location'],
                          'author_description'      => $followed['description'],
                          'author_url'              => $followed['url'],
                          'is_protected'            => $followed['is_protected'],
                          'total_followers'         => $followed['followers']
                     );
               }
          } catch (Exception $e) { $form_error = 17; }
     }
  }

/* Sort Follow Network */
     $follow_net      = sortData ($follow_net, 'compareFollowNet');

/* Format Follow Network */
     $display         = array();
     $default_pic     =
                    'http://static.twitter.com/images/default_profile_normal.png';
     foreach ($follow_net as $this_user_info) {
         $i = $this_user_info['follow_net'] + 1;
         $display[$i] .= "<a href='";
         $display[$i] .=
                        "http://twitter.com/".$this_user_info['author_username'];
         $display[$i] .= "' title='";
         $display[$i] .= htmlentities($this_user_info['author_fullname']);
         if ($this_user_info['author_location'] != '') {
             $this_location = htmlentities($this_user_info['author_location']);
             $display[$i] .= " ($this_location)";
             $locations[$i][$this_location.''] += 1;
         }
         $display[$i] .= " \n\n";
         if ($this_user_info['author_description'] != '') {
             $display[$i] .=
                     htmlentities($this_user_info['author_description'])." \n\n";
         }
         $display[$i] .= $this_user_info['total_followers']." Followers";
         if ($this_user_info['is_protected'] == 'true') {
             $display[$i] .= " [ PRIVATE ACCOUNT ]";
         }
         $display[$i] .= "'>";
         $display[$i] .= "<img src='";
         $display[$i] .= $this_user_info['author_avatar'];
         if ($this_user_info['is_protected'] == 'true') {
             $display[$i] .= "' height='16' width='16' style='border:2px solid
                 red";
             $stats[$i]['private'] += 1;
         }
         else {
             $display[$i] .= "' height='20' width='20' style='border:none";
         }
         $display[$i] .= ";'
                 alt='".htmlentities($this_user_info['author_fullname'])."' />";
         $display[$i] .= "</a>";
```

```php
                $stats[$i]['count'] += 1;
                $stats[$i]['followers'] += $this_user_info['total_followers'];
                if ($this_user_info['author_avatar'] == $default_pic) {
                    $stats[$i]['avatars'] += 1;
                }
        }

    }
}

/* Determine Feedback Response */
$default_response    = '';
if ($form_error < 0)
    { $show_message = ' style="display:none;"'; }
else {
    $author_avatar    = str_replace("_normal.","_bigger.",$author_avatar);
    $default_response = "
        <div id=\"uar_profile\">
            <div id=\"uar_avatar\">
                <a href='http://twitter.com/$author_username'><img src='";
    $default_response .= $author_avatar;
    $default_response .= "' alt='$author_username on Twitter' /></a>
            </div>
            <div id-\"uar_detail\">
                $author_profile<br />";
    if ($author_location != '')
    { $default_response .= "$author_location<br />"; }
    if ($author_description != '')
    { $default_response .= "<br />$author description<br />"; }
    if ($author_url != '') {
        $default_response .= "<br /><a href='$author_url'>$author_url</a><br />";
    }
    $default_response .= "<br />$total_followers Followers";
    $default_response .= " | $total_following Following";
    $default_response .= " | $total_tweets Tweets";
    if ($is_protected == 'true')
    { $default_response .= "<br />PRIVATE ACCOUNT"; }
    $default_response .= "
            </div>
        </div>";
}
$form_response        = getResponse($form_error,$default_response);

/* Clean Up */
apiRequest($cURL,$cURL_source['end_session']);
curl_close($cURL);

/* Render Interface */
getHeader($app_title,'css/uar.css');
$stats                = array(
    groupStats($stats[0],$locations[0]),
    groupStats($stats[1],$locations[1]),
    groupStats($stats[2],$locations[2])
);
$div_columns          = <<<DIV_COLUMNS
```

```
<div id="uar_columns">
    <div id="uar_info"$show_info>
        <div id="uar_left">
            <h4><a href="#" title="{$stats[0]}">Followers</a> &raquo;</h4>
            <p>$author_profile does not follow these people</p>
            {$display[0]}
        </div>
        <div id="uar_right">
            <h4>&raquo; <a href="#" title="{$stats[2]}">Following</a></h4>
            <p>These people do not follow $author_profile</p>
            {$display[2]}
        </div>
        <div id="uar_center">
            <h4><a href="#" title="{$stats[1]}">Mutuals</a></h4>
            <p>$author_profile and these people follow each other</p>
            {$display[1]}
        </div>
    </div>
</div>
DIV_COLUMNS;
$html_info              = array(
    'title'            => $app_title,
    'url'              => $this_dir,
    'hide_username'    => '',
    'username'
        => htmlspecialchars($twitter_username, ENT_QUOTES, 'UTF-8'),
    'reset'            => '',
    'info'             => '',
    'label'            => $submit_button_label,
    'show_message'     => $show_message,
    'message'          => $form_response,
    'supplemental'     => '',
    'columns'          => $div_columns
);
getInterface($html_info);
getFooter();
```

Now let's take a look under the hood.

Get user profile

Every status object coming from the Twitter API contains a certain amount of detail about the author of the tweet. It does not include enough of the statistics, however, to allow your application to make intelligent guesses about how many requests will be needed to API methods to obtain a member's full follow network. This important information (and more) can be found in the extended user object containing the details of a Twitter profile (see "User Objects" on page 192).

The API method URIs stored into $cURL_source will sometimes have a placeholder—[id]—that is used to customize the request for a specific Twitter member. The application would get an error or some other nonsense if this placeholder were left alone, so the first order of business is to substitute the `$twitter_username` value into the URI using the `str_replace( )` function in PHP.

When the edited request URI is sent through the open cURL channel, the Twitter API should return an HTTP status of 200, indicating the XML contains information goodness and not error-filled sorrow. The XML string (`$twitter_data`) can be turned into an array of arrays using the custom function `parseXML( )`. That array—which should contain only one author—is then harvested to get all of the information needed to show a nice profile summary for the user.

Just as importantly, the application now has access to the total number of followers and members followed for this user. Since each API request can yield up to 100 users at a time, we can tell PHP to perform simple math to calculate the number of pages that need to be requested from the API in order to get everyone in the user's follow network:

```
$followers_pages = ceil($total_followers/100);
```

The entire parsing process is wrapped in a `try...catch` statement. This is useful because in some instances, the Twitter API is interrupted by network traffic or server hiccups and fails to return all of the XML. Invalid XML can cause the parser to freak out. Rather than killing the application completely, this structure allows runtime errors to be trapped and flagged so the page can still be displayed.

Get follow network

Using the estimated number of pages as an upper limit, the application creates a loop to retrieve all of the followers and followed members the user has in her network. As with the user profile, the method URI in `$cURL_source` must be customized for the authenticated account by replacing `[id]` with `$twitter_username`. The requested URI also requires some query string parameters—`page` and `count`—to tell the Twitter API which chunk of the follow network to return. This string is given to `apiRequest( )`, which returns the HTTP status code and an XML string as a response. Each page is parsed in the same way described for the user profile, turning the structured string into an array of data PHP can use (`$follow_net`).

Because each member's username is a key in the associative array, all of the people in the follow net are mixed together. The three columns are formed by manipulating the value of a new key added to the `$follow_net` array. That key holds a value to separate the mutuals from the followers and the followed. If the value is less than zero (`-1`), that member is a follower whom the authenticated user does not follow in return. A value of zero indicates a mutual, and a positive value (`1`) indicates someone that the user is following who does not follow back.

The API rate limit may prevent larger follow networks from being processed in their entirety. The various constraints Twitter injects into the process of gathering this data will impose a hard maximum of about 10,000 members. Most Twitter users are well under this threshold, but other popular applications (such as TweetDeck) will eat into that maximum with normal use, making the practical limit much smaller. If the user's rate limit is exceeded, the page will still complete, but it will not display the full network.

Sort follow network

The `$follow_net` array at this point is a hodgepodge of member information. There is no order to it, even though the code has given PHP some hooks to use to give it order. The network needs to be sorted into three major groups—followers, mutuals, and followed—based on the value (`-1`, `0`, or `1`) assigned to the `follow_net` key. To give the network more visual meaning, the application also considers additional dimensions that group private accounts and members with similar locations together.

Since sorting on more than one value can be complicated, the code relies on one of the included custom functions: `sortData( )`. It takes two parameters: the `$follow_net` array, and the name of the sorting algorithm to be used. In this case, that algorithm is also a custom job (`compareFollowNet`). `sortData( )` will return the same array of data, but it does so in an order that makes our web page useful. For more detail on how this function works, see "Data Sorting Functions" on page 252.

Format follow network

A lot of little parts go into displaying each little user icon in the member's follow network. The profile picture is important, obviously, but the application also needs to construct a link to the member's Twitter profile page, determine whether the account is private, and create the profile text for the mouseover action. By default, Twitter's brown icon is used, but most members have taken the time to upload their own profile pictures.

Although most of this process is fairly straightforward XHTML, a couple of quirky things are happening in this part of the code. Statistics are being tabulated with each loop through the `$follow_net` array, and the cumulative counts are loaded into the `$stats` and `$locations` arrays for use a bit later, when rendering the web page.

Network Viewer uses the data gathered to compose a profile summary for each member. This text becomes the value for the `title` attribute in the link surrounding each little icon. When the user moves the mouse over a member's profile picture, a small box displaying the text in the `title` attribute will appear.

Use the `title` attribute with some awareness of its limitations: not everyone will have the same experience with its content. Most visual browsers will display the content as a "tooltip," but the small box will appear for only a few seconds before disappearing. Audio browsers will attempt to read the title, but its display is dependent on moving a mouse over a link, and the text cannot be resized.

All of the formatting is stored as strings in an array ($display) to be used during the rendering of the web page.

Render interface

This web page is unlike any of the other applications because it requires three columns. The application goes a step further and adds some group statistics calculated from all of the members in each column. The text to use in the `title` attribute in each header link is formatted in a custom function—`groupStats( )`—that requires the stats and locations arrays created earlier during the formatting process. When the user moves the mouse over the column headers, a little box appears briefly to show the calculated statistics for that group of users. For more detail on how this function works, see "Statistics Functions" on page 253.

Shifting Gears

Interest in Twitter networks is currently high, with a number of applications and research efforts looking for ways to analyze or visualize them to reveal hidden meaning. Although it may require a lot of effort and many brain cells to come up with some new algorithm for this analysis, there are a few features you could add with relative ease to improve the Network Viewer:

Scalability for larger networks

If A-list blogger and media critic Robert Scoble tried to use the Network Viewer to explore his enormous follow network, he would likely see one column filled with a lot of icons. His network is much too big to handle the constraints of only 100 requests to the Twitter API per hour. One way to help would be to offload the data-gathering chores to the main account, which may be able to be whitelisted to raise the rate limit to 20,000 hits per hour. The downside of this approach is that member authentication also controls the kind of information returned by the API, so there may be some holes in the data set.

Another approach would be to start a long-running process and tell Scoble to come back later. With this solution, there is no instant gratification for the über-users, as the largest networks may still take hours or even days to complete. Finding a suitable solution for this type of Twitter user may be an important part of generating buzz about your application.

Ability to browse other networks

Currently, clicking on one of the profile icons opens up a new web browser window with that person's Twitter profile. With some data management that collects network data as people request it, you may be able to reengineer that link to show that person's own three-column Network View. This would create an aspect of discovery as you browse from one to member to the next, allowing you to see at a glance how their networks are configured.

Dynamics over time

If you look at the Network Viewer today and then return a week later, you will likely see some minor differences on the page. That is because our networks are not static; they change every time someone makes a decision to follow or unfollow someone else. This is an area that is largely unexplored in the Twitosphere—the big exception is TwitterCounter (*http://twittercounter.com*), which keeps tabs on how many followers each member has and the rate of growth in the users' follow networks. Finding a way to highlight new additions or track which members have recently dropped out of their networks would be a highly useful tool to help members analyze their follow networks.

Best of Twitter API

One of the most underutilized aspects of Twitter is its bookmarking feature, or the ability to save tweets as "favorites." Only a very small percentage of overall users (many of whom are Japanese) favorite other members' tweets.* A big reason for the lack of interest in this feature is that the Twitter API makes it quite difficult to get information about favorites out of the system.

There is no public stream of bookmarked tweets readily available for developers to use, nor is there any way for the API to tell an individual which of her tweets have been marked as favorites. The process of collecting a good repository of favorited status updates requires a shotgun approach: every active member has to be checked to see whether they have ever favorited any tweets.

This situation creates a vicious cycle. Developers don't focus on bookmarking because Twitter doesn't provide useful methods to access this information. Twitter doesn't prioritize new methods for this purpose because people are clamoring for other things. People don't favorite because there are no tools to give them value. This is where a third-party developer can fill an important gap simply by creating a repository of bookmarked tweets and making that data available as a second-generation API. This is exactly what Summize did for searching Twitter status updates.

In a very rudimentary form, that is the goal of the Best of Twitter API—to create a simple API for developers to use to build bookmarking tools.

There is no web interface to describe in this section, as was the case with the other sample applications. Best of Twitter is comprised of two automated tasks on the back-end: one looks for active users, and the other pulls down their lists of favorited tweets to aggregate into one system (see "Queue Users" on page 349 and "Collect Favorites" on page 352). These tasks work together to create the database from which one

---

* My own research indicates that less than 1% of people have favorited at least one tweet. However, there do appear to be communities within the larger Twitter community that use this feature regularly.

sample API method can be used to pull data from the server. This method—
all_time—returns the 20 most popular tweets.

The list of existing applications that explore favorites is short. Favrd (*http://favrd
.com*) is a pretty site that asks for people to voluntarily register to get on the site's radar
(see "Tools for Search" on page 58), and Ono Matope's Favotter (*http://favotter.matope
.com/en/*) has cataloged over 1.4 million bookmarked tweets. A solid API for favorites
might change the limited appeal to developers.

Take the App for a Spin

The Best of Twitter API is not found in the header links on the sample application
pages, but you can reach it directly by loading *all_time.php* from the "favorites" directory wherever you uploaded your application files (for example, *http://makice.net/uar/
favorites/all_time.php* in my development environment). Doing so will return an XML
document containing data pulled from the Twitter favorites collected in the local
database.

The sample method returns the most favorited tweets detected by the application.
There are two simple parameters—id and since—that allow developers to further filter
the full set down to something useful. Only 20 results are returned. Although this may
or may not seem useful to you, please remember that this method is merely an illustration of what can be done.

The XML generated by the Best of Twitter API intentionally mimics the structure used
by Twitter. That is, it is a truncated version of a status object with one new element
added to the results (see Example 7-8). The addition, favorites_count, contains a count
of the total number of members who have bookmarked a particular tweet.

Example 7-8. A status update object from the Best of Twitter API

```
<statuses type="array">
    <status>
        <created_at>Wed Nov 05 19:34:59 -0700 2008</created_at>
        <id>992176676</id>
        <text>We just made history. All of this happened because you gave your
            time, talent and passion. All of this happened because of you.
            Thanks</text>
        <favorites_count>48</favorites_count>
        <user>
            <id>813286</id>
            <screen_name>BarackObama</screen_name>
            <profile_image_url>http://s3.amazonaws.com/twitter_production/
                profile_images/25901972/iconbg_normal.jpg</profile_image_url>
        </user>
    </status>
</statuses>
```

For more detail on these and other elements that are returned as XML by the Twitter
API, see "User Objects" on page 192 and "Status Objects" on page 198.

Scalability will be an issue when creating an API. In less than a month of regular monitoring, this sample application had already accumulated 200,000 users and 1.4 million bookmarks. The database load grows exponentially larger with each new application that relies on your API.

Check Under the Hood

The PHP script to generate the sample method for the Best of Twitter API is very similar in nature to the one that creates an RSS feed in Tweet Broadcast (see "Broadcast Feed" on page 300). Other than the kind of content in the output, it mimics the same logic.

There are some distinctions, though. For one thing, the Best of Twitter API is building an XML document, not an RSS feed (which is much more specific and constrained XML). It also accepts multiple parameters that can filter the data, rather than a single identifier determining which member's aggregation to retrieve. Finally, this method will accept either POST or GET methods, which requires a slightly different approach to deal with user input. The script is shown in Example 7-9.

Example 7-9. PHP to render the XML for the all-time favorites method

```php
/* Include External Functions */
$root_path = str_replace('/public_html', '/uar', $_SERVER['DOCUMENT_ROOT'])
                          .'/includes/';
include $root_path.'database.php';
include $root_path.'sql_queries.php';
include $root_path.'parse_data.php';

/* Initialize Values */
$twitter_username    = '';
$bookmarks_stored    = array();

/* Parse Input */
if ($_SERVER['REQUEST_METHOD'] == 'POST') {
    $id                = $_POST['id'];
    $since             = $_POST['since'];
}
else {
    $id                = $_GET['id'];
    $since             = $_GET['since'];
}

if ($id == '')        { $id = 0; }
if ($since == '')     { $since = 0; } else { $since = strtotime($since); }

$this_url             = "http://".$_SERVER['HTTP_HOST'].$_SERVER['REQUEST_URI'];
$this_dir             = $this_url;
if (strpos($this_dir, basename($this_url)) !== false) {
    $this_dir = reset(explode(basename($this_url), $this_dir));
}
```

```
try {

/* Prepare Database Interaction */
    $db_connection          = openDB();
    if (!(is_int($id+0))) { $id = strtolower($id); }
    $sql_variables          = array(
        'id'                    => $id,
        'since'                 => $since
        );
    $sql_query              = getQueries($sql_variables);

/* Retrieve Stored Data */
    $sql_result             = mysql_query($sql_query['Retrieve_Favorites']);
    while ($row = mysql_fetch_assoc($sql_result)) {
        $bookmarks_stored[] = $row;
    }
    mysql_free_result($sql_result);
    closeDB($db_connection);

} catch (Exception $e) {
    $status_message = "Could not parse tweet XML for $this_user_name";
}

/* Initiate XML */
$xml                    = createXMLshell();

/* Add Bookmarks */
foreach ($bookmarks_stored as $this_bookmark) {
    $this_date          = date("D M d G:i:s O
                          Y",strtotime($this_bookmark['created_at']));
    $status             = array (
        'created_at'        => $this_date,
        'id'                => $this_bookmark['status_id'],
        'text'              => $this_bookmark['tweet'],
        'favorites_count'   => $this_bookmark['favorited']
    );
    $bookmark = addItem($xml,'status',$status);
    $user               = array (
        'id'                  => $this_bookmark['author_user_id'],
        'screen_name'         => $this_bookmark['author_user_name'],
        'profile_image_url'   => $this_bookmark['author_avatar']
    );
    $author             = addItem($bookmark,'user',$user);
}

/* Render RSS Feed */
echo $xml->asXML();
```

Let's take a closer look at what's going on in this code.

Parse input

API methods are more valuable if the developers have some control over the content they return. By default, Best of Twitter will return a list of the 20 most popular tweets. This sample method will also accept two optional parameters:

id
> The tweet author's username or ID

since
> A date that can be used to ignore older bookmarks

Both follow the format and nomenclature Twitter uses for its API methods. For kicks, this method will accept those parameters with either a GET or a POST request.

If the variables are passed to the script using GET, the name/value pairs are included in the query string and will appear in the `$_GET` array. For posted data, the parameters will show up in `$_POST`. This script uses an `if...else` statement to examine the value in `$_SERVER['REQUEST_METHOD']` to see which array to use.

> Technically, it is possible to send parameters using POST with query string variables appended to the end of the requested URI. In that situation, both `$_GET` and `$_POST` could have parameter values.
>
> This script logic will give precedence to the POST data and ignore the query string.

Add bookmarks

An RSS feed has certain extra expectations in terms of how it is formatted. Some of the elements require specific names that must be present for feed readers to know what to do with them. XML is a more generalized structure, but because I chose to mimic the data objects that Twitter provides with its API, this method also has some constraints in how it is built.

To start the XML file, the application calls a custom function made available to PHP through the include statements at the beginning of the code. `createXMLshell()` creates the header and the top-level tags into which the content will be stuffed.

As was the case with the Tweet Broadcast RSS feed, the `addItem()` custom function becomes the means to this end. The script loops through the `$bookmarks_stored` array, which contains all of the data retrieved from the database earlier in the script. The contents of each record in the data set are scrubbed a bit, placed into the `$status` array, and passed to `addItem()` as a parameter. Unlike with Tweet Broadcast, this XML document has nested elements, so the custom function needs to be called twice for each record. The XML object returned during the first call (`$bookmark`) is passed as a parameter in the second call. This gives the latter bundle of data a new starting point in the hierarchy.

Shifting Gears

This sample method for the Best of Twitter API has a long way to go in terms of development before it is production-ready. Here are a few suggested areas to attack as you use this sample script to build a solid second-generation API:

Improve the database efficiency of the query and schema

As with the Tweet Broadcast RSS feed, use of caching and static page management should improve the performance of this method and help make it production-ready. Another technique that could help is to create new easy-to-query tables that contain the results of common queries. You can repopulate the tables with an automated task running every so often, and then point the method queries to them instead of to the much larger tables used to collect all of the bookmark data. Be aware, however, that there is a trade-off of increased redundancy to avoid bottlenecks that occur when a lot of complicated requests are being made on large tables.

Add more methods and parameters

A list of the most popular tweets is only going to be so useful. Creating new methods to offer different views of the same data would give developers more parts to combine to make unexpected tools. A method to view the most recent bookmarks, for example, might feed a third-party application differently than a list of the most popular tweets.

 API design and maintenance quickly becomes an art. Ask Twitter's API guru Alex Payne about some of the headaches that come from casual decisions about things like nomenclature that are made early in the development of an API.

Because you are inviting other developers to build new and exciting things using your API data, there is an implicit demand to support their work even as you try to improve your own. If the Best of Twitter API is meant to be an extension of Twitter, adopting Twitter's XML and method request conventions is a good idea to help with consistency.

Allow pagination to search for full histories

As use of the favorites feature in Twitter grows, so will the size of the individual data sets. I have 15 pages' worth of bookmarked tweets, starting with the first tweet by creator Jack Dorsey in 2006. Without support for pagination, the tools that can be created with your API are limited to the top of whatever lists the methods provide. Adding the ability to query a certain chunk of the full data set is easy with MySQL's `LIMIT` clause, which lets you point to the starting point and specify how many records to include in the query results.

CHAPTER 8

Automated Tasks

 kmakice Look Ma, no hands! Find out how to make your applications run by themselves.

The suite of sample applications is almost complete. In Chapter 6 you saw how to set up the environment in which the tools function, and in Chapter 7 you got a tour of the web interfaces users will see when they interact with the tools. This chapter examines the code used to run the behind-the-scenes operations that give the tools their functionality.

Automated tasks run in the background at scheduled intervals to perform work without user oversight. They draw from what has been saved in the database through the web interfaces and what they have collected through the Twitter API. Servers manage the launching of these applications using commands set in a *crontab* file. For details on how to set up an automated task, see "A Place to Call /home" on page 126.

There are five automated tasks that power the suite of sample applications:

RSS to Tweet
> This script asks the database for a list of all the RSS or Atom URIs that Twitter members have registered through the Auto Tweet tool, as well as for each user's authentication information, to form a queue of news feeds to turn into tweets. The stored credentials are checked against the Twitter API to make sure they work, and the feeds of any members whose credentials do not validate are disabled from future processing. Each remaining feed is then retrieved and parsed. If the most recent article in the feed is more recent than the last time the URI was processed, its title and link are published to that member's timeline.

Aggregate Broadcast
> To give Tweet Broadcast the content it needs to create a custom RSS feed, this script retrieves from the database a list of all of the Twitter members included in such feeds. For each member, new tweets are fetched from the Twitter API and stored in the database. The script also prunes any content older than 20 days.

Scan Tweets

The Scan Tweets script checks the Twitter search API for recent instances of tweets that contain desired keywords. If a match is found, a list of the members who requested notifications about that term is obtained from the database, and each of those members is sent a direct message. The master password for the application's main Twitter account is retrieved and decoded to use when sending the alerts.

Queue Users

Two automated tasks are needed to build the repository of bookmarked status updates in the Best of Twitter API. This is the first one, designed to discover and add new users to the database. A check is performed to see whether each Twitter member encountered is already in the queue before adding a new record.

Collect Favorites

This second task for the API retrieves batches of tweets that members have already marked as favorites. A segment of the full roster of registered members is selected and processed, with the new favorites returned from the Twitter API for each person in the queue. Every favorite is recorded, but only new tweets are added to the database.

Each of these automated tasks creates a log file that keeps track of what the script does and when it was launched. This can be helpful when troubleshooting, or simply if you want to get some information on activity.

As with the other code in the suite of sample applications, I intended for these scripts to function and to inspire iteration. If you don't like the way something works, change it. Improve it. For some suggestions on what kinds of edits might be helpful, see any of the "Shifting the Gears" sections in Chapter 7.

 As in the previous chapter, the descriptions of the code in this chapter build on each other. The first application will be discussed in more detail than the later ones because they share a lot of code structure and logic. If you want a refresher on part of the code that's not explained here, please review in Chapter 7.

RSS to Tweet

The Auto Tweet application turns aggregated information into a single status update added to a member's timeline. For it to do this, something has to run in the background to do the work of fetching the content from a URI, parsing it into chunks, and figuring out whether one of those chunks should become a new tweet.

This script serves as that workhorse. It is invoked with a *crontab* pointing to a file called *uar_rss_to_tweet.php* that lives in the *automated* directory created outside of the web path (see "Automation" on page 128). I scheduled my installation of this application to fire four times a day, or once every six hours. Most bloggers have trouble posting even once a day, so four checks is probably overkill for them. News sources, on the other hand, may spew out dozens or even hundreds of RSS items each day, so limiting them to a sampling of four seems merciful to those Twitter members who would otherwise have to read all of that content. You can set your own schedule.

Once launched, RSS to Tweet will ask the database for a list of all of the feed URIs submitted by Twitter members using the Auto Tweet tool. This becomes the processing queue that the application uses to make sure all of the new tweets get published. For a description of how the web interface collects feeds to process, see "Auto Tweet" on page 282.

The database query also returns other information, such as the last time the account was processed and the authentication information for Twitter. The former is needed to avoid publishing the same tweet every six hours, and the latter is an API requirement to be able to post the status update at all. For each member in the queue, the stored credentials are checked against the Twitter API to make sure they work. If they don't, the application sets a flag in that member's profile in the database to disable that feed from future processing.

Each feed is retrieved using cURL and parsed into variables PHP can understand. If the timestamp of the newest article in the feed is more recent than the time at which the user's feed was last processed, the article's title and link are published to the member's timeline. The database record for that member is then updated with the current time-stamp to let the application remember on its next run where it left off. When all of the members in the queue have been processed, the task ends.

Check Under the Hood

Because this is an automated task that doesn't require user input, the code can focus on getting things done without spending any processor resources on web output. Still, much of the core structure of these automated tasks will look very familiar if you have reviewed the code in Chapter 7. Here are the steps the code performs:

1. Include required custom functions.
2. Initialize values, particularly those needed for logging what has been done.
3. Start logging activity of the task.
4. Initialize connections to the Twitter API and your database.
5. ***Do stuff.***
6. Clean up the open connections.

I'll provide a fuller description of the code in this first task (see Example 8-1) than of the code for the other tasks covered. Their code will look very familiar in structure. For details on any code you don't see explained here, please refer back to Chapter 7.

Example 8-1. PHP to post tweets from RSS feeds

```php
/* Include External Functions */
$root_path            = realpath('./../includes/')."/";
include $root_path.'validate_data.php';
include $root_path.'api_config.php';
include $root_path.'pw_manage.php';
include $root_path.'database.php';
include $root_path.'sql_queries.php';
include $root_path.'parse_data.php';
include $root_path.'log_manage.php';

/* Initialize Values */
$status_signature     = '';
$status_message       = '';
$post_ok              = 0;

/* Initiate Logging */
$path_to_logs         = realpath('logs/')."/";
$log_file             = 'auto_tweet.txt';
$log                  = openFile($path_to_logs.$log_file,'a');
$app_title            = 'Auto Tweet';

/* Configure API Requests */
list($master_username,$cURL_source) = prepAPI();

/* Initiate cURL */
$cURL                 = prepRequest($app_title);
curl_setopt($cURL, CURLOPT_POST, false);

/* Prepare Database Interaction */
$db_connection        = openDB();
$sql_variables        = array(
    'file_id'                => basename(__FILE__)
    );
$sql_query            = getQueries($sql_variables);

/* Retrieve Stored Data */
$sql_result = mysql_query($sql_query['Retrieve_Stored_RSS'])
    or die('Error, selection query failed');
while ($row = mysql_fetch_assoc($sql_result)) {
    $this_record_id      = $row['record_id'];
    $this_user_name      = $row['user_name'];
    $this_scrambled      = $row['password'];
    $this_rss_feed       = $row['rss_url'];
    $this_date           = $row['date_processed'];
    $status_signature    = time()." | $this_user_name | $this_rss_feed | ";
    $sql_query['Disable_Profile'] = "
        UPDATE    autotweet_profiles
        SET       is_enabled = 0
        WHERE     record_id = $this_record_id
        ";
    $sql_query['Update_Profile'] = "
        UPDATE    autotweet_profiles
        SET       date_processed = now()
        WHERE     record_id = $this_record_id
```

```php
            ";
    $this_password       = unscramblePassword($this_scrambled);
    curl_setopt ($cURL, CURLOPT_USERPWD, "$this_user_name:$this_password");
    if (!(hasAccess($cURL,$cURL_source)))      {
        $status_message = 'Could not authenticate to Twitter. Please re-enter your
                        username and password.';
        mysql_query($sql_query['Disable_Profile'])
            or die('Error, disable query failed');
    }
    else {
        list($thisFeed,$foo) = parseFeed($this_rss_feed,$this_date);
        if (sizeof($thisFeed) > 0) {
            $tweet           = $thisFeed[0]['title'];
            $link            = file_get_contents(
                'http://tinyurl.com/api-create.php?url='.$thisFeed[0]['link']);
            if (strlen($link) > 0) { $tweet .= " $link"; }
        }
        else { $tweet = ''; }
        if (strlen($tweet) > 0) {
            $status_message    = 'A new item has been detected.';
            $tweet_encoded     = urlencode(stripslashes(urldecode($tweet)));

/* Post Message */
            curl_setopt ($cURL, CURLOPT_POSTFIELDS, "status=$tweet_encoded");
            curl_setopt ($cURL, CURLOPT_POST, true);

            list($cURL_status,$twitter_data) =
                            apiRequest($cURL,$cURL_source['post_tweet']);
            if ($cURL_status == 200)      {
                $status          = parseXML($twitter_data);
                $new_status_id = $status[0]['status_id']; ;
                mysql_query($sql_query['Update_Profile'])
                    or die('Error, update query failed');
                $status_message .= " | status ID $new_status_id";
            }
            else {
                $status_message .= " | API ERROR: $cURL_status";
            }

        }
    }
    if (strlen($status_message) > 0) {
        writeFile($log,$status_signature.$status_message);
    }
}

/* Clean Up */
mysql_free_result($sql_result);
apiRequest($cURL,$cURL_source['end_session']);
curl_close($cURL);
closeDB($db_connection);
closeFile($log);
```

The following sections explore this code in detail. You may want to refer back to these discussions when you look at the code for the rest of the automated tasks.

Include external functions

Like their web counterparts, these automated tasks rely on custom functions contained in included files (see "Included Functions" on page 227). There's no need to include functions that handle things like feedback responses and formatting XHTML output; instead, the application relies on support for logging activity in text files.

The location of the include files is also a little different. Because this task isn't invoked from a web page request, there is no $_SERVER['DOCUMENT_ROOT'] value from which PHP can get its bearings in the directory hierarchy. The application instead uses a built-in PHP function, realpath( ), to determine where to look for these included files:

```
$root_path = realpath('./../includes/')."/";
```

The initial series of dots and forward slashes tells PHP to start in the current directory and go up one level before looking for a directory called *includes*. This relative reference assumes that you have placed the *automated* and *includes* directories in the same part of the server hierarchy. This new full path is stored in $root_path for the automated task to use to find the specific included files, as was the case with the Chapter 7 web applications.

Initiate logging

Since this script is automated, there is no human being clicking buttons and monitoring the results in real time. But at some point, you may need to review what this task has actually accomplished in order to write reports, debug problems, or plan for future iterations. Therefore, it is smart to create some text files to log information about the script's activities, so you can review them later.

First, the code has to tell PHP where to put this information: I created a subdirectory of the *automated* folder to hold all of the text files. The log file for this task also needs a name—in this case, *auto_tweet.txt*—that will differentiate it from the logs we'll create for the other tasks later in this chapter. If you have any questions about the task's performance, you can view the file's contents as plain text, and you can rename the file if you want to start a new version.

Opening a file is like opening a real book: after figuring out where it is, you turn the cover to get to the page where you want to place the data. There isn't much to the built-in PHP functions for manipulating files, but we've wrapped that code in a custom function called openFile( ). This function accepts two parameters: the full path and name of the log file, and a file command code to either write ('w', the default) or append ('a') to this file. If the file doesn't exist, it will be created. If it does exist, any new text written to the file will be tacked onto the end of whatever content is already there.

Prepare database interaction

Since all of these automated tasks rely on information stored in a MySQL database, a connection has to be opened to the database. The only difference here is in what we pass as the file_id value to the custom function getQueries( ).

The web applications discussed in Chapter 7 are all requested with HTTP protocols, which means there is an environment variable—$_SERVER['SCRIPT_NAME']—whose value can be used to automatically differentiate one web application from the next. With scripts called through a *crontab*, however, that value is empty. To identify which application is calling the function, PHP instead has to rely on the value contained in __FILE__.

The __FILE__ variable always refers to the full path and filename of the script. Because that value is different when evaluated in an included file than it is in the script that invoked the custom function, the script has to evaluate it locally and pass that value as a parameter to getQueries( ) (see "SQL Queries" on page 235).

Retrieve stored data

The purpose of this part of the code is to turn all of the member records that need to be processed into an array that can be looped through. The script also needs to define some SQL statements based on the particular record ID of each member profile in the queue.

There is a lot of data in each of those records, including a scrambled password that must be run through the custom function unscramblePassword( ) to become useful in a request to the Twitter API. The automated task must be able to retrieve a member's username and password in order to be able to successfully use the API to post content to that member's timeline. After running the credentials through the hasAccess( ) custom function to make sure that they are still valid, the script will start retrieving and parsing the registered feed URIs. If the credentials return an error from the API, the member profile is disabled to remove it from future queues.

The URI for the RSS or Atom feed is passed along with the date and time at which this member was last processed to the custom function parseFeed( ), which returns an array of articles published since that time. The title of and link to the newest article—which is converted into a TinyURL using the file_get_contents( ) PHP function—are extracted from that array. If this process produces something to make into a status update, the new tweet text is encoded to prepare it for delivery to the Twitter API.

Post message

The main function of this script, of course, is to post new tweets to member timelines. To achieve that goal, the cURL configuration has to be adjusted to match the expectations of the API. Namely, the Post a Tweet method requires that the POST method be used and that the content be sent using CURLOPT_POSTFIELDS. Success, indicated by an HTTP status code of 200, leads to parsing the XML response returned by the Twitter API in order to identify the new status ID. This ID is then stored in the member's profile in the database, making it available to filter the feed content for the next check in six hours.

Clean up

This is the part where the script closes all of its open connections, including the one to the log file. This is done with a custom function—`closeDB( )`—using the open file handle as a parameter (see "Log Management Functions" on page 254).

Log output

Each automated task has a log file associated with it. Activity from this script is stored in a file named *auto_tweet.txt*. Although you can make changes to record whatever you want in this file, I chose to log:

- A Unix timestamp to indicate when this attempt happened
- The username of the member account
- The URI for the news feed used to create the tweet
- A message indicating what happened
- The new status ID

The first three items are part of a signature format that is repeated for many of the other log files. All of this information is recorded as a single line of text (see Example 8-2), but only if there was some content to post to the member's timeline.

Example 8-2. Sample output from the Auto Tweet log

```
1231573563 | anonymous_ | http://www.blogs
chmog.net/feed | A new item has been detected. | status ID 1108697026
```

Aggregate Broadcast

One way for Tweet Broadcast to generate its RSS content would be to ask the Twitter API for that information whenever it is needed. The big drawback to that solution is that the more subscribers there are to the custom feed, the more times the application will have to return to Twitter for the same information. Not only is that inefficient, but it is also stressful to the Twitter servers. Instead, I created this script to routinely go to Twitter and ask for just the newest tweets to be stored locally for later querying.

The *crontab* to launch this task points to a file called *uar_collect_broadcast.php* located in the *automated* directory outside the web path. I scheduled my *crontab* to run this script just once per day, gathering and saving the data it needs. The reason the task doesn't run more often is because it isn't necessary. The Tweet Broadcast feeds are aggregations of all the tweets that were published each day. Whether someone looks at the RSS feed early in the morning or late in the evening, the previous day's tweets will still be the same.

The Aggregate Broadcast script gives Broadcast Feed the content it needs to create a custom RSS feed for Tweet Broadcast to disseminate. This script asks the database to give it a list of all of the Twitter members included in these daily aggregations, forming a queue to process for the duration of the run. For a description of how the web interface determines the groups of usernames to process and outputs them as RSS, see "Tweet Broadcast" on page 291 and "Broadcast Feed" on page 300.

The new status updates for each member in the queue are fetched from the Twitter API and stored in the database. The API can tell what is new because the application passes the ID of the last recorded status update for each member to Twitter with the method request. Since Broadcast Feed includes only 20 daily summaries in its feed, the Aggregate Broadcast script also does a little housecleaning by pruning any content older than 20 days. The remaining data is what the feed uses to dynamically fill its XML structure with content

Check Under the Hood

This automated task has a different function to achieve than the RSS to Tweet script: Aggregate Broadcast must communicate with the database to first pull out a list of names and then store whatever new content it discovers through making requests of the Twitter API. Otherwise, the structure and logic of this code (see Example 8-3) is essentially the same as that for the previous automated task. For explanations about the parts of this code not covered here, please review "RSS to Tweet" on page 332 and the relevant parts of Chapter 7.

Example 8-3. PHP to aggregate several members into one daily feed

```
/* Include Functions */
$root_path          = realpath('./../includes/')."/";
include $root_path.'api_config.php';
include $root_path.'log_manage.php';
include $root_path.'database.php';
include $root_path.'sql_queries.php';
include $root_path.'parse_data.php';

/* Initiate Logging */
$path_to_logs       = realpath('logs/')."/";
$log_file           = 'tweet_broadcast.txt';
$log = openFile($path_to_logs.$log_file,'a');
$status_signature   = '';
$status_message     = '';
$app_title          = 'Tweet Broadcast';

/* Configure API Requests */
list($master_username,$cURL_source) = prepAPI();

/* Initiate cURL */
```

```
$cURL                = prepRequest($app_title);

/* Prepare Database Interaction */
$db_connection       = openDB();
$sql_variables       = array(
    'file_id'             => basename(__FILE__)
    );
$sql_query           = getQueries($sql_variables);

/* Retrieve Stored Data */
$sql_result = mysql_query($sql_query['Retrieve_Stored_Group'])
    or die('Error, selection query failed');
# loop through each user
while ($row = mysql_fetch_assoc($sql_result)) {
    $this_user_name     = $row['other'];
    $last_status_id     = $row['last_status_id'];
    $status_signature   = gmdate("Y-m-d H:i:s",time()).
        " | $this_user_name | Last: $last_status_id | ";
    $recent_tweets      =
                str_replace("[id]",$this_user_name,$cURL_source['user_timeline']);
    $recent_tweets      .= "?&count=200";
    if ($last_status_id > 0) { $recent_tweets .= "&since_id=$last_status_id"; }
    list($cURL_status,$twitter_data) = apiRequest($cURL,$recent_tweets);
    if ($cURL_status > 200) {
        $status_message     = "Could not retrieve tweets for $this_user_name";
        $status_message     .= " | API ERROR: $cURL_status";
        $status_message     .= " | $recent_tweets";
        $status_message     .= "\n\n$twitter_data\n\n";
    }
    else {
        try {
            $status_message = "Parsing XML data ... ";
            $count          = 0;
            $tweets         = parseXML($twitter_data);
            foreach($tweets as $tweet) {
                foreach($tweet as $key => $value) {
                    $tweet[$key] = mysql_real_escape_string($value);
                }
                $tweet_sql = $tweet['tweet_text'];
                $tweet_html_sql = $tweet['tweet_html'];
                $sql_query['Add_Tweet'] = "
                    INSERT INTO tweetbroadcast_tweets
                        (status_id,
                        author_username,author_fullname,author_avatar,
                        tweet_text,tweet_html,pub_date)
                    VALUES (
                        {$tweet['status_id']}, '{$tweet['user_name']}',
                        '{$tweet['full_name']}', '{$tweet['avatar']}',
                        '$tweet_sql','$tweet_html_sql',
                        '{$tweet['pub_date']}')
                ";
                $foo = mysql_query($sql_query['Add_Tweet'])
                    or die('Error, insert query failed');
                $count += mysql_affected_rows();
            }
```

```
            $status_message .= " $count tweet(s) found and saved";
        } catch (Exception $e) {
            $status_message = 'Could not parse tweet XML for $this_user_name';
        }
    }
    if (strlen($status_message) > 0) {
        writeFile($log,$status_signature.$status_message);
    }
}
mysql_free_result($sql_result);

/* Purge Old Stored Data */
$sql_result = mysql_query($sql_query['Remove_Old_Tweets'])
    or die('Error, deletion query failed');
$deleted_records = mysql_affected_rows();
$status_message = "PURGED older tweets | Records deleted: $deleted_records";
writeFile($log,$status_message);

/* Clean Up */
curl_close($cURL);
closeDB($db_connection);
closeFile($log);
```

Let's take a closer look at the salient parts of this code.

Retrieve stored data

Once the application has successfully negotiated with the database to get a list of members to process, the looping begins to retrieve those members' latest tweets. The username and the status ID of the last tweet captured for each member are used to formulate a request to the Twitter API. The application requests up to 200 of the newest tweets authored by that member, skipping any status updates older than the ones already in the database.

For each of the new tweets the script detects, a record is inserted into the database with all of the data that will be used later by Broadcast Feed. The fields of interest include: the status ID, the author's username, the author's full name (which is usually different from the username), the link to the author's Twitter profile picture, the tweet text, and the date and time at which it was published (GMT).

The parsing operation is wrapped in a try...catch block to allow the code to continue processing if the XML returned by Twitter is improperly formatted or (more likely) interrupted by network hiccups.

Purge old stored data

This application isn't meant to be an archive. It only needs to keep as many tweets as are relevant to create a 20-item RSS feed for the people who have requested one. That means we can keep the database smaller and faster by getting rid of any material this script has captured that is older than 20 days. After executing the SQL query to remove the old tweets, this application records the result of the purge in the log file.

Log output

The log file for this automated task, *tweet_broadcast.txt*, is located in the same directory as the other log files. Two kinds of activities are logged. For each new member included as part of someone's custom RSS feed, a summary line is added that includes:

- A Unix timestamp to indicate when this attempt happened
- The member's username
- The status ID of the most recent tweet processed by this task
- A message indicating what the task was doing
- The number of new tweets found and saved during this run

The other kind of log entry is the one describing the purging of old data. This is a single line that includes "PURGED older tweets" and the number of records deleted that day. Both kinds of entry are illustrated in Example 8-4.

Example 8-4. Sample output from the Tweet Broadcast log

```
2008-12-11 19:27:46 | wnryan | Last: 1043701296 | Parsing XML data ...  5 tweet(s)
found and saved
PURGED older tweets | Records deleted: 78
```

Scan Tweets

Not everyone you follow will say things that are relevant to you in every tweet. Conversely, every once in a while people you don't choose to follow will post things that are of interest to you. Simply using Twitter's follow and unfollow functions to manage the flow of information through your timeline won't help you find those hidden gems. That is where automation and the Twitter search API come in handy.

The Scan Tweets script is responsible for querying the Twitter search API with a list of user-submitted keywords and phrases to find matches in the status updates published to the public timeline. It is launched with a *crontab* that points to the *uar_scan_tweets.php* file, which lives in the *automated* directory outside the web path. I've scheduled this script to run every 15 minutes, checking the public timeline and alerting users of any new matches. I find that to be a good pace for this task because it is run often enough to make any matches relevant without putting undue burden on either the server or the people who might be tracking more popular terms.

Scan Tweets begins by asking the database for the last status ID that was encountered while checking for matches. Using this value, the API requests are filtered so that only new material is included. A list of all search terms is then retrieved to form a queue to process for the run of the task. For a description of how the tracking terms are gathered, see "Tweet Alert" on page 305.

For each term, the Twitter timeline is checked for matches. If a match is found, the application obtains from the database a list of the members who requested notifications about that term and sends each of them a direct message, using the master Twitter account. The script finishes by updating the log kept in the database to point to a new status ID that can be used as a filter for the next run.

Check Under the Hood

The description of the code for the Auto Tweet application talks about a one-to-one relationship, with each member using that web tool limited to a single RSS or Atom news feed. With the Scan Tweets automated task, the relationship is many-to-many: each person can track several keywords or phrases, and any given term might have multiple members interested in tracking tweets about it.

This may not seem like that big a distinction, but it means that the code for the Scan Tweets task (see Example 8-5) has to handle its queue a little differently. The script focuses first on asking Twitter whether there are any matches for each unique term, and if a match is found it follows that with another query to find out whom to notify.

Example 8-5. PHP to scan the timeline for keyword matches

```
/* Include Functions*/
$root_path            = realpath('./../includes/')."/";
include $root_path.'validate_data.php';
include $root_path.'api_config.php';
include $root_path.'log_manage.php';
include $root_path.'pw_manage.php';
include $root_path.'database.php';
include $root_path.'sql_queries.php';
include $root_path.'parse_data.php';
include $root_path.'html_template.php';

/* Initiate logging */
$path_to_logs         = realpath('logs/')."/";
$log_file             = 'tweet_alert.txt';
$log                  = openFile($path_to_logs.$log_file,'a');
$status_signature     = '';
$status_message = "TWEET ALERT | scanning underway at ".time();
writeFile($log,$status_message);
$app_title            = 'Tweet Alert';

/* Configure API Requests */
list($master_username,$cURL_source) = prepAPI();

/* Initiate cURL */
$cURL                 = prepRequest($app_title);

/* Prepare Database Interaction */
$db_connection        = openDB();
$sql_variables        = array(
    'file_id'               => basename(__FILE__)
    );
$sql_query            = getQueries($sql_variables);
```

```php
/* Retrieve Master Password */
$sql_result = mysql_query($sql_query['Retrieve_Master_Password'])
    or die('Error, selection query failed ... '.$sql_query
['Retrieve_Master_Password']);
$row                = mysql_fetch_assoc($sql_result);
$master_password    = unscramblePassword($row['password']);
mysql_free_result($sql_result);
curl_setopt ($cURL, CURLOPT_USERPWD, "$master_username:$master_password");
if (!(hasAccess($cURL,$cURL_source)))      {
    $status_message     = 'The Master password is incorrect. Please use the
                            administration tool to correct this.';
    writeFile($log,$status_message);
}
else {

/* Retrieve Last ID */
    $sql_result = mysql_query($sql_query['Retrieve_Last_Status'])
        or die('Error, selection query failed');
    $row = mysql_fetch_assoc($sql_result);
    $max_status_id      = $row['last_status_id'];
    $new_max_status_id  = $max_status_id;
    mysql_free_result($sql_result);

    $keyword_count      = 0;
    $matches_count      = 0;
    $messages_count     = 0;

/* Retrieve Stored Data */
    $sql_result = mysql_query($sql_query['Retrieve_Stored_Alerts'])
        or die('Error, selection query failed');
    $keyword_queue      = array();
    while ($row = mysql_fetch_assoc($sql_result)) {
        $keyword_queue[]      = $row['keyword'];
    }
    mysql_free_result($sql_result);

    foreach ($keyword_queue as $keyword) {
        $keyword_count    += 1;

/* Check for Matching Tweets */
        try {
            $search_query     =
                "?q=".URLEncode($keyword)."&since_id=$max_status_id&rpp=100";
            list($thisFeed,$search_title) =
                            parseFeed($cURL_source['search'].$search_query);
            $web_link         = $cURL_source['search_web'].$search_query;
            $tweet_count      = sizeof($thisFeed);
            if ($tweet_count > 0) {
                $matches_count    += 1;
                foreach ($thisFeed as $this_tweet) {
                    $full_id = $this_tweet['id'];
                    list($foo,$bar,$most_recent_id) = split(':',$full_id);
                    if ($most_recent_id > 0) break;
                }
                if ($most_recent_id > $new_max_status_id) {
```

```
                    $new_max_status_id = $most_recent_id;
                }
                if ($new_max_status_id > $max_status_id) {

/* Format Message */

                    $message = "'$keyword' has $tweet_count new matches ... ";
                    $link = file_get_contents(
                            'http://tinyurl.com/api-create.php?url='.$web_link);
                    if (strlen($link) > 0) {
                        $message .= " $link";
                    }
                    $message_encoded =
                                urlencode(stripslashes(urldecode($message)));
                    $status_message = "===> '$keyword' found $tweet_count new
                                matches for";

/* Retrieve Users */

                    $keyword_sql = mysql_real_escape_string($keyword);
                    $sql_query['Retrieve_Users'] = "
                        SELECT    distinct user_name
                        FROM      tweetalert_profiles
                        WHERE     keyword = '$keyword_sql'
                        ";
                    $sql_result = mysql_query($sql_query['Retrieve_Users'])
                        or die('Error, selection query failed');
                    $user_queue    = array();
                    while ($row = mysql_fetch_assoc($sql_result)) {
                        $this_user        = $row['user_name'];
                        $status_message .= " $this_user";

/* Confirm Follower Status */

                        if (!(in_array($this_user, array_keys($user_queue)))) {
                            $user_queue[$this_user] = FALSE;
                            $cURL_query =
                                    "?user_a=$this_user&user_b=$master_username";
                            curl_setopt ($cURL, CURLOPT_POST, false);
                            curl_setopt ($cURL, CURLOPT_POSTFIELDS, "");
                            list($cURL_status,$confirmation) = apiRequest($cURL,
                                $cURL_source['confirm_follow'].$cURL_query);
                            if ($confirmation == '<friends>true</friends>') {
                                $user_queue[$this_user] = TRUE;
                            }
                        }

/* Notify Users */

                        if ($user_queue[$this_user]) {
                            curl_setopt ($cURL, CURLOPT_POST, true);
                            curl_setopt ($cURL, CURLOPT_POSTFIELDS,
                                "user=$this_user&text=$message_encoded");
                            list($cURL_status,$twitter_data) = apiRequest(
                                $cURL,$cURL_source['post_message']);
                            if ($cURL_status == 200)     {
                                $messages_count    += 1;
```

```
            }
            else {
                $status_message .= " (API error $cURL_status)";
            }
        }
        else {
            $status_message .= "*";
        }
        $status_message .= " /";

    }
    writeFile($log,$status_message);
    mysql_free_result($sql_result);

/* Log Activity */

    $sql_query['Add_Log'] = "
        INSERT INTO tweetalert_log
            (status_id,scan_datetime,keywords,matches,messages)
        VALUES
            ($new_max_status_id, current_timestamp, $keyword_count,
                $matches_count, $messages_count)
        ";
    $sql_result = mysql_query($sql_query['Add_Log'])
        or die('Error, log insertion query failed');
    $status_message = "Logged results | status IDs $max_status_id
                        to $new_max_status_id ($keyword_count
                        keywords, $matches_count matches,
                        $messages_count messages)";
    writeFile($log,$status_message);
    $sql_result = mysql_query($sql_query['Prune_Log'])
        or die('Error, log deletion query failed');
    }
  }
} catch (Exception $e) {
    $status_message = 'Could not get search data';
    writeFile($log,$status_message);
    }
  }
}

/* Clean Up */
curl_close($cURL);
closeDB($db_connection);
closeFile($log);
```

Let's explore this code in a little more detail.

Retrieve master password

In order to send direct messages to alert members of matches, the application requires that the recipient be following the main Twitter account (see "Confirm follower status" on page 311) and that the master account be the one making the request to the Twitter API. This is where the administration tool comes in handy (see "Administration

Tool" on page 267). That tool made it possible to store the password for the main Twitter account in the database for later retrieval, and now is the time to go get it.

After querying the SQL database for a scrambled version of the password, the script needs to turn the gibberish that's returned into usable text that can be sent as credentials to the API. The companion to the custom function that scrambled the plain-text password in the first place (see "Password Management Functions" on page 246), unscramblePassword( ), is used to transform the stored string back into its original form. The open cURL connection is then configured to check the Twitter API to see whether the credentials from the master account are still valid. If not, the script effectively ends with the error written to the log file. Otherwise, the script continues.

Retrieve last ID

If the script didn't bother to keep track of where it finished a run, each run would detect the same matching tweets and keep sending redundant alerts to members. That would be both annoying and not very helpful. Fortunately, this automated task does save the last status ID checked, so only fresh notifications are delivered. The script queries the database for this value and stores it in $max_status_id for later use by PHP. It also copies this value to $new_max_status_id, a variable that will be used to identify the last status ID checked on the current run.

Check for matching tweets

After retrieving all of the unique keywords and phrases Twitter members have requested to track (stored in the variable $keyword_queue), the script prepares the open cURL connection to check the Twitter search API for matches to each term. The URI for the Keyword Search method accepts three parameters of interest: the query term, q; the since_id value of the last ID checked ($max_status_id); and rpp, the number of tweets to return in each page (100 is the maximum).

The data that is returned is not like the standard XML generated by other Twitter API methods; instead, it looks more like a news feed (see "Search Objects" on page 205). Rather than using the open cURL connection to retrieve data, only to send it on to the parsing function, this script takes care of both tasks at once using the custom function parseFeed( ) and the search method URI as a parameter. Any matching tweets are saved in $thisFeed.

The last step for this part of the code is trying to determine what the latest status ID is and whether it is the most recent tweet for the entire loop. The status ID isn't as easy as other field values to retrieve because it is embedded in an ID string. The script loops through all the tweets and saves the status ID of the first one it can successfully parse using the split( ) function. If that value is greater than $new_max_status_id, it becomes the status ID to beat.

The processing of each search term in the queue is wrapped in a `try...catch` block. This allows the script to continue even if it encounters errors, limiting any failure to just the current term.

Format message

If any new tweets containing the current search term are found, a direct message needs to be sent to each member who wanted to know about matches for that term. The message composed by the automated task identifies which term was searched—remember, some people will track more than one keyword or phrase—and provides a TinyURL linking back to the web version of the same search this script just conducted. This message content is encoded so that it can be sent to the Twitter API correctly.

Retrieve users

Because Scan Tweets involves a many-to-many relationship, it is possible that several people will have been responsible for placing the current search term in the queue to be processed. The script therefore asks the database to return a list of all distinct usernames associated with this search term.

Confirm follower status

Knowing who is interested in the current search term only gets you halfway there: you must also notify the interested users of matches via direct messages. To receive these messages, the users must be following the account sending them (`$master_username`). This script checks the Twitter API to confirm that this relationship exists for each user in the list. If so, the `$user_queue` array item for this user is set to `TRUE` (the default value is `FALSE`). The keys in this array where the value is `TRUE` become the mailing list receiving direct message notifications for this search term.

Notify users

Direct messaging is a POST method operation, which demands that the open cURL connection be configured as such. For each member on the mailing list, the username and the content of the message are set as `CURLOPT_POSTFIELDS` parameter values. The cURL connection is passed to the custom function `apiRequest( )`, returning an HTTP status code. If the code is 200, the message was sent and the counter is incremented to reflect the number of members that have been notified about the new tweets. A log entry is also written to summarize the activity for the current term.

Log activity

The most important bit of information at this juncture is stored in `$new_max_status_id`. Storing the maximum status ID value in the database enables the automated task to pick up where it left off when it is next fired 15 minutes later. Consequently, this is one case where it isn't sufficient to simply write to a text file to log activity. Other stats are gathered, too, such as how many terms were matched by how many tweets, and how many direct messages were sent. These may be helpful for some later report, so why not take the time to tally and save them now?

Each log record inserted into the database is tied to the current search term. That is, the statistics are not accumulated for the entire run. Depending on how often you schedule this task and the number of terms in your search, the log table can fill up quickly. To keep the database footprint small, regular pruning is done to get rid of the oldest records.

Log output

On the server, the log file for this automated task is *tweet_alert.txt*, located in the same directory as the other logs. Two kinds of activities are logged (see Example 8-6). Every term will have a summary line that includes:

- A label of "TWEET ALERT"
- A Unix timestamp to indicate when the term was processed
- The search term
- The number of new matches found
- A list of the members who requested an alert

If a member username is flagged with an asterisk (*), that person did not receive a direct message because he was not following the main Twitter account for the application.

The other kind of log entry summarizes everything that happened during this run of the automated task. This one line of logged results includes:

- The range of status IDs checked, from the stored ID to the maximum encountered
- A summary of the number of keywords, matches, and messages sent

Example 8-6 illustrates the two types of log entry. If errors are encountered, the details will be logged as a separate line item.

Example 8-6. Sample output from the Tweet Alert log

```
TWEET ALERT | scanning underway at 1229112001
===> ' papyrus' found 15 new matches for mzhartz /
Logged results | status IDs 1049868566 to 1053907272 (1 keywords,
 1 matches, 1 messages)
```

Queue Users

As described in "Best of Twitter API" on page 324, making sense of the bookmarking done in Twitter is somewhat difficult. There are no easy ways to get a list of the tweets you have published that others have flagged as favorites, for example. Building a new API from the data available in the Twitter API seems like a good way to fill this gap.

This script is the first of two backend automated tasks to maintain the data needed to drive this new second-generation API. It is invoked with a *crontab* pointing to the file *uar_queue_users.php*, which is located in the *automated* directory outside the web path. I scheduled my installation of this application to run every two minutes: because of caching in Twitter, querying more than once per minute is redundant, and I slowed down that pace a little to give my server a break and create a slightly larger window for the second script, Collect Favorites, to do its thing.

The public timeline API method this script uses only returns 20 new tweets at a time, but Twitter's posting rate is considerably higher than 10 tweets per minute (in fact, as of January 2009 Tweet Rush estimated it at about 1.8 million tweets a day, or 1,250 per minute). There is no expectation that the script will be able to capture all tweets, so I've settled for regular sampling.

 Twitter does have a few other options to get public tweets. See "Other Data Options" on page 181 for more details.

This application is designed to discover and add new users to the database for use by the other automated task for the Best of Twitter API. After it launches, the script fetches a set of recent tweets from the public timeline. This part of the application is not interested in the status updates themselves, but rather their authors. A check is performed to see whether each Twitter member encountered is already in the queue; if not, the author's data is added as a new member record. For a description of how the second-generation API refers to this stored data, see "Collect Favorites" on page 352.

Check Under the Hood

There are no surprises at this point. Everything you have already read in this chapter about the automated task code structure and logic applies here as well; only the primary function is different. The section of this code (see Example 8-7) that I'll describe here deals with checking the public timeline for new users who favorite.

 This automated task records information to a log file, but that file is shared by a second task that helps power the API. I'll discuss how the log file works at the end of the next section.

Example 8-7. PHP to find new users to track

```
/* Include Functions */
$root_path            = realpath('./../includes/')."/";
include $root_path.'api_config.php';
include $root_path.'log_manage.php';
include $root_path.'database.php';
```

```php
include $root_path.'parse_data.php';

/* Initiate Logging */
$path_to_logs        = realpath('logs/')."/";
$log_file            = 'best_of_twitter.txt';
$log = openFile($path_to_logs.$log_file,'a');
$status_signature    = '';
$status_message      = '';
$app_title           = 'Best of Twitter';

/* Configure API Requests */
list($master_username,$cURL_source) = prepAPI();

/* Initiate cURL */
$cURL                = prepRequest($app_title);

/* Prepare Database Interaction */
$db_connection       = openDB();

/* Mine New Users*/
list($cURL_status,$twitter_data) =
                        apiRequest($cURL,$cURL_source['public_timeline']);
if ($cURL_status > 200) {
    $status_message  = "Could not retrieve authors from the public timeline.";
    $status_message .= " | API ERROR: $cURL_status";
    $status_message .= " | $recent_tweets";
    $status_message .= "\n\n$twitter_data\n\n";
}
else {
    # Parse the XML file
    try {
        $status_message = "Parsing XML data from public timeline ... ";
        $count           = 0;
        $authors         = parseXML($twitter_data);
        foreach ($authors as $author) {
            foreach($author as $key -> $value) {
                $ author [$key] = mysql_real_escape_string($value);
            }
            # check to see if this user is in the queue
            $sql_query['Check_Queue'] = "
                SELECT  record_id
                FROM    bestof_queue
                WHERE   user_id = {$author['user_id']}
                ";
            $sql_result = mysql_query($sql_query['Check_Queue']);
            if (mysql_num_rows($sql_result) < 1) {
                $sql_query['Add_to_Queue'] = "
                    INSERT INTO bestof_queue
                        (user_id, user_name, user_avatar)
                    VALUES
                        ({$author['user_id']},'{$author['user_name']}',
                        '{$author['avatar']}')
                    ";
                $sql_result = mysql_query($sql_query['Add_to_Queue']);
                $count      += mysql_affected_rows();
```

```
            }
        }
        $status_message .= " $count authors(s) found and saved";
    } catch (Exception $e) {
        $status_message = 'Could not parse the XML for the public timeline';
    }
}
writeFile($log,$status_signature.$status_message);

/* Clean Up */
curl_close($cURL);
closeDB($db_connection);
closeFile($log);
```

Only one part of this code is new; we'll explore that section now.

Mine new users

When checking the public timeline for tweets, the application automatically gets some
basic information on the authors of those status updates. Unfortunately, the number
of times those authors have declared tweets to be their favorites will not be found in
that data set. The only way to get that information would be to request the extended
user profile for each member. We could do that here, at a cost of up to 20 hits against
the API rate limit each time this task runs, but it turns out it is more economical to
simply collect all users and try to download their lists of favorites in the other automated
task.

In this brute-force method, the script first requests some new tweets from the public
timeline. Wrapping the parsing in a `try...catch` block, the application attempts to
parse the XML returned by the API, looping over each of the 20 tweets. The code checks
the database for the existence of each tweet's author, inserting a new record for that
member if none exists.

 I have the application keep track of the new member count. Even though
it has already identified about 200,000 unique members, every run of
this task finds that as many as half of the recent posters have not been
registered. At the rate I am collecting information and with the technique I am using, I doubt that will change. The rate of growth on Twitter
is staggering.

Collect Favorites

The second of the automated tasks for the Best of Twitter API is responsible for querying
the list of favorites for known members and saving a local copy of any status updates
that those members have marked as favorites. This script is invoked as a *crontab* that
points to the file *uar_collect_favorites.php*, which lives in the *automated* directory outside the web path.

My *crontab* is scheduled to launch this application only once per hour. The reason for this is the constraint of the API rate limit (see "Accessing the API" on page 134), which resets after an hour. This script is written to continue grabbing data until it encounters an error, which will most likely be the rate limit error after about 100 requests.

 My master account for this suite of sample applications has been granted whitelist access to the API, which means the limits are turned off for that account. While in theory that gives me unfettered access to the API data, I am also concerned about the toll that continued sampling takes on my host server. Once per hour is enough to get some goods for a sample API method that you are likely to improve for production anyway (hint, hint).

The Collect Favorites task starts by retrieving a selection of known users from the list the Queue Users task has been assembling. The selection favors new members who have not yet been processed, then goes back and gets the ones for whom it has been the longest time since the program has checked for new bookmarks. For each member, the database returns the basic information—user ID, username, and last processed status ID—that the script will need to make intelligent guesses about what to request from the Twitter API.

The Twitter API sends the application a batch of tweets that a particular member has favorited. The script loops over each batch, examining the status object for each tweet to determine whether it should process it. If so, the favorite relationship between the current member and that status ID is recorded, and if the tweet is new (i.e., has not been favorited before), it is added to the database. For a description of how the second-generation API refers to this stored data, see "Best of Twitter API" on page 324.

The default logic for this tool is to stop whenever there is a problem. That problem could be an error returned from the API, an interruption in the network connection that messes up the XML, or that the tweets being encountered are older than what is already in the database. It will start over with the next run, excluding anything it has already processed.

Check Under the Hood

A lot has to happen here to get a comprehensive list of all favorited tweets into one local database for the Best of Twitter API to use to fuel its sample method. The application cannot assume that a user will ever join the subgroup of Twitter users who bookmark their favorite tweets, so no user placed into the queue can ever be removed (although those who don't use this feature can get a lower priority).

Similarly, because Twitter does not include the favorites count in the short-form user object when describing the authors in the public timeline (see "User Objects" on page 192), Twitter gives no hint when a member has not bookmarked anything. Consequently, the script has to assume that everyone has favorited at least one tweet; only after checking will the application know whether that assumption is true.

This section covers how the queue of users collected by the Queue Users automated task is used to feed the local repository of favorited tweets. If you encounter any part of the code (see Example 8-8) not explained in this section or earlier in this chapter, please review the appropriate sections in Chapter 7.

Example 8-8. PHP to collect favorited tweets

```php
/* Include Functions */
$root_path          = realpath('./../includes/')."/";
include $root_path.'validate_data.php';
include $root_path.'api_config.php';
include $root_path.'log_manage.php';
include $root_path.'pw_manage.php';
include $root_path.'database.php';
include $root_path.'sql_queries.php';
include $root_path.'parse_data.php';

/* Initiate Logging */
$path_to_logs       = realpath('logs/')."/";
$log_file           = 'best_of_twitter.txt';
$log                = openFile($path_to_logs.$log_file,'a');
$status_signature   = '';
$status_message     = '';
$app_title          = 'Best of Twitter';

/* Configure API Requests */
list($master_username,$cURL_source) = prepAPI();

/* Initiate cURL */
$cURL               = prepRequest($app_title);

/* Prepare Database Interaction */
$db_connection      = openDB();
$sql_variables      = array(
    'file_id'               => basename(__FILE__)
    );
$sql_query          = getQueries($sql_variables);

/* Retrieve Master Password */
$sql_result = mysql_query($sql_query['Retrieve_Master_Password'])
            or die('Error, selection query failed);
$row = mysql_fetch_assoc($sql_result);
$master_password    = unscramblePassword($row['password']);
mysql_free_result($sql_result);

curl_setopt ($cURL, CURLOPT_USERPWD, "$master_username:$master_password");
if (!(hasAccess($cURL,$cURL_source)))      {
    $status_message = 'The Master password is incorrect.
 Please use the administration tool to correct this.';
    writeFile($log,$status_message);
```

```
        curl_setopt ($cURL, CURLOPT_USERPWD, "");
}

/* Retrieve Queue */
$continue_loop         = 1;
$users_processed       = 0;
$default_last_status_id = 0;
$sql_result = mysql_query($sql_query['Retrieve_Queue'])
    or die('Error, selection query failed');
while (($row = mysql_fetch_assoc($sql_result)) && ($continue_loop)) {
    $this_user_id        = $row['user_id'];
    $this_user_name      = $row['user_name'];
    $last_status_id      = $row['last_status_id'];
    $status_signature    = gmdate("Y-m-d H:i:s",time()).
                            " | $this_user_name | Last: $last_status_id | ";

/* Retrieve Favorites */
    $max_status_id     = $last_status_id;
    $page_count        = 1;
    $continue          = 1;
    $bookmark_count    = 0;
    while ($continue) {
        $this_bookmark_count = 0;
        $recent_bookmarks    =
                    str_replace("[id]",$this_user_name,$cURL_source['bookmarks']);
        $recent_bookmarks    .= "?page=$page_count";
        list($cURL_status,$twitter_data) = apiRequest($cURL,$recent_bookmarks);
        if ($cURL_status > 200) {
            $status_message    = "Could not retrieve favorites for $this_user_name";
            $status_message    .= " | API ERROR: $cURL_status";
            $status_message    .= " | $recent_bookmarks";
            $continue = 0;
            $continue_loop = 0;
            break;
        }
        else {
            $status_message = "Parsing favorites XML data for $this_user_name
                            (total pages $page_count) ... ";
            $bookmarks = parseXML($twitter_data);
            foreach ($bookmarks as $bookmark) {
                foreach($bookmark as $key => $value) {
                    $bookmark[$key] = mysql_real_escape_string($value);
                }
                $status_id         = $bookmark['status_id'];
                $author_user_id    = $bookmark['user_id'];
                $author_user_name  = $bookmark['user_name'];
                $author_avatar     = $bookmark['avatar'];
                $tweet             = $bookmark['tweet_text'];
                $pub_date          = $bookmark['pub_date'];
                if ($status_id > $last_status_id) {
                    $sql_query['Add_Favorite'] = "
                        INSERT INTO bestof_favorites
                            (status_id, user_id, created_at)
                        VALUES
                            ($status_id,$this_user_id,CURRENT_TIMESTAMP)
```

```
                    ";
                    $foo = mysql_query($sql_query['Add_Favorite'])
                        or die('Error, insert query failed');
                    if (mysql_affected_rows() > 0) {
                        $sql_query['Update_Tweet'] = "
                            UPDATE      bestof_tweets
                            SET         favorited = favorited + 1
                            WHERE       status_id = $status_id
                        ";
                        $foo = mysql_query($sql_query['Update_Tweet'])
                            or die('Error, update query failed');
                        if (mysql_affected_rows() < 1) {
                            $sql_query['Add_Tweet'] = "
                                INSERT INTO bestof_tweets
                                    (status_id, author_user_name,
                                     author_user_id, author_avatar,
                                     tweet, created_at)
                                VALUES
                                    ($status_id,'$author_user_name',
                                     $author_user_id, '$author_avatar',
                                     '$tweet','$pub_date')
                            ";
                            $foo = mysql_query($sql_query['Add_Tweet'])
                                or die('Error, update query failed');
                        }
                        if ($status_id > $max_status_id) {
                            $max_status_id = $status_id;
                        }
                        $bookmark_count       += 1;
                        $this_bookmark_count += 1;
                    }
                }
                else { $continue = 0; break; }
            }
        }
        if ($this_bookmark_count < 1)    { $continue = 0; }
        else                             { $page_count += 1; }
    }
    if ($max_status_id > $default_last_status_id) {
        $default_last_status_id = $max_status_id;
    }
    if ($max_status_id > $last_status_id) {
        $last_status_id = $max_status_id;
    }
    if ($last_status_id < 1) {
        $last_status_id = $default_last_status_id;
    }

/* Update Queue */
    $sql_query['Update_Queue'] = "
        UPDATE    bestof_queue
        SET       last_status_id = $last_status_id,
                  last_checked_date = CURRENT_TIMESTAMP
        WHERE     user_id = $this_user_id
    ";
```

```
    $foo = mysql_query($sql_query['Update_Queue'])
        or die('Error, update query failed');
    $users_processed += mysql_affected_rows();
    $status_message  .= " $bookmark_count tweet(s) found and saved";
    writeFile($log,$status_signature.$status_message);
}
mysql_free_result($sql_result);
$status_message = "$users_processed users processed from the queue.";
writeFile($log,$status_message);

/* Clean Up */
curl_close($cURL);
closeDB($db_connection);
closeFile($log);
```

Let's take a closer look at what's new in this code.

Retrieve master password

You may be asking yourself why this script fetches the password for the master Twitter account and confirms the credentials, as this automated task doesn't post any content or communicate through direct messages. The answer is, rate limits.

Without authenticating with my master account for this suite of sample applications, I wouldn't be able to take advantage of the whitelisting status I requested from Twitter. It is possible to work with the View Favorites method in the Twitter API without authenticating, but the requests will be capped out at 100, based on the IP address of the server making those hits. Using the master account allows me to open up the throttle.

> Unlike with the other tasks that rely on the master Twitter account, it isn't a deal killer if the credentials should fail. This script is designed to start hunting for bookmarks, regardless.

Retrieve queue

The application begins looping through the queue of Twitter members by setting some counters and asking the database for a list of member records that need to be checked for new favorites. Preference is given to new users and those who have not been scanned in a while (see "SQL Queries" on page 235), which includes all of the new usernames that have never been processed.

> As discussed in the section on the Queue Users task, the current combination of *crontab* schedule and rate of new posters encountered in the public timeline will keep the unknowns growing at a faster rate than those who have been checked already. Adjustments must be made to the timing and coordination of these two automated tasks to enable you to re-check members known to bookmark for new favorites.

The script processes the results of the SQL query one at a time, fetching the user ID, username, and status ID of the last bookmark processed. By default, this number is zero for members when they are first added to the database, indicating that the filters should be shut off and the full archive of favorites from this member should be collected.

Retrieve favorites

The method in the Twitter API to retrieve a given member's list of favorited tweets is accessible even if it returns no status updates. The most efficient way to automatically figure out whether a member has ever bookmarked a tweet is not to check that member's user profile—the only place the API will include a cumulative favorites count— but to simply start gathering bookmarks on the assumption that there are some tweets to gather.

For each page of favorites, the parseXML() custom function converts the XML data returned by the Twitter API into a form understandable by PHP (see "Data Parsing Functions" on page 240). The application is interested in the status ID, text, and publication date of each bookmarked tweet, as well as the user ID, username, and link to the profile picture of the author. If the script finds a favorited tweet to save, it records the relationship between the status update and the current member being processed.

Next, the script creates a new record for the bookmarked tweet with the information it found in the API data. If this tweet has already been recorded, that record will simply be updated, incrementing the data column that keeps a running count of the number of people who have marked it as a favorite. Other counters used later in the script are also advanced, and the script moves on to the next tweet.

There are four scenarios of interest that cause Collect Favorites to stop processing the current page of favorited tweets:

- There are no more status updates in the member's list of favorites.
- A tweet is encountered with a status ID lower than the last one stored in the database.
- There are no more users left in the task's queue.
- An error is encountered as a response from the API.

The first scenario either ends the current iteration of the loop and moves to the next page, or—if no tweets were found on the current page—declares the list of favorites exhausted, causing the script to move on to the next user. The second scenario tells the script that there are no more new bookmarks to process, signaling it to abandon the current user for the next one.

The latter two scenarios, on the other hand, effectively kill the entire task. If all the users in the queue have been processed, the script can conclude naturally. If an error is encountered, the assumption is that continuing will lead to more errors. If you aren't using a whitelisted master account, the most common API error encountered will be the one indicating that you've exceeded your rate limit. In both cases, no more data mining will be done until the task fires again in an hour.

> If you are using a whitelisted account, the assumption that any error you encounter should halt processing is faulty. You won't run into the fatal problem of exceeding your rate limit, but you may encounter other kinds of errors, such as a formerly public user switching her feed to private. Ideally, these errors will be handled differently and the task will be able to continue to run to completion. Maybe that is an improvement you can make to the code.

This particular method of favorite mining assumes that people only favorite new material. For frequent users of this Twitter feature, that assumption may not hold. (I would not be able to favorite Jack Dorsey's historic first tweet unless it was my first bookmark, for example.) The logic is a trade-off, however, between redundancy and progress. Here, we stop processing a member's list as soon as we encounter a bookmark that has already been recorded, assuming that he will not have retroactively bookmarked any older tweets. The alternative to making this assumption would be to retrieve everyone's full archive with each encounter.

> Take time once in a while to reflect on your code and how it fits in an ever-changing environment. The balance will change as the Best of Twitter API is used. The more attention developers pay to favorites, the more people will use them. The more they discover cool tweets in the archives, the more likely they will be to bookmark older tweets. As it's currently coded, this Collect Favorites script would never see those connections.

Update queue

Once a member has been processed, her member record in the database is updated with the last status ID encountered in her list of favorites and the current timestamp. Since the query this script uses to draw out a sample of users from the full queue relies on an ordering by last date checked, this member then falls to the back of the line. Counters are also advanced to increment the number of users processed, and a log entry is added to summarize the data mining activity for this user.

Log output

The log file for both automated tasks that powers the Best of Twitter API is called *best_of_twitter.txt*, located in the same directory as the other logs. Three kinds of activities are logged in this file. From the Queue Users task, the number of new members pulled from the public timeline each run will be added as a line item, prefaced by

"Parsing XML data from public timeline." From the Collect Favorites task, the result of the data mining for each user is summarized as:

- The date and time the member was processed
- The member's username
- The status ID of the last favorite found and stored for this member
- The total number of API pages requested for this member
- The total number of bookmarks found and stored for this member

At the end of the task—whether or not an API error ended the script prematurely—the total number of members processed from the queue will be logged for posterity. The three kinds of log entries are illustrated in Example 8-9.

Example 8-9. Sample output from the Best of Twitter log

```
Parsing XML data from public timeline ...  13 authors(s) found and saved
2008-12-12 20:13:03 | muskabot | Last: 0 | Parsing favorites XML data for muskabot
(total pages 1) ...  0 tweet(s) found and saved
18 users processed from the queue.
```

Twitter API Reference

Don't have time to reread all the prior poetry about the Twitter API? Fine. Here's a methods cheat sheet that gives you the basics you will need to program your Twitter application. The hierarchy listed here is based on the server paths used by Twitter—the technical order, based on path and method name—rather than the functional groups I used in Chapter 4 of this book.

Twitter tracks two kinds of rate limits: one for unauthenticated requests (which is not possible for the methods that require authentication), and the other for requests made per account when authentication is used. POST method requests, used whenever you need to make a change to the server, don't cost anything. There are also a few methods that are exempt from the rate limit.

For more information on the current nuances of using the API, check out the Twitter API FAQ (*http://apiwiki.twitter.com/FAQ*).

 In this appendix, I use the *.xml* format to describe the methods. Remember, you can substitute *.json* for all of the Twitter API methods and *.atom* or *.rss* for some of them.

Status Methods

Delete a Tweet

Removes a single status update from the Twitter timeline.

Path	/statuses/destroy/*id*.xml
Requires authentication	Yes (the account owns the existing update).
Charged against rate limit	No.

HTTP method type	POST or DELETE.
Required parameters	
id	Provides the record ID for an existing status update owned by the authenticating user. The id parameter is passed as part of the URL request.
Successful output	See "Publishing" on page 151.

View Followers

Returns a list of people who follow you.

Path	/statuses/followers.xml
Requires authentication	Yes (authenticating user must be allowed by the author to view a private list of followers).
Charged against rate limit	Yes.
HTTP method type	GET.
Optional parameters	
id	Indicates the user ID or username of the Twitter account whose follower list you want to view. The id parameter is passed as part of the URL request: /statuses/followers/id.xml.
page	Indicates which page of 100 users to return. The default is 1 (users most recently created).
Successful output	See "The Follow Network" on page 157.

View Members Being Followed

Returns a list of people you follow.

Path	/statuses/friends.xml
Requires authentication	Yes, if the account is private (authenticating user must be allowed by the author to view the list of friends).
Charged against rate limit	Yes.
HTTP method type	GET.
Optional parameters	
id	Indicates the user ID or username of the Twitter account whose following list you want to view. The id parameter is passed as part of the URL request: /statuses/friends/id.xml.
page	Indicates which page of 100 users to return. The default is 1 (users most recently followed).
Successful output	See "The Follow Network" on page 157.

 There are newer methods that allow you to get the entire list of followers and friends as user IDs. No other information is included in the Twitter API response, but it does save on pagination. See "Get All Followers" on page 160 and "Get All Friends" on page 161.

View a Friends Timeline

Returns the most recent status updates made by people you follow.

Path	`/statuses/friends_timeline.xml`
Requires authentication	Yes.
Charged against rate limit	Yes.
HTTP method type	GET.
Optional parameters	
`since`	Ignores information older than the specified time (which must be within the last 24 hours). The value must be encoded in the format "Mon, 3 Nov 2008 18:39:12 GMT".
`since_id`	Returns only the most recent updates (those made since the specified record ID was created).
`count`	Limits the most recent status updates to the number of records specified. The maximum count is 200, and the default is 20.
`page`	Indicates which page of 20 items to return. The default is 1 (the most recent status updates).
Successful output	See "The Information Stream" on page 152.

View the Public Timeline

Returns the most recent status updates from public accounts with custom pictures.

Path	`/statuses/public_timeline.xml`
Requires authentication	No.
Charged against rate limit	No.
HTTP method type	GET.
Successful output	See "The Information Stream" on page 152.

View Replies

Returns the most recent status updates from people who have replied to you.

Path	`/statuses/replies.xml`
Requires authentication	Yes (replies are to the authenticating user).
Charged against rate limit	Yes.
HTTP method type	GET.
Optional parameters	
`since`	Ignores information older than the specified time (which must be within the last 24 hours). The value must be encoded in the format "Mon, 3 Nov 2008 18:39:12 GMT".
`since_id`	Returns only the most recent updates (those made since the specified record ID was created).

count	Limits the most recent replies to the number of records specified. The maximum count is 200, and the default is 20.
page	Indicates which page of 20 items to return. The maximum value is currently 40, and the default is 1 (the most recent status updates).
Successful output	See "The Information Stream" on page 152.

Show a Tweet

Returns a single status update with the given ID.

Path	/statuses/show/*id*.xml
Requires authentication	Yes, if the status update is private (authenticating user must be allowed by the author to view the text).
Charged against rate limit	Yes.
HTTP method type	GET.
Required parameters	
id	Provides the record ID for an existing status update owned by the authenticating user. The id parameter is passed as part of the URL request.
Successful output	See "The Information Stream" on page 152.

Post a Tweet

Creates a new status update authored by you.

Path	/statuses/update.xml
Requires authentication	Yes (this account owns the status update).
Charged against rate limit	No.
HTTP method type	POST.
Required parameters	
status	Indicates the text used to update the authenticating user's status. This string is limited to 140 characters after URL encoding.
Optional parameters	
in_reply_to_status_id	Provides the record ID of an existing status update to which the new update will be attached.
source	Identifies the name of the tool used to publish the tweet (as in "web" or "twitterrific").
Successful output	See "Publishing" on page 151.

View an Individual Timeline

Returns the most recent status updates for a specific account.

Path	`/statuses/user_timeline/id.xml`
Requires authentication	Yes, if the account is private (authenticating user must be allowed by the author to view the timeline).
Charged against rate limit	Yes.
HTTP method type	GET.
Required parameters	None, if authenticated (Twitter assumes the authenticating user is the `id`).
Optional parameters	
`id`	Provides the user ID or username for the Twitter account whose timeline you want to view. The `id` parameter is passed as part of the URL request.
`since`	Ignores information older than the specified time (which must be within the last 24 hours). The value must be encoded in the format "Mon, 3 Nov 2008 18:39:12 GMT".
`since_id`	Returns only the most recent updates (those made since the specified record ID was created).
`count`	Limits the most recent status updates to the number of records specified. The maximum count is 200, and the default is 20.
`page`	Indicates which page of 20 items to return. The default is 1 (the most recent status updates).
Successful output	See "The Information Stream" on page 152.

Users Methods

Show Member Profile

Returns your profile and statistical details.

Path	`/users/show/id.xml`
Requires authentication	Yes, if the account is private (authenticating user must be allowed by the author to view the profile).
Charged against rate limit	Yes.
HTTP method type	GET.
Required parameters	One of the following is required:
`id` or email	Indicates the user ID or username of the Twitter member whose profile you want to view. The `id` parameter is passed as part of the URL request. An email address can be used if you do not know the user ID or username.
`user_id`	Accepts the user ID of an existing Twitter member as a parameter, to help disambiguate when `screen_name` is a number. This parameter is passed as a query string variable.
`screen_name`	Accepts the current `screen_name` of the Twitter member. This parameter is passed as a query string variable.
Successful output	See "The Follow Network" on page 157.

Direct Message Methods

List Received Messages

Returns the most recent direct messages you have received.

Path	/direct_messages.xml
Requires authentication	Yes (list owned by authenticating user).
Charged against rate limit	Yes.
HTTP method type	GET.
Optional parameters	
since	Ignores information older than the specified time (which must be within the last 24 hours). The value must be encoded in the format "Mon, 3 Nov 2008 18:39:12 GMT".
since_id	Returns only the most recent updates (those made since the specified record ID was created).
page	Indicates which page of 20 items to return. The default is 1 (the most recent messages).
count	Limits the most recent messages to the number of records specified.
Successful output	See "Communication" on page 165.

Delete a Message

Deletes an existing direct message received by you.

Path	/direct_messages/destroy/*id*.xml
Requires authentication	Yes (authenticating user owns the message).
Charged against rate limit	No.
HTTP method type	POST or DELETE.
Required parameters	
id	Provides the record ID for an existing message owned by the authenticating user. The id parameter is passed as part of the URL request.
Successful output	See "Communication" on page 165.

Create a Message

Creates a new direct message sent from you to another user.

Path	/direct_messages/new.xml
Requires authentication	Yes (authenticating user authors the message).
Charged against rate limit	No.
HTTP method type	POST.

Required parameters

user	Provides the user ID or username of the intended recipient of this message.
text	The text message sent by the authenticating user. This string is limited to 140 characters after URL encoding.

Successful output   See "Communication" on page 165.

List Sent Messages

Returns the most recent direct messages you have sent.

Path	/direct_messages/sent.xml
Requires authentication	Yes (list owned by authenticating user).
Charged against rate limit	Yes.
HTTP method type	GET.
Optional parameters	

since	Ignores information older than the specified time (which must be within the last 24 hours). The value must be encoded in the format "Mon, 3 Nov 2008 18:39:12 GMT".
since_id	Returns only the most recent updates (those made since the specified record ID was created).
page	Indicates which page of 20 items to return. The default is 1 (the most recent messages).
count	Limits the most recent messages to the number of records specified.

Successful output   See "Communication" on page 165.

Friendship Methods

Follow a Member

Creates a new follow relationship between you and another Twitter member.

Path	/friendships/create/*id*.xml
Requires authentication	Yes.
Charged against rate limit	No.
HTTP method type	POST.
Required parameters	

id	Provides the user ID or username of an existing Twitter member not already followed by the authenticating user. The id parameter is passed as part of the URL request.
follow	Adds device notifications for this friend, in addition to following that member. See "Turn On Notification" on page 374.

Successful output   See "The Follow Network" on page 157.

Unfollow a Member

Removes an existing follow relationship with another Twitter member.

Path	/friendships/destroy/*id*.xml
Requires authentication	Yes.
Charged against rate limit	No.
HTTP method type	POST.
Required parameters	
id	Provides the user ID or username of an existing Twitter member already being followed by the authenticating user. The id parameter is passed as part of the URL request.
Successful output	See "The Follow Network" on page 157.

Confirm a Follow

Verifies whether one Twitter member is following another.

Path	/friendships/exists.xml
Requires authentication	Yes.
Charged against rate limit	Yes.
HTTP method type	GET.
Required parameters	
user_a	Indicates the user ID or username of the existing Twitter member whom you want to confirm is following user_b.
user_b	Provides the user ID or username of the existing Twitter member whom you want to check if user_a is following.
Successful output	See "The Follow Network" on page 157.

Social Graph Methods

Get All Friends

Returns the full list of people you follow.

Path	/friends/ids.xml
Requires authentication	Yes, if the account is private (authenticating user must be allowed by the author to view the list of friends).
Charged against rate limit	Yes.
HTTP method type	GET.
Optional parameters	

id	Indicates the user ID or username of the Twitter account whose following list you want to view. The `id` parameter is passed as part of the URL request: `/friends/ids/`*`id`*`.xml`.
Successful output	See "The Follow Network" on page 157.

Get All Followers

Returns the full list of people who follow you.

Path	`/followers/ids.xml`
Requires authentication	Yes (authenticating user must be allowed by the author to view a private list of followers).
Charged against rate limit	Yes.
HTTP method type	GET.
Optional parameters	
id	Indicates the user ID or username of the Twitter account whose follower list you want to view. The `id` parameter is passed as part of the URL request: `/followers/ids/`*`id`*`.xml`.
Successful output	See "The Follow Network" on page 157.

Account Methods

End a Member Session

Tells Twitter that your application is finished using your access credentials.

Path	`/account/end_session.xml`
Requires authentication	Yes (affects authenticating user).
Charged against rate limit	No.
HTTP method type	POST.
Successful output	See "API Administration" on page 174.

Check Rate Limit Status

Checks to see how many hourly hits on the API are left for your account.

Path	`/account/rate_limit_status.xml`
Requires authentication	No. If authenticated, returns the rate limit for that Twitter account. If unauthenticated, returns the rate limit for the IP address used to make the request.
Charged against rate limit	No.
HTTP method type	GET.
Successful output	See "API Administration" on page 174.

Update the Delivery Device

Selects a device for you to use to receive updates.

Path	`/account/update_delivery_device.xml`
Requires authentication	Yes (changes device for authenticating user).
Charged against rate limit	No.
HTTP method type	POST.
Required parameters	
`device`	Must be one of the two valid options supported by Twitter, namely `sms` or `im`. To turn off device notifications, the value should be none.
Successful output	See "Member Account" on page 168.

 There is currently no Twitter support for IM notifications.

Update Member Location

Changes the location information stored in your profile.

Path	`/account/update_location.xml`
Requires authentication	Yes (changes location of authenticating user).
Charged against rate limit	No.
HTTP method type	POST.
Required parameters	
`location`	Provides the text to be displayed in the location field in the authenticating user's member profile. The text must be encoded.
Successful output	See "Member Account" on page 168.

 The `update_location` method has been deprecated in favor of the `update_profile` method, which contains an optional parameter for location. To keep your application from breaking in the future, avoid using `update_location`.

Update Member Profile

Sets the values of selected fields found in the "Account" tab under the settings on the Twitter website.

Path	`/account/update_profile.xml`
Requires authentication	Yes (changes profile for authenticating user).

Charged against rate limit	No.
HTTP method type	POST.
Required parameters	At least one parameter must be included.
Optional parameters	Only the requested parameters are changed.
`name`	The full name of the person or organization owning the authenticating account. The maximum length is 40 characters.
`email`	Must be a valid and unique email address of no more than 40 characters in length.
`url`	The URL link to a website, displayed on the member's profile web page. The maximum length is 100 characters. "http://" will be added to the beginning of the string, if not already provided.
`location`	Contains the text to be displayed in the location field in the authenticating user's member profile. The maximum length is 30 characters.
	Note: this is an open text field. No geocoding or other normalization is done by Twitter.
`description`	This text describes the authenticating member. The maximum length is 160 characters.
Successful output	See "Member Account" on page 168.

Update Background Image

Changes the background image on the authenticating user's member profile web page.

Path	`/account/update_profile_background_image.xml`
Requires authentication	Yes (changes the image for authenticating user).
Charged rate limit	No.
HTTP method type	POST.
Required parameters	
`image`	Must contain raw multipart data, not a URL to an image located on the Web. This method accepts GIF, JPG, or PNG images with a maximum of 2,048 pixels. Larger images will be scaled down, provided they are less than 800 KB.
Successful output	See "Member Account" on page 168.

Update Profile Colors

Changes the color scheme applied to the authenticating member's profile page.

Path	`/account/update_profile_colors.xml`
Requires authentication	Yes (changes device for authenticating user).
Charged against rate limit	No.
HTTP method type	POST.
Required parameters	At least one parameter must be included.
Optional parameters	Must be valid hexadecimal values (e.g., #f1c or #ff11cc).

`profile_background_color`	The background color, visible only if no background image is used for the member profile.
`profile_text_color`	The color of the primary text in the profile.
`profile_link_color`	The color of the links used on the page.
`profile_sidebar_fill_color`	The shading used in the righthand sidebar.
`profile_sidebar_border_color`	The border colors used for lines in the sidebar.
Successful output	See "Member Account" on page 168.

Update Profile Image

Changes the picture associated with the authenticating member's account and displayed with that user's tweets.

Path	`/account/update_profile_image.xml`
Requires authentication	Yes (changes image for authenticating user).
Charged against rate limit	No.
HTTP method type	POST.
Required parameters	
`image`	Must contain raw multipart data, not a URL to an image located on the Web. This method accepts GIF, JPG, or PNG images with a maximum of 500 pixels. Larger images will be scaled down, provided they are less than 700 KB.
Successful output	See "Member Account" on page 168.

Verify Credentials

Confirms that the supplied user account credentials are valid.

Path	`/account/verify_credentials.xml`
Requires authentication	Yes.
Charged against rate limit	Yes.
HTTP method type	GET.
Successful output	See "API Administration" on page 174.

Favorite Methods

View Favorites

Returns a list of all status updates you've flagged as favorites.

Path	/favorites.xml
Requires authentication	Yes, if the favorites are private (authenticating user must be allowed by the author to view the bookmarks).
Charged against rate limit	Yes.
HTTP method type	GET.
Optional parameters	
id	Indicates the user ID or username of the Twitter account whose list of favorite updates you want to view. The id parameter is passed as part of the URL request: /favorites/*id*.xml.
page	Indicates which page of 20 items to return. The default is 1 (the most recent status updates).
Successful output	See "The Information Stream" on page 152.

Create a Favorite

Flags a status update as a favorite.

Path	/favorites/create/*id*.xml
Requires authentication	Yes.
Charged against rate limit	No.
HTTP method type	POST.
Required parameters	
id	References the ID of an existing status update. The id parameter is passed as part of the URI request.
Successful output	See "The Information Stream" on page 152.

Delete a Favorite

Removes an existing flag on one of the authenticating member's favorite status updates.

Path	/favorites/destroy/*id*.xml
Requires authentication	Yes.
Charged against rate limit	No.
HTTP method type	POST or DELETE.
Required parameters	
id	References the ID of an existing status update that the authenticating user has already made a favorite. The id parameter is passed as part of the URL request.
Successful output	See "The Information Stream" on page 152.

Notification Methods

Turn On Notification

Tells Twitter to start sending an author's updates to the preferred device.

Path	/notifications/follow/*id*.xml
Requires authentication	Yes (affects authenticating user).
Charged against rate limit	No.
HTTP method type	POST.
Required parameters	
id	Provides the user ID or username of another member to be followed by the authenticating user. The id parameter is passed as part of the URL request.
Successful output	See "Member Account" on page 168.

Turn Off Notification

Tells Twitter to stop sending an author's updates to the specified device.

Path	/notifications/leave/*id*.xml
Requires authentication	Yes (affects authenticating user).
Charged against rate limit	No.
HTTP method type	POST.
Required parameters	
id	Provides the user ID or username of another member followed by the authenticating user. The id parameter is passed as part of the URL request.
Successful output	See "Member Account" on page 168.

Block Methods

Block a Member

Keeps another member from following your updates.

Path	/blocks/create/*id*.xml
Requires authentication	Yes.
Charged against rate limit	No.
HTTP method type	POST.
Required parameters	

id	Provides the user ID or username of an existing Twitter member not already blocked by the authenticating user. The id parameter is passed as part of the URL request.
Successful output	See "The Follow Network" on page 157.

Remove a Block

Allows another member to once again follow your updates.

Path	/blocks/destroy/*id*.xml
Requires authentication	Yes.
Charged against rate limit	No.
HTTP method type	POST or DELETE.
Required parameters	
id	Supplies the user ID or username of an existing Twitter member already blocked by the authenticating user. The id parameter is passed as part of the URL request.
Successful output	See "The Follow Network" on page 157.

Help Methods

Test

Verifies whether your application's connection to the Twitter API is working.

Path	/help/test.xml
Requires authentication	No.
Charged against rate limit	No.
HTTP method type	GET.
Successful output	See "API Administration" on page 174.

Search Methods

Keyword Search

Searches for keyword matches in tweet content.

Path	search.twitter.com/search.atom?q=*query*
Requires authentication	No.
Charged against rate limit	No.
HTTP method type	GET.

Required parameters

    q   Contains the encoded keywords and other parameters used for the search.

Optional parameters

since
: Ignores information older than the specified time (which must be within the last 24 hours). The value must be encoded in the format "Mon, 3 Nov 2008 18:39:12 GMT".

since_id
: Returns only the most recent updates (those made since the specified record ID was created).

page
: Indicates which page of items to return, with the size of the page determined by rpp. The default is 1 (the most recent messages).

rpp
: Indicates the size of a given result page. The maximum is 100 items per page, and the default is 16.

geocode
: There are three parts to the geocode parameter: latitude, longitude, and radius of interest. The resulting comma-delimited string (e.g., "39.123456,-86.345678,10km") must be URL-encoded. The radius must be specified in units of either mi (miles) or km (kilometers).

lang
: Contains an accepted ISO 639-1 code (e.g., "en") to indicate the language of all returned tweets.

show_user
: When set to true, tags the beginning of each tweet returned in the search results with a username and a colon (e.g., "kmakice:Writing").

callback
: (JSON only.) A callback allows a program to pass a reference to a dynamic function on the application side.

Successful output   See "Search" on page 176.

Monitor Trends

Returns the current top keyword trends in the public timeline.

Path	search.twitter.com/trends.json
Requires authentication	No.
Charged against rate limit	No.
HTTP method type	GET.
Successful output	Ten keywords and search links (JSON output format only)

Index

Symbols

" (double quotes), 98, 143
\# (hash), 92, 121, 170, 178
$ (dollar sign), 98
& (ampersand), 143
(') single quotes, 98
* (asterisk), 92
, (commas), 92
. (full stop/period), 92, 113
// (double-slash), 121
< and > (angle brackets), 143
=.^..^=, 16
@ (at sign) command, 8
 (spaces), 92

A

accessing
    Twitter API, 134–149
account methods, 369–372
account spam, 32
accounts (see member accounts; Twitter accounts; users)
activism (see social change)
addChild() method, 116
adding
    bookmarks, 328
    daily updates, 303
addItem() function, 246
Administration Tool sample application, 263, 267–276
advertising
    opt-in advertising, 22
    potential for profit on Twitter, 21

affiliate linking
    success of, 34
Aggregate Broadcast automated task, 331, 338–342
aggregation tools
    web applications, 64–67
ambient intimacy
    defined, 3
ampersand (&), 143
angle brackets (< and >), 143
anthropomorphism
    using Twitter for, 35
API configuration functions, 230–234
API requests
    configuring, 272
apiRequest() function, 233
APIs (see Summize API; Twitter API)
applications, 260
    (see also automated tasks; sample applications; uses of Twitter; web applications)
    stylesheet for the sample applications, 260
arrays
    PHP, 98
array_search() function, 100, 102
asterisk (*), 92
asXML() method, 117
at sign (@) command, 8
Atom (Atom Syndication Format), 139
attacks
    types of, 97
authentication, 140
    (see also passwords)
    checking rate limit status, 175

We'd like to hear your suggestions for improving our indexes. Send email to *index@oreilly.com*.

Twitter API, 140
author element, 208
authorized element, 209
Auto Tweet sample application, 264, 282–291
automated tasks, 331–360
    Aggregate Broadcast, 331, 338–342
    Collect Favorites, 332, 352–360
    Queue Users, 332, 349–352
    RSS to Tweet, 331, 332–338
    Scan Tweets, 332, 342–349
    scheduling jobs, 128
avatars, 172, 219

B

back channel messaging system, 165
background color property
    stylesheets, 95
background images
    updating, 171
base64_encode() function, 100
basename() function, 100, 229
Best of Twitter sample application, 264, 324–
      329
bike couriers
    history of Twitter, 12
bin2hex() function, 100
block tags, 85
blocking
    members, 164, 374
blocks
    removing, 165, 375
blocks of properties
    stylesheets, 96
bookmarks
    adding, 328
borders
    stylesheets, 93
Botanicalls, 36
Broadcast Feed sample application, 300–305
browsers
    recognizing styles, 95
Buchanan, Ben
    on the Twitter experience, 9
bytes
    limits on number of, 12

C

caching

public timeline, 154
callback option, 181
callback parameter, 147, 376
capacity constraints to Twitter growth, 16
Cascading Style Sheets (see CSS)
ceil() function, 100
celebrities
    using Twitter, 38
ChaCha search engine, 36
changing
    information in MySQL databases, 125
characters
    limits on number of, 12
Check Rate Limit Status method, 369
checking, 148
    (see also verifying)
    rate limit status, 148, 175
checkInput() function, 249, 273
children() method, 116
clean up, 338
closeDB() function, 235
closeFile() function, 255
Collect Favorites automated task, 332, 352–
      360
color property
    stylesheets, 95
colors
    profiles, 170
comedians
    using Twitter, 38
commands, 149
    (see also custom functions; functions;
    statements)
    cURL, 149
commas (,), 92
communication methods, 165–168
compareFollowNet() function, 252
comparePassword() function, 247
comparing
    groups, 298
configuring
    API requests, 272
    Twitter accounts, 217–221
    Twitter API, 230–234
confirming
    follower status, 311, 348
    follows, 163, 368
constructs
    compared to functions in PHP, 115

contact lists
    on web-based servers, 216
content
    searching, 177
content element, 207
context
    importance of in Twitter, 2
    threaded conversations, 8
conversations, 8
    (see also threaded conversations)
    one-to-one, 165
    Twitter as, 8
    web application tools, 55–58
count parameter, 145, 154, 363, 365, 366, 367
Create a Favorite method, 373
Create a Message method, 366
CREATE TABLE statement, 123
createDOMfromURL() function, 243
created_at element, 197, 200, 204
createParserFromString() function, 244
createRSSshell() function, 244
createXMLshell() function, 244
creating
    databases, 222–227
    favorites, 156
    includes directory, 227
    messages, 166
    tables in MySQL, 123
creativity
    using Twitter for, 37
credentials
    verifying, 174
CRLF injection attacks, 97
crontab files, 129
CSRF attacks, 98
CSS (Cascading Style Sheets), 90–96
    about, 90
    decorating web pages, 94
    style recognition by browsers, 95
    stylesheet for the sample applications, 260
    web page layout, 93
culture
    importance of in Twitter, 2
    Twitter impact on, 43
cURL
    about, 118
    commands, 149
    configuration, 230
    handling URLs for API methods, 233
    initiating, 272
    PHP communication with APIs, 232
    security of user account information, 140
CURLOPT_HTTPGET option, 118
CURLOPT_HTTPHEADER option, 233
CURLOPT_POST option, 119
CURLOPT_POSTFIELDS option, 119
CURLOPT_RETURNTRANSFER option, 119, 232
CURLOPT_SSL_VERIFYPEER option, 233
CURLOPT_URL option, 119
CURLOPT_USERAGENT option, 119, 232
CURLOPT_USERPWD option, 119, 232
curl_close() function, 120
curl_exec() function, 120
curl_getinfo() function, 120
curl_init() function, 118
curl_setopt_array() function, 119
curl_setopt() function, 118
Curry, Ian
    on staying in contact with people, 2
custom functions
    PHP, 113–115

D

data
    format, 139
    manipulating in PHP, 100–104
    POST data, 136
    purging, 341
    remote data, 98
    retrieving, 191, 288, 297, 337, 341
    saving, 273
data mining feed
    Twitter API, 181
    using, 181
data parsing functions, 240–246
data sorting functions, 252
data validations functions, 249–251
database functions, 234
databases
    connecting to in PHP, 111
    creating, 222–227
    interaction with, 272, 337
    MySQL, 124
date() function, 101
debugging
    error hash objects, 211
    PHP, 120

dechex() function, 101
declarations
    location of, 271
dedicated servers, 127
Delete a Favorite method, 373
deleting
    favorites, 156, 373
    files, 255
    messages, 167, 366
    process deletion requests, 289, 297
    tweets, 152, 361
    URL resources, 137
delivery notices
    updating, 172
description element, 196
description parameter, 146, 169, 371
detailed user objects, 193
detweet
    defined, 4
developers
    strategic role, 23
device parameter, 143, 370
die() function, 109, 274
digital pets
    Japanese tweet traffic, 16
direct message elements, 204
direct message methods, 366
direct messages, 202
directories
    includes directory, 227
disabling
    profiles, 287
disasters
    Twitter to the rescue, 30
display property
    stylesheets, 94
Does Follow application, 74
dollar sign ($), 98
DOM (Document Object Model)
    PHP, 117
DOMDocument() method, 117
Dorsey, Jack
    inspiration for Twitter, 12
double quotes ("), 98, 143
double-slash (//), 121
Dunbar Number, 9

E

echo() construct, 122

education
    using Twitter for, 38
Edwards, John
    presidential campaigns, 32
elements
    direct message elements, 204
    entry elements, 207
    feed elements, 206
    hash elements, 210
    ID elements, 208
    response elements, 209
    status elements, 200
    user elements, 195–198
email addresses
    Twitter, 215
email parameter, 144, 169, 365, 371
emergencies
    using Twitter for, 30
emoticons
    in search requests, 178
empty values, 224
encryption
    passwords, 247
ending
    member sessions, 176, 369
entertainment
    using Twitter for, 38
entry elements, 207
environment functions, 229
environmental variables
    PHP, 104
    web servers, 271
error element, 211
errors
    debugging PHP, 120
    hash objects, 211
exit() function, 109
explode() function, 101
external files
    importing stylesheet properties, 96
external functions
    including, 336

F

Fail Whale, 16
favorite methods, 372
favorited element, 202
favorites
    creating, 156

deleting, 156
retrieving, 358
favorites method, 156
favourites_count element, 198
Favrd application, 63
fclose() function, 110
feed elements, 206
feeds, 289
(see also data mining feed; RSS feeds)
fieldset tag, 89
files
in includes directory, 228
including, 113
managing in PHP, 109
picture files, 219
file_get_contents() function, 110
filters
meta filters, 178
firehose data stream, 182
floating elements in stylesheets, 93
Follow a Member method, 367
Follow Cost application, 70
follow network methods, 157–165
follow network tools
web applications, 74–80
follow networks
formatting, 322
getting, 321
rate limit constraints, 313
sorting, 322
follow parameter, 145, 162, 367
follower status
confirming, 311, 348
followers
getting, 160
viewing, 159
followers_count element, 196
following
limits of, 9
members, 161
following element, 198
follows
confirming, 163
font-family property, 94
font-size property, 95
FoodFeed application, 58
fopen() function, 109
for statement, 107
foreach statement, 107

form tags, 87
format
data, 139
status codes, 138
formatting
follow networks, 322
formatTweetAsXHTML() function, 245
forms
web forms, 106
freemium service, 21
Friend Or Follow application, 76
friends, 160
(see also followers)
getting, 161
use of term, 161
friends element, 209
friends timeline method, 154
friendship methods, 367
friends_count element, 198
full stop (.), 92
functions, 227–260
(see also commands; methods)
API configuration functions, 230–234
compared to constructs in PHP, 115
custom functions, 113–115
data parsing functions, 240–246
data sorting functions, 252
data validations functions, 249–251
database functions, 234
environment functions, 229
external functions, 336
HTML template functions, 257
includes directory, 227
log management functions, 254
MySQL and PHP, 111
password management functions, 246–249
PHP, 100
SQL queries functions, 235–240
statistics functions, 253
fwrite() function, 110

G

games
for selling children's books, 34
using Twitter for, 34
geocode
Update Member Location method, 168
geocode parameter, 146, 180, 376
Get All Followers method, 369

Get All Friends method, 368
GET method, 135, 150
getAttribute() method, 118
getDBconfiguration() function, 234
getElementsByTagName method, 117
getFooter() function, 260
getHeader() function, 258, 275
getHTTPpath() function, 230
getInterface() function, 258
getName() method, 116
getQueries() function, 235
getResponse() function, 256
getServerPath() function, 229
getting
    follow networks, 321
    followers, 160
    friends, 161
    user profiles, 320
GIF formats, 171
gmdate() function, 101
Gnip, 182
God
    worshiping with Twitter, 29
Gospelr, 30
Green Tweets application, 60
groups
    comparing, 298
    saving, 298
groupStats() function, 253
growth
    of Twitter, 14–20
guidelines for using Twitter, 4

H

hasAccess() function, 251
hasCredentials() function, 251
hash (#), 92, 121, 170, 178
hash elements, 210
hash objects, 209–212
    errors, 211
hash() function, 101
@having, 58
help
    using Twitter for, 36
help methods, 375
hexadecimal values, 170
history of Twitter, 9–25
    bike couriers, 12
    developers' role, 23

growth, 14–20
microblogging, 10
profitability and monetization, 20
host servers
    web applications, 126–130
hourly-limit element, 211
HTML template functions, 257
htmlentities() function, 101
HTTP
    requests, 134–137
    status codes, 137, 175
HTTPS
    use of, 134
Hurricane Katrina
    IRC response, 31
hyperlink tags, 85

I

id element, 195, 201, 204, 206, 207, 208
ID elements, 208
ID objects, 208
id parameter, 135, 143, 144, 152, 154, 156, 159,
        161, 328, 362
IDs
    retrieving last, 347
if statement
    PHP, 106
IM (instant messaging)
    availability of with Twitter, 7
    status reports and Twitter, 13
    support for, 173
image parameter, 146, 171, 371, 372
image tags, 86
images
    updating, 171
implode() function, 101
includes directory
    creating, 227
include() statement, 113
including
    external functions, 270, 336
individual timeline method, 155
information streams
    methods, 152–156
    web applications, 51–55
initializing values in PHP, 271
initiating
    cURL, 272
    XML, 303

initiating logging, 336
inline tags, 85
input
    parsing, 272, 280, 287, 302, 328
input tag, 87
instant messaging (see IM)
Instant Relay Chat (see IRC)
interaction
    databases, 272, 337
interfaces
    rendering, 275, 281, 299, 323
in_reply_to_screen_name element, 201
in_reply_to_status_id element, 202
in_reply_to_status_id parameter, 364
in_reply_to_user_id element, 201
IRC (Instant Relay Chat)
    Hurricane Katrina, 31
    origins of, 10
    Twitter as, 3
isSubmitted() function, 250
isValidTweet() function, 250
is_int() function, 102

J

Jaiku, 23
JSON (JavaScript Object Notation)
    about, 139

K

Keyword Search method, 375
keywords
    monitoring trends, 181
    searching for, 177

L

lang parameter, 146, 180, 376
LazyTweet, 36
Least Dangerous Game, 34
libraries
    cURL, 118
    list of, 213
link element, 206, 207
link tag, 96
links
    filtering, 178
List Received Messages method, 366
List Sent Messages method, 367
list tags, 85

listing messages sent and received, 166
lists
    sort order, 160
LiveTwitting application, 56
load() method, 117
location element, 195
location field
    reliability of, 146
location parameter, 143, 146, 169, 370
log management functions, 254
logging
    initiating, 336
logic flow
    PHP, 106–109
logs
    automated tasks, 338, 342, 348, 359
London Bridge, 35

M

margins
    stylesheets, 93
marketing
    sales, 34
    using Twitter for, 31
master passwords
    retrieving, 346, 357
member accounts, 214
    (see also Twitter accounts; users)
    methods, 168–174
member locations
    updating, 168
member profiles, 320
    (see also profiles)
    showing, 157
    updating, 169
member sessions
    ending, 176
members
    being followed, 159
    blocking, 164
    deleted, 158
    following, 161
    unfollowing, 163, 368
message objects, 202
messages, 166
    (see also status updates; tweets)
    API methods, 165–168
    creating, 166
    listing, 166

posting, 280, 337
  sending and receiving, 165
  showing, 168
meta filters
  content searching, 178
methods, 361–376
  (see also functions; commands; custom functions; external functions)
  account methods, 369–372
  API administration, 174–176
  block methods, 374
  communication methods, 165–168
  direct message methods, 366
  favorite methods, 372
  follow network methods, 157–165
  friendship methods, 367
  help methods, 375
  information streams, 152–156
  member accounts, 168–174
  notification methods, 374
  publishing methods, 151
  search method, 375
  social graph methods, 368
  status methods, 361–365
  users methods, 365
metrics (see statistics)
microblogging, 10
monetizing Twitter
  history of, 20
monitoring
  network changes, 159
  web applications, 47
monitoring keyword trends, 181, 376
Mr. Tweet application, 77
mt_rand() function, 102
MySQL
  about, 222
  communicating with PHP, 272
  functions an PHP, 111
  web programming, 122
mysql_affected_rows() function, 112
mysql_close() function, 112
mysql_connect() function, 111
mysql_fetch_array() function, 112
mysql_free_result() function, 112
mysql_num_rows() function, 112
mysql_query() function, 111
mysql_real_escape_string() function, 112
mysql_select_db() function, 111

N

name element, 195
name parameter, 145, 169, 371
NASA
  twittering away, 28
nested arrays
  PHP, 99
nested styles, 93
Network Viewer sample application, 264, 313–324
news
  using Twitter for, 27
nodeValue() method, 118
notifications
  delivery notices, 172
  methods, 374
  receiving, 220
  turning on/off, 173
  usefulness of, 162
  users, 198, 348
NULL values, 224
number_format() function, 102

O

OAuth
  Twitter API security, 187
  Twitter future plans, 140
Obama, Barack
  presidential campaign, 32
objects, 191–212
  hash objects, 209–212
  ID objects, 208
  message objects, 202
  PHP, 98
  response objects, 209
  search objects, 205–208
  status objects, 198–202
  user objects, 192–198, 192–198
ok element, 209
Omnee application, 78
Open API (see Twitter Open API)
open source service model
  competition with, 22
openDB() function, 235
openFile() function, 254
openSearch:itemsPerPage element, 207
operators
  keyword searches, 179

opt-in advertising, 22
output, 191
    (see also objects)
    logs for automated tasks, 338, 342, 349,
        359

P

pack() function, 102
padding
    stylesheets, 93
page parameter, 145, 154, 180, 362, 363, 365,
        367, 373, 376
pages (see web pages)
parameters
    keyword searches, 180
    Twitter API, 143–147
parseFeed() function, 240
parseXML() function, 242
parsing
    input, 272, 280, 287, 302, 328
    RSS feeds, 243, 284
passwords
    authentication, 140
    management functions, 246–249
    master passwords, 346
    sample applications, 265
    setting, 219
    Twitter API, 182–189
period (.), 92, 113
phishing, 182–189
    (see also twishing)
Phoenix probe
    tweeting back to earth, 28
phones
    getting updates on, 219
PHP
    attacks, 97
    communicating with MySQL, 272
    connecting to databases, 111
    cURL, 118
    custom functions, 113–115
    data manipulation, 100–104
    debugging, 120
    DOM, 117
    environmental variables, 104
    file management, 109
    initializing values, 271
    logic flow, 106–109
    SimpleXML, 116

strings, arrays and objects, 98
    web programming, 96–122
picture files
    size of, 219
political process
    Twitter in, 32
posting
    data, 136
    messages, 280, 337
    tweets, 151, 364
preg_replace() function, 102
prepAPI() function, 230
prepRequest() function, 232
presidential campaigns
    Barack Obama and John Edwards, 32
print() command, 122
prioritization
    of styles by browsers, 91
privacy
    member accounts, 218
private accounts
    versus protected accounts, 218
process deletion requests, 289, 297
profile colors
    updating, 170
profile images
    updating, 172
profiles, 320
    (see also member profiles)
    disabling, 287
    getting user profiles, 320
    saving, 290
profile_background_color element, 197
profile_background_color parameter, 146,
        372
profile_background_image_url element, 196
profile_background_tile element, 196
profile_image_url element, 196
profile_link_color element, 197
profile_link_color parameter, 146, 372
profile_sidebar_border_color element, 197
profile_sidebar_border_color parameter, 146,
        372
profile_sidebar_fill_color element, 197
profile_sidebar_fill_color parameter, 146, 372
profile_text_color element, 197
profile_text_color parameter, 372
profitability
    history of Twitter, 20

protected accounts
    following, 162
    security fix, 158
    versus private accounts, 218
protected element, 196
protocols (see format; XML)
public timeline
    caching, 154
public timeline method, 153
published element, 207
publishing applications, 48–51
publishing methods, 151
purging data, 341

Q

q parameter, 144, 177, 376
Queue Users automated task, 332, 349–352
queues
    retrieving, 357
    updating, 359
Qwitter application, 75

R

rate limits
    about, 147
    follower networks, 313
    status, 148, 175
receiving notifications, 220
recipient element, 204
recipient_id element, 204
recipient_screen_name element, 204
registering new Twitter accounts, 215
remaining-hits element, 210
remote data
    CSRF attacks, 98
remote servers
    deleting URLs from, 137
removing blocks, 165, 375
rendering
    interfaces, 275, 281, 299, 323
    RSS feeds, 304
replies
    integrity of threads, 152
    location of reply indicator, 155
    viewing, 155
request element, 211
request-rate surcharges, 22
requests

API requests, 272
    HTTP, 134–137
reset-time element, 210
reset-time-in-seconds element, 210
reset() function, 102
resource codes, 201
response elements, 209
response objects, 209
RESTful systems
    principles adopted by Twitter, 134
retrieving
    data, 124, 191, 288, 297, 337, 341
    favorites, 358
    last ID, 347
    master passwords, 346, 357
    queues, 357
    update timestamps, 303
    users, 348
retweet
    defined, 4
$root_path variable, 113
rpp parameter, 376
RSS feeds
    about, 139
    generating, 291
    parsing, 243, 284
    rendering, 304
RSS to Tweet automated task, 331, 332–338
rumors
    propagation of in the Twitosphere, 28

S

sales
    marketing, 31
    using Twitter for, 34
sample applications, 263–329
    (see also automated tasks; web applications)
    Administration Tool, 263, 267–276
    authentication in sample applications, 265
    Auto Tweet, 264, 282–291
    Best of Twitter, 264, 324–329
    Broadcast Feed, 300–305
    Network Viewer, 264, 313–324
    Tweet Alert, 264, 305–313
    Tweet Broadcast, 264, 291–300
    Tweet Publisher, 263, 277–282
    variables used in, 105
saving
    data, 273

groups, 298
profiles, 290
scalability
Twitter growing pains, 16
Scan Tweets automated task, 332, 342–349
scheduling (see automated tasks)
science
using Twitter for the study of, 28
Scoble, Robert, 26
scramblePassword() function, 248, 287
screen_name element, 195
screen_name parameter, 144, 365
search API (see Summize API)
search methods, 176–181, 375
search objects, 205–208
search tools
web applications, 58–64
search-and-replace
function for, 102
searching
for keywords, 177
tweet content, 24
SecretTweet application, 50
secure certificates
verification, 233
securePassword() function, 247
security
first security Twitter issue, 13
password management, 246–249
POST data, 136
protected accounts, 158
SQL injection attacks, 236
Twitter API, 182–189
user account information and cURL, 140
SELECT statement, 124
self-selecting advertising (see opt-in
advertising)
sender element, 204
sender_id element, 204
sender_screen_name element, 204
sent messages
listing, 166
$_SERVER variable, 105
servers
deleting URLs from, 137
handling server requests, 104
host servers, 126–130
remote content without cURL, 120
Twitter server scalability, 17

sessions (see member sessions)
shared events
using Twitter for, 41
shared hosting, 127
short-form user objects, 192
Show a Tweet method, 153, 364
Show Member Profile method, 157, 365
showing
member profiles, 157
messages, 168
show_user parameter, 146, 181, 376
SimpleXML
PHP, 116
SimpleXMLElement() method, 116
simplexml_load_string() method, 116
since parameter, 144, 154, 159, 179, 328, 363,
365, 366, 367, 376
since_id parameter, 145, 154, 180, 363, 365,
367, 376
single quotes ('), 98
sizeof() function, 102
SnapTweet application, 49
social change
using Twitter for, 32
social graph methods, 368
sort order
lists, 160
sortData() function, 252, 322
sorting
follow networks, 322
source element, 201
source parameter, 364
spaces (), 92
spam
challenges for on Twitter, 32
sports
using Twitter for, 39
SportyTweets, 40
SQL (Structured Query Language), 123
(see also MySQL)
statements, 299
SQL injection attacks, 97, 236
SQL queries functions, 235–240
statements (see commands; custom functions;
functions; methods)
statistics
functions, 253
web applications, 67–73
status

confirming follower status, 311
rate limit status, 148, 175
status codes
for deleted members, 158
HTTP, 137
status element, 197
status elements, 200
status messages functions, 255
status methods, 361–365
status objects, 198–202
status parameter, 151, 364
status reports
IM, 13
status updates, 25
(see also tweets)
statuses_count element, 198
stealthing Twitter accounts, 185
streams (see information streams)
strings
PHP, 98
stripslashes() function, 102
strlen() function, 103
strnatcmp() function, 103
strpos() function, 103
strrev() function, 103
strtolower() function, 103
strtotime() function, 103
Structured Query Language (SQL), 123
(see also MySQL)
statements, 299
structures
assigning styles to in CSS, 92
str_pad() function, 102
str_replace() function, 103
str_rot13() function, 103
styles
assigning to structures in CSS, 92
recognizing by browsers, 95
stylesheets
for the sample applications, 260
structure of, 90
substr() function, 104
Summize API, 24, 148, 176, 205
switch statement
PHP, 108

T

tables
building, 223

MySQL, 123
tags
form tags, 87
terrorism
potential for, 40
test method, 174, 375
text element, 200, 204
text parameter, 167, 367
text-align property
stylesheets, 94
textarea tag, 88
texting, 11
tf8_encode() function, 104
threaded conversations
context in, 8
integrity of, 152
threads
filtering, 179
time zone, 218
timelines
public timeline, 153
viewing favorites, 156
timestamps
update timestamps, 303
time_zone element, 198
tips (see guidelines)
title attribute, 322
title element, 206, 207
Track This application, 55
tracking
network changes, 159
web applications, 47
trends
monitoring keywords, 181
trim() function, 104
truncated element, 201
try statement
PHP, 108
Turn Off Notification method, 374
Turn On Notification method, 162, 374
Twalala application, 54
twam, 32
Twappi application, 65
tweeple/tweeps, 4
Tweet Alert sample application, 264, 305–313
Tweet Broadcast sample application, 264, 291–300
Tweet Publisher sample application, 263, 277
Tweet Scan application, 62, 305

TweetBeep application, 61, 305
TweetRush application, 4, 16
tweets, 25
  (see also status updates)
  defined, 2, 4
  estimated number of, 4
  matching, 347
  number of, 16
  posting, 151
  size of, 251
TweetStats application, 68
tweetup
  defined, 4
twethics, 5
twishing, 184–187
  (see also phishing)
Twist application, 67
TwitDir application, 2, 15, 59
Twitree application, 79
Twitscoop application, 65
Twittads, 171
Twitter, 1–44
  (see also sample applications; uses of
  Twitter; web applications)
  cultural change, 43
  history of, 9–25
  uses of, 25–42
  "What are you doing?", 2–9
Twitter accounts, 168–174
  (see also member accounts; users)
  importance of for development work, 214
  establishing, 214–221
  estimated number of, 2, 15
  security and cURL, 140
Twitter API, 133–189
  about, 46
  accessing, 134–149
  data mining feed, 181
  history of, 23
  methods, 150–181, 361–376
  security, 182–189
Twitter Color War, 35
Twitter Digest, 291
Twitter Grader application, 71
Twitter Matrix application, 53
twitter:source element, 207
Twitterank application, 72, 182
Twitterfeed application, 48
TwitterLit, 34

Twitterrific application, 7, 46
Twittervision application, 52
Twitties, 25
twoosh
  defined, 4
twply, 183

U
unfollowing
  members, 163, 368
  users, 174
unlink() function, 110
unscramblePassword() function, 248
Update Background Image method, 371
Update Member Location method, 370
Update Member Profile method, 370
Update Profile Colors method, 371
Update Profile Image method, 372
Update the Delivery Device method, 370
update timestamps
  retrieving, 303
updated element, 207
updates
  adding, 303
updating
  background images, 171
  delivery notices, 172
  member locations, 168
  member profiles, 169
  profile colors, 170
  profile images, 172
  queues, 359
url element, 196
url parameter, 145, 169, 371
URL resources
  deleting from remote servers, 137
urlencode() function, 104
user element, 202
user elements, 195–198
user parameter, 167, 367
user profiles, 320
  (see also member profiles; profiles)
usernames
  authentication, 140
users
  estimated financial value of, 21
  intentions of, 27
  methods, 365
  notifying, 198, 348

retrieving, 348
user_a parameter, 368
user_b parameter, 368
user_id parameter, 144, 365
uses of Twitter, 25–42
    anthropomorphism, 35
    creativity, 37
    education, 38
    emergencies, 30
    entertainment, 38
    for evil, 40
    games, 34
    help, 36
    marketing, 31
    news, 27
    sales, 34
    science, 28
    shared events, 41
    social change, 32
    sports, 39
    utilitarianism, 26
    worship, 29
using
    Twitter, 6
usort() function, 104
utc_offset element, 198

V

validating
    access, 273
variables, 104
    (see also environmental variables)
    declaring, 271
    PHP, 98
    used in sample applications, 105
    versatility of, 115
verifying
    credentials, 174, 372
    feeds, 289
    secure certificates, 233
viewing
    favorites, 156, 372
    followers, 159, 160, 362
    friends timeline, 154, 363
    individual timeline, 364
    members being followed, 159, 362
    public timelines, 363
    replies, 155, 363
    timelines, 153–155

virtual pets
    Japanese tweet traffic, 16
VPS (Virtual Private Server), 127

W

web applications, 45–81
    aggregation tools, 64–67
    conversation tools, 55–58
    CSS, 90–96
    follow network tools, 74–80
    host servers, 126–130
    information streams, 51–55
    publishing, 48–51
    search tools, 58–64
    statistics, 67–73
    tracking, 47
    Twitter Open API, 46
web forms
    processing variables, 106
web pages
    decorating in CSS, 94
    layout in CSS, 93
    XHMTL, 84
web programming, 83–131
    MySQL, 122
    PHP, 96–122
    XHTML, 83–89
Westwinds church
    worshiping with Twitter, 29
"What Are You Doing?", 2–9
What's Your Tweet Worth? application, 67
while statement
    PHP, 107
whitelisting
    Twitter API, 148
width property
    stylesheets, 93
Wilson, Fred
    on monetizing Twitter, 20
worship
    using Twitter for, 29
writeFile() function, 254
writing
    Twitter as creative medium, 37

X

XHTML
    web programming, 83–89

XML (eXtensible Markup Language)
    about, 139
    initiating, 303
    Twitter use of, 191
    use of, 138

About the Author

Kevin Makice is currently a Ph.D. student at the Indiana University School of Informatics, the first such doctoral program in the nation. His research interests center around the local use of technology and Phatic Design, the application of relational psychology to complexity and design. Prior to completing his Masters of Science in Human-Computer Interaction in 2006, Kevin was the primary Internet programmer for TicketsNow, a clearinghouse for sports, theatre, and entertainment tickets available in the secondary market. Along with three others, he won the CHI 2005 student competition by designing a concept for an ad-hoc volunteering system for elderly residents in assisted-living centers. His past research includes political wikis, tangible interfaces for children's games, machinima, and network analysis of ball movement in basketball. Much of his blogging and academic efforts over the past year have focused on exploring Twitter as a means of community building.

Colophon

The animal on the cover of *Twitter API: Up and Running* is a white-breasted nuthatch (*Sitta carolinensis*). This small songbird is 5 to 6 inches in length with a wingspan of 8 to 11 inches. It has a large head, short tail, and a white face and dark crown. The name *nuthatch* refers to its habit of gathering nuts and seeds, jamming them into tree bark, and then hammering or "hatching" them open with their strong beaks.

A common species, the white-breasted nuthatch has an estimated total population of 10 million. It lives in woodland areas across North America, from southern Canada to southern Mexico. At least nine subspecies exist, although the differences between them are small (mainly plumage color) and change gradually across the range. Like other nuthatches, the white-breasted nuthatch is able to walk headfirst down tree trunks and can hang upside down from branches. This behavior is the reason for its several nicknames, including topsy-turvey bird, devil-down-head, and tree mouse.

The nuthatch is omnivorous, feeding on acorns and hickory nuts in the winter and insects in the summer. It builds nests 10 to 50 feet up in trees, usually in a hole lined with fur, grass, or bark. In spring the female nuthatch lays 3 to 10 eggs, which are white with reddish brown spots. Its main predators are hawks, owls, and snakes.

The cover image is from the *Dover Pictorial Archive*. The cover font is Adobe ITC Garamond. The text font is Linotype Birka; the heading font is Adobe Myriad Condensed; and the code font is LucasFont's TheSansMonoCondensed.